Feminist Activism in the Supreme Court

Law and Society Series
W. Wesley Pue, General Editor

Gender in the Legal Profession: Fitting or Breaking the Mould
Joan Brockman

Regulating Lives: Historical Essays on the State, Society, the Individual, and the Law
Edited by John McLaren, Robert Menzies, and Dorothy E. Chunn

Taxing Choices: The Intersection of Class, Gender, Parenthood, and the Law
Rebecca Johnson

Collective Insecurity: The Liberian Crisis, Unilatelarism, and Global Order
Ikechi Mgbeoji

Murdering Holiness: The Trials of Franz Creffield and George Mitchell
Jim Phillips and Rosemary Gartner

Unnatural Law: Rethinking Canadian Environmental Law and Policy
David R. Boyd

People and Place: Historical Influences on Legal Culture
Edited by Jonathan Swainger and Constance Backhouse

Compulsory Compassion: A Critique of Restorative Justice
Annalise Acorn

The Heiress vs the Establishment: Mrs. Campbell's Campaign for Legal Justice
Constance Backhouse and Nancy L. Backhouse

Christopher P. Manfredi

Feminist Activism in the Supreme Court: Legal Mobilization and the Women's Legal Education and Action Fund

UBCPress · Vancouver · Toronto

09 08 07 06 05 04   5 4 3 2 1

Printed in Canada on acid-free paper

National Library of Canada Cataloguing in Publication

Manfredi, Christopher P. (Christopher Philip), 1959-
   Feminist activism in the Supreme Court : legal mobilization and the Women's Legal Education and Action Fund / Christopher P. Manfredi.

   (Law and society)
   Includes bibliographical references and index.
   ISBN 0-7748-0946-9

   1. Equality before the law – Canada. 2. Feminism – Canada. 3. Canada. Canadian Charter of Rights and Freedoms. 4. Women's Legal Education and Action Fund. 5. Canada. Supreme Court. 6. Women – Legal status, laws, etc. – Canada. 7. Constitutional history – Canada. 8. Sociological jurisprudence. I. Title. II. Series: Law and society series (Vancouver, B.C.)

HQ1236.5.C2M349 2004   342.7108'5   C2004-900058-6

Canadä

UBC Press gratefully acknowledges the financial support for our publishing program of the Government of Canada through the Book Publishing Industry Development Program (BPIDP), and of the Canada Council for the Arts, and the British Columbia Arts Council.

This book has been published with the help of a grant from the Canadian Federation for the Humanities and Social Sciences, through the Aid to Scholarly Publications Programme, using funds provided by the Social Sciences and Humanities Research Council of Canada.

UBC Press
The University of British Columbia
2029 West Mall
Vancouver, BC V6T 1Z2
604-822-5959 / Fax: 604-822-6083
www.ubcpress.ca

This book is dedicated to my wife, Paula Bontá, and our daughter, Sophie Manfredi.

Contents

Tables / viii

Acknowledgments / ix

Introduction / xi

1 Legal Doctrine, Legal Mobilization, and LEAF / 1

2 The Path to Substantive Equality / 35

3 Gaining Ground / 63

4 Family Matters: Breakdowns and Benefits / 91

5 A Difficult Dialogue / 112

6 Making a Difference: The Policy Consequences of Legal Mobilization / 149

Conclusion / 193

Notes / 198

Bibliography / 223

Cases Cited / 229

Index / 232

Tables

1.1 LEAF revenue and expenses, 1999-2002 / 14

1.2 LEAF participation, position, and success in the Supreme Court / 16

1.3 Origin and outcome of LEAF cases / 19

1.4 Individual judicial support for LEAF / 21

1.5 Court voting on LEAF issues, 1988-2000 / 22

1.6 Dissent behaviour in LEAF cases / 25

1.7 Government participants in LEAF cases / 25

1.8 Other nongovernment interveners in LEAF cases / 27

5.1 Sexual assault cases in the Supreme Court, 1986-2000 / 115

5.2 *O'Connor* regimes: Lamer and L'Heureux-Dubé compared / 134

5.3 Comparison of the Criminal Code "privacy shield" and the alternative *O'Connor* regime / 139

6.1 Extrinsic evidence cited by LEAF / 152

6.2 Supreme Court use of LEAF material and arguments / 154

6.3 Citation frequencies for LEAF cases / 165

6.4 Supreme Court citation of LEAF cases / 167

6.5 Therapeutic abortions among Canadian women, 1978-98 / 182

6.6 Abortion rates per 100 live births (selected years, by province) / 182

6.7 Abortion rates per 1,000 women (age 15-44), 1998-99 (by province) / 183

6.8 Sexual assault rates per 100,000 population, 1983-2001 / 185

6.9 Unfounded incidents and clearance rates, 1983-95 (sexual assault and all Criminal Code offences) / 187

6.10 Sexual assault conviction rates, acquittal rates, and sentences / 187

Acknowledgments

This book is the product of a Standard Research Grant from the Social Sciences and Humanities Research Council of Canada. I am grateful for the financial support this organization has provided me not only for this project, but throughout my academic career. I also benefited from the financial support of the Donner Canadian Foundation for portions of the research on which the book is based.

The book could not have been completed without the assistance of several able graduate research assistants, including Troy Riddell, Julia Gray, and Matt Hennigar. In addition, I twice had the opportunity to explore the ideas contained in this book in the Honours Seminar in Canadian Politics at McGill University. I thank the students in that seminar during the fall terms of 2001 and 2002 for their critical input. Finally, four scholars – Lori Hausegger, Rainer Knopff, Ian Brodie, and James Kelly – read all or parts of the manuscript and offered constructively critical comments. None of these people, of course, should be held responsible for the book's content or argument.

Much of the book is based on the analysis of factums submitted by the Women's Legal Education and Action Fund (LEAF) in Supreme Court cases, and of the decisions rendered by the Court in those cases. In 1996, LEAF published all of the factums it submitted during its first ten years of activity in a book entitled *Equality and the Charter: Ten Years of Feminist Advocacy Before the Supreme Court of Canada* (Toronto: Emond Montgomery). I have relied on this collection for those factums. Factums for subsequent years were available on LEAF's website, and made available for public use with acknowledgment. I had hoped to acknowledge the direct participation of lawyers who prepared factums and argued LEAF cases before the Court, but circumstances beyond my control made that impossible. The original research design for this project anticipated written contact and interviews with every lawyer who had participated in two or more LEAF cases. My initial contacts with these individuals generated relatively positive responses, but in the end none of these lawyers – citing various reasons – participated in the research project.

With respect to the analysis of judicial decisions, I benefited from the fact that the decisions and reasons for decision of the Supreme Court of Canada fall within the terms of the Reproduction of Federal Law Order, P.C. 1996-1995, December 19, 1996, SI/97-5, and may be reproduced, in whole or in part and by any means, without further permission from the Supreme Court of Canada.

Finally, I am grateful for permission from Oxford University Press to use and quote from my book *Judicial Power and the Charter: Canada and the Paradox of Liberal Constitutionalism, 2d ed.* (2001), especially material found on pp. 60, 62-65, 90-97, 116-35, and 176-83.

Introduction

This book examines legal mobilization by the Canadian feminist movement in the post-Charter era. As such, the project by necessity explores contested terrain, since neither "feminism" nor "legal mobilization" is a sharply defined concept with a universally accepted meaning. Political activism by women in Canada has been and is a complex and dynamic phenomenon even as its history and development have paralleled similar activism in other countries.[1] Early-nineteenth-century activists were motivated to a large degree by a general reform impulse, and they viewed greater participation by women in social, economic, and political life as an antidote to the "moral decay" they associated with increased immigration and urbanization. Their activism focused on establishing women's access to basic civil and political rights, especially in the areas of property ownership and voting. Legal mobilization played an important, if subsidiary, role during this early period. Later, and most famously, five prominent members of the movement – Henrietta Edwards, Louise McKinney, Irene Parlby, Nellie McClung, and Emily Murphy – challenged the conventional interpretation of the word "persons" in section 24 of the British North America Act, 1867 (now the Constitution Act, 1867). As interpreted by the Canadian Supreme Court, "persons" in this section of the Act did not include women, thereby preventing them from being appointed to the Senate. However, on appeal to the Judicial Committee of the Privy Council (JCPC), these women persuaded the JCPC that the BNA Act should be viewed as a "living tree capable of growth and expansion within its natural limits."[2] Consequently, twelve years after women had obtained the right to vote in federal elections, the JCPC recognized them as "persons" under Canadian constitutional law.

As early objectives were achieved throughout the first half of the twentieth century, the movement shifted its target in the 1960s, toward a more comprehensive strategy of liberating women from the constraints imposed by traditional notions of their role in society. This strategy provided the impetus for the establishment in 1967 of the Royal Commission on the

Status of Women, which would eventually issue 167 recommendations for improving the position of women in Canadian society.[3] In 1972 the commission's recommendations led to the formation of the National Action Committee on the Status of Women (NAC) by approximately thirty women's groups. NAC was to serve as an umbrella organization to lobby for, and monitor the implementation of, the commission's recommendations.[4] The federal government itself responded to the commission by establishing the Canadian Advisory Council on the Status of Women (CAC), which had the task of amplifying and transmitting the demands of women's groups to government. The women's movement expanded at a rapid rate during the 1970s, and by the 1980s it possessed a strong organizational structure linked together in a network with NAC at its centre.[5] However, as Sylvia Bashevkin notes, this apparently "smooth pattern of growth ... masked growing internal conflict." By the mid-1980s, according to Bashevkin's account, the leaders of the established women's organizations who initially dominated NAC gave way to a more militant set of activists.[6] The tensions generated by this shift in leadership have been evident in the development of feminist legal strategies and activism.

At the risk of oversimplification, the common thread running through the suffrage-oriented activism of the nineteenth century to the multifaceted activism of late-twentieth-century feminism is the "organized pursuit of women's social, political, and economic equality."[7] In this sense, the objective of post-Charter feminist legal mobilization has been relatively straightforward: to articulate a constitutional doctrine of substantive equality and use that doctrine as the standard for evaluating the legal rules and other public policies most relevant to women's interests. To a large degree, this objective became part of the women's movement's strategic agenda as a result of its experiences during the 1970s.

Although Canadian feminists achieved important legislative victories at the national level during that decade, they found themselves on the losing side in every case crucial to their interests decided by the Supreme Court of Canada between 1973 and 1982.[8] Three judgments in particular – *Lavell*, *Morgentaler*, and *Bliss* – epitomize this futility. In *Lavell* the Court upheld a provision of the federal Indian Act which stipulated that Aboriginal women, but not Aboriginal men, lost their status under the Act by marrying non-Aboriginals. The Court defined "equality before the law" to mean "equality of treatment in the enforcement and application of the laws." The Court reasoned that, because the impugned provision applied equally to all Aboriginal women, it satisfied this principle of equality. In *Morgentaler*, decided only three years after the United States Supreme Court's landmark abortion rights decision, *Roe* v. *Wade*,[9] the Court declined the opportunity to review Canada's abortion law on the grounds that it had no place in "the loud and continuous public debate" on this policy question.[10] In the Court's view, it had no warrant to overturn Parliament's judgment that "the desire of a woman to be relieved of her pregnancy is not, of itself, justification for performing an abortion." At issue in *Bliss* were provisions of the Unemployment Insurance Act that treated benefit applications based on pregnancy differently from regular applications or disability-based claims. The Court rejected Stella Bliss's assertion that these differential rules discriminated on the basis of sex, since in principle they applied equally to men and women. To the obvious objection that only women would ever be in a position to claim pregnancy-based benefits, the Court replied that "any inequality between the sexes in this area is not created by legislation but by nature."[11]

Although these failures in the 1970s might have turned the women's movement away from legal mobilization, they in fact had the opposite effect. Women's groups took full advantage of the opportunity that emerged between 1980 and 1982 to shape the content of the most important constitutional modification in Canadian history. In the end, the text of the Charter of Rights and Freedoms reflected their successful effort to broaden the document's equality rights section, to exempt affirmative action programs from that section, and to add an interpretive clause guaranteeing the Charter's equal application to women and men.[12] Consequently, the Charter's adoption made possible a period of successful interest-group litigation and broader legal mobilization unprecedented in Canadian history. Indeed, according to Sylvia Bashevkin, even during a period of conservative control of national politics (1984-93), the Canadian women's movement saw its combined legislative and judicial success rate increase from 50 to 87 percent.[13] The change was particularly impressive in the area of litigation, where the success rate increased from zero to almost 90 percent.

A Reversal of Fortunes

The emergence of the Canadian women's movement as an influential and effective participant in constitutional politics and litigation is a remarkable case of successful entry into the field of legal mobilization, particularly when set against the experience of its counterpart in the United States. During the 1970s, the American women's movement enjoyed uncommon success in both the political and legal arenas. Indeed, almost 70 percent of its national legislative and judicial initiatives were successful during the decade, successes that included important legal victories in the areas of equal rights, family law, reproductive freedom, and employment.[14] Most importantly, in 1972, after almost fifty years of effort by the movement, the US Congress sent the Equal Rights Amendment (ERA) to the states for ratification. The amendment provided that "equality of rights under the law shall not be denied or abridged by the United States or any State on account of sex," and it gave Congress the power to enforce the amendment through appropriate legislation.

By modifying the national constitution and providing Congress with an independent source of legislative power to regulate against sex discrimination, the ERA contributed to the movement's political agenda in at least two ways. First, it created new opportunities to legislate sexual equality on a national basis, thereby providing for federal regulation of matters normally within state jurisdiction. Second, it supported the movement's existing litigation strategy by creating the possibility that sex-based classifications would become subject to a "strict scrutiny" standard of constitutional review.[15] With presidential support, broad consistency with existing constitutional and statutory rules, and overwhelming approval by both houses of Congress, the ERA moved rapidly toward ratification.[16] Indeed, by early 1973 a positive outcome seemed certain, with thirty of the necessary thirty-eight states having voted for ratification. As the 1970s ended, however, the American movement experienced a drastic reversal of fortune. In particular, according to Jane Mansbridge, the ERA ratification process stalled, and pro-ERA sentiment diminished as its opponents argued that it would produce "major substantive changes" in public policy through federal judicial interpretation.[17] In 1978 Congress attempted to salvage the ERA by extending the ratification deadline, but in 1982, just as Canadian feminist activists were acquiring the most powerful legal tool in their history, this new deadline passed with the amendment still three states short of ratification.

Canadian Feminists in the Constitutional Arena

The decision by Canadian feminists to concentrate significant resources on achieving policy reform through the development of legal rules provides an excellent opportunity to examine both the process by which legal doctrine changes and the impact of those changes on politics and society. To exploit this opportunity, this book pursues two lines of analysis. First, it examines how Canadian feminists became key constitutional actors and explores the role of the Canadian women's movement during three periods of intense debate about formal amendment of the Canadian constitution. It was during these debates that the movement successfully sought to incorporate, and then to preserve, a constitutional doctrine of equality that would serve its broader policy goals. The second line of analysis is to examine the manner in which the movement mobilized this doctrine through litigation to support its policy agenda. The focus in this second part of the analysis is on the Women's Legal Education and Action Fund (LEAF), which is the most active and visible feminist litigating organization in Canada. Based in part on strategies and tactics developed by women's groups in the United States, LEAF's activity has contributed to reversing the litigation defeats of the 1970s, to protecting important legislative victories, and to expanding women's rights in areas such as reproductive freedom and family law.

Not surprisingly, other scholars have also analyzed these two elements of feminist constitutional activism. It is rare, however, to find work that offers a combined analysis of both Charter litigation and participation in the broader politics of constitutional change. For example, two widely cited early works on equality rights litigation and LEAF contain either none or only a brief reference to the politics of constitutional amendment.[18] William Bogart's discussion of women and the courts is also singularly focused on litigation, as is a later study of feminist litigation by Morton and Allen.[19]

Although these studies share a similar subject matter, they reach varying conclusions about the utility of litigation. In 1989, just as the Supreme Court decided its first Charter equality rights case, the Canadian Advisory Council on the Status of Women offered a pessimistic assessment of sex equality litigation during the first three years that section 15 of the Charter was in effect.[20] After analyzing almost six hundred decisions delivered by courts at all levels, the study's authors (Gwen Brodsky and Shelagh Day, who were instrumental in founding LEAF) concluded that "the news is not good. Women are initiating few cases, and men are using the Charter to strike back at women's hard-won protection and benefits."[21] Brodsky and Day found only seven cases (1.2 percent of the total) in which women had initiated an equality rights claim.[22] Similarly, thirty-five of the forty-four cases involving sex discrimination claims concerned challenges by men, particularly against sexual offence provisions of the Criminal Code.

Despite this record, Brodsky and Day did not join those critics who questioned Charter-based legal mobilization. In their view, the problem was not litigation per se, but certain structural features of litigation that were nevertheless amenable to change. Women, they argued, faced outdated theories of equality and interpretive tests, as well as barriers to accessing the judicial process. They also faced a generation of judges who were either hostile to, or simply unfamiliar with, feminist equality claims. The solution to these problems, Brodsky and Day implied, was not retreat but, rather, stronger engagement in advocating appropriate theories and interpretations of equality, articulating more generous rules of standing and intervener participation, and paying greater attention to judicial appointments and continuing legal education for both judges and lawyers. In retrospect, the findings of the 1989 study and the strategy that emerged from it form an important part of the feminist legal mobilization story since 1990.

In 1991, Sherene Razack echoed Brodsky and Day's observations about the difficulty of making feminist gains in the courts. The organizing theme of her book about LEAF is the contradiction between litigation and feminism. The essence of this contradiction, she argued, is that litigation requires the articulation of "women's stories in a language and a setting structured to deny the relevance of women's experiences."[23] This tension affected LEAF in its formative years, since its focus on litigation privileged a relatively homogeneous group of legally trained feminists. Not surprisingly, this meant that technical legal considerations, rather than community consultation and consensus building, drove the process of case selection. While this may have facilitated achievement of LEAF's early objectives, Razack argued, it limited its integration into the broader feminist community and led to charges of elitism.[24]

For Razack, the important question raised by LEAF's activity was the fate of feminism once it entered the legal arena. Could feminism, in other words, adapt to the demands of legal discourse and process without losing its ability to challenge an oppressive social order?[25] In many ways, according to Razack, this, rather than decisional outcomes, was the more important measure of litigation success. Indeed, Razack offered the paradoxical proposition that the success of feminist rights-based litigation should be its ability to challenge "rights thinking" itself.[26] To her, at least in 1991, LEAF's success in this sense was still an open question.

Although published more than a decade after Razack's book, a collection of essays edited by Radha Jhappan touches on similar themes. In her introduction, Jhappan notes the same paradox as Razack: feminist litigation at the same time that "feminist theorists regard law as an integral, formalized carrier of patriarchal relations."[27] The strategies adopted by LEAF, in particular, to overcome this paradox constitute the focus of many of the contributions to the volume. Authors such as Sheila McIntyre and Lise Gotell document changes in LEAF strategies (e.g., greater consultation and coalition building) and approaches to equality (e.g., shifting from essentialist to particularistic analyses of women's equality). In the end, however, Jhappan herself suggests that future success lies in constructing an approach based on justice, especially as conceptualized by critical race theorists, rather than on equality.[28]

Although less pessimistic or skeptical than these works, Bogart's analysis was nevertheless cautious. He suggested that the Charter had made an important difference for women's success in the courts, with "feminist issues" gaining credence especially in the Supreme Court. Yet at the core of Bogart's analysis is what he called the "dangers of victory."[29] Two issues in particular attracted his attention in 1994: abortion and pornography. Both areas could be justifiably described as post-Charter successes for the women's movement, with the Supreme Court nullifying the Criminal Code abortion provision while upholding criminal prohibitions against obscenity. Yet in both cases the judicialization of these policy areas generated new, and in some ways more intractable, conflicts. In the case of abortion, for example, Bogart observed that feminist legal victories in both Canada and the United States fuelled anti-abortion movements of varying strength. The apparent victory on the issue of pornography regulation proved divisive among feminists themselves. Bogart's point was that legal victories are a mixed blessing because legal success can generate a false sense that law itself can drive transformative policy change. As a result he was able to offer only qualified support for the strategy of legal mobilization.

The Morton/Allen study offers by far the most positive assessment of feminist legal activism, largely because it refines the definition of success. More precisely, they take this definition beyond mere outcome to measure a decision's impact on the "policy status quo" and on the development of legal rules.[30] Underlying this operationalization of success is the point that litigation can take different forms and serve different purposes, from offensive litigation to achieve favourable policy change to defensive litigation to preserve the policy status quo. As Morton and Allen point out, this means that success is not just a function of raw outcome (i.e., whether a group is on the "winning" side in a case). It also depends on whether a group is mobilizing offensively or defensively, and whether the outcome changes the policy status quo. The most valued outcome is an offensive win that generates policy change; the least valuable is a defensive loss that produces negative policy change.

These measures of success have a dramatic effect on Morton and Allen's assessment of feminist legal mobilization. Although women were on the losing side in fourteen of the forty-seven cases they examined, only three of these losses (21.4 percent) resulted in negative policy change. By contrast, seventeen of thirty-three nominal wins produced positive change (51.5 percent).[31] Moreover, in eleven cases where no policy change occurred, feminists still managed to acquire legal rules with future value for further litigation. Policy success was highest in the areas of private sector discrimination and family law, and success was much more likely in non-Charter cases.[32] To Morton and Allen, these findings raised questions about earlier skepticism.

While the four studies discussed above share an emphasis on litigation, Alexandra Dobrowolsky's 2000 book, *The Politics of Pragmatism*, offers a comprehensive treatment of the important role played by the Canadian women's movement during the three most recent episodes of what Peter Russell calls "mega-constitutional" politics.[33] Based on an extensive survey of documentary sources, as well as interviews with key actors, Dobrowolsky's book attempts to leverage the case study of Canadian women's constitutional activism to "reconsider the meaning and forms of representation."[34] The case study is impressive, as Dobrowolsky discusses to at least some degree the constitutional activism of forty-two women's organizations, both feminist and nonfeminist. The book provides a wealth of information about the development of lobbying strategies and tactics, and tells a story of multiple strategies and the establishment of creative alliances to overcome internal divisions, particularly within the feminist movement. The story leads

Dobrowolsky to conclude that "representation is about both interest and identity,"[35] and demonstrates how feminist participation in constitutional politics became more complicated as the identities it sought to represent expanded and became more complex. In this sense, Dobrowolsky's book is a good complement to Razack's discussion of the internal contradictions that eventually emerged in LEAF's litigation activity. However, Dobrowolsky devotes only three paragraphs to "courts and the charter."[36]

These separate studies of feminist litigation and constitutional activism constitute an undeniably rich empirical and theoretical contribution to our knowledge of the Canadian women's movement, legal mobilization, and constitutional politics. Yet, they arguably miss an important phenomenon captured in Mansbridge's observation that the US Equal Rights Amendment became fatally controversial only when its opponents linked the amendment to rights-based litigation. As I have argued elsewhere,[37] Mansbridge's observation points to the value of broadly conceptualizing constitutions and the politics of constitutional modification. Constitutional rules impose constraints on political choice, and these constraints operate systematically to favour some outcomes over others. In this sense, the politics of constitutional modification is a competitive process of institutional design, in which the objective is to modify existing rules in order to change the dynamics of political power, alter the status of competing interests, and affect policy outcomes.[38] At the macrolevel, constitutional modification takes place through formal amendment, which is characterized by political bargaining conducted according to the formal rules of the amending process. At the microlevel of constitutional politics, rule modification occurs through judicial interpretation triggered by constitutional litigation. At both levels, constitutional rules are valuable legal resources that state-based actors distribute, and for which society-based actors compete, to serve their broader policy objectives.[39]

Purpose and Plan

Although this book focuses on LEAF's litigation activity in the Supreme Court of Canada, it situates that activity within the broader context of feminist constitutional activism in the formal amendment process. It also situates this detailed study of LEAF within the broader theoretical literature on legal mobilization, which has not yet been well exploited by Canadian scholars.[40] Placing the study in this context is important because a carefully constructed theoretical framework enriches the descriptive narrative of the Canadian women's movement's campaign. As this literature suggests, legal mobilization offers individuals, interest groups, and social movements both opportunities and challenges.[41] On the one hand, legal rights are an important tactical and strategic resource in the personal and political conflicts in which individual and collective actors find themselves enmeshed. On the other hand, the process and discourse required to acquire and vindicate legal rights imposes its own unique set of constraints. This book seeks to understand how the Canadian women's movement exploited these opportunities and dealt with the challenges of operating in the legal arena during a twenty-year period spanning the 1980s and 1990s.

To achieve this objective, the book is divided into seven chapters. The first chapter moves from a general discussion of the sources of change in legal doctrine, including judicial attitudes, political environment, and the activities of interest groups and social movements, to a general overview of LEAF's participation in Supreme Court cases. Tying these two topics together is a theoretical discussion of legal mobilization as a strategic and tactical instrument for achieving policy change. Chapters 2 through 5 constitute the substantive core of the book, since in these chapters I provide a detailed discussion of feminist constitutional activism at both the macro (formal amendment) and micro (litigation) levels. My focus, especially in Chapters 3 to 5, is on LEAF's legal and policy arguments and their reception by the Court. My methodological approach is inspired by Lee Epstein and Joseph Kobylka's observation that "it is *the law and legal arguments as framed by legal actors* that most clearly influence the content and direction of legal change."[42] My approach assumes that neither traditional legal nor microlevel behavioural analysis is completely adequate for understanding the development, resolution, and impact of legal mobilization. On the one hand, traditional legal analysis ignores, or at least downplays, the political environment of legal mobilization. On the other hand, the behaviouralist focus on voting and judicial attitudes does not capture the complexity involved in developing the legal arguments necessary to mobilize constitutional rules in a favourable direction. My discussion of LEAF's activity in the policy areas covered by these chapters thus combines traditional analysis (since legal argumentation and doctrine are important for understanding the policy significance of legal mobilization) with certain aspects of extralegal analysis (since deciding these cases is a profoundly political exercise).

Chapter 6 steps back from this detail to analyze and assess the accomplishments of LEAF's litigation activity, as well as the impact of that activity on broader social conditions. In this chapter I offer three separate measures of impact: the Court's use of, and reference to, LEAF evidence and arguments; the jurisprudential influence of LEAF cases as measured by their citation in subsequent Court judgments; and changes in social practices that might be attributable to the legal rules developed in LEAF cases. Finally, the Conclusion uses this specific case of legal mobilization to reflect on some of the more general issues raised in the literature about the wisdom of this strategy and the conditions under which it may or may not be successful. It also offers some thoughts on the development of a feminist theory of the Charter.

No single book, of course, can do complete justice to the complex realities of either the Canadian feminist movement or legal mobilization. However, the success or failure of legal mobilization depends heavily on the skill with which litigants use the tools available to them in the litigation process, and on their ability to adjust to the structural constraints of adjudication. I hope that this book, by examining how a key actor within a particular movement applied its skills and adjusted to these constraints in a series of cases over several policy areas, and by situating its activity within an established theoretical framework, makes at least a modest contribution to understanding both the Canadian feminist movement and legal mobilization.

Feminist Activism in the Supreme Court

1
Legal Doctrine, Legal Mobilization, and LEAF

On 4 May 1989 the Supreme Court of Canada delivered its judgment in *Brooks* v. *Canada Safeway*.[1] At issue was the legality under Manitoba's Human Rights Act of a private employer's disability plan that excluded pregnant women from benefits during a seventeen-week period. The apparent reason for the exclusion was the availability of alternative benefits under the federal Unemployment Insurance Act during the exclusion period. When complaints were first filed in *Brooks*, the Manitoba statute did not explicitly prohibit discrimination on the basis of pregnancy. The complainants thus relied on the Act's general prohibition against sex discrimination to challenge the legality of the private plan's eligibility rules. This, of course, posed the same question that the Court had confronted during the pre-Charter era in *Bliss*: Does discrimination on the basis of pregnancy constitute sex discrimination? Writing for a unanimous Court, Chief Justice Brian Dickson held that "*Bliss* was wrongly decided," and that discrimination based on pregnancy is indeed created by legislation rather than by nature.[2] In Dickson's view, any analysis of "pregnancy-based discrimination" must recognize the biological fact that the "capacity to become pregnant is unique to the female gender."[3] Pregnancy discrimination, he declared, *is* sex discrimination. Thus, Dickson expressly overruled the legal principle underlying one of the women's movement's most visible legal defeats of the 1970s.

Brooks was the fourth case heard by the Supreme Court in which the Women's Legal Education and Action Fund appeared as an intervener. Both the nature of LEAF's intervention and the outcome of the case illustrate important aspects of post-Charter feminist legal mobilization. First, the objective of mobilization – to achieve judicial recognition of a new theory of equality – is clearly evident in *Brooks*. LEAF's factum in *Brooks* criticized existing theories of equality as "incomplete," and it proposed an alternative model that recognized the "social subordination of women to men."[4] Second, the Court's acceptance of this theory to reverse a unanimous judgment less than a decade old is testimony to the successful achievement of this objective. Although LEAF accepted the possibility that the Court might simply distinguish *Brooks* from *Bliss*, it had invited the Court to take the more radical step of declaring that *Bliss* had in fact been "wrongly decided."[5] That the Court accepted this invitation is a dramatic indicator of the inherent potential of legal mobilization.

Yet, the Court did not decide *Brooks* in a vacuum, nor can LEAF be given sole credit for the outcome. Other developments, including federal and provincial legislative initiatives, doctrinal developments in other areas of the law, and changes in judicial personnel, contributed to the Court's judgment in *Brooks*. For example, the federal government had signalled its disagreement with the legal principle established in *Bliss* by amending the Unemployment Insurance Act to provide the very benefits denied by the Court in 1979.[6] Similarly, by 1989 several provinces had included "pregnancy" among the prohibited grounds of discrimination in their human rights codes.[7] In the judicial arena, the Supreme Court had declared in 1987 that the "special nature" of human rights legislation required a broad interpretive approach.[8] Finally, five of the seven justices who decided *Bliss* were no longer on the Court for *Brooks*, including Justice Roland Ritchie, who had authored many of the Court's prominent pre-Charter equality decisions.[9]

As this brief description suggests, the change in legal doctrine from *Bliss* to *Brooks* confirms the observation that the composition of the bench and the legal and political environments are all important factors in determining the success of legal mobilization by organized movements.[10] In the remainder of this chapter, this observation provides the background for a general overview of LEAF's litigation activity in the Supreme Court. The next section of the chapter summarizes the important role played by judicial attitudes and political context in doctrinal change, with particular attention to the changing judicial and political context in which LEAF has functioned. The second section focuses more specifically on legal mobilization and outlines the debate about its utility as an instrument for achieving legal changes that have immediate policy consequences. The final section of the chapter paints a broad portrait of LEAF's activity in the Supreme Court.

Explaining Legal Change:
The Background to Feminist Legal Mobilization

For more than half a century, the study of judicial decision making has been dominated by what is widely known as the "attitudinal model" of judicial behaviour.[11] Among the first empirical demonstrations of the link between judicial attitudes and decisional outcomes was C. Herman Pritchett's now classic study of the US Supreme Court during the 1940s.[12] Observing the obvious fact that justices often disagreed about important questions of constitutional law, Pritchett concluded that the result in nonunanimous cases "was influenced by judicial preferences as to public policy." His pioneering work also documented the existence of judicial voting blocs, as well as "shifting alignments and progressive deterioration" of those blocs.[13]

The attitudinal model rests on two assumptions. One is that judges, like other political actors, are goal-oriented and seek to advance their goals through legal judgments. Second, the model assumes that judicial goals include policy preferences that have been shaped by the personal background and experiences of individual judges. According to the attitudinal model, judges, particularly those on national high courts, are free to decide disputes according to their attitudinally and experientially determined policy preferences because of the ambiguity of legal rules and institutional provisions such as security of tenure and formal independence from legislatures and executives. From this perspective, changes in legal doctrine are the product of attitudinal shifts caused by changes in judicial personnel.

Although the attitudinal model has been elaborated most fully in the US case, scholars have also applied it to other courts, including the Supreme Court of Canada. In general, the Canadian studies confirm the model's basic premise that "the attitudes and values that justices hold have an influence on their voting behaviour."[14] Certainly, differences in attitudes and values are one possible explanation for variations in individual justices' support for Charter claims. Between 1982 and 1999, according to data compiled by James Kelly,[15] individual support for Charter claims ranged from a low of 22 percent (Justice William McIntyre) to a high of 55 percent (Justice Bertha Wilson). Individual justices also differed in their willingness to accept government justifications for Charter limits under section 1, and to exclude evidence under section 24(2). Among those justices who participated in at least ten Charter judgments, individual acceptance of section 1 defences ranged from a low of 13 percent (Justice – and then Chief Justice – Beverley McLachlin) to 41 percent (Chief Justice Brian Dickson). Similarly, Justice Claire L'Heureux-Dubé was least likely to vote to exclude evidence (16 percent of cases), while Justice Wilson voted to exclude evidence in 73 percent of the relevant cases.

Individual justices also exhibit varying attitudes toward different types of Charter claims. A common and useful distinction is the one made between criminal rights claims and "post-material" policy claims involving, in particular, equality rights.[16] For example, although Justice L'Heureux-Dubé's aggregate support for Charter claims (31 percent) is close to the Court's support as a whole (33 percent), this conceals an important difference in the structure of her support. Although she is among the least supportive of criminal rights claims (24 versus the Court's 35 percent), she is an extremely strong supporter of post-material claims (63 versus the Court's 48 percent).[17]

The impact of individual justices, and changes in judicial personnel, is evident in the Court's sexual orientation jurisprudence. In *Egan* v. *Canada*

(1995), a narrow majority (five to four) upheld a provision of the federal Old Age Security Act against a claim that it constituted unreasonable discrimination on the basis of sexual orientation.[18] By early 1998, Justices Michel Bastarache and Ian Binnie had replaced two members of the *Egan* majority, Justices Gérard La Forest and John Sopinka. Although Justice Bastarache's overall support rate for Charter claims (23 percent) is somewhat lower than his predecessor La Forest's (29 percent), his support rate for post-material policy claims is much higher (57 versus 34 percent). Similarly, while Justice Binnie's overall support rate is not very different from the late Justice Sopinka's (39 versus 37 percent), his support for post-material claims is almost twice as high (67 versus 34 percent).

Justices Bastarache and Binnie shifted the Court's median attitude toward the post-material end of the decisional continuum, which contributed to overwhelmingly favourable gay rights decisions in the Court's next two cases concerning sexual orientation, *Vriend* v. *Alberta* (nine to zero) and *M.* v. *H.* (eight to one).[19] These appointments themselves would have been sufficient to transform the five-to-four loss by the gay rights movement in *Egan* into six-to-three victories in *Vriend* and *M.* v. *H.*, even if Chief Justice Lamer and Justice Major had not switched their votes from the anti- to the pro-sexual orientation position.

The fate of feminist legal mobilization in the post-Charter era, therefore, cannot be understood without reference to the Canadian Supreme Court's composition throughout the 1980s and 1990s. At least two important changes in the Court's composition have affected LEAF's legal mobilization efforts: the (inevitable) retirement of Justice Roland Ritchie and the appointment of women to the Court. As noted above, Ritchie's retirement in 1984 created an opportunity for the Court to reconsider its equality jurisprudence. Born in Halifax in 1910, Ritchie followed a typical path to the legal profession for his era by reading law with a prominent Halifax lawyer. Called to the bar in 1934, he practiced with the firm of Steart, Smith, MacKeen and Rogers until beginning his war service in 1940. Upon his return to civilian life in 1944 he began his own practice and received his appointment to the Supreme Court from John Diefenbaker in 1959. Ritchie came to the Court without having held judicial office, and his entire legal career had been deeply concerned with the concrete and practical.

Despite his lack of prior judicial experience, Ritchie compiled an impressive record of authoring landmark judgments during his twenty-five-year career on the Court. In 1963 he wrote the majority judgment in *Robertson and Rosetanni* v. *The Queen*, the Court's first Bill of Rights decision and one in which it upheld the 1905 federal Lord's Day Act on the basis of what commentators would widely criticize as a "frozen concepts" theory of rights. Six years later, however, Ritchie appeared to abandon this cautious approach in *R.* v. *Drybones*, which marked the first (and only) occasion on which the

Court nullified a statutory provision on Bill of Rights grounds. *Drybones* raised commentators' expectations that the Court was ready to strike out on an activist path, but Ritchie himself dashed those expectations in *Lavell* and *Bliss*. Ritchie's cautious approach to the Bill of Rights in all these cases, with the exception of *Drybones*, may have reflected the practical orientation of his professional background. Certainly, his training and experience had not emphasized abstract legal principles. In any event, his retirement from the Court at the dawn of the Charter era was symbolic of the idea that the new document was not simply a continuation of the existing federal statute in constitutional form.

The elevation of women to the Court began with Justice Bertha Wilson in 1982. In an article implicitly confirming the basic premise of the attitudinal model, Justice Wilson argued that the appointment of more women judges would make a difference to the development of the law.[20] Quoting from Carol Gilligan's book, *In a Different Voice*,[21] Wilson argued that a distinctively female form of moral reasoning would make contextual factors much more important in the adversarial process. To the extent that one objective of feminist legal mobilization is to bring a feminist method that challenges the norms of the adversarial process into the courtroom,[22] Wilson appeared to suggest that this would be facilitated by increasing the number of women justices on the Court. Although Wilson cast only sixteen votes in LEAF cases before her retirement in 1991, eleven of those votes supported LEAF's position. Her three negative votes were on issues on which the Court was unanimous.

Three other women have been appointed to the Court during the period covered by this book: Claire L'Heureux-Dubé (1987), Beverley McLachlin (1989, elevated to Chief Justice in 2000), and Louise Arbour (1999). Each has been highly supportive of positions advocated by LEAF, and McLachlin and L'Heureux-Dubé have dissented together to support LEAF's position against a majority composed entirely of their male colleagues. According to McCormick, through 1999 McLachlin and L'Heureux-Dubé were "isolated at one edge of the Court," suggesting that they had not been "absorbed into the male-dominated" Court, at the price of "being left outside the dominant decision-making coalitions."[23] Justice Arbour's orientation toward LEAF claims at the end of 2000 is more difficult to evaluate, but it is suggestive of a positive stance. Her general support for LEAF claims in a limited number of cases includes a telling dissent in *Little Sisters Book and Art Emporium* v. *Canada* (2000) in support of LEAF's argument that customs legislation, by allegedly targeting gay and lesbian erotica, violates freedom of expression on its face as well as in its application.[24] However, whether gender itself explains this dissent is unclear, since Arbour joined two male colleagues in voting against McLachlin and L'Heureux-Dubé.

LEAF also may have benefited from a shift in individual judicial behaviour by Beverley McLachlin in the early 1990s. In the eight LEAF-related votes that McLachlin cast through 1991, her support for LEAF was actually quite low (25.0 percent). By contrast, since 1991 her support level has been 81.3 percent (twenty-six of thirty-two votes cast). The significance of 1991 is that it marks her much-criticized judgment in *Seaboyer*,[25] in which she led a majority of the Court in nullifying the so-called "rape shield" provisions of the Criminal Code. *Seaboyer* was a major doctrinal loss for LEAF, and McLachlin's judgment provoked a sharp dissent from Justice L'Heureux-Dubé. Quoting approvingly from LEAF's factum, L'Heureux-Dubé charged the majority with perpetuating sexual stereotypes and "rape myths." Whether the negative reaction to *Seaboyer* affected McLachlin's subsequent voting behaviour is obviously a matter of speculation, but it points to the fact that judges decide cases in an institutional and political context that affects how they translate their attitudes into votes, and perhaps even shapes and changes those attitudes themselves.[26]

Indeed, as James Gibson argues, judicial decision making is a "function of what [judges] prefer to do, tempered by what they think they ought to do, but constrained by what they perceive is feasible to do."[27] The attitudinal model obviously speaks directly to judicial preferences, but these preferences are filtered through individual role orientations that affect judicial beliefs about the appropriateness of using personal attitudes as a guide to decision making.[28] Feasibility is determined by both legal and institutional constraints. Legal constraints include the facts of particular cases and controlling legal doctrine,[29] while institutional constraints include internal court rules, interpersonal dynamics, and external political conditions.[30] In particular, institutional constraints force justices to "consider the preferences of others ... the choices they expect others to make, and the institutional context in which they act."[31] These considerations, in turn, generate a wide range of strategic behaviour.[32]

From a doctrinal standpoint, LEAF's litigation activity certainly benefited from the Supreme Court's developing jurisprudence in relation to human rights statutes. Three decisions in particular – *O'Malley*, *Bhinder*, and *Action Travail des Femmes*[33] – illustrate this development. In *O'Malley* and *Bhinder*, the Court explicitly recognized "adverse effects discrimination" as grounds for complaint under provincial human rights legislation. In *Action Travail des Femmes*, it approved quota-based affirmative action programs as an appropriate remedial measure under the Canadian Human Rights Act. In these decisions the Court accepted the basic principles that would later be advocated by LEAF in the constitutional context, namely substantive equality and the need for broad remedies for sex discrimination. However, while these decisions increased the power of human rights tribunals and the scope of human rights legislation, they had little impact on the basic distribution of political power between the judiciary and other branches of government.

Indeed, had they so desired, the provincial and federal governments could have overridden these decisions simply by enacting ordinary legislative amendments restricting the jurisdiction of human rights tribunals and commissions. Instead, governments generally took the opposite route by specifically amending these statutes to affirm the Court's construction of human rights statutes and the additional administrative powers to which it had given its blessing. Certainly, this made it more feasible for the Court to accept LEAF's argument that these principles of human rights jurisprudence should be transformed into constitutional law under the Charter.

Fortunately for LEAF, the strategic context of Charter decision making has also been favourable since 1988. One of the most important strategic considerations that affects judicial decision making is the relationship between courts and other political institutions. More precisely, because the achievement of immediate judicial policy goals depends to a significant degree on a court's institutional power and prestige,[34] courts must simultaneously maximize their policy preferences and minimize threats to their institutional legitimacy. Consequently, they must be cognizant of the capacity of other institutions to negate specific policy decisions or to challenge the legitimacy of the court itself.

In this respect, the most important strategic variable the Canadian Court must consider is the legislative override provision found in section 33 of the Charter. Section 33 allows federal and provincial legislatures to declare for five-year renewable periods that a law shall operate "notwithstanding" the fundamental freedoms, legal rights, and equality rights provisions of the Charter. The inclusion of section 33 in the Charter means that the Constitution Act, 1982, is deliberately ambiguous about the ultimate institutional source of constitutional authority, at least with respect to the interpretation and application of rights and freedoms. On the one hand, section 52 of the Act declares the principle of constitutional supremacy and authorizes courts to nullify unconstitutional statutes. On the other hand, section 33 gives legislatures the authority to override judicial decisions, or even to immunize legislation from judicial review under the Charter altogether. The presence of this clause makes it more difficult in principle for the Court to assert final authority over the articulation and enforcement of constitutional rights because it provides a clear institutional mechanism for legislatures to resist assertions of judicial constitutional supremacy.

Use of the legislative override thus represents a double threat to the achievement of judicial policy goals. First, it can negate the effects of the Court's immediate intervention in the policy process. Second, it can challenge the Court's long-term institutional authority by immunizing an issue from judicial review. In every Charter case, the justices must assess the long-term impact of their actions by posing the following question: How far can we intervene before provoking a negative reaction from other political actors? The Court's strategic dilemma is that, to maintain its Charter-based policy-making authority, it cannot simply avoid participating in controversial policy debates. Yet, uncertainty about whether judicial intervention will trigger a legislative override forces the Court to calibrate the nature of its intervention carefully.

The constraining effect of this strategic dilemma obviously depends on the probability that legislatures will invoke section 33; by 1990, events had significantly reduced the likelihood that governments would directly confront judicial power by resorting to the legislative override.[35] In 1988, in response to the Court's judgment in *Ford* v. *Québec*,[36] Quebec enacted new language legislation (Bill 178) that contained a notwithstanding clause. The legislation permitted the use of English on interior commercial signs but continued the prohibition of English on exterior signs. The decision had immediate consequences: three anglophone ministers resigned from Premier Robert Bourassa's cabinet; Manitoba premier Gary Filmon withdrew a resolution to ratify the Meech Lake constitutional accord from his province's legislature; and general public support for the accord declined precipitously outside Quebec.[37]

Prime Minister Brian Mulroney reacted by attacking the notwithstanding clause's inclusion in the Charter. Speaking in the House of Commons, the prime minister called section 33 "that major fatal flaw of 1981, which reduces your individual rights and mine." Section 33, Mulroney continued, "holds rights hostage" and renders the entire constitution suspect. Any constitution, he concluded, "that does not protect the inalienable and imprescriptible individual rights of individual Canadians is not worth the paper it is written on."[38] Even astute constitutional scholars such as Patrick Monahan changed their attitude toward section 33 after Bill 178 and the subsequent demise of the Meech Lake Accord. In his 1987 book on the Charter, Monahan argued that section 33 does not "legitimate tyranny" but merely ensures "that the political process will not be subject to unreasonable or perverse judicial interpretations."[39] However, writing about the downfall of the Meech Lake Accord four years later, he concluded that "the inclusion of the notwithstanding clause in the 1982 constitution was clearly a very serious mistake." Reflecting on events between 1988 and 1990, Monahan argued that section 33 had created an unforeseen political dynamic that would eventually divide Quebec and the rest of Canada. In contrast to his relatively strong support for section 33 in his 1987 book, Monahan's 1991 study of the Meech Lake process lamented that "the notwithstanding clause has become truly embedded in the charter in a permanent way."[40]

Quebec's Bill 178 marks the last time any legislature has successfully invoked the notwithstanding clause in a major piece of legislation, leading one observer to conclude that constitutional convention now virtually prohibits its use.[41] Indeed, in March of 1998 the Alberta government learned a very hard lesson about the political status of section 33. On 10 March, Alberta introduced a bill to compensate victims of provincial eugenics laws that were in effect from 1929 to 1972. One element of the bill was a provision to prohibit victims from suing for additional compensation, and the government proposed to shield that provision from judicial review through the notwithstanding clause. Using the notwithstanding clause against this vulnerable group smacked of mean-spiritedness, and one day after introducing the bill the provincial Attorney General withdrew it under intense political pressure. Alberta's premier explained the decision to withdraw the bill in the following terms: "It became abundantly clear that to individuals in this country the Charter of Rights and Freedoms is paramount and the use of any tool ... to undermine [it] is something that should be used only in very, very rare circumstances."[42]

The decline, if not the actual death, of section 33 has had a profound impact on the legislative-judicial relationship in Canada, in favour of judicial power. Nevertheless, the Court does not operate in an infinitely accommodating strategic environment. Although it enjoys strong public support at both the institutional and decisional level,[43] commentators have observed that it "seems to be influenced by arguments that it has been too activist and should defer more to legislatures and craft its decisions in a narrower fashion."[44] In fact, this is one explanation for the Court's failure to nullify a single statute, federal or provincial, during 2000.[45]

To summarize, the targets of feminist legal mobilization are individual justices operating within a particular institutional context. By 1989 judicial personnel changes and a shifting balance of power from legislatures to the Court established an hospitable environment for LEAF. Yet this emphasis on judicial personnel and context should not be understood as devaluing LEAF's own efforts. LEAF is an example of the type of "rights-advocacy organization" that is both an important element and beneficiary of the legal support structure underlying any "rights revolution."[46] According to Charles Epp, this support structure is important because successful legal mobilization depends on sustained litigation throughout the judicial system, and individual litigants generally lack the financial and other resources to undertake this sustained effort. Organized groups such as LEAF, by contrast, have the resources to sustain litigation campaigns on particular issues. Whether the outcome of these efforts is "revolutionary" or not is the subject of some controversy in the legal mobilization literature, and it is to this literature which I now turn.

Legal Mobilization and Social Reform

The term legal mobilization refers to a host of related phenomena. It is a "process by which legal norms are invoked to regulate behavior;"[47] the translation of desires into demands "as an assertion of one's rights;"[48] a "planned effort to influence the course of judicial policy development to achieve a particular policy goal."[49] Underlying each of these descriptions is the idea that the law can be an effective instrument for social and political change. This is true with or without litigation or the direct participation of courts.

The use of legal mobilization as an instrument of sociopolitical reform traces its roots to the early twentieth century, when the National Consumers' League used litigation to advance the interests of working women and children in the United States.[50] In Canada, the 1930s saw business interests use federalism litigation as a political tactic to oppose economic regulation, especially in Alberta.[51] However, credit for the systematic development of this type of litigation usually goes to two groups: the American Civil Liberties Union (ACLU) and the National Association for the Advancement of Colored People (NAACP). Although both organizations oriented legal mobilization around a "leading case" approach,[52] the NAACP initially took a more programmatic approach than did the ACLU.[53] Indeed, the NAACP explicitly developed "a strategic plan for cumulative litigation efforts aimed at achieving specified social objectives."[54]

The NAACP turned to legal mobilization because restrictive election laws and voting requirements, not to mention poverty and the legacy of slavery, ensured that African-Americans remained a "discrete and insular minority,"[55] unable to defend or advance their interests through normal democratic political participation. Thus, in 1915, the NAACP entered the judicial arena to defend the existing legal rights of African-Americans, and in 1939 it established an independent Legal Defense and Education Fund (LDF) to undertake a systematic program of social reform through legal mobilization.[56] These legal struggles achieved important victories against restrictive property covenants and segregated education, and in favour of voting rights.[57] The crowning achievement, of course, was the US Supreme Court's unanimous declaration in 1954 *(Brown* v. *Board of Education)* that segregated public education violates the constitutional guarantee of equal protection of the laws. Indeed, *Brown* has been credited with making judicial activism possible,[58] and with being "such a moral supernova in civil liberties adjudication that it almost single handedly justifies the exercise."[59] To be sure, these victories required further legal and political action to become even partially effective, but the NAACP's apparent success came to define the method and potential of legal mobilization.

By the end of the 1960s, conventional wisdom suggested that legal mobilization was an effective instrument for social and political reform by disadvantaged groups. By the middle of the 1970s, this conventional wisdom was under attack. In perhaps the most widely cited article in the law and society literature, Marc Galanter argued that only repeat player (RP) litigants were likely to be successful in mobilizing the law programmatically to achieve long-term objectives.[60] In contrast to one-shot (OS) litigants, RP litigants are more interested in law reform than client service, and they enjoy an advantage in the judicial process because of their accumulated expertise and extensive legal resources. As repeat players, moreover, they also have access to better than average political resources, such as diffuse financial support.[61] It became apparent, in venturing "beyond the political disadvantage theory," that groups without political resources were also unlikely to possess the legal resources necessary to sustain systematic litigation campaigns.[62] Indeed, even the NAACP had political resources in the form of financial support from philanthropic organizations and influential (or merely dedicated and hard-working) individuals with ties to the majority political community.[63] These observations led to the following conclusion: legal mobilization, which appears superficially to be the exclusive province of political outsiders, actually belongs as much, and perhaps more, to political insiders.[64]

The 1960s ideal of legal mobilization as an instrument for improving the position of the politically disadvantaged also began to fade as scholars questioned whether the achievements of groups such as the NAACP were more apparent than real. Again, 1974 was a key year; Stuart Scheingold observed that "two decades after the *Brown* decision, [Americans] are still struggling inconclusively with school desegregation." According to Scheingold, the "continued vitality of litigation," despite the unfulfilled promise of *Brown*, could "be read as a triumph of myth over reality."[65] In his view, litigation could produce social reform at best indirectly, by contributing to a broader process of political mobilization in which interests are activated, organized, and realigned.[66] Scheingold's observations foreshadowed an important debate about legal mobilization that took place between Gerald Rosenberg and Michael McCann, among others, during the 1990s. The debate opened with Rosenberg's 1991 book, *The Hollow Hope*.[67] Rosenberg examined six areas (civil rights, abortion and women's rights, environment, reapportionment, and criminal law) and posed a simple question: Did judicial decisions produce significant social reform? His findings were not optimistic, and he concluded that systematic institutional factors, including the limited nature of constitutional rights, limited judicial independence, and limited judicial implementation capacity, made legal mobilization an exceptionally unreliable path to social reform.[68]

In 1992 Michael McCann described *The Hollow Hope* as "bold, compelling, and important," yet ultimately unconvincing.[69] Although McCann raised concerns about evidence, interpretation, and conceptualization, he argued that Rosenberg's approach missed the "constitutive capacity of law" in which "legal knowledge prefigures in part the symbolic terms of material relations and becomes a potential resource in ongoing struggles to refigure those relations."[70] McCann's own study of legal mobilization and pay equity, published in 1994 as *Rights at Work*,[71] led him to conclude that legal mobilization provides important political payoffs, even in the absence of directly positive effects.[72] In particular, the mobilization of rights discourse by marginalized groups, according to McCann, can be a source of empowerment that facilitates long-term improvement in their disadvantaged status.[73] In his review of *Rights at Work*, Rosenberg argued that McCann's "de-centred" approach had missed important phenomena – such as union activism – that affected the degree of successful legal mobilization in the pay-equity field.[74] According to Rosenberg, a close analysis of McCann's findings actually supported the central thesis of *The Hollow Hope*, that "courts can help progressive forces, but only under conditions that both occur infrequently and are virtually determinative of change on their own."[75]

One of the most important lessons of the McCann-Rosenberg debate is that measuring either the success or influence of legal mobilization is extremely difficult. Success is not a simple concept, nor is it identical to influence. Success can mean favourable outcomes in individual cases, or the development of desired legal doctrine. Yet even accomplishing these two difficult objectives does not guarantee achieving the broader socioeconomic and political changes at which legal mobilization aims. Moreover, case outcomes, doctrinal developments, and broader policy shifts may be entirely independent of group participation.

LEAF in the Supreme Court: An Overview

Whether seeking to press existing advantages or mobilizing to overcome political disadvantage, organized group litigants face several strategic and tactical choices. The basic strategic choice is between direct sponsorship of test cases and participation as an intervener. Direct sponsorship maximizes control of litigation but is expensive; intervener participation is less costly but provides far less control over the development of legal rules.[76] The strategic choices that interest groups make are closely related to the principal tactical choices they face: selecting specific cases and determining the arguments to make in those cases. The incremental character of judicial policy making means that the ultimate legal objectives of a litigation campaign can be achieved only through the gradual development of discrete rules that eventually form the basis for a new, overarching constitutional doctrine. In practical terms, this means that cases raising the easiest constitutional questions must be identified and litigated first, before moving on to cases raising more problematic constitutional issues.

Both sets of choices are to a large extent affected by a group's organizational structure and resources. LEAF is organized both geographically and functionally. Geographically, it consists of a national office – located in Toronto – and eleven regional branches (four of which are also located in

Ontario). The national office houses LEAF's administrative apparatus, including its executive director, litigation director, and staff lawyers. Functionally, LEAF has two main governing bodies: the board of directors and the national legal committee (NLC). The board is responsible for setting general organizational policy, including case selection criteria. In addition, it plays a key role in LEAF's public education and law reform activities. The NLC's function, whose chair is a member of the board, is to select cases for LEAF support. The NLC is expected to follow the board's selection criteria, but otherwise it exercises autonomous decision-making authority in this realm. The criteria it follows include the following: (1) cases must promote substantive equality and promise significant gains for women (or gains for a significant number of women); (2) Charter cases and other cases that raise novel legal issues have precedence; (3) cases must lend themselves to resolution on equality rights grounds, as well as to remedies that promise concrete progress toward substantive equality for women; (4) preference is given to cases involving dual discrimination.[77] Although cases come to the NLC's attention in a variety of ways, most are the result of referrals from lawyers and other women's rights activists.

As Table 1.1 indicates, two sources typically provide more than half of LEAF's revenue: the LEAF Foundation and in-kind legal services. Formed in 1989 as a separate corporation, the LEAF Foundation manages an investment portfolio and makes annual operating grants to LEAF. The foundation is an incorporated, registered charitable foundation with its own board of directors. From 1999 to 2001 it also assumed regular annual fundraising responsibilities for LEAF. Between 1999 and 2001 the contribution of operating grants from the foundation grew from 20.6 to 42.2 percent of annual LEAF revenues, but dropped off slightly to 41.7 percent in 2002. In-kind legal services represent the value of the pro bono legal work by counsel acting on LEAF's behalf. The proportional contribution of this revenue source remained relatively constant from 1999 to 2001, ranging from a low of 32.2 percent in 2000 to a high of 35.9 percent in 1999. However, in 2002 this proportion dropped to 27.9 percent. Another important revenue stream comes from public and quasi-public sources such as the Women's Program of the federal secretary of state, the Court Challenges Program, and the Ontario Litigation Fund. In both 1999 and 2000, these sources provided more than 20 percent of LEAF's revenue, but in 2001 there was a sharp drop in contributions from the Women's Program and the Court Challenges Program before a substantial recovery in 2002.

LEAF responded to this drop in revenue by decreasing its administrative costs from an average of 28.8 percent in the previous two years, to 20.4 percent in 2001. Yet in 2002 administrative costs rose to 28.6 percent of expenses. In all four years, legal activities accounted for approximately 60 percent of expenses. Interestingly, there was a significant annual increase in

Table 1.1

LEAF revenue by source and LEAF expenses by type, 1999-2002

LEAF revenue by source

Year	Total revenue	Donations	In-kind legal services	LEAF Foundation	Status of Women Canada: Women's Program	Court Challenges Program Act	Other grants	Ontario Litigation Fund	Miscellaneous
2002	746,172	53,936 (7.2)	208,017 (27.9)	310,919 (41.7)	72,898 (9.8)	54,914 (7.4)	20,000 (2.7)	295 (0.04)	25,193 (3.4)
2001	908,295	71,818 (7.9)	306,983 (33.8)	383,000 (42.2)	55,000 (6.1)	24,285 (2.7)	12,500 (1.4)	20,903 (2.3)	33,806 (3.7)
2000	1,204,389	90,370 (7.5)	387,592 (32.2)	327,157 (27.2)	196,000 (16.3)	126,142 (10.5)	3,901 (0.3)	22,073 (1.8)	51,154 (4.2)
1999	1,508,804	275,758 (18.3)	541,096 (35.9)	310,853 (20.6)	190,000 (12.6)	111,749 (7.4)	6,272 (0.4)	10,406 (0.7)	62,670 (4.2)

LEAF expenses by type

Year	Total	Legal	Public education	Administration	Fundraising	Transition expenses
2002	744,083	457,782 (61.5)	71,890 (9.7)	212,873 (28.6)		1,538 (0.2)
2001	920,989	580,450 (63.1)	152,802 (16.6)	187,737 (20.4)		
2000	1,215,648	727,597 (59.9)	126,714 (10.4)	360,966 (29.7)	371 (.03)	
1999	1,494,795	896,339 (60.0)	96,780 (6.5)	417,955 (27.9)	83,721 (5.6)	

Sources: LEAF annual report, 2001-2002; LEAF annual report, 2000-2001; LEAF annual report, 1999-2000.

expenditures on public education activities for three years, from 6.5 percent of expenses in 1999 to 16.6 percent of expenses in 2001. Two important initiatives were at the core of this activity: a program to educate teenage girls about the implications of developments in sexual assault law, and workplace standards seminars for unions, lawyers, and employers. Indeed, in LEAF's 2000-2001 annual report, its executive director, Nancy Radclyffe, revealed that "LEAF and the LEAF Foundation are well into discussions and planning to make way for ground-breaking and vital changes to much that LEAF does."[78] However, the public education program appeared to run out of steam in 2002, with LEAF spending less than half on this activity than it had in 2001.

Although LEAF has directly sponsored cases in lower courts,[79] and one of its regional affiliates (West Coast LEAF) continues to do so, with only one exception its participation in the Supreme Court has been as an intervener. During the 1980s the Court changed its rules governing intervener status several times, often in response to pressure from academic criticism, advocacy groups similar to LEAF, and LEAF itself.[80] Although the rules continue to make intervener participation a matter for judicial discretion, the Court has been generous in accepting applications for leave to intervene. From 1987 to 1999, the intervener application success rate fell below 80 percent only once (79 percent in 1992), and from 1985 to 1999 the Court did not reject a single LEAF application for leave to intervene.[81] As a result, LEAF has intervened more frequently than any other nongovernment group, with only the Canadian Civil Liberties Association coming close to LEAF's intervention frequency.

What is the overall character and record of LEAF's Supreme Court activity? Between 1988 and 2000 the Supreme Court of Canada decided thirty-six cases in which LEAF participated (see Table 1.2). Ironically, given LEAF's organizational focus on equality issues, the *legal* rights provisions of the Charter (sections 7 to 14) actually constituted the most frequent type of case in which LEAF participated (twelve cases). By contrast, section 15(1) equality rights accounted for nine cases, fundamental freedoms cases for five cases, and one case encompassed both equality rights and a fundamental freedom (expression). Nine LEAF cases did not involve the Charter at all, although LEAF advanced equality-based arguments in each of them. It has intervened slightly more frequently to defend existing policy (twenty-three cases) than to advocate changes in the status quo (thirteen cases). Reflecting its geographic strength in British Columbia and Ontario, more than one-third of LEAF's cases have originated in these two provinces (eight in BC and seven in Ontario). Not surprisingly, given LEAF's position as a national organization, the federal court system has also contributed five cases to its docket.

Table 1.2

LEAF participation, position, and success in the Supreme Court

Case	Year	LEAF action	Issue	LEAF position	Result
Canadian Newspapers	1988	Intervener	Expression restricted	No	Loss
			Restriction justified (publication ban)	Yes	Win
Andrews	1989	Intervener	Substantive equality	Yes	Win
			Analogous groups protected	Yes	Win
Janzen	1989	Intervener	Sexual harassment as sex discrimination	Yes	Win
Brooks	1989	Intervener	Pregnancy distinctions as sex discrimination	Yes	Win
Borowski	1989	Intervener	Mootness	Yes	Win
			Fetal personhood	No	N/A
Daigle	1989	Intervener	Fetal personhood	No	Win
Keegstra	1990	Intervener	Expression restricted	No	Loss
			Restriction justified (hate speech)	Yes	Win
Andrews (90)	1990	Intervener	Criminal Code hate propaganda provisions constitutional	Yes	Win
Taylor	1990	Intervener	Hate communication provision of the Canadian Human Rights Act consistent with expressive freedom	Yes	Loss
			If inconsistent, then reasonable limit	Yes	Win
Sullivan	1991	Intervener	Fetal personhood	No	Win
			Fetus "in and of" the mother	Yes	N/A
Seaboyer	1991	Intervener	Sexual assault: sexual reputation admissible	No	Win
			Sexual assault: sexual history admissible	No	Loss
Canadian Council of Churches	1992	Intervener	Standing for public interest groups	Yes	Loss
Norberg	1992	Intervener	Consent defence	No	Win
Moge	1992	Intervener	Variation of spousal support orders easy	No	Win

▶

◄ *Table 1.2*

Case	Year	LEAF action	Issue	LEAF position	Result
Schachter	1992	Co-litigant	Section 52 remedy: reading in	Yes	Win
			Section 24(1) remedy: extend benefits	Yes	Loss
Butler	1992	Intervener	Expression restricted	No	Loss
			Restriction justified (pornography)	Yes	Win
M.(K.) v. *M.(H.)*	1992	Intervener	Statute of limitations on incest claims	No	Win
Weatherall	1993	Intervener	Formal equality in treatment of prisoners	No	Win
M. (M.L.)	1994	Intervener	Consent defence	No	Win
Whitley	1994	Intervener	Consent defence	No	Win
O'Connor	1995	Intervener	Disclosure of medical and therapeutic records by Crown	No	Loss
			Disclosure of medical and therapeutic records by third parties	No	Loss
Beharriel	1995	Intervener	Disclosure of medical and therapeutic records	No	Loss
Thibaudeau	1995	Intervener	Child support taxable	No	Loss
Gordon	1996	Intervener	Control over relocation of female custodial parent	No	Win
R. v. S.	1997	Intervener	Apprehension of judicial bias	No	Win
Eldridge	1997	Intervener	Right to sign-language interpretation in provision of health care	Yes	Win
Winnipeg Child and Family Services	1997	Intervener	Province may exercise *parens patriae* over fetus	No	Win
Vriend	1998	Intervener	Sexual orientation must be included in human rights statute	Yes	Win
			"Reading in" as appropriate remedy	Yes	Win
Ewanchuk	1999	Intervener	Implied consent as defence to sexual assault	No	Win

►

◄ *Table 1.2*

Case	Year	LEAF action	Issue	LEAF position	Result
M. v. H.	1999	Intervener	Same sex partners must be included in definition of spouse	Yes	Win
			Remedy: nullification with suspension	Yes	Win
BC (Public Service Employee Relations Commission)	1999	Intervener	Fitness test bona fide occupational qualification	No	Win
New Brunswick (Minister of Health and Community Services) v. G.(J.)	1999	Intervener	Parental right to security of the person in custody proceedings	Yes	Win
Mills	1999	Intervener	Fair trial: disclosure of medical and therapeutic records	No	Win
Blencoe	2000	Intervener	Unreasonable delay in human rights proceedings: s. 7 of Charter violated	No	Win
Darrach	2000	Intervener	Fair trial: revised "rape shield" provisions unconstitutional	No	Win
Little Sisters	2000	Intervener	Customs legislation violates freedom of expression	Yes	Win
			Violation of expression justified	No	Loss
			Customs legislation violates equality rights (gay and lesbian pornography)	Yes	Loss

Despite the difficulty of measuring success, several indicators suggest that LEAF has either selected its cases well or made strong arguments before the Court (see Tables 1.2 and 1.3). In terms of raw outcome, LEAF's success rate is 83.8 percent, in the sense that the Court has treated the appellate court ruling as LEAF argued it should (i.e., dismissed appeals when LEAF argued

Table 1.3

Origin and outcome of LEAF cases

Case	Origin	LEAF supports	Objective	Outcome
Canadian Newspapers	Ont. Ct. Appeal	Appellant	Allow	Allowed
Andrews	B.C. Ct. Appeal	Respondent	Dismiss	Dismissed
Janzen	Man. Ct. Appeal	Appellant	Allow	Allowed
Brooks	Man. Ct. Appeal	Appellant	Allow	Allowed
Borowski	Sask. Ct. Appeal	Respondent	Dismiss	Dismissed
Daigle	Queb. Ct. Appeal	Appellant	Allow	Allowed
Keegstra	Alta. Ct. Appeal	Appellant	Allow	Allowed
Andrews (90)	Ont. Ct. Appeal	Respondent	Dismiss	Dismissed
Taylor	Fed. Ct. Appeal	Respondent	Dismiss	Dismissed
Sullivan (A)	B.C. Ct. Appeal	Appellant	Allow	Allowed
Sullivan (B)	B.C. Ct. Appeal	Appellant	Allow	Dismissed
Seaboyer	Ont. Ct. Appeal	Respondent	Dismiss	Dismissed**
Canadian Council of Churches	Fed. Ct. Appeal	Appellant	Allow	Dismissed
Norberg	B.C. Ct. Appeal	Appellant	Allow	Allowed
Moge	Man. Ct. Appeal	Respondent	Dismiss	Dismissed
Schachter	Fed. Ct. Appeal	Respondent	Dismiss	Allowed
Butler	Man. Ct. Appeal	Respondent	Dismiss	Allowed*
M.(K.) v. M.(H.)	Ont. Ct. Appeal	Appellant	Allow	Allowed
Weatherall	Fed. Ct. Appeal	Respondent	Dismiss	Dismissed
M. (M.L.)	N.S. Ct. Appeal	Appellant	Allow	Allowed
Whitley	Ont. Ct. Appeal	Respondent	Dismiss	Dismissed
O'Connor	B.C. Ct. Appeal	Respondent	Dismiss	Dismissed
Beharriel	Ont. Ct. Appeal	Appellant	Allow	Allowed
Thibaudeau	Fed. Ct. Appeal	Respondent	Dismiss	Allowed
Gordon	Sask. Ct. Appeal	Respondent	Dismiss	Allowed (in part)*
R. v. S.	N.S. Ct. Appeal	Appellant	Allow	Allowed
Eldridge	B.C. Ct. Appeal	Appellant	Allow	Allowed
Winnipeg Child and Family Services	Man. Ct. Appeal	Respondent	Dismiss	Dismissed
Vriend	Alta. Ct. Appeal	Appellant	Allow	Allowed
Ewanchuk	Alta. Ct. Appeal	Appellant	Allow	Allowed

▶

◄ *Table 1.3*

Case	Origin	LEAF supports	Objective	Outcome
M. v. H.	Ont. Ct. Appeal	Respondent	Dismiss	Dismissed
BC (Public Service Employee Relations Commission)	B.C. Ct. Appeal	Appellant	Allow	Allowed
New Brunswick (Minister of Health and Community Services) v. *G.(J.)*	N.B. Ct. Appeal	Appellant	Allow	Allowed
Mills	Alta. Ct. Q.B.	Appellant	Allow	Allowed
Blencoe	B.C. Ct. Appeal	Appellant	Allow	Allowed
Darrach	Ont. Ct. Appeal	Respondent	Dismiss	Dismissed
Little Sisters	B.C. Ct. Appeal	Appellant	Allow	Allowed (in part)

*　Outcome loss, but issue win.
**　Outcome win, but issue loss.

to dismiss, allowed appeals when LEAF argued to allow). LEAF's success rate on specific issues is also high. In its thirty-six cases, LEAF advanced substantive arguments on fifty separate issues, and on thirty-five of those issues the Court reached a decision consistent with the position advocated by LEAF. While this success rate (70.0 percent) is lower than its success rate on raw outcomes, it is still impressive. Given that the overall success rate of Charter claims is about 33 percent,[82] LEAF's ability to choose the winning side is remarkable. Moreover, even in two cases where it lost on outcome *(Butler, Gordon)*, LEAF won on the substantive issue.

By these two measures, therefore, LEAF has reason to be pleased with its intervention activity. Other research also supports the conclusion that LEAF has been successful. Lori Hausegger calculated LEAF's success rate on outcomes at 83 percent, and its success rate on doctrine at 78 percent.[83] Morton and Allen's method, described in the Introduction, produces a blended success rate for feminist issues (which includes non-LEAF cases) of 70 percent.[84]

One reason for LEAF's success is the broad support that individual justices have provided to its positions. Between 1988 and 2000, eighteen justices cast 393 separate votes in the thirty-six Supreme Court cases in which LEAF participated (see Table 1.4). Two-thirds of those votes (262) were cast in agreement with the position advocated by LEAF. This aggregate support does conceal some individual variation in support for LEAF, however. For example, among the thirteen justices who cast at least ten votes in LEAF cases, six had support levels below 70 percent. This group included Chief

Justice Lamer (65.6 percent) and Justices Gonthier (69.0 percent), Wilson (68.8 percent), Major (65.2 percent), La Forest (56.8 percent), and Sopinka (43.3 percent). The seven justices who cast at least ten votes in LEAF cases and had support levels at or above 70 percent are Chief Justices Dickson (71.4 percent) and McLachlin (70.0 percent) and Justices Bastarache (83.3 percent), L'Heureux-Dubé (74.0 percent), Binnie (72.7 percent), Iacobucci (72.4 percent), and Cory (70.0 percent).

As one might expect, given this overall support level, LEAF cases have not been particularly divisive. As Table 1.5 shows, the Court decided thirty-two of fifty LEAF issues unanimously. The justices' dissent behaviour also provides some indication of the level of individual judicial support for LEAF (see Table 1.6). On the positive side, the justices whose net nonmajority votes favoured LEAF were Justices L'Heureux-Dubé (+3) and Gonthier (+2). At the other end of the spectrum, Justices Sopinka (-5), Major (-3), La Forest

Table 1.4

Individual judicial support for LEAF

Justice	Issues decided	For	Against	Neutral/Not applicable	% support
Beetz	2	2			100.0
Bastarache*	12	10	2		83.3
McIntyre	8	6	1	1	75.0
L'Heureux-Dubé*	50	37	9	4	74.0
Binnie*	11	8	3		72.7
Iacobucci*	29	21	8		72.4
Dickson	14	10	3	1	71.4
Cory	30	21	8	1	70.0
McLachlin*	40	28	10	2	70.0
Gonthier*	42	29	10	3	69.0
Wilson	16	11	3	2	68.8
Lamer	32	21	9	2	65.6
Major*	23	15	8		65.2
Arbour*	5	3	2		60.0
Lebel*	5	3	2		60.0
La Forest	37	21	11	5	56.8
Sopinka	30	13	15	2	43.3
Stevenson	7	3	3	1	42.9
Total	393	262	107	24	66.7

* Active as of 6 August 2001.

(-3), and Lamer (-2) were more likely to vote against the majority in order to oppose the position supported by LEAF. Two final phenomena from which LEAF has benefited are its partnership with governments and the relative absence of opposing nongovernmental interests in its cases (see Tables 1.7 and 1.8).

LEAF has intervened on the side of governments in twenty cases, and against governments in twelve. In three of its six outcome losses, LEAF opposed some governmental interest. However, on four occasions LEAF managed to be on the winning side despite the opposition of more than two governments. With respect to other groups, LEAF has been the sole nongovernmental intervener in eleven cases, and in an additional thirteen cases

Table 1.5

Court voting on LEAF issues, 1988-2000

Case	Issue	Vote	Dissents
Canadian	Expression restricted	0-6	
Newspapers	Restriction justified (publication ban)	6-0	
Andrews	Substantive equality	6-0	
	Analogous groups protected	6-0	
Janzen	Sexual harassment as sex discrimination	6-0	
Brooks	Pregnancy distinctions as sex discrimination	6-0	
Borowski	Mootness	7-0	
	Fetal personhood	N/A	
Daigle	Fetal personhood	9-0	
Keegstra	Expression restricted	0-7	
	Restriction justified (hate speech)	4-3	La Forest, Sopinka, McLachlin
Andrews (90)	Hate propaganda provisions constitutional	4-3	La Forest, Sopinka, McLachlin
Taylor	Hate propaganda constitutionally protected	0-7	
	If protected, limit reasonable	4-3	La Forest, Sopinka, McLachlin
Sullivan	Fetal personhood	8-0	
	Fetus "in and of" mother	0-1-8	L'Heureux-Dubé (remainder of Court chooses not to decide issue)

▶

◄ *Table 1.5*

Case	Issue	Vote	Dissents
Seaboyer	Sexual assault: sexual reputation admissible	9-0	
	Sexual assault: sexual history admissible	2-7	L'Heureux-Dubé, Gonthier
Canadian Council of Churches	Standing for public interest groups	0-7	
Norberg	Consent defence	5-0	
Moge	Variation of spousal support orders easy	6-0	
Schachter	Section 52 remedy: reading in	5-0-2	La Forest, L'Heureux-Dubé see no reason to decide this issue
	Section 24(1) remedy: extend benefits	0-5-2	La Forest, L'Heureux-Dubé see no reason to decide this issue
Butler	Expression restricted	0-9	
	Restriction justified (pornography)	9-0	
M.(K.) v. M.(H.)	Statute of limitations on incest claims	7-0	
Weatherall	Formal equality in treatment of prisoners	7-0	
M. (M.L.)	Consent defence	9-0	
Whitley	Consent defence	9-0	
O'Connor	Disclosure of medical and therapeutic records by Crown	4-5	La Forest, L'Heureux-Dubé, Gonthier, McLachlin
	Disclosure of medical and therapeutic records by third parties	0-5-4	La Forest, L'Heureux-Dubé, Gonthier, McLachlin argue that issue should not be decided since not raised by case
Beharriel	Disclosure of medical and therapeutic records	0-7	
Thibaudeau	Child support taxable	2-5	L'Heureux-Dubé, McLachlin
Gordon	Control over relocation of female custodial parent	9-0	

►

◄ *Table 1.5*

Case	Issue	Vote	Dissents
R. v. S.	Apprehension of judicial bias	6-3	Lamer, Sopinka, Major
Eldridge	Right to sign-language interpretation in provision of health care	9-0	
Winnipeg Child and Family Services	Province may exercise parens patriae over fetus	7-2	Sopinka, Major
Vriend	Sexual orientation must be included in human rights statute	8-0	
	"Reading in" as appropriate remedy	7-1	Major
Ewanchuk	Implied consent as defence to sexual assault	9-0	
M. v. H.	Same sex partners must be included in definition of spouse	8-1	Gonthier
	Remedy: nullification with suspension	8-0	
BC (Public Service Employee Relations Commission)	Fitness test bona fide occupational qualification	9-0	
NB (Minister of Health and Community Services) v. G.(J.)	Parental right to security of the person in custody proceedings	7-0	
Mills	Fair trial: disclosure of medical and therapeutic records	7-1	Lamer
Blencoe	Unreasonable delay in human rights proceedings: s. 7 of Charter applies	5-4	Iacobucci, Binnie, Arbour, Lebel (dissent based on administrative law principles)
Darrach	Fair trial: revised "rape shield" provisions unconstitutional	9-0	
Little Sisters	Customs legislation violates freedom of expression (gay and lesbian pornography)	9-0	
	Violation of expression justified	3-6	Iacobucci, Arbour, Lebel
	Customs legislation violates equality rights	0-9	

Table 1.6

Dissent behaviour in LEAF cases[*]

Justice	Dissents	For LEAF	Against LEAF	Difference
L'Heureux-Dubé	7	5	2	+3
Gonthier	4	3	1	+2
McLachlin	6	3	3	0
Arbour	2	1	1	0
Iacobucci	2	1	1	0
Lebel	2	1	1	0
Binnie	1		1	-1
Lamer	2		2	-2
La Forest	7	2	5	-3
Major	3		3	-3
Sopinka	5		5	-5

[*] Dissent is defined here as voting differently from the majority.

Table 1.7

Government participants in LEAF cases

Case	Supporting LEAF	Opposing LEAF	Outcome
Canadian Newspapers	CAN, ON, QC		Win
Andrews		BC, ON, QC, NS, SK, AB	Win
Janzen			Win
Brooks	MB		Win
Borowski	CAN		Win
Daigle	CAN, QC		Win
Keegstra	AB, CAN, ON, QC, NB, MB		Win
Andrews (90)	ON, CAN, QC, NB, MB		Win
Taylor	CAN, ON, QC, MB		Win
Sullivan (A)		BC	Win
Sullivan (B)	BC		Loss
Seaboyer	ON, CAN, QC, SK		Win (issue loss)
Canadian Council of Churches		CAN	Loss
Norberg			Win

▶

◄ *Table 1.7*

Case	Supporting LEAF	Opposing LEAF	Outcome
Moge			Win
Schachter		CAN, ON, QC, NB, BC, SK, AB, NFLD	Loss
Butler	MB, CAN, ON, QC, BC, AB		Loss (issue win)
M.(K.) v. M.(H.)			Win
Weatherall	CAN, ON, QC, BC		Win
M. (M.L.)	NS		Win
Whitley	ON		Win
O'Connor	BC, CAN, ON		Win
Beharriel	ON, CAN, MB		Win
Thibaudeau		CAN, QC	Loss
Gordon			Loss (in part)
R. v. S.			Win
Eldridge		BC, CAN, ON, MB, NFLD	Win
Winnipeg Child and Family Services		MB, YK	Win
Vriend	CAN (In part)	AB, ON	Win
Ewanchuk	AB, CAN		Win
M. v. H.		ON*	Win
BC (Public Service Employee Relations Commission)		BC*	Win
NB (Minister of Health and Community Services) v. G.(J.)		NB, MB, BC, AB	Win
Mills	AB, CAN, ON, QC, NS, MB, BC, PEI, SK		Win
Blencoe	ON, BC		Win
Darrach	ON, CAN, QC, MB, BC		Win
Little Sisters		CAN, BC, ON	Win (in part)

*   In both of these cases, although the two governments opposed LEAF, the provincial human rights commissions supported LEAF.

Table 1.8

Other nongovernment interveners in LEAF cases

Case	Supporting LEAF	Opposing LEAF
Andrews	COPOH, CAUT/OCUFA	Federation of Law Societies
Borowski		REAL Women, Interfaith
Daigle	CARAL, CCLA	REAL Women, Campaign Life Coalition
Keegstra	B'nai B'rith, Interamicus, Canadian Jewish Congress	CCLA
Andrews (90)	Canadian Jewish Congress, League for Human Rights of B'nai B'rith Canada, Interamicus	CCLA
Taylor	Canadian Jewish Congress, League for Human Rights of B'nai B'rith Canada, Canadian Holocaust Remembrance Association, Canadian Civil Liberties Association	
Sullivan		REAL Women
Seaboyer	CCLA (sexual reputation)	CCLA (sexual history)
Canadian Council of Churches	CDRC, B'nai B'rith, COPOH	
Schachter	Minority Advocacy and Rights Council (reading in)	Minority Advocacy and Rights Council (benefit extension)
Butler	Group Against Pornography	MBCLA/CCLA, BCCLA
Weatherall	Coalition of Provincial Organizations of the Handicapped, Minority Advocacy and Rights Council	
O'Connor	Aboriginal Women's Council, Canadian Association of Sexual Assault Centres, DisAbled Women's Network of Canada, Canadian Mental Health Association, Canadian Foundation for Children, Youth and the Law	
Beharriel	Canadian Foundation for Children, Youth and the Law, Aboriginal Women's Council, Canadian Association of Sexual Assault Centres, DisAbled Women's Network Ontario	Criminal Lawyers Association

▶

◄ *Table 1.8*

Case	Supporting LEAF	Opposing LEAF
Thibaudeau	SCOPE, Charter Committee on Poverty Issues, Federated Anti-Poverty Groups of British Columbia, National Action Committee on the Status of Women	
R. v. S.	National Organization of Immigrant and Visible, Minority Women of Canada, African Canadian Legal Clinic, Afro-Canadian Caucus of Nova Scotia, Congress of Black Women of Canada	
Eldridge	DisAbled Women's Network Canada, Charter Committee on Poverty Issues, Canadian Association of the Deaf, Canadian Hearing Society and Council of Canadians with Disabilities	
Winnipeg Child and Family Services	Canadian Civil Liberties Association, Canadian Abortion Rights Action League, Women's Health Clinic, Metis Women of Manitoba, Native Women's Transition Centre, Manitoba Association of Rights and Liberties	Evangelical Fellowship of Canada, Christian Medical and Dental Society, Catholic Group for Health, Justice and Life, Alliance for Life, Association des Centres jeunesse du Québec, South-east Child and Family Services, West Region Child and Family Services
Vriend	Alberta Civil Liberties Association, Equality for Gays and Lesbians Everywhere (EGALE), Foundation for Equal Families, Canadian Human Rights Commission, Canadian Labour Congress, Canadian Bar Association – Alberta Branch, Canadian Association of Statutory Human Rights Agencies (CASHRA), Canadian AIDS Society, Alberta and Northwest Conference of the United Church of Canada, Canadian Jewish Congress	Christian Legal Fellowship, Alberta Federation of Women United for Families, Evangelical Fellowship of Canada, Focus on the Family (Canada) Association

►

◄ *Table 1.8*

Case	Supporting LEAF	Opposing LEAF
Ewanchuk	DisAbled Women's Network Canada, Sexual Assault Centre of Edmonton	
M. v. H.	Foundation for Equal Families, Equality for Gays and Lesbians Everywhere (EGALE), United Church of Canada	Evangelical Fellowship of Canada, Ontario Council of Sikhs, Islamic Society of North America, Focus on the Family, REAL Women of Canada
BC (Public Service Employee Relations Commission)	DisAbled Women's Network Canada, Canadian Labour Congress	
New Brunswick (Minister of Health and Community Services) v. *G.(J.)*	Canadian Bar Association, Charter Committee on Poverty Issues, National Association of Women and the Law, DisAbled Women's Network Canada, Watch Tower Bible and Tract Society of Canada	
Mills	Canadian Mental Health Association, Canadian Psychiatric Association, Child and Adolescent Services Association, Alberta Association of Sexual Assault Centres, Sexual Assault Centre of Edmonton	Criminal Lawyers' Association (Ontario), Association québécoise des avocats et avocates de la défense, Canadian Civil Liberties Association, Canadian Council of Criminal Defence Lawyers
Darrach	Canadian Association of Sexual Assault Centres, DisAbled Women's Network Canada, National Action Committee on the Status of Women	
Little Sisters	Canadian AIDS Society, Canadian Civil Liberties Association, Canadian Conference of the Arts, EGALE Canada Inc., PEN Canada	Equality Now

its position has been unopposed by any other society-based interest. The groups most frequently opposed to LEAF have been REAL Women (on abortion and fetal rights issues) and the Canadian Civil Liberties Association (CCLA) (on sexual assault trial procedure and freedom of expression issues). Despite its opposition to LEAF on some issues, the CCLA has nevertheless supported LEAF's position in several cases. The DisAbled Women's Network (DAWN) has been the single most frequent women's movement group to intervene on LEAF's side. LEAF also forged important coalitions with gay and lesbian rights organizations, such as Equality for Gays and Lesbians Everywhere (EGALE) and the Foundation for Equal Families, in the latter half of the 1990s. Other groups with multiple interventions in conjunction with LEAF include the Coalition of Provincial Organizations of the Handicapped (COPOH), the Canadian Abortion Rights Action League (CARAL), and the Canadian Jewish Congress (CJC). The importance of these partnerships and coalitions, along with the relative absence of nongovernmental groups on the opposing side, lies in the signal it sends to the Court about general social support for the positions advocated by LEAF.

LEAF's participation in the Supreme Court does not, of course, provide a complete picture of feminist legal mobilization in the post-Charter era. Most obviously, LEAF itself has been active in litigation outside the Supreme Court, as well as in making submissions to various legislative committees. These activities play a crucial role in advancing LEAF's agenda. In addition, although LEAF understands itself as a feminist organization,[85] the agenda of Canadian feminism goes well beyond the issues litigated by LEAF. Finally, as Table 1.8 illustrates, LEAF is not the only organization that litigates on behalf of women. Other feminist groups often appear before the Supreme Court in conjunction with, or in the absence of, LEAF.

The importance of looking beyond LEAF can be illustrated by a brief discussion of four cases that do not appear in Table 1.2: *Morgentaler, Smoling and Scott* v. *The Queen* (1988), *R.* v. *Morgentaler* (1993), *Symes* v. *Canada* (1993), and *R.* v. *Daviault* (1994).[86] Although the 1988 *Morgentaler* decision provided Canadian feminists with a key policy victory by nullifying the existing abortion provisions of the Criminal Code, no feminist group – indeed no nongovernmental group of any kind – participated directly in the case. Although Henry Morgentaler's lawyer, Morris Manning, had links to the pro-choice movement and to CARAL, the *Morgentaler* (1988) litigation was more the product of its main protagonist's individual efforts than of an organized social movement.[87] The absence of organized pro-choice participants in *Morgentaler* (1988) may be one explanation for the Court's relatively cautious judgment. Only Justice Bertha Wilson was willing to base her judgment on a conception of liberty broad enough to encompass reproductive freedom and prohibit all government regulation of abortion during at least the early stages of pregnancy. Inspired by the Chief Justice, who declared that it was "neither necessary nor wise" to "explore the broadest implications" of liberty in analyzing the abortion provisions,[88] a plurality of the Court focused on the impact of the statute's administrative structure. According to these four justices, administrative deficiencies produced unjustified delays in securing abortions, which in turn infringed security of the person in both its physical and psychological dimensions. In addition, two justices (including the Chief Justice) found that these deficiencies created unequal access to a criminal defence in violation of the principles of fundamental justice. While these procedural grounds were sufficient to nullify the existing law, they were narrow enough to leave room for the reestablishment of criminal regulation of abortion under a different administrative scheme.

Consequently, LEAF's involvement in abortion litigation began in earnest as the legal status quo established in 1988 came under attack from both individuals and governments. Thus, as Table 1.2 shows, LEAF intervened successfully in *Daigle* (1989) and *Borowski* (1989). However, it did not intervene in *Morgentaler* (1993), which concerned a provincial law designed to prohibit the establishment of private, free-standing abortion clinics by requiring that abortions be performed in provincially administered hospitals. Instead, CARAL took responsibility for articulating the feminist position, albeit under the direction of LEAF founding member Mary Eberts. This non-LEAF intervention was successful, as the Court nullified the requirement on the grounds that it intruded on the federal government's criminal law power.

LEAF's absence from *Symes* is a more complicated story, and it illustrates some of the tensions underlying feminist legal mobilization. At issue in *Symes* was whether self-employed professionals could deduct child-care expenses as business expenditures under the Income Tax Act (ITA). Elizabeth Symes, a lawyer, argued that the ITA's failure to permit the deduction of child-care expenses from business income violated section 15 because of its disproportionate impact on women. The case thus raised several issues of obvious relevance to the women's movement's policy agenda and LEAF's doctrinal objectives. From a policy perspective, the case was about access to child care, which is a key precondition for women's participation in the public sphere. From a legal perspective, the case challenged the doctrine of formal equality and relied on "adverse effects" discrimination to advance its section 15 claim. Certainly Justices McLachlin and L'Heureux-Dubé, who dissented from their male colleagues' denial of Symes's claim, saw the case as challenging an important impediment to "the attainment of substantive equality for women."[89]

In one sense, LEAF was not entirely absent from *Symes*.[90] Both the appellant (Elizabeth Symes) and her lawyer (Mary Eberts) had strong connections to LEAF. They were coauthors of the document that gave birth to

LEAF, and both had served on LEAF's national legal committee. However, neither LEAF nor any other explicitly feminist organization intervened in *Symes*. Indeed, the women's movement was skeptical about the policy benefits that might derive from a legal victory in *Symes*. According to Razack, this "approach to the child care problem was explicitly rejected by the Canadian Day Care Advocacy Association as being beneficial to middle- and upper-class women at the expense of others."[91] The ITA changes demanded by Symes could have undercut support from an influential constituency for a national, publicly funded day care policy.[92] In addition, others within the women's movement were critical of the exploitative relationship between privileged, mostly white professional employers and their marginalized, mostly immigrant, domestic employees.[93] In sum, the *Symes* litigation did not appear to be for the collective benefit of women as a group. Indeed, ten years after the judgment, a former member of LEAF's national litigation committee criticized those who supported the *Symes* litigation for ignoring its "fundamental commodification of racialized women as tax write-offs."[94]

The final non-LEAF case that merits attention is *Daviault*. At issue was whether the defence of extreme intoxication could be invoked in sexual assault cases.[95] In 1977 the Supreme Court had declared that intoxication was not available as a defence for general intent offences, and in 1987 the Court had added sexual assault to the list of such offences. Although there was some judicial ambivalence about these rules, it was still remarkable that a trial judge would acquit Henri Daviault of sexual assault on the grounds that his intoxication had rendered him unable to form the minimal intent necessary to meet the *mens rea* of this offence. The Quebec Court of Appeal overturned the trial verdict and Daviault appealed to the Supreme Court. Surprisingly, the Court overturned its previous rule by a six-to-three margin and held that the categorical exclusion of intoxication as a defence to sexual assault violates a defendant's Charter rights.

One possible explanation for LEAF's failure to intervene in *Daviault* is that it reached the Court as an appeal by right. As Chief Justice McLachlin told the Canadian Bar Association in August 2001, these cases rarely raise novel legal issues that require the Supreme Court's attention.[96] Such appeals are usually dealt with summarily and generally result in the Court's affirming the appellate court ruling. Consequently, there may have been little reason to anticipate that the Court would use *Daviault* to make new law contrary to the women's movement's interests, especially since the appellate court ruling had affirmed the existing legal rule. In addition, LEAF had a low profile in Quebec, which may have affected its assessment of the case's significance.[97] For example, only 7 of the 104 women who served on LEAF's board of directors from 1985 to 1995 were francophone. Similarly, during this period, only three of fifty-nine members of LEAF's National Legal Committee, and one of fifty-nine members of its national staff were francophone.

Only two francophone women served as counsel for LEAF before the Supreme Court, and only two of its Supreme Court cases originated in Quebec (and one of these, *Thibaudeau*, actually came through the federal court system). Finally, by 1995, LEAF litigation outside the Supreme Court included only one case in Quebec. As Radha Jhappan notes, "LEAF has never, in fact, been as widely accepted or promoted in Quebec as it has been in Ontario or elsewhere in Canada."[98]

Through LEAF's efforts, the Supreme Court has become an important site of feminist activism. Although this activism has been perhaps more passive and defensive than LEAF might have originally preferred, it has been on one level successful. LEAF has enjoyed broad judicial support, and this support has translated into high rates of success in terms of both outcome and doctrine. Whether this activism has improved the social, economic, or political status of women is a more complicated question.

Conclusion

Where do LEAF's achievements in the Supreme Court stand in relation to the various findings of the legal mobilization literature? By any measure, LEAF falls within Galanter's repeat player category. LEAF did not emerge in explicit opposition to the state, or at least to the federal state. Its founding document was a report commissioned by the federally funded Canadian Advisory Council on the Status of Women.[99] Its subsequent legal research and litigation activities have also depended heavily on federal financial support. For example, in 1999-2000 LEAF received over 25 percent of its revenue from Status of Women Canada (within the Department of Canadian Heritage) and the Court Challenges Program (CCP).[100] The CCP funding is particularly significant because LEAF was instrumental in lobbying the federal government to expand the program to cover equality rights; in pressuring the newly elected Liberal government to restore the program in 1994 after it had been cancelled by the Progressive Conservatives in 1992; and in managing the program since 1997.[101] LEAF's cooperation with the federal state has also extended to litigation itself, with LEAF aligning itself with the federal government in sixteen cases before the Supreme Court. Its status, which is the product of several factors, has allowed it to become the most frequent nongovernmental participant in the Supreme Court.[102]

LEAF has also benefited from the level of legal expertise that one would expect from a repeat player litigant. The core group of activists who founded LEAF had strong connections to the elite levels of the Canadian legal profession. For example, Mary Eberts was an LLM graduate of Harvard Law School, and at the time of LEAF's founding she was a partner in the prestigious Toronto law firm, Tory Tory DesLauriers and Binnington. Lynn Smith, to cite another example, was a professor at the University of British Columbia Law School, and would eventually be appointed to the BC Supreme

Court. Other founders of LEAF had similarly prestigious pedigrees. Indeed, perceptions of elitism sometimes generated tensions between LEAF and other feminist organizations.

One of the underlying principles of LEAF is that "law can be an effective tool for egalitarian social change."[103] Whether LEAF's belief in this principle is warranted or is simply a function of Scheingold's "myth of rights," there is no question that in the early 1980s the Canadian feminist movement perceived new opportunities to pursue law reform. The introduction of a constitutionally entrenched rights document, the changing composition of the Supreme Court, favourable developments in analogous areas of the law, and a maturing litigation support structure created the potential for a feminist rights revolution. The Canadian feminist movement mobilized to exploit this opportunity to become a repeat player in the equality rights field. As this chapter suggests, it did so with at least a modicum of success in the Supreme Court. In the chapters that follow, I explore in more detail how, and to what effect, the movement mobilized law in the arenas of constitutional politics and Supreme Court litigation to promote its objective of substantive equality.

2
The Path to Substantive Equality

The objective of feminist legal mobilization since 1980 has been to establish and apply a constitutional rule of substantive equality. As a legal concept, substantive equality does not mean equal treatment. Indeed, equal treatment is neither necessary nor sufficient for the existence of substantive equality. It is unnecessary because substantive equality anticipates differential (i.e., ameliorative) treatment of historically disadvantaged groups, and equal treatment is insufficient precisely because it does not account for the cumulative effects of alleged past discrimination. The doctrine of substantive equality demands that law and policy be concerned with actual differences in the social and political condition of specified groups rather than with the neutral application of formal rules to similarly situated individuals. For Canadian feminists, the negative judicial outcomes of the 1970s were the inevitable result of a superficial emphasis on legal equality.[1]

Although this objective has led the women's movement to litigation in the Supreme Court, it began in – and twice returned to – the political arena of formal constitutional amendment. It is therefore important to begin the discussion of feminist legal mobilization with some general reflections on the politics of constitutional modification, including the relationship between the macroconstitutional politics of formal amendment and the microconstitutional politics of litigation.[2] Whether macro or micro, the politics of constitutional modification is always about rules. The *primary* rules of a constitution are those found in its text, while *secondary* rules refer to those derived from the text through judicial review and interpretation. For the Canadian women's movement, therefore, the path to substantive equality has required macro- and microconstitutional mobilization around a specific set of primary and secondary rules. The political dynamics of the broader process of constitutional modification thus form an important backdrop to the movement's activities, particularly during the period from 1980 to 1992. In this chapter I elaborate this backdrop more fully, examine the women's movement's activity in the macroconstitutional arena during three periods of comprehensive constitutional modification, and analyze LEAF's interventions in the Supreme Court in five cases concerning the definition of equality and discrimination.

The Politics of Constitutional Modification

The aim of any model of constitutional modification is to understand why some modifications succeed and others fail. The model I employ focuses on the ability of constitutional actors to predict and control the specific policy consequences of new constitutional rules.[3] Three institutional variables – *institutional rigidity, interpretive flexibility,* and *litigation potential* – form the core of the model. The basic thrust of the argument is that the very features of a constitutional rule that make it attractive to its sponsors – indeterminate language that facilitates litigation to generate a wide range of specific policies that are difficult to reverse – are precisely what makes constitutional modification more difficult to achieve. In this section of the chapter I elaborate on this model and apply it to the Canadian case, with particular emphasis on its impact on feminist participation in macroconstitutional politics.

An Institutional Design Model

How difficult is it to amend a constitution? Is its language broad and open-ended, or is it narrow and specific? To what extent are nongovernmental actors able and willing to use constitutional litigation as an instrument to advance their interests? In an institutional design model of constitutional modification, the answers to these questions provide some insight into the conditions under which constitutional rules can be changed. A very rigid amendment process, for example, affects the probability of successfully implementing formal constitutional amendment in two ways. First, the procedural complexity of an institutionally rigid amendment process makes the barriers to formal modification exceptionally high. Second, institutional rigidity enhances uncertainty by increasing the costs of miscalculating the impact of proposed amendments. The difficulty of implementing amendments in the first instance means that it will also be difficult for either state or society-based actors to remedy any unanticipated negative consequences of a successful amendment through a formal counter-amendment. As a result, the politics of formal constitutional modification becomes a set of discrete zero-sum games. Institutional rigidity thus suppresses the incentive, which is common in the more fluid legislative process, of competing groups to compromise on their demands in order to form and maintain policy coalitions. This exacerbates the level of conflict surrounding formal amendment proposals. Moreover, institutional rigidity provides amendment opponents with the means to defeat the proposal.

Although institutional rigidity significantly reduces the frequency of formal amendment, it does not obviate the basic necessity of periodic modification in every constitutional system. In stable constitutional systems characterized by both institutional rigidity and the doctrine of constitutional supremacy, the most common alternative to formal amendment is modification through judicial interpretation.[4] This practice points to the importance of both interpretive flexibility and litigation potential.

Interpretive flexibility refers to the capacity of a constitutional rule to support a wide range of meaning. Some constitutional rules are "phrased in general terms and have the potential to influence a wide variety of policy outcomes," while others are "indistinguishable in form from the rules contained in ordinary legislation" and affect "a limited set of policy outcomes."[5] The more general the rule, the more interpretive flexibility it permits, and this has two implications for the political dynamics of constitutional modification. On the one hand, it allows the proponents of constitutional change to conceal their ultimate policy objectives behind a veil of linguistic ambiguity. On the other hand, their opponents can exploit that very ambiguity by exaggerating the likely policy impact of the rule.

Interpretive flexibility is a key determinant of the litigation potential of any constitutional rule. The ambiguous nature of highly flexible rules virtually guarantees that litigation will be necessary to clarify their meaning. In addition, litigation potential depends on the existence and variety of political actors able to exploit constitutional litigation opportunities. The existence of systematic, repeat-player litigants in a policy area broadly affected by a proposed constitutional amendment increases the probability that a proposed rule will generate unanticipated policy consequences through litigation and judicial interpretation.

How do these institutional variables affect the success or failure of formal amendment proposals? The combined impact of institutional rigidity, interpretive flexibility, and high litigation potential increases policy uncertainty by entrenching rules whose future meaning and impact is subject to the dynamics of constitutional litigation. Under these conditions, political actors have a strong incentive to mobilize against proposed amendments in order to prevent unfavourable policy outcomes. At a minimum, this opposition will take the form of interpretive rule demands, which are designed to limit the manoeuvrability of judicial decision makers. These demands are likely to be contentious and to meet resistance from the initial sponsors of an amendment.

Thus, where constitutional actors are faced with an attempt to add an interpretively flexible amendment with high litigation potential to an institutionally rigid constitution, the likelihood increases that the politics of constitutional modification will generate a degree of uncertainty under which the process may collapse. In an important sense, this dynamic is a by-product of the interaction between the macrolevel constitutional politics of formal amendment and the microlevel constitutional politics of litigation and judicial interpretation.

Perhaps the most relevant way to illustrate this dynamic is with reference to the decline in fortunes of the Equal Rights Amendment in the United States. By the end of 1972, the amendment's ratification seemed certain, but ten years later, despite Congress's extension of the ratification period, it was dead. Jane Mansbridge has explained the ERA's failure by observing that "no really controversial amendment has passed [in the United States] since Prohibition was repealed."[6] At first glance, this conclusion is puzzling, given that the ERA had a long political gestation during which its supporters successfully built a consensus around the general principle of gender equality.[7] Indeed, a constitutional guarantee of the equal rights of men and women had attracted the support of every US president from Harry Truman to Jimmy Carter. Moreover, the principle of gender equality underlay Title VII of the 1964 Civil Rights Act, which prohibits discrimination on the basis of sex. Finally, Congress itself passed the ERA by large majorities in both the House of Representatives (354 to 23) and the Senate (84 to 8). How, then, were the ERA's opponents able to defeat it?

According to Mansbridge, pro-ERA sentiment diminished as its opponents focused on possible judicial interpretation of the amendment. In terms of the institutional design model of constitutional modification, the ERA became controversial when the focus of the ratification debate explicitly shifted toward its potential redistributive impact within an institutional context that made this impact extremely difficult to predict. The ERA's redistributive implications became particularly apparent following the Supreme Court's abortion decision in late January of 1973. In that decision – *Roe* v. *Wade* – the Court revolutionized US constitutional law by holding that women could claim a virtually unrestricted right to abortion during the first two trimesters of pregnancy. What made this decision especially controversial was the Court's inability to demonstrate convincingly that either the general right to privacy or the specific right to abortion could be found in the express language or "manifest tenor" of the constitution. For opponents of abortion, the ERA was problematic because it could be interpreted as providing a more solid constitutional foundation for the right to abortion. This interpretation would have complicated legislative efforts by the pro-life movement to limit the impact of *Roe*.[8] In addition, the ERA made further "feminist" constitutional gains possible. If the Court could extract a right to abortion from the distantly relevant language of the First, Third, Fourth, and Fifth Amendments, ERA opponents asked, what might it do with an amendment directly linked to the interests of the women's movement?

To the ERA's opponents, the decision in *Roe* clearly signalled the impossibility of predicting the amendment's policy consequences. They were thus able to use *Roe* to attack the ERA as the prelude to a more comprehensive feminist litigation campaign, the outcome of which would be to eliminate existing protections for women while imposing new obligations on them such as compulsory military service in combat roles. Congressional supporters of the ERA responded to the opposition's strategy by attempting to attach interpretive rules to the amendment that would foreclose the policy consequences that the ERA's opponents were using to attack it. These attempts were opposed by ERA supporters, who argued that interpretive rules would undermine the amendment's symbolic value and make it more difficult to mobilize activists at the state level who were unwilling to expend energy on anything less than fundamental constitutional modification. Moreover, from their perspective, these interpretive rules contributed to a different kind of redistributive indeterminacy by making it less likely that the ERA would have its intended positive policy impact. In the final analysis, the institutional dynamics of the US amending process – multiple actors engaged in a one-shot competition over an interpretively fluid constitutional rule – generated a high level of redistributive indeterminacy that transformed virtually certain ratification into failure when the process collapsed over the issue of interpretive rules designed to reduce that indeterminacy.

To return to Mansbridge's observation: the ERA was controversial because of its redistributive indeterminacy. To a large degree, that indeterminacy was a direct result of an amending process characterized by high levels of amending process rigidity, interpretive fluidity, and institutional inclusiveness. Nevertheless, indeterminacy need not have been fatal; it could have been mitigated by a set of interpretive rules designed to assure opponents that the ERA would not have the redistributive consequences they feared. Ironically, this would have reversed the direction of indeterminacy, a fact recognized by the ERA's proponents, who therefore rejected such rules. The amendment could not survive the regulative and interpretive rule demands of its opponents because the ERA's supporters would not accommodate those demands.

The Dynamics of Constitutional Modification in Canada, 1980-1992

More than any other advanced, liberal-democratic regime, Canada's recent history has been dominated by the politics of comprehensive constitutional modification involving fundamental regime principles. Indeed, between 1980 and 1992, Canada undertook three successive attempts at mega-constitutional politics to reconfigure its institutional framework through formal amendment. Although characterized by acrimonious intergovernmental negotiations, lengthy parliamentary hearings, a controversial Supreme

Court decision, and profound opposition in Quebec, the first attempt succeeded in 1982 in modifying Canada's constitution to include a domesti-
cally controlled amending formula and a judicially enforceable Charter of
Rights and Freedoms.[9] The second effort produced the 1987 Meech Lake
Accord, which attempted to ameliorate the perceived shortcomings of the
1982 modifications by recognizing Quebec as a distinct society and including a revised amending formula and important provisions concerning immigration policy, Supreme Court appointments, and federal spending
powers. Despite initial public support (56 percent approval), unequivocal
ratification by the federal House of Commons (242 to 16), and ratification
by eight of the ten provinces within the first twelve months of the ratification process, the Meech Lake Accord could not be ratified by its June 1990
deadline.[10]

Convinced that Meech Lake failed because it emerged from a closed negotiation process that focused too narrowly on Quebec's concerns, Canadian
political leaders changed tactics by making the process of framing constitutional amendments more participatory, and by providing for ratification by
popular referendum. The federal government issued a new set of constitutional reform proposals in September 1991. Containing twenty-eight recommendations, these proposals covered eight principal subjects: the nature
of Canada, Quebec as a distinct society, changes to the Charter, Aboriginal
self-government, senate reform, the Supreme Court, economic union, and
the division of powers. The task of gathering public reaction to the proposals was delegated to a committee supplemented by five constitutional confer-
ences. The committee met for two weeks in a closed-door session to produce
a 125-page report recommending changes to all the federal proposals.

The final step in the process was a meeting of First Ministers and territo-
rial and Aboriginal leaders at Charlottetown in August of 1992. The *Consensus Report of the Constitution* issued after that meeting dealt with six issues:
unity and diversity, social and economic union, parliamentary reform, the
federal division of powers, Aboriginal self-government, and the constitutional amendment process. Despite the efforts at public consultation, and
the attempt, through the Charlottetown Accord, to address concerns raised
by a wide range of political actors, Canadian voters rejected it by a significant margin.[11]

Why was Canada unable to reproduce the relative success of 1980-82?
Prior to 1982, the absence of specific written rules made the formal amendment process institutionally flexible. Indeed, the process was so flexible
that it took a series of three Supreme Court decisions in the early 1980s to
establish even the basic legal framework governing formal amendment.[12]
As a result, despite the inability of political leaders to agree on a domestic
amending formula, Canada formally amended its constitution several times
between 1870 and 1982.[13] Moreover, the constitution continuously evolved

through the emergence and development of various informal constitutional conventions.[14] The key to this institutional flexibility was the practice of negotiating amendments among federal and provincial government leaders through a closed process of elite accommodation.

As in most modern constitutional democracies, the indeterminate language of many provisions in the Constitution Act, 1867, combined with the practice of judicial review to generate interpretive flexibility. The most explicit statement of this flexibility is found in the 1930 decision by the Judicial Committee of the Privy Council (JCPC) that "the B[ritish] N[orth] A[merica] Act planted in Canada a living tree capable of growth and expansion within its natural limits."[15] Canadian judges also found sufficient flexibility in these rules to extract an "implicit" bill of rights from the constitution even in the absence of specific protection for individual rights such as freedom of speech and the press.[16] Although interpretive flexibility did produce some unexpected policy consequences, especially with respect to federal and provincial powers, its political impact was mitigated by the institutional flexibility of the amending process. Indeed, the available evidence suggests that federal and provincial governments have been reasonably adept at adapting to adverse constitutional interpretations, as they did in 1940 by amending the constitution to transfer jurisdiction over unemployment insurance to the federal government.[17]

The political impact of interpretive flexibility was also constrained by the relatively low litigation potential of pre-1982 rules. With constitutional litigation focused on federalism issues, the most that interest groups could achieve from litigation was the indirect, and often temporary, benefit of a redistribution of power between levels of government. The low political utility of constitutional litigation is reflected in the fact that constitutional cases represented less than 3 percent of the Supreme Court's decisions from 1962 to 1971, a proportion that increased to a still low 5.5 percent between 1972 and 1981.[18] Nor was litigation potential enhanced by the adoption of a quasi-constitutional Bill of Rights in 1960. Indeed, between 1960 and 1981 only thirty-four Bill of Rights cases reached the Supreme Court, and only five of these were successful.[19]

The litigation utility of the Bill of Rights was diminished by two key factors. First, and most obviously, the Bill lacked constitutional status, which weakened any claim that it could be used legitimately to nullify legislation or impose policy obligations on the federal government (the only level of government to which it applied). Second, its recognition of rights and freedoms that "have existed and continue to exist" discouraged judicial creativity in the definition and enforcement of civil liberties. This second factor, in particular, signalled to potential litigants that the Bill would not be an effective tool for altering policy.[20] The Bill's text, combined with a tradition of judicial restraint, significantly suppressed its litigation potential.

The comprehensive constitutional modification project of 1980-82 thus took place against an institutional background in which two of the determinants of policy uncertainty (institutional rigidity and litigation potential) were in large measure absent. Nevertheless, the package of reform proposals contained in this project was sufficiently controversial that eight provinces engaged for more than a year in political and legal manoeuvring to block the project. The principal source of controversy was the policy uncertainty generated by the proposed Charter of Rights and Freedoms, which was the subject of parliamentary hearings in late 1980 and early 1981. During those hearings, the federal government sought to generate societal support for its efforts by inviting key interest groups to participate in the construction of the Charter. These groups responded by pressing for "a charter with terms which were as broad and potent as they could be."[21] This demand proved politically easy to satisfy, and the result was a new set of interpretively flexible substantive rights that created an unprecedented opportunity for interest groups to pursue their policy objectives in the microconstitutional arena of Charter-based constitutional litigation. Indeed, had the constitutional modification project of 1980-82 been subject to a ratification process any less flexible than the one ultimately specified by the Supreme Court in September 1981, it is possible that it would not have survived the policy uncertainty it generated.

The relative absence of interpretive rigidity permitted the project to succeed for several reasons. First, by declaring that the *legal* rules of formal amendment in Canada were so flexible that the federal government could proceed unilaterally, the Supreme Court diluted any veto power that the blocking coalition of provinces might expect to exercise. Second, by also declaring that the *conventional* rules of formal amendment required substantial provincial consent, the Court negated the political legitimacy of any unilateral move by the federal government. The overall impact of this definition of the formal rules of amendment was to force the parties back to the bargaining table, where institutional flexibility permitted the entrenchment of a rule that gave governments some measure of control over the policy impact of Charter litigation.[22] Ultimately, only Quebec refused to agree to the comprehensive constitutional modification embodied in the Constitution Act, 1982.

Although the litigation potential inherent in the Charter of Rights and Freedoms enhanced the policy uncertainty of the modifications proposed between 1980 and 1982, the institutional flexibility of the formal amendment process provided an instrument for managing the conflict generated by that uncertainty. Thus, in the final analysis, the flexible rules and process of executive federalism successfully produced comprehensive constitutional modification in 1982. Consequently, this was the process adopted during the 1987-90 period, and it functioned reasonably well in generating the Meech Lake Accord and in securing quick ratification by the federal parliament and most provincial legislatures. However, the elite-level negotiators of the Meech Lake Accord failed to understand the single most important institutional consequence of the 1982 modification. This was that the adoption of specific ratification rules increased the institutional rigidity of the amendment process by replacing the closed process of executive negotiation with an open process of legislative ratification. The ratification of the Meech Lake Accord thus took place in an institutional environment characterized by each of the determinants of policy uncertainty.

The same could be said even more strongly about the Charlottetown process. By 1992 the degree of institutional rigidity inherent in the 1982 amending formula was apparent to all constitutional actors. Thus, these actors were not willing to postpone discussion of their objectives to future constitutional rounds. There was a general consensus that Charlottetown represented a one-shot opportunity to effect constitutional change, and that opportunities missed were opportunities lost. This generated unprecedented demands for constitutional rule changes, which contributed in part to the Charlottetown Accord's ballooning to sixty amendments – a dramatic increase from the seven amendments contained in the Meech Lake Accord.

Interpretive fluidity and litigation potential played a similarly important role. Constitutional actors understood the potential significance of interpretive clauses on the redistributive impact of existing constitutional language. By 1992, an institutionally flexible process relatively unaffected by the unique interpretive flexibility of rights-based litigation had become an inflexible process dominated by judicial interpretation of individual rights. Even the threat of Quebec separatism, which hung over the process, could not negate the effects of these institutional factors.

The Women's Movement and Constitutional Modification

The institutional dynamics of the constitutional modification process from 1980 to 1992 affected the role that women's groups played in the macroconstitutional political arena, both in terms of framing the constitution of 1982 and in preserving the movement's apparent gains from that period. In this section I focus on gender equality as a constitutional issue, and on the activities of its principal advocates.

Framing the Charter

Not surprisingly, the women's movement was determined to reverse the restrictive 1970s interpretation of equality through its participation in the framing of the Charter. Although the various issues on the constitutional agenda from 1980 to 1982 generated conflict within Canada's principal feminist organization, the National Action Committee on the Status of

Women, or NAC,[23] six groups specifically representing women eventually made submissions to the Special Joint Committee on the Constitution. These groups included an ad hoc committee of NAC activists, the Canadian Advisory Council on the Status of Women (CAC), the National Association of Women and the Law (NAWL), and the Canadian Congress for Learning Opportunities for Women (CCLOW). In addition, the Native Women's Association of Canada (NWAC) and Indian Rights for Indian Women (IRIW) made representations on behalf of their particular constituencies. NAC, CAC, and NAWL, in particular, took advantage of the opportunity provided by the committee's hearings to lobby the federal government on the Charter's equality provisions. By contrast, NWAC, IRIW, and CCLOW confined their presentations to more narrow issues of direct interest to their members. NWAC, for example, appeared before the committee to "declare the sovereignty of our peoples and to serve notice that we intend to relate to Confederation as equal partners with the provincial and federal orders of government."[24] CCLOW's presentation was even more specific: it focused on women's "right to learn" and argued that this right could be advanced by defining women as a disadvantaged group in the affirmative action clause of the Charter's equality rights provision.[25]

The Canadian feminist movement's broad concerns about the Charter became evident in the presentations made by NAC, CAC, and NAWL on 20 November 1980 (NAC, CAC) and 9 December 1980 (NAWL). NAC began its presentation with the stark prediction that "women could be worse off if the proposed charter of rights and freedoms is entrenched in Canada's constitution."[26] According to NAC, the proposed charter would have a positive impact only if the federal government adopted three key recommendations.[27] First, NAC argued that the clause imposing general limitations on guaranteed rights and freedoms (the "reasonable limits" clause that is now section 1 of the Charter) had to be removed.[28] This clause, NAC asserted, would allow governments to justify almost any infringement on rights. Second, NAC argued for changes to the equality provisions. These included "a new clause to specify the human right to equality as a positive objective"; amendments to include marital status, sexual orientation, and political belief among the prohibited grounds of discrimination; and the elimination of the three-year moratorium on equality rights litigation.[29] Finally, NAC argued for a constitutional guarantee that women would be proportionately appointed to Canadian courts, including the Supreme Court.[30] NAC's overall objective was to provide constitutional direction for the judicial interpretation of equality so as to avoid results like those in *Lavell* and *Bliss*.[31]

This last point was at the centre of the CAC and NAWL presentations. Although CAC announced its strong support for "an entrenched charter of rights which guarantees equal rights for women," it also warned that it "must be clearly understood by the public, by the courts and the legislatures that Canadians intend to enshrine in the Constitution a *genuine* principle of equal rights."[32] The key problem, CAC argued, was constitutional uncertainty, which could be avoided by including "language, meant as a clear signal to the courts that whatever they may think about other bases of distinction, certain bases of distinction should never be regarded as reasonable."[33] Sex led CAC's list of absolutely prohibited bases of distinction, which also included race, colour, national or ethnic origin, and religion.[34] CAC thus proposed "two tiers of protection within the context of a general guarantee [of equality]."[35] As NAWL would explain in its presentation, the legal implication of this two-tier approach was to require that "the judiciary should apply a different, a more stringent, test to laws which distinguish on the basis of the invidious or the suspect categories, such as sex or race, than to laws distinguishing on other bases, age, handicap, etc."[36]

The essence of NAWL's proposal was to entrench within the constitution a modified version of the US Supreme Court's equality rights jurisprudence. The US Court applies different standards of constitutional review to legislative distinctions, depending on the nature of the classification involved. The most stringent standard is strict scrutiny, which applies to legislative distinctions affecting fundamental rights (e.g., voting) or suspect classifications (e.g., race). To survive strict scrutiny, governments must show that a legislative distinction is *necessary* to achieve a *compelling* state interest, a test that has been described as "strict in principle, fatal in practice."[37] A less exacting standard of review – the "rational basis test" – applies to most other statutory classifications (with the exception of gender, which is subject to intermediate or heightened scrutiny).[38] Both NAWL and CAC wanted to define "sex" as a suspect classification (which the US Court had never done) and to codify this two-tier analysis in the constitution. The purpose of this recommendation, in tandem with the recommendation to eliminate the reasonable limits clause,[39] was to prohibit virtually all legislation containing gender-based distinctions.

The objective of the macroconstitutional political strategy pursued by NAC, CAC, and NAWL during the Joint Committee proceedings was to construct a constitutionally entrenched interpretive framework around the Charter's equality rights that would reduce the possibility of negative judicial interpretations of those provisions. As NAWL put it, the objective was to replace "legislative ambiguity" with "legislative certainty" by "indicat[ing] to the court what the standard is that you expect the court to supply to you in their decisions."[40] Although these groups failed to entrench the US-inspired hierarchy of equality rights in section 15, or to have those provisions exempted from the "notwithstanding" clause (section 33), their efforts were in other respects successful. As a result, LEAF would start its history much farther ahead than the US groups (e.g., the American Civil Liberties Union's Women's Rights Project) after whom it modelled itself.[41]

To begin with, NAWL succeeded in persuading the government to add "equal protection" and "equal benefit of the law" to the rights protected by section 15.[42] Feminist groups were also successful in changing the title of section 15 from "Non-Discrimination Rights" (with its connotation of negative rights) to the more positively oriented title "Equality Rights."[43] Moreover, feminist groups succeeded in adding a separate interpretive section to the document (section 28) which provides that the Charter's rights and freedoms "are guaranteed equally to male and female persons," and which is exempt from the "notwithstanding" clause.[44] This achievement required significant effort, and only the interventions of the opposition in Parliament ensured that section 28 would not be subject to section 33.[45] Finally, feminist groups were instrumental in ensuring that the Charter's guarantee of equality would not suddenly "de-constitutionalize" affirmative action programs. With the US experience as background, feminists successfully persuaded the Charter's drafters to provide explicit constitutional protection for such programs in section 15 itself. In this instance, feminists sought an interpretive rule that would prevent their macroconstitutional gains from becoming microconstitutional losses. In the end, despite their initial distrust of the federal government's constitutional agenda, feminist organizations became important federal allies in the intergovernmental dispute over entrenching the Charter.[46]

Preserving the Status Quo
The Charter advanced the constitutional status of women's rights in Canada for several obvious reasons. First, despite their initial opposition to the federal government's plan to proceed unilaterally, women were able to make themselves part of the coalition that would potentially benefit from the Charter's policy impact. Second, women were able to use their position in this coalition to broaden the equality rights language of the Charter and to ensure that the only interpretive rule attached to that language (which exempts affirmative action programs from the general equality requirements) worked to their advantage. Finally, as we will see throughout the remainder of this chapter, they were able to establish an active litigation program to exploit the unprecedented litigation potential created by the Charter. These accomplishments gave Canadian feminists something to protect in any subsequent constitutional modification project.

As a result, the Anglophone women's movement opposed the Meech Lake Accord project. The movement's concern stemmed from the distinct society clause, which it perceived as a new interpretive rule that could dilute the meaning of equality contained in the Charter and advanced through litigation.[47] This concern, which a broad spectrum of minority rights advocates expressed, was that the distinct society clause would affect judicial interpretation of what constitutes a "reasonable limit" on rights. More specifically, various groups suggested that Quebec might be permitted to restrict rights in ways that were prohibited to the federal government and other provinces, thereby undermining the establishment of a *national* standard of individual rights. The First Ministers fuelled this perception by adding an interpretive clause to the Accord that protected the rights of Aboriginal Canadians and multicultural groups from potentially negative judicial interpretations of the distinct society clause.

To the women's movement, this action confirmed that recently entrenched rights were threatened. As Doris Anderson, former head of CAC, said, "As far as women are concerned, the wording in Meech Lake is muddy and unclear, and all our hard won gains under the Charter are threatened."[48] In particular, the movement was concerned that the pursuit of equality would be sacrificed to provincial demands for greater power.[49] Led by a coalition of five organizations – NAC, CAC, LEAF, NAWL, and NAC's Ad Hoc Committee on the Constitution – the movement demanded that section 28 of the Charter be transformed into an interpretive rule that would safeguard equality rights from any negative consequences of the Meech Lake Accord.[50] When this demand was not met, women's organizations played a pivotal role in buttressing anti-Meech sentiment in both New Brunswick and Manitoba.[51]

Two years after the demise of the Meech Lake Accord, the story was similar. Although the Charlottetown Accord affirmed in its preamble that "Canadians are committed to the equality of female and male persons," this affirmation was only one among eight similar commitments, including the commitment to recognize Quebec as a distinct society. Moreover, the gender equality commitment referred only to "Canadians," while other commitments, for example to the "vitality and development of official language minority communities," included references to "Canadians and their *governments*" (emphasis added). In addition, the chairperson of NAC argued that the emphasis in the Charlottetown Accord on provincial equality represented a return to notions of formal equality and to the primacy of male-dominated governments in the political process.[52] NAC also opposed the Accord's dilution of the federal spending power, and sought a formula for Senate representation that would improve women's representation in the upper house.[53] Finally, the failure to ensure that the Charter would apply to Native women in the provisions for Aboriginal self-government intensified NAC's opposition.[54] In the final analysis, NAC opposed the Charlottetown Accord because of its belief that it negatively affected the constitutional status that the women's movement had succeeded in acquiring in 1982.[55]

The negative reaction of the women's movement to the Meech Lake and Charlottetown Accords stemmed from the "possibility that the Charter's equality rights, fought for so recently and with such tenacity by English-Canadian feminists, could in any way be diminished by the accords."[56] In neither instance would Canadian feminists, after struggling so hard in the political arena of formal amendment, accept a set of constitutional rules that appeared to provide the worst of all possible outcomes. The rules of Meech Lake and Charlottetown failed to entrench feminist policy preferences further in the constitution and simultaneously appeared to reduce the value of the constitutional resources the women's movement had acquired in 1982. Women thus had a strong incentive to safeguard their position in any future attempt at constitutional modification.

To put these political dynamics in terms of the institutional design model, in the Meech Lake and Charlottetown Accord periods, governments proposed comprehensive constitutional modification against a post-1982 background of institutional rigidity in which formal amendment was no longer a simple matter of agreement among government leaders. This meant it would be that much more difficult to reverse the consequences of modification, and that political actors concerned about those consequences would have both the incentive and the opportunity to prevent ratification. For example, the interpretive flexibility and litigation potential of Meech Lake's "distinct society" clause made its policy impact uncertain. The federal government attempted to deal with some of the controversy generated by this uncertainty by attaching to the distinct society clause interpretive rules that were designed to address the concerns of Aboriginal and multicultural Canadians. The clause remained controversial from the perspective of women's groups, however, and they took advantage of the more rigid amendment process to support nonratification.[57] A similar dynamic contributed to the collapse of the Charlottetown Accord. In both cases, the institutional environment of the formal amendment process, which had changed significantly as a result of the modification of 1982, fuelled controversy over the uncertain policy impact of proposed comprehensive modification, making successful ratification difficult.

Litigating Equality: Arguments and Outcome

One reason for the women's movement's resistance to the Meech Lake and Charlottetown proposals is that they appeared to threaten not only the movement's macroconstitutional accomplishments but also the work it had done in the microconstitutional arena of litigation. Not surprisingly, it soon became apparent that the movement's success before the Special Joint Committee in 1980 represented only the first stage in the feminist effort to redesign Canadian institutions through constitutional modification. As NAWL had noted in its testimony before the committee, one of the perceived strengths of an entrenched rights document was its potential for providing an "alternative forum" for the enforcement of basic rights and freedoms.[58] In 1984, CAC published a report on how feminists could realize the Charter's potential to generate litigation-driven social change.[59] The report recommended "the establishment of a single national fund, the direct sponsorship of (preferably winnable) cases, and a complementary strategy of education and lobbying."[60] This document gave birth to the Women's Legal Education and Action Fund.

The first step in the microconstitutional campaign for substantive equality was "to build a theory of equality which is accepted by academics, lawyers, and the judiciary" by publishing articles in respected law journals, presenting papers at seminars, and participating in judicial training sessions.[61] In the absence of legal precedent for novel claims, social movement litigants require alternative authorities for those claims. Law review articles, in particular, can play this role because they provide judges with necessary principles and modes of application. This part of the campaign led to the establishment of the *Canadian Journal of Women and the Law* by NAWL in 1985. This new journal contributed to a marked increase in the amount of scholarly literature concerning equality issues in general, and women's equality in particular.[62] For example, between 1961 and 1980, the *Index to Canadian Legal Periodical Literature* contained only fifty entries on equality-related subjects. By contrast, there were 283 entries concerning this subject for the 1981-92 period. During this period, about 25 percent of the equality literature (seventy-three entries) dealt with women and equality, with seven of LEAF's founders (Beth Atcheson, Marilou McPhedran, Elizabeth Symes, Shelagh Day, Gwen Brodsky, Mary Eberts, and Lynn Smith) accounting for more than thirty books and articles themselves.[63] This literature tended to be proscriptive and prescriptive rather than retrospective and descriptive in tone, suggesting that the feminist movement's use of "legal literature was part of a long-term approach, in which indirect influence in the form of shaping the climate of opinion" was the key objective.[64]

The second step in the substantive equality campaign, of course, was litigation itself. Although all LEAF's interventions in the Supreme Court have involved equality-based arguments, five cases have been especially concerned with the definition of equality and discrimination. These include *Andrews* (1989), *Janzen* (1989), *Brooks* (1989), *Weatherall* (1993), and *BC Public Service Employee Relations Commission* (1999). All these cases resulted in favourable outcomes for LEAF. Most importantly, LEAF's intervention in *Andrews* (1989) played a key role in establishing the basic framework for future equality rights litigation. I turn now to a discussion of these cases.

Andrews (1989)

LEAF's first intervention in the Supreme Court was perhaps also its most important, since it came in the Court's first equality rights case. At issue in *Andrews* was the constitutionality of section 42 of the British Columbia Barristers and Solicitors Act, which required that applicants for admission to the practice of law in British Columbia be Canadian citizens, regardless of their other educational and professional qualifications.[65] Although *Andrews* clearly involved legislation that imposed a direct disadvantage on a group of individuals, it did not involve any of the expressly prohibited grounds of discrimination listed in section 15. Indeed, as Andrews's own case illustrated (he eventually acquired citizenship and was admitted to the legal profession in British Columbia), the citizenship requirement did not constitute a permanent barrier to the practice of law in British Columbia. The Court could have used these factual circumstances to begin its section 15 jurisprudence with a "minimalist" decision, but that did not occur.[66] LEAF's intervention, along with interventions by the Coalition of Provincial Organizations of the Handicapped, the Canadian Association of University Teachers, and the Ontario Confederation of University Faculty Associations, aimed at ensuring that *Andrews* did not lead to a post-Charter version of the "frozen concepts" theory in the area of equality rights.

LEAF's factum, authored by Mary Eberts and Gwen Brodsky, offered "no comment on the facts" of the case. Nor did LEAF take a "position on the constitutional validity of the citizenship requirement."[67] Instead, from its position as an "advocate for women's equality," LEAF restricted its "arguments to the question of what approach should be taken" by the Court in analyzing section 15 "and in determining its relationship to section 1."[68] The immediate target of LEAF's intervention was the approach articulated by the British Columbia Court of Appeal in its review of the statute. The BC court had held that unequal treatment in itself did not constitute a *prima facie* violation of section 15 because its reference to "discrimination" meant that the Charter prohibited only "unreasonable" or "unfair" legislative distinctions. By including the question of reasonableness within the substantive definition of equality, this approach imposed an additional burden on equality seekers that reduced the potential for successful claims. Eberts and Brodsky argued instead that section 15 should be interpreted in substantive as well as process terms, and that it should be interpreted to the benefit of historically disadvantaged groups whether listed in section 15 (i.e., "enumerated") or not (i.e., "nonenumerated").

Although the Court had not yet rendered a decision on section 15, Eberts and Brodsky did not have to construct their argument for *Andrews* out of whole cloth. To begin with, the Court had articulated a set of general principles of Charter interpretation in its earliest Charter judgments. In a conscious effort to avoid the charge of narrow legalism that flowed from its Bill of Rights decisions, the Court had declared that the overarching principle of Charter interpretation should be to engage in a "broad, purposive analysis, which interprets specific provisions of a constitutional document in light of its larger objects."[69] The Court had derived this principle from the "classical principles of American constitutional construction" articulated by US Chief Justice John Marshall in *Marbury* v. *Madison* and *McCulloch* v.

Maryland.[70] The Court would eventually link these principles to the JCPC's notion of the Canadian constitution as a "living tree."[71]

LEAF's factum therefore began by reminding the Court that it had adopted this purposive approach,[72] and from this starting point its task was to establish that LEAF's own objectives regarding equality were consistent with the purposes of section 15. More precisely, LEAF wanted to demonstrate that the purpose of section 15 is to promote the substantive equality of particular disadvantaged groups while simultaneously preventing dominant groups from undermining legislation and policy designed to improve the condition of the disadvantaged. To advance this argument, LEAF drew on three sources: (1) the Court's general comments about equality in other Charter judgments; (2) judicial construction of domestic human rights statutes; and (3) extralegal literature concerning the legislative history of section 15.

As LEAF pointed out, the Court had singled out the "commitment to social justice and equality" as one of the "values and principles essential to a free and democratic society."[73] Moreover, the Court had determined that socially dominant groups should not capture the Charter. This idea first emerged in *Edwards Books and Art* v. *The Queen* (1986), where the Court cautioned against the adoption of "rigid and inflexible standards" of judicial review in circumstances where legislatures had limited rights in order to promote the interests of less advantaged groups.[74] There was a certain irony in the adoption of this argument in *Andrews*, of course, since Mark Andrews himself was a white, male lawyer of British descent, which hardly qualified him as a member of an oppressed group.[75] However, because LEAF had no interest in the concrete facts of the case but only in the Court's construction of equality, this irony had little relevance.

Judicial construction of human rights statutes, along with scholarly commentary on that construction, supported LEAF's argument that Canadian public policy had moved "toward increasing the substantive equality of those groups previously excluded from power and full participation in society."[76] In particular, LEAF noted the extension of human rights legislation to cover a wider range of characteristics, as well as judicial recognition that the concept of discrimination includes indirect and unintentional discrimination.[77] In LEAF's view, these policy developments were also at the core of the legislative history and purpose of section 15. It argued that the language of section 15 was an explicit attempt to avoid the exclusive focus on equal process that characterized Bill of Rights equality decisions, and to direct judicial attention to promoting the substantive equality of "the powerless, excluded, and disadvantaged."[78]

LEAF's ability to rely on extralegal literature was partly the result of the women's movement's own equality scholarship strategy. Although the factum cited some "traditional" commentaries by authors like Peter Hogg and

Walter Tarnopolsky, it relied most heavily on commentaries produced by many of the women involved in the Joint Committee proceedings and LEAF's founding. These included Eberts herself, Lynn Smith, Colleen Sheppard, Beverley Baines, and Mary Jane Mossman. Particularly prominent among these sources was the collection of essays coedited by Eberts and Anne Bayefsky, *Equality Rights and the Canadian Charter of Rights and Freedoms*. LEAF also made good use of material prepared for the Parliamentary Committee on Equality Rights and the Commission on Equality in Employment chaired by Rosalie Abella.

Although none of the six justices who participated in rendering judgment in *Andrews* referred specifically to LEAF's factum, the judgment effectively adopted the position articulated by Eberts and Brodsky. One justice – Gérard La Forest – agreed with the interpretation of section 15 followed by the British Columbia Court of Appeal, but concurred with his colleagues that there was a violation of section 15 in this case. More importantly, five justices united behind Justice William McIntyre's interpretation, which was completely consistent with the position advocated by LEAF. However, although McIntyre (with Justice Antonio Lamer) concluded that the citizenship requirement for entry into the legal profession constituted a reasonable limit on the right to equality, four other justices reached a different judgment. As a result, the Court nullified the impugned provision of the British Columbia law. For LEAF, of course, this ultimate result was unimportant: the objective of its intervention was achieved in McIntyre's discussion of the principles that should guide the interpretation of section 15.

McIntyre's reasons for judgment on this question represented a relatively comprehensive survey of the major issues raised by section 15. His first task was to determine the meaning of the concept of equality guaranteed by section 15(1), and he began by emphasizing that the Charter could not guarantee abstract social equality or the equal treatment of individuals and groups in their private interactions. Section 15(1), he declared, is concerned only with equality in the application of the law.[79] According to McIntyre, however, this concern did not mean that courts must restrict themselves to enforcing a conception of formal equality in which the sole burden on government is to ensure that similarly situated individuals receive identical treatment. McIntyre rejected this approach to equality because experience suggested that it too easily permitted unjust outcomes. Citing as examples laws passed in Nazi Germany and the "separate but equal" doctrine adopted by the US Supreme Court in *Plessy* v. *Ferguson* (1896), McIntyre argued that the similarly situated test of equality could easily be applied to justify laws that discriminate equally against entire classes of people. At the same time, he argued that this test could also exclude socially desirable legislation by failing to recognize the injustice of "equal treatment of unequals." For McIntyre, the meaning of equality could not be defined by any rigid formula;

instead, it required the sensitive accommodation of differences. From this perspective, courts faced two key tasks: first, to determine which legislative distinctions deny equality, and second, to determine whether the failure to make legislative distinctions under certain circumstances violates equality rights.[80]

Following the approach outlined by Chief Justice Dickson in *Big M Drug Mart*, McIntyre attributed two related objectives to section 15.[81] First, it aimed at overcoming the narrow protection of equality provided by the 1960 Bill of Rights, whose shortcomings had been revealed in *Lavell* and *Bliss*. McIntyre quite correctly took as evidence of this purpose the fact that section 15(1) added additional equality rights to the protection of equality before the law found in the Bill of Rights. This brought the constitutional protection of equality into line with the broad definition of discrimination found in the statutory language and judicial interpretation of federal and provincial human rights legislation. Moreover, in a particularly important passage, McIntyre inferred from this similarity between human rights legislation and section 15 that intent did not constitute an essential element of discrimination under the Charter.[82] The second purpose of section 15, McIntyre argued, was to remedy discrimination, and this purpose justified legislative departures from formal equality in order to redress deeper inequalities. According to McIntyre, this objective explained the specific reference to discrimination in section 15(1) and the constitutional protection afforded affirmative action in section 15(2). Consequently, section 15 could not be interpreted in a way that might undermine legislation designed to address certain inequalities through differential treatment. Both of these conclusions paralleled the arguments presented by LEAF, and two of the sources cited by LEAF found their way into McIntyre's reasons for judgment.

As important as this discussion was, it did not really get McIntyre any closer to resolving the specific question before the Court, since citizenship is not one of the enumerated characteristics in section 15. LEAF had also urged the Court not to adopt a narrow approach to these characteristics, arguing instead that "a non-enumerated ground may appear as proxy for an enumerated ground."[83] McIntyre accepted this basic principle and turned to whether the impugned ground of distinction in the statute (citizenship) could be considered analogous to any of the enumerated classifications. He concluded after a single paragraph that legislative classifications based on citizenship are among those prohibited by section 15, offering as his rationale for this decision the observation that noncitizens are "a good example of a 'discrete and insular minority' who come within the protection of s.15."[84]

In essence, LEAF's intervention in *Andrews* appears to have contributed to the establishment of three interrelated rules: (1) equality should be measured in substantive, rather than formal, terms; (2) impact is more relevant than intent in determining discrimination; and (3) courts may extend equality

rights protection on the basis of characteristics other than those enumerated in section 15, although perhaps not infinitely.[85] This last point had
important implications for LEAF's future litigation plans. Indeed, in addition to citizenship, its factum singled out pregnancy discrimination and
sexual harassment as nonenumerated aspects of sex discrimination that could
nevertheless be scrutinized under section 15. Not surprisingly, both of these
issues would become subjects of LEAF interventions.

Brooks (1989) and *Janzen* (1989)

In discussing the desirability of a broad interpretation of the characteristics
enumerated in section 15, the LEAF factum in *Andrews* attacked the women's
movement's most infamous loss of the 1970s. According to Eberts and
Brodsky, a narrow approach to the enumerated grounds would be inappro-
priate because "a ground which seems to be non-enumerated – e.g. pregnancy – is actually an aspect of a 'sex' distinction. Since only women become
pregnant, any disadvantage visited upon a pregnant person is inevitably a
disadvantage visited upon a woman. The intervenor criticizes in this regard
the decision in *Bliss* v. *A.-G. Canada.*"[86]

As we saw in the introduction to Chapter 1, LEAF had an opportunity to
expand this argument in *Brooks* v. *Canada Safeway* (1989). The argument
was successful, with the Court equating pregnancy discrimination with sex
discrimination and thereby reversing its judgment in *Bliss*.

The *Andrews* factum also foreshadowed the issue that would arise in *Janzen*
v. *Platy Enterprises* (1989): sexual harassment. The case involved two women
(Dianna Janzen and Tracy Govereau) who brought sexual harassment complaints against a cook at the restaurant where they worked as waitresses.
Although the Manitoba Human Rights Act did not explicitly cover sexual
harassment, both a human rights adjudicator and the Manitoba Court of
Queen's Bench found that harassment fell within the prohibition against
sex discrimination. The Manitoba Court of Appeal, however, reversed the
lower court decision on the grounds that sexual harassment, while vexa-
tious, was not necessarily a form of discrimination. The case thus presented
two issues to the Supreme Court: (1) whether sexual harassment is sex discrimination; and (2) whether employers can be held liable for harassment
committed by their employees.

To some degree, LEAF faced a more difficult task in *Janzen* than in *Brooks*
because, in principle at least, harassment is obviously not as gender specific
as pregnancy. Indeed, LEAF's factum conceded that "victims and perpetra-
tors of sexual harassment can be male or female,"[87] but devoted twelve of
forty-four paragraphs in its factum to analyzing the unique impact of sexual
harassment on women. Relying on Catherine MacKinnon's analysis of sexual
harassment in the United States and similar work for Canada by Constance
Backhouse and Leah Cohen,[88] LEAF stressed that sexual harassment is both

a product of, and contributor to, "a fundamental imbalance of power between men and women in the workplace and society."[89] This part of the factum was exactly the sort of feminist approach to litigation to which LEAF had aspired at its founding. It attempted to articulate the experience of harassment from a uniquely female perspective, and link that experience to broader issues of gender relations. Sexual harassment, the factum argued, is part of a social construction of sex that presents women as powerless and submissive. It is "a way of exploiting ... economic control to secure sexual access to women," and is "a tool for maintaining dominance and reminding women of their dependent, vulnerable, and precarious status in the workplace."[90] "Sexual harassment of women by men," the factum continued, "would rarely occur if women and men were social equals."[91] Despite its apparent gender neutrality, therefore, sexual harassment operated uniquely to the disadvantage of women and had to be included within the definition of sex discrimination.

As in *Andrews*, six justices participated in the judgment in *Janzen*, with Chief Justice Brian Dickson delivering a unanimous "judgment of the Court." The judgment adopted the same position as that advocated by LEAF and supported its holding with numerous references to material cited in LEAF's factum. For example, the Court quoted from the books by MacKinnon and by Backhouse and Cohen; it quoted an article from the *Manitoba Law Journal* to which LEAF had referred,[92] as well as another study of sexual harassment cited by LEAF;[93] and it referred to the findings and recommendations of the Royal Commission on Equality in Employment. Moreover, the judgment quoted directly from the LEAF factum that "sexual harassment is a form of sex discrimination because it denies women equality of opportunity in employment because of their sex."[94] The Court thus restored the trial court judgment, as well as the human rights adjudicator's even more generous damages award. As it did in *Brooks*, LEAF achieved a double victory in *Janzen*: it persuaded the Court to reverse an unfavourable appellate court decision and in the process to adopt LEAF's preferred doctrine on the definition of sex discrimination.

Weatherall (1993) and *British Columbia (Public Service Employee Relations Commission)* (1999)

The depth of the Court's commitment to the doctrine of substantive equality first articulated in *Andrews* is evident in *Weatherall* and *British Columbia (Public Service Employee Relations Commission)* (hereafter *BCPSERC*), where the judgments were both consistent with the position advocated by LEAF. At issue in *Weatherall* (1993) were surveillance practices in Canadian penitentiaries. Male inmates argued that cell patrols and frisk searches conducted by female correctional officers violated their rights to security of the person and privacy as guaranteed by sections 7 and 8 of the Charter. In addition, they argued that the protection of female, but not male, inmates from cross-gender searches violated their right to equality under section 15. The federal government opposed these claims for two reasons. First, a positive outcome for the inmates would have introduced greater administrative complexity into procedures that Corrections Canada considered essential for maintaining security in penitentiaries. Second, a prohibition on cross-gender searches in male institutions would have curtailed an employment equity initiative designed to increase the number of female correctional officers. Given the demographic profile of Canadian penitentiary inmates (98 percent are male), the number of positions available for women would be severely limited if they were restricted to female institutions.

The case was a delicate one for LEAF, however, since prisoners could obviously be counted among the socially disadvantaged whom LEAF had identified as the principal beneficiaries of section 15. Its factum admitted this and argued that the state had a duty to protect inmates' privacy and dignity. However, the factum also argued that the performance of surveillance activities by female correctional officers did not in itself pose any special risk to male inmates so long as these activities did not exceed the minimum level necessary for security and were conducted according to proper procedures.[95] For LEAF, the question was essentially one of relative disadvantage. Although male inmates were clearly disadvantaged, they were less so than female inmates. However, LEAF's failure at the outset to recognize the "racialized" nature of the correctional officer-inmate relationship – where most of the female officers were white and large numbers of the male inmates came from "racialized communities" – caused one member of the national litigation committee to resign.[96]

The male inmates' equality rights claim rested entirely on the idea of equal treatment in insisting that the rule against cross-gender searches that applied in women's prisons should also apply in male correctional institutions. LEAF's reaction to this argument was obviously to stress the substantive dimension of equality. On the one hand, LEAF supported the absence of a ban on cross-gender searches in men's prisons on the grounds that it promoted employment opportunities for women in a nontraditional profession. On the other hand, it opposed cross-gender searches in women's prisons on the following grounds:[97]

(a) Women's bodies and female nudity are sexualized in our society in a manner and degree that is not paralleled for men.
(b) The majority of women prison inmates have histories of childhood and adult sexual abuse at the hands of men.
(c) Women justifiably fear sexual violence at the hands of men, particularly men in positions of power.

(d) The imbalance of power resulting from the authority that men guards would have over women inmates compounds the normal imbalance of power produced by gender relations in our society.

Together, these factors meant that "the social meaning of cross-gender surveillance is different and more threatening for women than for men."[98]

Weatherall generated a short (six paragraphs), unanimous judgment of the Court that denied all the male inmates' claims. Despite its brevity, the judgment contained perhaps the Court's most explicit statement of the substantive equality doctrine. According to the Court,

> The jurisprudence of this Court is clear: equality does not necessarily connote identical treatment and, in fact, different treatment may be called for in certain cases to promote equality. Given the historical, biological and sociological differences between men and women, equality does not demand that practices which are forbidden where male officers guard female inmates must also be banned where female officers guard male inmates. The reality of the relationship between the sexes is such that the historical trend of violence perpetrated by men against women is not matched by a comparable trend pursuant to which men are the victims and women the aggressors. Biologically, a frisk search or surveillance of a man's chest area conducted by a female guard does not implicate the same concerns as the same practice by a male guard in relation to a female inmate. Moreover, women generally occupy a disadvantaged position in society in relation to men. Viewed in this light, it becomes clear that the effect of cross-gender searching is different and more threatening for women than for men. The different treatment to which the appellant objects thus may not be discrimination at all.

The clarity with which this passage expresses the doctrine of substantive equality is almost as remarkable as the identity of its author, Justice Gérard La Forest. Among those justices who cast at least ten votes in LEAF cases, his support level for LEAF (56.8 percent) was the lowest of all but Justice Sopinka. La Forest also dissented five times from majority judgments that otherwise supported LEAF. In more general terms, he had voted to uphold Canada's abortion law in *Morgentaler, Smoling and Scott* (1988), and he was the sole justice not to join Justice McIntyre's interpretation of section 15 in *Andrews* (1989).

Although La Forest did not refer specifically to LEAF's factum, it appears to have influenced his judgment for the Court in several ways. Consider, for example, the similarity between the passage quoted above and the following language in LEAF's factum: "This Court has explicitly recognized that 'same treatment' may in fact exacerbate social disadvantage. In many cases, inequality will only be remedied by a recognition that groups socially, politically, and/or economically unequal may require different treatment in order to achieve equality of results."[99] In particular, the penultimate sentence in the passage from La Forest's judgment ("the effect of cross-gender searching is different and more threatening for women than for men") is identical to a key point in LEAF's factum (paragraph 38). Although *Weatherall* became a touchstone for later equality rights judgments, Justice La Forest himself did not pursue the boldness of his own judgment. Indeed, he very quickly reverted to his more conservative jurisprudence in cases involving sexual orientation *(Egan* v. *Canada)* and sex discrimination *(Gould* v. *Yukon Order of Pioneers).*[100]

The participation of women in "nontraditional" occupations was also at the core of LEAF's intervention in *BCPSERC*. At issue was a test developed for the BC Forest Service to determine the occupational fitness of forest firefighters. A female firefighter, Tawney Meiorin, who had worked on an Initial Attack Crew for almost three years, lost her position when she failed the running component of the test by forty-nine seconds on her fourth attempt.[101] Her union filed a grievance on her behalf, and an arbitrator held that she had established a *prima facie* case of adverse effects discrimination and that the government had not accommodated her "to the point of undue hardship." The arbitrator ordered that Ms. Meiorin be reinstated and awarded lost wages and benefits. However, the government successfully appealed to the British Columbia Court of Appeal, which held that there was no discrimination because the aerobic capacity standard was necessary for the safe and efficient performance of Ms. Meiorin's duties and she had been individually tested against it.

The appeal to the Supreme Court raised two issues, one broad and the other narrow. The narrow issue, of course, was whether the Court of Appeal was correct in concluding that the BC government had not discriminated against Ms. Meiorin when it terminated her employment as a firefighter. Although the resolution of this issue depended in part on factual matters, it also depended on the broader issue of the legal test for determining discrimination under human rights legislation. Although LEAF and its coalition partners (the DisAbled Women's Network and the Canadian Labour Congress) offered arguments on both issues, two of its three submissions and thirty-six of its factum's seventy-three paragraphs dealt with the broader issue.

The gravamen of LEAF's argument was that the "purpose of human rights legislation is to remedy systemic discrimination and achieve substantive equality." The argument did not simply question the impact of "social norms" on disadvantaged groups, but the very content of those norms themselves. The elimination of systemic barriers to substantive equality, according to

LEAF, requires more than simply accommodating those who are "different": it requires standards that do not exclude them in the first place.[102] This is particularly true for cases involving sex discrimination because these standards affect more than single individuals or small minorities, which might be the case with standards that exclude on the basis of religion.[103] Given that the Court's human rights jurisprudence had been developed for the most part in cases involving religious discrimination, LEAF argued, it was necessary to reconsider the Court's approach to discrimination in this context. In this sense, LEAF's position had come full circle from *Andrews*. Whereas in that case it had argued that the interpretation of section 15 should be informed by human rights jurisprudence, it now argued that judicial construction of human rights statutes should "be consistent with equality rights jurisprudence under ... the Charter."[104]

The key doctrinal change advocated by LEAF was for the Court to abandon the conceptual distinction between direct and adverse effect (indirect) discrimination. According to LEAF, this bifurcation allows employers – private or public – to leave inherently discriminatory practices in place so long as they demonstrate either (a) that directly discriminatory practices constitute a "bona fide occupational requirement," or (b) that accommodation is made for individuals adversely affected by indirect discrimination.[105] An approach more consistent with the goals of eliminating systemic barriers and achieving substantive equality would broaden the notion of accommodation to include a requirement that standards be changed rather than simply requiring that individual exceptions be made to existing standards.

Writing for a unanimous Court, Justice Beverley McLachlin agreed that there was "a compelling case for revising the analysis" of discrimination under human rights statutes.[106] Quoting extensively from an article published in the *Canadian Bar Review* by LEAF activists Shelagh Day and Gwen Brodsky, McLachlin agreed with their observation that the conventional approach "does not challenge the imbalances of power, or the discourses of dominance, such as racism, ablebodyism and sexism," and that "accommodation is assimilationist" in the sense that it "does not challenge deep-seated beliefs about the intrinsic superiority of such characteristics as mobility and sightedness."[107] The principal defect of the conventional approach, McLachlin held, is that it "bars courts and tribunals from assessing the legitimacy of the standard itself," and thus undermines the quest for substantive equality and the elimination of systemic discrimination.[108] This reinterpretation of human rights legislation required that accommodation should occur in the construction of standards rather than in their application to individual employees.[109]

The analysis resulted in a new three-pronged test for determining whether a facially discriminatory standard qualifies as a bona fide occupational requirement.[110] First, the reason for adopting the standard must be rationally connected to the performance of the job. Second, the employer must demonstrate that the standard's adoption stemmed from a good faith belief that it is necessary to the fulfillment of the work-related purpose. Finally, the standard must be reasonably necessary to the accomplishment of the purpose, which the employer demonstrates by showing that it is impossible to accommodate individual employees with the relevant characteristic without imposing undue hardship on the employer. In undertaking the third step in this analysis, according to McLachlin,

> Courts and tribunals should be sensitive to the various ways in which individual capabilities may be accommodated. Apart from individual testing to determine whether the person has the aptitude or qualification that is necessary to perform the work, the possibility that there may be different ways to perform the job while still accomplishing the employer's legitimate work-related purpose should be considered in appropriate cases. The skills, capabilities and potential contributions of the individual claimant and others like him or her must be respected as much as possible.[111]

In this judgment, McLachlin moved the Court away from the sensitive accommodation of differences standard implicit in Justice McIntyre's *Andrews* judgment and toward denying the very relevance of certain differences. Given that *Andrews* was considered a progressive step from McLachlin's own appellate court judgment in the case, her reasoning in *BCPSERC* demonstrates a significant evolution in her understanding of equality rights.

Without any doubt, this test significantly reduces the range of standards that might be considered bona fide occupational requirements. This, of course, was precisely the point of LEAF's factum, and Justice McLachlin's judgment constitutes wholesale agreement with the position advocated by LEAF, including the particular standard under review.[112] In fact, the judgment implicitly accepted LEAF's view that lower standards might be necessary to remedy systemic discrimination. There is a subtle shift in the Court's language in the course of two paragraphs, from "reasonably necessary" in paragraph 72 to "minimally necessary" in paragraph 74. Given that it might be reasonable in some contexts to set the employment standard above the minimum, the implication of this language shift seems to be that even reasonable standards may not be bona fide, and that employers must aim at the minimal standard in order to be as inclusive as possible.

Summary and Conclusion
With the possible exception of section 7,[113] no Charter provision applies to as wide a range of public policy as section 15. Moreover, by identifying certain groups as deserving of enhanced constitutional recognition, section 15 provides them with an opportunity to "stake preferential claims on the

political resources of the state or on the political process itself."[114] Indeed, various groups and social movements recognized the importance of explicit inclusion within section 15 during the framing of the Charter, and the Joint Committee received proposals to add mental and physical disability, marital status, sexual orientation, and political belief to the list of constitutionally recognized sources of inequality. For the most part, these efforts at macrolevel constitutional modification failed, with only mental and physical disability being added to the text of section 15. However, as the prescient justice minister predicted, this failure only moved the quest for constitutional recognition into the microlevel arena of litigation.[115] As a result, two additional categories – citizenship and sexual orientation – have been added to section 15 through judicial interpretation.[116]

The story of section 15 in the Supreme Court, therefore, is largely the story of a self-described process of "equality seeking," in which groups have sought recognition under section 15 and mobilized that recognition to extract favourable policy outputs from governments. Among the groups involved in this process have been the Aboriginal Women's Council, the Canadian Association of Sexual Assault Centres, the Canadian Civil Liberties Association, the Canadian Disability Rights Council, the Canadian Jewish Congress, the Charter Committee on Poverty Issues, the Coalition of Provincial Organizations of the Handicapped, the DisAbled Women's Network Canada, Equality for Gays and Lesbians Everywhere, the National Action Committee for the Status of Women, and the Native Women's Association of Canada. Even workers' compensation claimants and male prisoners have staked claims under section 15.[117] However, the Canadian women's movement has been the most active equality seeker under section 15.

This activity has had significant consequences for broader constitutional reform in Canada. Between 1972 and 1992, both the United States and Canada experienced unsuccessful efforts to implement comprehensive constitutional modification. To be sure, these efforts differed in significant ways. Most obviously, Canada's Meech Lake and Charlottetown Accords were much broader proposals than the US Equal Rights Amendment, since they concerned the identity, nature, and fundamental principles of the Canadian political community. In addition, while the ERA's failure constituted a defeat for US gender equality activists, the defeats of the Meech Lake and Charlottetown Accords can be attributed to a significant degree to the opposition of Canadian feminists. However, despite these differences, these failed attempts at constitutional modification share several common features. First, all three proposals initially enjoyed the support of important political elites and began the ratification process with relatively high levels of public approval. Second, especially in the cases of the ERA and Meech Lake, the initial support of both elites and the public translated into strong early momentum in favour of ratification, with close to the necessary levels of approval reached within approximately twelve months in both cases. Finally, opponents of all three proposals eventually halted, and to some degree reversed,[118] the momentum toward ratification, leading ultimately to the rejection of each proposal. Amendment proposals that once seemed certain to succeed went down to ignominious defeat.

An important aspect of this chapter is its use of a common framework of analysis to understand these instances of amendment failure. The framework, which attempts to explain why proposed amendments become too controversial to survive ratification, focuses on the institutional factors that make the policy impact of comprehensive amendments uncertain. It identifies three such factors: institutional rigidity, interpretive flexibility, and litigation potential. The strong presence of these variables in the institutional design of a regime's process of constitutional modification renders it difficult to predict, control, or reverse the specific policy consequences of a formal amendment. Opponents of a proposal are able to exploit this situation to make amendments controversial from the perspective of undecided and risk-averse ratifiers. What makes amendments controversial is not necessarily opposition to the principles they embody but uncertainty about the specific policy consequences that may flow from those principles. Interpretive flexibility and litigation potential increase the likelihood that constitutive rules will generate constitutionally entrenched policies, which institutional rigidity will make exceedingly difficult, if not impossible, to reverse through future formal amendment.

Mansbridge's observation that the ERA was too controversial for ratification can be traced back to the institutional rigidity, interpretive flexibility, and litigation potential that permeates the institutional design of constitutional modification in the United States. The institutional context of constitutional modification generated a level of policy uncertainty that ERA supporters were unwilling to quell by attaching regulative or interpretive rules to the amendment. Similarly, the post-1982 formal amendment failures in Canada can, ironically, be attributed to the successful comprehensive modification of 1980-81, which brought the institutional design of constitutional change in Canada much closer to the US model. As a result, the slow death of the Meech Lake Accord and the unequivocal rejection of the Charlottetown Accord were the product of the same political dynamic that undermined the ERA campaign. Gender equality activists in Canada were able to take advantage of this political dynamic to protect the gains they had made in pre-1982 macroconstitutional politics and in post-1982 microconstitutional politics.

3
Gaining Ground

The positions advocated by LEAF gained ground in three key areas of the law: reproductive choice and fetal rights,[1] regulation of expression (especially pornography),[2] and sexual orientation.[3] LEAF was involved in eleven cases in these areas, and its success rate with respect to outcome is 83.3 percent. Its "issue" success rate in these interventions is lower, at 72.2 percent (thirteen of eighteen decided issues).[4] Moreover, individual judicial support for LEAF's position has been very strong. For example, individual justices in the reproductive choice and fetal rights cases cast thirty-one votes for, and only three against, LEAF's position. Similarly, LEAF's position received thirty-one of the thirty-three votes cast on the four issues in the two sexual orientation cases. Only in the regulation of expression cases has LEAF met some resistance, with thirty-three issue votes for and forty-seven against. Nevertheless, in the key case involving criminal regulation of pornography, LEAF's position prevailed by a unanimous nine-to-zero vote.

LEAF's success in these cases illustrates three distinct ways in which social movements can gain ground through legal mobilization. First, it secured constitutional protection for existing policies favoured by the women's movement, defending them against immediate challenge and immunizing them from future threats. Second, in areas characterized by a policy vacuum, legal mobilization prevented the introduction of policies adverse to the movement's interests. Finally, legal mobilization proved effective in promoting policy change in the movement's preferred direction. One reason for this success is that, in most of these cases, LEAF's position also enjoyed strong governmental support. This was true in three of four reproductive choice and fetal rights cases; in four of five expression cases; and even to some degree in both sexual orientation cases (in one, the Canadian Human Rights Commission and the Canadian Association of Statutory Human Rights Associations – both governmental bodies – took the same position as LEAF). This chapter examines LEAF's arguments and the Court's response in each of these policy areas.

Reproductive Choice and Fetal Rights

The United States Experience

Reproductive choice, particularly in the form of access to contraception and legal abortion, is one of the defining issues of the post–Second World War women's movement.[5] In the United States, the constitutional attack against restrictions on reproductive choice bore fruit in three key decisions: *Griswold* v. *Connecticut* (1965), *Eisenstadt* v. *Baird* (1972), and, finally, *Roe* v. *Wade* (1973).[6] In *Griswold*, the Court struck down a Connecticut statute prohibiting the use of contraceptives by married couples on the grounds that the law violated the implicit constitutional right to privacy that the Court purported to discover in the "penumbral emanations" of several provisions of the Bill of Rights. According to the Court, these amendments each protected an aspect of personal privacy which, viewed in their entirety, pointed to a general right to privacy.[7] In *Eisenstadt*, the Court extended this right to privacy to cover nonmarital relationships by holding that it belongs to individuals and not relationships per se. Finally, in *Roe*, seven justices agreed that this general right "is broad enough to encompass a woman's decision whether or not to terminate her pregnancy." The majority held that this right is absolute during the first trimester of pregnancy, but that states may regulate abortion in the interests of maternal health during the second trimester and prohibit it entirely during the third in order to protect the "potential" life of fetuses. Over time, despite attempts by Republican presidents to affect judicial policy in this area through the appointments process, the US Court has refused to reverse the essential holding in *Roe* that the right to abortion is constitutionally protected. In 2000 a five-justice majority of the Court held that a state ban on "partial birth" abortions constituted an "undue burden" on the right to abortion even during the third trimester.[8]

The Canadian Experience, 1969-88

As in the United States, the push for broader access to abortion in Canada achieved its first significant gains in the 1960s. Prior to 1969 the Criminal Code treated abortion as a form of homicide for which the only possible justification was the common law defence of necessity, which applied only in limited circumstances. As part of a comprehensive reform of the criminal law, a new section 251 of the Code created two categories of abortion: therapeutic abortions, which could be performed legally, and nontherapeutic abortions, which remained subject to criminal penalties. At the core of this provision were procedures designed to identify and approve legitimate requests for therapeutic abortions. To achieve this objective, section 251 permitted only those abortions approved by a therapeutic abortion committee of an accredited hospital. It further stipulated that this committee must include three physicians other than the physician intending to perform the abortion, and that abortions could be approved only where necessary to promote the health of the woman seeking the abortion. Failure to meet the conditions set forth in section 251 constituted an indictable offence, the maximum punishments for which were two years' imprisonment for women procuring (or self-performing) abortions, and life imprisonment for individuals performing abortions.

Not surprisingly, section 251 became the target of legal challenge. Ironically, the principal protagonists in these legal mobilization campaigns were both men: Dr. Henry Morgentaler and Joe Borowski.[9] Morgentaler operated private abortion clinics in direct defiance of section 251, which made him the target of prosecutors and eventually earned him a prison sentence. In 1976 Morgentaler failed to persuade the Supreme Court to nullify section 251 under the 1960 Bill of Rights, with Justice Brian Dickson declaring that the Court had no place in "the loud and continuous public debate on abortion."[10] At roughly the same time, Joe Borowski was meeting similar resistance from lower courts in his pro-life challenge to section 251. However, in 1981, over the dissent of Chief Justice Bora Laskin, the Court recognized that Borowski had legal standing to challenge section 251, holding that individuals could challenge legislation if they have "a genuine interest in the validity of the legislation and ... there is no other reasonable and effective manner in which the issue may be brought before the Court."[11] Consequently, although section 251 did not affect Borowski directly in any way, the Court granted him permission to return to the lower courts and continue his legal challenge on the merits.

The adoption of the Charter of Rights and Freedoms in 1982 obviously provided a new context for the respective legal struggles of Henry Morgentaler and Joe Borowski. Ultimately, Morgentaler's struggle reached the Court first in the post-Charter era, and in 1988 the Court delivered its judgment in *Morgentaler, Smoling and Scott* v. *The Queen*.[12] *Morgentaler, Smoling and Scott* (hereafter *Morgentaler 2*) presented the Court with a difficult dilemma. On the one hand, maintaining its Charter-based institutional authority to participate in controversial policy debates meant that it could not simply avoid the abortion issue, as it had in 1976. Reversing his earlier view that the Court should not participate in the public debate over abortion, Chief Justice Dickson solemnly declared in *Morgentaler 2* that the Court had to assume its "added responsibilit[y]" of ensuring that legislative initiatives "conform to the democratic values" inherent in the Charter.[13] On the other hand, various factors raised the possibility that judicial nullification of the federal abortion law might trigger a legislative override under section 33. *Morgentaler 2* was only the forty-ninth Charter case decided by the Court, and it was arguably the first case to engage the Court in an issue of broad public visibility and controversy. Moreover, unlike the nineteenth-century statute overturned by the US Court in *Roe*, the provision under review was a liberalizing one less than twenty years old. Finally, the government in power was politically conservative and contained a significant number of members who supported stricter regulation of abortion.

Public opinion over abortion was also divided.[14] In 1975, only 23 percent of Canadians surveyed by the Gallup organization supported unrestricted access to abortion. This figure declined to 16 percent in 1978 before gradually rising to 28 percent in a poll conducted shortly after the *Morgentaler 2* decision. Clearly, the Court was functioning in a climate of public opinion that supported some degree of legislative regulation of abortion. There was at least the possibility that the conservative government of the day could find public support to override a *Roe*-type declaration of a constitutional right to abortion.[15] If this had occurred, the Court would have "lost" its first direct confrontation with Parliament over a highly visible policy issue, and this loss would have damaged its future ability to claim constitutional supremacy in rights-based policy disputes.

The difficulty posed by the Court's dilemma is reflected in the exceedingly complex set of judgments generated by the justices. The seven members of the *Morgentaler 2* Court produced four separate reasons for judgment, ranging from support for the status quo (upholding the constitutionality of the existing law) to nullification based on a broad interpretation of liberty (right to reproductive freedom). At one end of the spectrum were Justices William McIntyre and Gérard La Forest, who based their judgment on the Charter's silence on the question of abortion rights and voted to support the existing law. According to McIntyre, "the proposition that women enjoy a constitutional right to have an abortion is devoid of support in the language of s.7 of the Charter or any other section."[16] Without such support, McIntyre argued, there was no constitutional reason to nullify the abortion law. At the other end of the spectrum was Justice Bertha Wilson, who argued that the right to liberty enumerated in section 7 of the Charter included reproductive freedom, which was essential to "modern woman's struggle to assert her dignity and worth as a human being."[17] This would have prohibited all government regulation of abortion during at least the early stages of pregnancy.

Between these two poles were the judgments of Justices Jean Beetz and William Estey and Chief Justice Brian Dickson and Justice Antonio Lamer. Beetz and Estey focused their attention on the delays women faced in securing permission for a legal abortion as a result of the procedural mechanisms contained in section 251 of the Criminal Code. In their view, these delays created an additional risk to women's health and thus threatened their section 7 right to physical security of the person. Dickson and Lamer broadened this procedural approach to include psychological and emotional integrity within the meaning of security of the person. Examining the procedural operation of section 251, Dickson characterized it as "a law which forces women to carry a foetus to term contrary to their own priorities and aspirations and which imposes serious delay causing increased physical and psychological trauma to those women who meet its criteria."[18] Dickson based this decision in large part on the 1977 Badgley Report, which concluded that the administrative framework for therapeutic abortions produced delays, uncertainty, and inequality of access.[19]

The Dickson-Lamer judgment aptly illustrates that one solution to the dilemma the Court faced was to nullify the existing abortion law while maximizing the feasible set of alternatives to legislative override. In fact, the combined plurality judgments excluded only two choices from Parliament's set of alternatives: the existing law and recriminalization of all abortions. To some degree, the available choices paralyzed Prime Minister Brian Mulroney's government, and after five months of indecision it asked Parliament to indicate by way of a free vote on 28 July 1988 its disposition toward several proposed abortion laws. The proposal that came closest to adoption was a pro-life resolution which would have restricted access to abortion even more than did section 251. This proposal was defeated by a vote of 118 to 105. No other proposal, including the one officially supported by the government itself, received more than seventy-six votes. The Mulroney government waited until after its reelection in November 1988 before introducing new legislation. On 29 May 1990, the House of Commons passed Bill C-43, which would have maintained the distinction between therapeutic and nontherapeutic abortions, but would have expanded the definition of health and liberalized the process for obtaining approval for legal abortions. However, as a result of a tie vote in February 1991 the Senate failed to approve Bill C-43 on third reading. The government subsequently announced that it would not attempt to enact new abortion legislation during the remainder of its mandate. No subsequent federal government has acted on the subject.

The Canadian Experience: *Borowski* (1989) and *Daigle* (1989)
Although LEAF did not participate directly in the litigation that culminated in *Morgentaler 2*, various feminist groups supported Dr. Henry Morgentaler's campaign against the regulation of therapeutic and nontherapeutic abortions set out in section 251 of the Criminal Code. LEAF's principal litigation activity came in defending the access to abortion provided by the judgment and the federal government's subsequent failure to relegislate. Indeed, it intervened in four cases that, by advancing fetal rights separate from those of a pregnant woman, threatened the pro-choice practices and principles ushered in by *Morgentaler 2*. The first of these cases was the product of Joe Borowski's legal activism, which finally reached the Court in October of 1988 (nine months after the *Morgentaler 2* judgment). Like Henry Morgentaler,

Borowski was challenging the constitutionality of section 251, but for not adequately protecting fetuses' constitutional right to life rather than for unduly restricting access to legal abortions. LEAF obviously intervened to oppose this interpretation of the Charter, and urged the Court to do one of two things: refuse to answer the constitutional questions posed by Borowski or hold that there are no fetal rights under the Charter.

LEAF's argument on the first point occupied twenty of its factum's sixty-seven paragraphs. The basis of the argument was the Court's invalidation of section 251 in January of 1988. According to LEAF, this meant that the "only rationale for Mr. Borowski's status to sue no longer exists."[20] In addition, LEAF urged the Court to follow the more cautious elements of both Chief Justice Dickson's judgment and Justice McIntyre's dissent in *Morgentaler 2*. Dickson had argued that it was "neither necessary nor wise ... to explore the broadest implications of s.7," while McIntyre had declared that courts should not manufacture constitutional rights "out of whole cloth."[21] In taking this position, LEAF articulated a Canadian version of the traditional American "case and controversy" doctrine, as well as of the more contemporary concept of "judicial minimalism."

Under the first doctrine, the US Supreme Court, at least, restricts itself to deciding concrete disputes between directly interested parties, on the grounds that only in this context is it possible to develop "the full exploration of the issue and an awareness of particular circumstances that illuminate the hazards as well as the benefits of a general rule."[22] Thus, according to LEAF, a fatal deficiency of Borowski's appeal was that the "evidentiary record... simply does not provide the factual basis to inform such a momentous legal decision as a determination that the foetus has constitutional status."[23]

Under the second doctrine, as described by University of Chicago law professor Cass Sunstein, judges exercising minimalist virtues "seek to avoid broad rules and abstract theories, and attempt to focus their attention only on what is necessary to resolve particular disputes." Minimalism is particularly appropriate in the face of "issues of high factual or ethical complexity that are producing democratic disagreement and debate."[24] The basic objective in these cases is to minimize decision-making costs and judicial error. As Sunstein argues, minimalism "allows the democratic process a great deal of room in which to adapt to coming developments, to produce mutually advantageous compromises, and to add new information and perspectives to legal issues."[25] As LEAF's factum presented it, *Morgentaler 2*, the judgment implicitly under attack in *Borowski*, was a paradigmatic example of judicial minimalism.[26]

On the second point of its argument, LEAF submitted that "the focus of rights concerns during pregnancy must be on the woman," who is a "live, independent, and autonomous person." Her rights, the factum continued, "cannot be sacrificed to a foetus, which may or may not become a person."[27]

LEAF naturally focused on the impact that fetal rights would have on access to legal abortion. The factum discussed this problem as an equality rights issue, arguing that such access was necessary to give women "more equal control of their reproductive capacities, more equal opportunity to plan their lives, and more equal ability to participate fully in society" than if it did not exist.[28] Moreover, constitutional recognition of fetal rights would prevent further discussion of the crucial issue left undecided in *Morgentaler 2:* whether women have a *right* to abortion under the Charter.[29]

On 9 March 1989, Justice John Sopinka delivered the judgment of the Court that Borowski's appeal should be dismissed on the grounds that Borowski had lost his standing to challenge the constitutionality of section 251. The judgment focused exclusively, therefore, on the doctrine of mootness. According to Sopinka, a case is moot when there no longer exists a "live controversy," in the sense that "the required tangible and concrete dispute has disappeared and the issues have become academic." Given that the issue Borowski's appeal raised – the constitutionality of section 251 – had already been decided in *Morgentaler 2* (albeit for different reasons), this description applied to his case. While this was undoubtedly sufficient to dispose of the case before the Court, and thus the properly minimalist approach, Justice Sopinka decided to hedge the Court's bets by discussing possible exceptions to the general principle under which the Court might nevertheless exercise discretion to decide moot cases. In determining whether to exercise this discretion, he argued, the Court should consider whether an adversarial context still exists, the importance of conserving judicial resources (including considerations of public importance), and the Court's proper law-making function. If the Court is faced with an issue of high public importance, fully argued by engaged adversaries, it *may* be beneficial to mobilize scarce judicial resources and establish legal rules even where a case is technically moot. Unfortunately for Joe Borowski, Justice Sopinka agreed with LEAF that his was not such a case.

The movement represented by Borowski did not abandon its legal campaign, however. Instead, it adopted a novel strategy designed to avoid a confrontation between the rights of adult women – who clearly had legal status as persons – and fetuses, whose legal status was at best ambiguous. This strategy took the form of "abortion injunction" cases, in which fathers sought to prevent former partners from aborting the child they had conceived together.[30] Although the injunctions sought to protect fetal rights, the presence of a directly affected legal person, asserting those rights on the fetus's behalf, complicated the analysis considerably. Nevertheless, cases brought in Alberta, Manitoba, and Ontario were largely unsuccessful, although an Ontario judge did issue a temporary injunction that was overturned within a week. On 17 July 1989, however, a Quebec Superior Court judge granted Jean-Guy Tremblay an injunction against his pregnant ex-girlfriend, Chantal

Daigle. Nine days later, the Quebec Court of Appeal upheld the injunction, and Daigle appealed to the Supreme Court. Given the urgency of the matter (Daigle was twenty weeks pregnant), the Court scheduled a expedited hearing for 8 August.

The legal dispute in *Daigle* v. *Tremblay* turned on whether the fetus was a human being under the Quebec Charter of Human Rights and/or had a separate juridical personality under the Quebec Civil Code. Along with the Canadian Abortion Rights Action League (CARAL) and the Canadian Civil Liberties Association (CCLA), LEAF intervened to oppose the injunction in this particular case, as well as the use of abortion injunctions generally. Although its factum attacked the lower courts for erroneously interpreting the Quebec Charter and Civil Code,[31] LEAF devoted most of its argument to establishing a conflict between those injunctions and the fundamental rights of pregnant women under the 1982 Charter. The injunctions violated the right to equality, LEAF argued, because they represented "an attempt by a man to control the life of a woman by forcing her, through government intervention, to become a mother."[32] Without citing evidence, the factum denied the proposition that men and women have the same relationship to the fetus: the women's relationship is deeper "biologically, socially [and] spiritually."[33] Repeating almost word-for-word a paragraph from its *Borowski* factum, LEAF described access to abortion as "a necessary means for women to survive in their unequal circumstances."[34] By establishing an even greater obstacle to abortion than the procedure nullified in *Morgentaler 2*, forcing women to justify their abortion decision in an injunction procedure would restrict access and promote inequality.

After a full morning of oral argument, the parties returned to the courtroom to learn from Daigle's lawyer that she had travelled to the United States and undergone an abortion. At this point the Court could have followed *Borowski* and declared the dispute moot, but it decided to continue with the proceedings and issue a decision on the merits. The Court delivered its unanimous decision quashing the injunction from the bench a few hours later but did not render its written judgment until 16 November 1989.[35] Although some of the pro-life participants in the case had argued that the term "everyone" in section 7 of the Charter of Rights and Freedoms includes fetuses, the Court avoided this constitutional question altogether. It declared that, since the case involved a civil action between two parties, it did not encompass a sufficient degree of government action to implicate the Charter. The Court then took issue with the lower courts' interpretation that fetuses were "human beings" with a "juridical personality" under Quebec law. This interpretation, the Court argued, rested exclusively on a "linguistic analysis," which was insufficient for settling "the difficult and controversial question of whether a foetus was intended by the National

Assembly of Quebec to be a person." The Court's analysis of the relevant *legal* authorities, by contrast, led it to conclude that the fetus did not have any legal personality under the Quebec Civil Code. Similarly, the Court concluded that the "treatment of a foetus in tort law, property law and family law reveals a similar situation as found under the Civil Code, namely, that the foetus has no rights in private law." The Court therefore concluded that "the foundation of substantive rights on which the injunction could possibly be founded is lacking."

The Canadian Experience: Litigating Fetal Rights
The *Daigle* judgment began to close off the possibility that a set of fetal rights might emerge to limit the scope of reproductive choice established by *Morgentaler 2* and its political aftermath. This possibility would diminish even further as a result of the Court's judgments in *Sullivan and Lemay* and *Winnipeg Child and Family Services*. At issue in *Sullivan and Lemay* was the criminal liability of two midwives for the death of a fetus they were attempting to deliver. The fetus died after its head had been delivered but before the rest of its body exited the birth canal. The midwives were charged with two counts of criminal negligence, one for causing death to another person (the fetus) and a second for causing bodily harm (to the mother). The trial court convicted on the first count but acquitted on the second. The British Columbia Court of Appeal reversed this decision, acquitting on the first count but convicting on the second (on the grounds that the fetus is part of the pregnant woman and its death constituted bodily harm to her). Sullivan and Lemay appealed this conviction on the second count, and the Crown cross-appealed their acquittal on the first count.

LEAF intervened to argue that the Supreme Court should uphold the Court of Appeal's judgment. Consequently, its factum focused on the impact that recognition of fetuses as persons under the Criminal Code might have on women's equality rights under the Charter. LEAF's approach, the factum argued, "focuses on the relationship between a pregnant woman and her foetus, aims to grasp its uniqueness, and situates pregnancy in the legal and social context of sex inequality in a way that makes clear the relationship of this case to women's equality rights in the reproductive area."[36] A seven-paragraph section of the factum, subtitled "The Foetus Is Not a Person," concluded with the warning that "clothing the foetus with independent legal and constitutional rights may lead to the foetus having a right to the use of a woman's body, or a right to medical treatment that overrides the welfare of the pregnant woman – rights to be asserted over the woman by the putative father, a doctor, a self-appointed foetal curator, or an arm of the state."[37] Instead, LEAF urged the Court to recognize that the fetus is "in and of" the pregnant woman, which must mean that "harm to a full-term foetus in the process of birth is harm to the woman giving birth."[38] Under the circumstances of the case, LEAF had no choice but to sacrifice the two female midwives in order to avoid legal recognition of fetuses as persons.

In the final analysis, the Court by margins of nine to zero and eight to one gave LEAF most of what it sought, and the two midwives *exactly* what they sought. With respect to the Crown's appeal of the acquittal on the count of criminal negligence causing death, which raised the issue of whether a fetus in the birth canal is a person, the Court unanimously held that Parliament had not intended to include fetuses within the term "person." Without elaborating on the point, Chief Justice Lamer noted that this result was "consistent with the 'equality approach' taken by L.E.A.F."[39] With respect to Sullivan and Lemay's appeal of their conviction for criminal negligence causing bodily harm, eight justices (L'Heureux-Dubé dissenting), found that the Court of Appeal did not have jurisdiction to substitute a conviction on this count for the trial court's acquittal. Although LEAF undoubtedly would have preferred the Court to have recognized the relationship of fetal dependency on pregnant women, the exclusion of fetuses from the definition of person was a crucial outcome. From the midwives' perspective, the result was entirely positive: they avoided conviction and punishment on both counts against them.

The last fetal rights case in which LEAF intervened was *Winnipeg Child and Family Services* (hereafter *WCFS*). This case involved a young pregnant Aboriginal woman (referred to as "G") addicted to solvents who had already lost custody of her three children to Winnipeg Child and Family Services. Two of these children had suffered permanent damage as a result of G's addiction, and the social agency obtained a court order committing her to its custody in order to undergo a mandatory course of medical and therapeutic treatment. The Manitoba Court of Queen's Bench issued the order pursuant to its *parens patriae* jurisdiction, but the Manitoba Court of Appeal set aside the order on appeal. At issue in the Supreme Court was whether a superior court's *parens patriae* jurisdiction could extend to an unborn child.

LEAF intervened to discourage the Supreme Court from creating "a coercive regime under which judges would mandate how women conduct their lives and manage their pregnancies."[40] Such a regime, LEAF argued, could only "be seen as a recent example of [the state's] long standing attempt to control women's sexual and reproductive lives."[41] For Aboriginal women like G, this was only the latest development in a history of state control over their reproductive and mothering capacities, a history that included removal of children, first to residential schools and then to the child welfare system. According to LEAF, coercive judicial control was simply a new instrument to achieve an old objective.

In addition to this historical argument, LEAF advanced three additional reasons why the Court should reject the principles underlying the original court order. First, it argued that "courts are ill equipped ... to engage in what would amount to the systematic regulation of pregnant women."[42] Second, LEAF objected to the extension of *parens patriae* jurisdiction to unborn children on the grounds of "established case law" that unborn fetuses do not have separate legal rights under common law, civil law, or the Quebec rights charter.[43] As LEAF had argued in *Borowski*, live birth provided an unambiguous starting point for recognizing legal rights.[44] Abandoning this "bright line test," as LEAF described it, would establish two sets of competing rights within the same body, and women would no longer control their own pregnancies.[45] LEAF's third objection was that a coercive regime of *parens patriae* jurisdiction over unborn fetuses would violate women's Charter equality rights. In particular, such a regime would operate disproportionately against multiply disadvantaged women like G.[46]

In a seven-to-two decision the Court acted consistently with LEAF's position and upheld the Court of Appeal's judgment. Writing for the majority, Justice Beverley McLachlin dismissed the appeal "on the ground that an order detaining a pregnant woman for the purpose of protecting her fetus would require changes to the law which cannot properly be made by the courts and should be left to the legislature."[47] According to McLachlin, the only issue before the Court was the *legal* status of fetuses, and that status was strictly determined by existing common law rules. Citing *Daigle*, McLachlin echoed LEAF's argument that "neither the common law nor the civil law of Quebec recognizes the unborn child as a legal person possessing rights."[48] She did not assert, however, that fetuses could *never* be legal persons. "If Parliament or the legislatures wish to legislate legal rights for unborn children or other protective measures," she wrote, "that is open to them, subject to any limitations imposed by the Constitution of Canada."[49]

There were at least two objections to these arguments. One objection was similar to a point made by John Hart Ely about the US Supreme Court's decision in *Roe*, which is that legal personhood and the possession of rights is not necessary for legal protection. As Ely noted, states protect all sorts of things that lack status as rights-bearing persons.[50] Similarly, it is not unusual for courts to issue protective injunctions in favour of nonpersons.[51] The second objection, which McLachlin anticipated, was that the Court is free to change the common law. Her response to this objection was that "judicial extension of common law principles" should be "confined to incremental change."[52] In her view, the changes required to uphold the original court order were major, affecting rights and remedies throughout tort law, involving moral choices, and creating conflicts between fundamental interests and rights.[53] Referring to one of the authorities cited by LEAF, McLachlin expressed particular concern about the implications of recognizing a cause of action for lifestyle choices that may affect others in the context of pregnancy.[54] In the final analysis, she concluded that "the changes to the law of tort that would be required to support the order for detention at issue are of such magnitude, consequence, and policy difficulty that they exceed the proper incremental law-making powers of the courts."[55] This was a task for legislatures, she argued.

Yet McLachlin warned legislatures that the Court would be waiting to review the constitutionality of any such change. This warning was relatively explicit in the judgment's twelfth paragraph, and McLachlin repeated it in her judgment's penultimate paragraph.[56] Noting that "some interveners [had] raised constitutional concerns," she nevertheless found it unnecessary to address those concerns because her judgment was based on the common law of tort and *parens patriae*. However, if legislatures took up the Court's invitation to establish a statutory basis for judicial intervention on behalf of the fetus, "its legislation in substance and procedure would fall to be assessed against the provisions of the Charter."

LEAF's legal mobilization in *Borowski, Daigle, Sullivan,* and *WCFS* constitutes a successful attempt to block various efforts to establish fetal rights under the Charter and other areas of Canadian law. The importance of this success to the issue of reproductive choice is obvious: recognition of fetal rights would greatly constrain women's decision-making autonomy in the context of pregnancy. Clearly the Court had decided that it would not fill the policy vacuum left by its decision in *Morgentaler 2*.

Regulation of Expression and Pornography
Almost 150 years ago John Stuart Mill observed that it was no longer even necessary to defend the proposition that freedom of expression is "one of the securities against corrupt or tyrannical government."[57] The importance of this freedom derives from the twin premises of human cognitive fallibility and the liberal democratic dedication to "government by rational and free public discussion among legally equal citizens."[58] In this sense, freedom of expression is vital to the enterprise of liberal democracy because it facilitates the "growth of knowledge and the nonviolent reform of constitutional democracy itself."[59] By providing a mechanism for testing the truth of opinions, freedom of expression improves the quality of collective decision making.[60] Moreover, this freedom makes it easier for "losing" minorities to accept the results of the majoritarian democratic process in two related ways. First, it gives the minority greater confidence that the majority decision is the product of "reflection and choice" rather than of the mere "accident and force" of its numerical superiority.[61] Second, freedom of expression provides the minority with a continuous opportunity to criticize, and perhaps alter, majority opinion.

Mill's discussion of expressive freedom was not limited to the political realm, however. In fact, *On Liberty* is as much a "defense of personal eccentricity, nonconformism, and deviance in the force of conscious peer-group pressures"[62] as it is a formula for effective collective decision making. Mill foreshadowed the contemporary liberal assumption that "equal citizens have different and indeed incommensurable and irreconcilable conceptions of the good,"[63] and argued that this was a benefit rather than a hindrance to society. According to Mill, the "despotism of custom is everywhere the standing hindrance to human advancement, being in unceasing antagonism to that disposition to aim at something better than customary, which is called, according to circumstances, the spirit of liberty, or that of progress or improvement."[64] Human progress requires that individual creativity be unleashed because "mental slavery" cannot produce an "intellectually active people."[65] Freedom of expression, and in particular the freedom to challenge entrenched conventions, is vital to cultural and intellectual development.

The centrality of expressive freedom to the liberal democratic enterprise has made its regulation one of the most difficult subjects of constitutional law. The US Supreme Court has dealt with it by attempting to distinguish between "protected" and "unprotected" speech under the First Amendment to the US constitution.[66] For example, in *Roth* v. *United States* (1957), the US Court held that obscene material, defined as "material which deals with sex in a manner appealing to prurient interest," did not fall "within the area of constitutionally protected speech."[67] Sixteen years later, in *Miller* v. *California* (1973), the Court clarified its definition of obscenity and directed triers of fact to consider three factors:[68]

1   Whether the average person, applying contemporary community standards, would find that the work, taken as a whole, appeals to the prurient interest.
2   Whether the work depicts or describes in a patently offensive way, sexual conduct specifically defined by the applicable state law.
3   Whether the work, taken as a whole, lacks serious literary, artistic, political, or scientific value.

However, despite leaving room for state regulation of obscene material, the Court did hold that the First Amendment prohibits the criminalization of mere private possession of obscene material.[69]

For American feminists like Catherine MacKinnon and Andrea Dworkin, the US Court's "moral corruption" rationale for excluding obscenity from constitutional protection was problematic because it focused on obscenity's impact on the consumer rather than on the broader social harm caused by depictions of women as sex objects. For the Canadian feminist movement, therefore, the objective was to defend existing regulations from constitutional challenge while establishing a more palatable rationale for those regulations. From this perspective, pornography regulation is a second policy area in which LEAF's intervention was largely, if not unequivocally, successful.

LEAF laid the foundation for its support of antipornography legislation in a series of interventions involving hate propaganda: *Taylor* v. *The Canadian Human Rights Commission* (1990), *R.* v. *Andrews and Smith* (1990), and *R.* v. *Keegstra* (1990).[70] In all these cases, of which *Keegstra* is the best known, LEAF argued for a narrow definition of expressive freedom that excluded hate propaganda. In the alternative, LEAF argued that any infringement of freedom of expression in this context should be considered a reasonable limit under section 1 of the Charter. At the core of both arguments was the principle that freedom of expression can be limited in order to promote equality rights. Although the Court unanimously rejected the proposition that section 15 could limit the substantive meaning of freedom of expression, a majority agreed that equality rights considerations are relevant in determining whether limits on expression are reasonable in a free and democratic society.[71] In the final analysis, the Court upheld the hate propaganda provisions of the Criminal Code in *Keegstra*.

University of Calgary law professor Kathleen Mahoney, who wrote LEAF's *Keegstra* factum, saw the judgment as an important tool in the women's movement's campaign against pornography.[72] She would get an opportunity to test this proposition in *R.* v. *Butler* (1992).[73] At issue in *Butler* was the constitutionality of the anti-obscenity provisions of the Criminal Code (section 163), which prohibit the production or distribution of publications "a dominant characteristic of which is the undue exploitation of sex, or of sex and any one or more of the following subjects, namely, crime, horror, cruelty and violence." *Butler* presented the Court with three questions: (1) What constitutes "undue" exploitation of sex? (2) Does freedom of expression extend to the undue exploitation of sex? And (3) Is the criminal prohibition of undue exploitation of sex a reasonable limit on freedom of expression? LEAF's factum addressed the second and third of these questions on the basis of a theory of pornography regulation new to Canadian law. This theory asserted that "pornography amounts to a practice of sex discrimination against individual women and women as a group."[74] As a result, the constitutional justification for regulating pornography was not anchored in the prevention of moral corruption, but in "a harms-based equality approach."[75] The impugned provisions of the Criminal Code, in other words, could be justified as preventing harm rather than promoting censorship.[76]

With this theory of pornography regulation as background, LEAF launched a three-pronged defence of section 163 of the Criminal Code. Two prongs attacked the extension of constitutional protection to obscene material. The first prong sought to characterize pornography as violence, which the Court had refused to include in its otherwise broad definition of expression in *Irwin Toy* v. *A.-G. Quebec* (1989).[77] LEAF argued that this exclusion meant that at least some forms of pornography were outside constitutional protection because they could only be made as a result of "violence against real people."[78] Moreover, citing a long list of social scientific studies, the factum asserted that some forms of pornography increase the risk of violence against women.[79] LEAF derived the second prong of its attack from section 28 of the Charter, arguing that it "requires a balancing of speech interests and equality interests" in determining whether freedom of expression should extend to pornography.[80] Again citing a variety of social science material, the factum argued that the inherently discriminatory effects of pornography rendered it unworthy of *prima facie* protection under the Charter. The final prong of LEAF's argument urged the Court to uphold section 163 as a reasonable limit even if it included pornography within the definition of expression. In terms of the *Oakes* test, LEAF argued that section 163 advanced the "compelling and concrete interest in eliminating systemic social subordination," and, when interpreted as promoting equality rather than censoring against immorality, it was neither vague nor overbroad.[81] Finally, the factum argued that the harm to women from the absence of regulation would be much greater than any harm to expressive freedom flowing from the criminal prohibition of obscene material.

Although the Court unanimously rejected the suggestion that obscenity falls outside the constitutional protection provided to expression under the Charter, it determined that section 163 constitutes a reasonable limit on expressive freedom for reasons almost identical to those advanced by LEAF. Most of the two principal judgments, authored, respectively, by Justices Sopinka and Gonthier, focused on the meaning of "undue exploitation" of sex and the justification for regulating it in a free and democratic society. In large measure the two judgments expressed similar views on the meaning of "undue exploitation," with Gonthier following Sopinka's analysis. Sopinka focused on three "tests" of undue exploitation (community standards of tolerance, degradation or dehumanization, and artistic merit) and applied them to three categories of obscene material: (1) explicit sex with violence, (2) explicit sex without violence but which subjects people to treatment that is degrading or dehumanizing, and (3) explicit sex without violence that is neither degrading nor dehumanizing. According to Sopinka, the link between these tests and the three types of obscene material was the concept of harm. In his view, material that "predisposes persons to act in an antisocial manner," defined as "conduct which society formally recognizes as incompatible with its proper functioning," will exceed the community standard of tolerance. Consequently, the first category of material will generally constitute undue exploitation, while the third is unlikely ever to do so. Material in the second category becomes more "undue" as the risk of harm increases.

But does obscene material, of whatever type, cause enough harm to justify the criminal prohibition of this expressive activity? According to Sopinka and six of his colleagues, the answer to this question was clearly yes, as long as Parliament defined harm as "antisocial attitudinal changes" rather than deviation from a "particular conception of morality."[82] In his view, although prevention of harm has always been the basis for anti-obscenity legislation, section 163 represented a shift in emphasis to harm in the former sense. Indeed, if the legislation only aimed at preventing harm in the sense of public morality, its objective would not be pressing and substantial in a post-Charter free and democratic society. It was this point, in particular, that provoked Justice Gonthier (along with L'Heureux-Dubé) to concur separately. They read Sopinka's judgment as establishing too strict a separation between social harm and public morality, whereas they interpreted these two concepts as more interdependent. Nevertheless, with the social harm objective in mind, Sopinka examined the rationality, level of impairment, and balance of social benefits of the prohibition. Granting wide deference to Parliament's interpretation of admittedly "inconclusive social science evidence,"[83] Sopinka found a rational basis for its conclusion that obscenity generates harmful antisocial attitudes, particularly toward women. Moreover, Sopinka found the Code's focus on the *public* display and distribution of *undue* sexual exploitation sufficiently narrow to impair freedom of expression minimally. As in most cases, Sopinka concluded with a summary discussion of the small individual costs and large social benefits of the legislation.

The similarities between Sopinka's judgment and the legal theory for pornography regulation advanced by LEAF are numerous. At the core of this theory was the proposition that the principal justification for regulating obscene materials is to prevent harm to society rather than to impose any particular standard of public or sexual morality. According to Sopinka, obscenity is harmful because it communicates a degrading and dehumanizing message that is "analogous to that of hate propaganda."[84] Consistent with LEAF's position, the Court declared that the particular harm avoided by regulating pornography is "the degradation which many women feel as 'victims' of the message of obscenity, and of the negative impact exposure to such material has on perceptions and attitudes towards women."[85] The Court also resolved the ambiguities in the social science literature about the causal links between pornography and harm to women in LEAF's favour by deciding that the constitutionality of the legislation did not require "proof of a causative link" but only a "reasoned apprehension of harm."[86] Finally, the Court rejected the argument made by competing groups such as the Canadian Civil Liberties Association that Parliament could address the problem less intrusively by restricting access to obscene materials rather than prohibiting them. According to Justice Sopinka, "Social problems such as violence against women require multi-pronged approaches by government. Education and legislation are not alternatives but complements in addressing such problems. There is nothing in the Charter which requires Parliament to choose between such complementary measures."[87] Especially when compared with the relative lack of success of its US counterparts in the same policy area,[88] *Butler* represented a triumph for LEAF of both principle and policy.

It was a bittersweet triumph, however. As *Ms.* magazine reported in 1995, elation quickly became disillusionment in many feminist circles, particularly among lesbians. The reason was that the *Butler* decision did not appear to affect "business as usual," which meant "the unfettered flow of most heterosexual porn and the targeting of alternative sexual representations – feminist, lesbian, and gay."[89] Lesbian activists attacked both the strategy and outcome of the *Butler* litigation in print.[90] Catherine MacKinnon and Andrea Dworkin, the best-known feminist antipornography activists in the United States, felt compelled to issue a press release in response to "untrue reports ... that our feminist work against pornography is responsible for the repression of feminist, gay, and lesbian materials in Canada."[91] Although MacKinnon had participated in *Keegstra* and *Butler* as a consultant to LEAF, Dworkin had opposed LEAF's position and argued against supporting any criminal obscenity law. The press release praised the *Butler* judgment for its equality rights approach to pornography regulation, but criticized the use of criminal regulation more generally on the grounds that it "empower[s] the state rather than the victims." MacKinnon and Dworkin argued that "homophobic seizures" by Canada Customs in the post-*Butler* context were simply the continuation of existing attitudes and practices that were, in fact, illegal under the *Butler* rationale for pornography regulation. Indeed, they suggested that any "crack down on importation of explicitly gay and lesbian material ... could be opposed under *Butler*, which made the restriction of material on the basis of a moral objection (such as homosexuality) conclusively unconstitutional for the first time."

This last point became the focus of LEAF's intervention in *Little Sisters Book and Art Emporium v. Canada* (2000).[92] In the wake of the post-*Butler* lesbian backlash against LEAF, it dispatched a member of its national legal committee, Karen Busby, to conduct a national consultation on the issue with a wide variety of feminist stakeholders. The Busby consultation took place just as the first stage in a long-running legal battle between the Little Sisters bookstore and Canada Customs reached its conclusion. Almost from the store's establishment in 1983, Little Sisters experienced administrative delays or seizures of erotic and other material imported from the United States. On 19 January 1996, following a three-month trial, the British Columbia Supreme Court declared that Canada Customs had construed and applied its legislative mandate against Little Sisters in a manner contrary to sections 2(b) and 15 of the Charter. However, the trial judge refused to declare the customs legislation itself unconstitutional. Little Sisters appealed to the British Columbia Court of Appeal, which declared that the customs legislation is a reasonable limit on freedom of expression and that it does not infringe section 15 of the Charter. Little Sisters appealed to the Canadian Supreme Court, which heard the case on 16 March 2000.

In a factum coauthored by Karen Busby, LEAF intervened to support the bookstore's constitutional challenge to the customs regime. LEAF attempted to reconcile the apparent tension between its *Little Sisters* position and the argument advanced in *Butler* by using an equality rights analysis to qualify the definition of obscenity in a way that excluded the material imported by Little Sisters. The gist of this argument was the following: (1) Obscenity is defined with reference to harmful consequences for women; (2) lesbian erotica is beneficial, rather than harmful, for women regardless of their sexual orientation; (3) therefore, lesbian erotica cannot be classified as obscene. From this perspective, the factum argued that the customs regime "is unconstitutional because it fails to provide mechanisms to guard against misuses of the censoring power and it is wholly unsuited to making the factual and legal determinations, including the constitutional equality analysis, which should be required before any materials are found to be 'obscene' and, as such, prohibited."[93] The customs regime, LEAF submitted, violated both expressive freedom and equality "by inappropriately limiting the free expression of sexual minorities in a discriminatory way."[94]

Implicit in LEAF's argument was the proposition that similar treatment of lesbian erotica and heterosexual pornography under the obscenity provisions reflected the discredited theory of formal equality, and that substantive equality "requires that lesbians and other constitutionally protected minority communities have the freedom to explore personal and community identities through writings, photography, drawing and other media."[95] Lesbian erotica, the factum argued, assists in forming individual lesbian identities and nurturing lesbian communities. Moreover, by challenging the inequalities inherent in conventional sexuality, such material benefits heterosexual women.[96] Thus, while affirming its support of the "harms-based equality approach to obscenity law" established in *Butler*, the factum argued for a strict test of harm. For harm to be shown, in other words, there must be "specific and compelling evidence" that "the materials increase propensity for violence, or they serve to foster and perpetuate the unequal position in society of those groups protected by the *Charter*'s equality guarantee."[97] As a blunt instrument, administered by harried and inexpert officials, the customs regime did not comply with this more equality-nuanced approach to determining harm.[98] LEAF had to focus on lesbian material for the simple reason that it had offered gay male material as examples of harmful obscenity in *Butler*.[99] To take a broader approach to same-sex erotica in *Little Sisters* would have been completely irreconcilable with its earlier position.

Although the Court noticed LEAF's arguments, they had little impact on the final result. In a six-to-three majority judgment (which included Chief

Justice McLachlin and Justice L'Heureux-Dubé, two of the three female justices on the Court), the Court essentially affirmed the original trial court
decision by upholding the constitutionality of the customs regime (with
the minor exception of a reverse onus provision) while criticizing customs
officials for applying it in a discriminatory fashion against Little Sisters.
Addressing LEAF's position that "sado-masochism performs an emancipatory
role in gay and lesbian culture and should therefore be judged by a different
standard from that applicable to heterosexual culture," the majority nevertheless concluded that "gay and lesbian culture as such does not constitute
a general exemption from the *Butler* test."[100] Even the dissenting justices
(Iacobucci, Arbour, and LeBel) agreed with the majority that the *Butler* obscenity test did not need modification and "applies equally to all materials
regardless of the sexual orientation of the individuals involved or the char-
acters depicted."[101] Their dissent was about whether customs officials could
be trusted to eliminate the unconstitutional application of the regime without judicial nullification of the relevant customs tariff. Writing for the dissenters, Justice Iacobucci argued that nullification would foster an important
dialogue that would fundamentally improve the statutory framework of
the customs regime.[102]

On one level, LEAF's intervention in *Little Sisters* might be considered a
failure. The Court – both majority and dissenters – either ignored (the list of
authors cited includes only one item referred to in LEAF's factum) or rejected most of its substantive arguments (although the dissenters would
have given LEAF the remedy it requested). The intervention, however, was
as much about healing wounds within the feminist movement as it was
about achieving a particular legal objective. In this instance, legal mobilization served the organizational purposes identified by Stuart Scheingold in
the mid-1970s. Indeed, as Miriam Smith pointed out more recently, legal
mobilization is frequently about creating "political community and organization."[103] In LEAF's case in *Little Sisters*, it was about mending divisions
within the feminist political community.

However, even in this respect, the intervention was not entirely successful. Equality Now, which describes itself as "an international human rights
organization dedicated to action for the civil, political, economic and social
rights of girls and women,"[104] intervened in *Little Sisters* against LEAF's position. Janine Benedet of Osgoode Hall Law School, who served as counsel for
Equality Now in *Little Sisters*, would subsequently publish an article highly
critical of the bookstore's case, if not of LEAF's intervention directly.[105]
Benedet criticized the positive media portrayals of the case and bookstore,
described the bookstore's claim of a fifteen-year government legal campaign
against it as "disingenuous," and accused Little Sisters of simply ignoring
the inherent harm of even gay and lesbian pornography.[106] In fact, *Little
Sisters* might be understood as the final part of a trilogy of interventions in

which LEAF reached out to the lesbian faction of the feminist movement. The next section discusses the other two cases in that trilogy.

Sexual Orientation

The constitutional status of distinctions based on sexual orientation first reached the Supreme Court in *Canada* v. *Mossop* (1993).[107] At issue was whether denial of bereavement leave for a public service employee to attend the funeral of his same-sex partner constituted discrimination on the basis of "family status" under the Canadian Human Rights Act (CHRA), and the case thus came to the Court strictly as a matter of statutory interpretation (i.e., whether "family status" included same-sex conjugal relationships). Although the Court invited Mossop to challenge the Act's constitutionality "on the basis of the absence of sexual orientation from the list of prohibited grounds of discrimination," he chose not to do so.[108] The Court thus restricted itself to the statutory interpretation issue and held that Parliament did not intend to prohibit discrimination on the basis of sexual orientation when it added "family status" to the CHRA in 1983.

The Court finally got its opportunity to consider sexual orientation from a constitutional perspective in *Egan* v. *Canada* (1995).[109] At issue was the constitutionality of a provision of the federal Old Age Security Act (OAS), which defined "spouse" as a person of the opposite sex. The ultimate resolution of this issue fractured the Court, with the nine justices producing four separate reasons for judgment. The plurality judgment by Justice La Forest (with Chief Justice Lamer and Justices Gonthier and Major) held that the legislation did not infringe section 15(1). Two dissenting judgments, by Justices Cory (with Iacobucci and McLachlin) and L'Heureux-Dubé, held that the statutory definition of "spouse" constituted an unreasonable denial of equality. Finally, Justice Sopinka cast the deciding vote by holding that the definition infringed section 15 but was justified under section 1. The final outcome: a five-to-four majority of the Court upheld the definition's constitutionality.

Despite the Court's divisions on substantive outcome, it was unanimous on a key issue: that "sexual orientation" is an analogous ground of discrimination that should be read into section 15 of the Charter. As La Forest indicated, establishing this point did not present any "great hurdle" for the appellants because the federal government conceded it at the outset. Putting aside his "ordinary reservations about concessions of constitutional issues," La Forest had "no difficulty accepting the appellants' contention that whether or not sexual orientation is based on biological or physiological factors, which may be a matter of some controversy, it is a deeply personal characteristic that is either unchangeable or changeable only at unacceptable personal costs, and so falls within the ambit of s. 15 protection as being analogous to the enumerated grounds."[110] Thus, despite the issue loss in

Egan, constitutional recognition of sexual orientation provided the gay and lesbian rights movement new opportunities for legal mobilization.

The movement thus returned to the Supreme Court in *Vriend* v. *Alberta* (1998).[111] Delwin Vriend had worked as a laboratory coordinator at a religiously affiliated college in Edmonton, Alberta. In 1991, the college terminated Vriend's employment because he refused to comply with its recently established policy against homosexual practice. Vriend attempted to file a complaint under Alberta's Individual Rights Protection Act (IRPA), but the Alberta Human Rights Commission advised him that he could not do so because the IRPA did not prohibit discrimination on the basis of sexual orientation. In association with the Gay and Lesbian Awareness Society of Edmonton (GALA), the Gay and Lesbian Community Centre of Edmonton Society, and Dignity Canada Dignité for Gay Catholics and Supporters, Vriend challenged the constitutionality of this exclusion in the Alberta Court of Queen's Bench. The trial court agreed with Vriend and read sexual orientation into the Act, but the Alberta Court of Appeal reversed. Vriend and his coappellants therefore appealed to the Supreme Court, which heard arguments on whether Alberta's conscious refusal to include sexual orientation in the IRPA constituted an unreasonable limitation of the right to equal benefit of the law without discrimination.

Not surprisingly, given its organizational focus, LEAF intervened "to ensure that lesbians and lesbian inequality are and remain visible in the legal determinations before this Court, so that gender neutral reasoning is not applied to the analysis or remedy with respect to inequalities which are not gender neutral in their effects."[112] Much of the factum authored by Claire Klassen, who would serve as Karen Busby's cocounsel in *Little Sisters*, focused on the specific impact on lesbians of what LEAF called the "watertight compartments" approach to interpreting human rights instruments.[113] According to LEAF, this approach (most obviously evident in *Mossop*) treated prohibited grounds of discrimination as mutually exclusive categories. As a result, the "scope of the grounds has come to be defined narrowly by reference to those claimants who are most visible to lawmakers and decision-makers and least 'different' from society's most dominant groups." This approach was particularly bad for groups, such as lesbians, whose socioeconomic and political disadvantage could not be reduced to a single source of discrimination.

The optimal solution, Klassen argued, was for lesbian discrimination to be recognized and redressed "as a distinctive form of 'sex' discrimination." This would allow for consideration of the particular types of sexual harassment, employment discrimination, and economic disadvantage from which lesbians uniquely suffered. However, in addition to, and certainly in the absence of, a complete reconstruction of human rights theory along these lines, LEAF obviously supported the appellants' argument that the exclusion of "sexual orientation" as a prohibited ground of discrimination in human rights statutes violated the Charter's equality rights. Moreover, LEAF supported the remedy of reading the words "sexual orientation" into the relevant sections of the IRPA.

In contrast to the division that characterized *Egan*, agreement typified the *Vriend* Court, which unanimously held that the exclusion of sexual orientation from the IRPA was an unjustifiable infringement of section 15, and seven of eight justices endorsed the remedy of reading sexual orientation into the Act (Justice Major, the only Albertan on the Court, dissented on this point). Justices Cory and Iacobucci collaborated on the lead judgment, with Cory writing on section 15 issues and Iacobucci addressing the section 1 analysis and remedy. Following his approach in *Egan*, Cory focused on whether the legislation created a discriminatory distinction, defined as one that denied equality on the basis of an enumerated or analogous ground. In his view, the IRPA created two such distinctions – one between homosexuals and other disadvantaged groups, and another between homosexuals and heterosexuals. These distinctions, Cory continued, denied gays and lesbians the benefit of the IRPA's remedial provisions while simultaneously promoting discrimination toward them. Describing the noninclusion of gays and lesbians from the Act's protection as a "particularly cruel form of discrimination," Cory held that it inflicted "psychological harm" by implying that "'all persons are equal in dignity and rights' except gay men and lesbians."[114] For his part, Justice Iacobucci could find no pressing and substantial objective that might justify this exclusion, and even if one did exist he declared that the exclusion could not possibly be rational since it was antithetical to the very purposes of the IRPA.[115]

On the level of substantive constitutional law and remedy, LEAF would obviously have to view the outcome in *Vriend* positively. On a deeper level, however, there was probably some reason for disappointment. With the exception of one sentence,[116] the judgment treated lesbians and gay men as a single, undifferentiated category. Thus, to the extent that one purpose of LEAF's intervention was to challenge the presumption that lesbians share "an identity of experience and interest" with gay men,[117] the effort was unsuccessful. Lesbians, per se, remained largely in the background throughout the *Vriend* judgment.

This would not be the case in the Court's next sexual orientation decision, *M. v. H.* (1999), in which LEAF also intervened.[118] The case involved a lesbian couple whose conjugal relationship broke down after approximately ten years. When one of the parties, M, applied for spousal support under Ontario's Family Law Act (FLA), H sought a summary judgment against the application on the grounds that the FLA defined spouse as a person of the opposite sex. However, the trial court held that this definition infringed section 15 of the Charter in a manner that could not be justified under section 1. Now joined by the Attorney General of Ontario as an intervener, H appealed to the Ontario Court of Appeal, which upheld the trial court judgment. H decided not to pursue her case to the Supreme Court, but the Court nevertheless granted leave to appeal to Ontario's Attorney General on the condition that M's costs be paid regardless of the appeal's outcome. Shortly before oral argument in the Supreme Court, M and H settled their financial dispute.

Since Ontario had conceded that the FLA denied a statutory benefit (the right to apply for spousal support) on the basis of sexual orientation (recognized as an analogous ground in *Egan*), LEAF devoted most of its factum (fifty-one of seventy-one paragraphs) to rebutting various section 1 arguments that might justify this infringement of section 15 of the Charter.[119] The first argument was that the Act's purpose was to protect economically vulnerable heterosexual women from the negative consequences of relationship breakdown, and that this was the type of pressing and substantial objective that justified limiting a Charter right. LEAF's response was that this purpose was at best only one of at least three objectives underlying the FLA.[120] Moreover, it pointed out that the Act's gender-neutral language belied the centrality of this purpose because it gave men the same right to apply for spousal support as women, and LEAF cited several cases where courts had in fact awarded support to men.[121] Finally, LEAF argued that there was no rational connection between the exclusion of same-sex relationships and any of the ostensible purposes of the FLA's support regime.

The second argument was that the Court should employ a deferential standard of review under section 1 because the FLA was enacted in a field where the legislature had to mediate among competing societal interests. In particular, lesbian activists themselves had been divided on the benefits of being included within the support regime. The source of this disagreement was the extent to which inclusion would erode the differences between lesbian and heterosexual relationships (assimilation), as well as government responsibility for the economic well-being of individuals (privatization). LEAF responded to both prongs of this argument by asserting that subsequent events had rendered them moot. The Court's abandonment of the "similarly situated" test for discrimination meant that "there is simply no need for lesbian litigants to portray their intimate relationships ... as if they were 'just like' their heterosexual counterparts."[122] With respect to the privatization prong, general government economic retrenchment made this concern irrelevant.[123] In any event, LEAF argued that "government should not be permitted to exploit the differences of political opinion that exist between members of equality-seeking groups to excuse its own unconstitutional action."[124]

The final argument concerned the availability of alternatives to the FLA regime in both common law and equity. LEAF argued that these alternatives were too narrow, inflexible, and expensive to be adequate responses to relationship breakdown. In fact, if they had been adequate, then Ontario never would have enacted the FLA in the first place.[125] To LEAF it was "particularly ironic ... that the government would attempt to justify its exclusion of lesbian women from [the spousal support regime] on the basis that they can always take advantage of the very remedies it recognized were inadequate to meet the needs of heterosexual women."[126]

LEAF's intervention in this case attracted the Court's attention. Not only did the majority judgment cite the same law reform commission reports and legislative debates as LEAF in constructing the FLA's legislative history, but Justice Iacobucci explicitly referred to LEAF's arguments in his section 1 analysis. In rejecting economic assistance for heterosexual women as the Act's sole purpose, he wrote that,

> As submitted by LEAF, the infrequency with which members of same-sex relationships find themselves in circumstances resembling those of many heterosexual women is no different from heterosexual men who, notwithstanding that they tend to benefit from the gender-based division of labour and inequality of earning power, have as much right to apply for support as their female partners.[127]

Similarly, Iacobucci adopted LEAF's submission that conventional equitable remedies were not a suitable alternative to the FLA's spousal support regime.[128] Whether he would have reached these conclusions without LEAF's submissions is uncertain, but his reference to them was precisely the type of impact that LEAF had hoped for from its intervention.

As in *Vriend*, Iacobucci shared responsibility for the majority judgment with Justice Cory. Cory's part of the judgment dealt with three topics: (1) the facts, statutory provisions, and lower court decisions; (2) mootness; and (3) discrimination under section 15. The second topic was necessary, of course, because M and H had resolved their dispute voluntarily and thus no longer had a vested interest in the case's outcome.[129] In Cory's view, however, since leave to appeal had actually been granted to the Ontario Attorney General, whose interest in the FLA's constitutionality was still obviously live, the mootness doctrine did not apply. Moreover, Cory argued that "even if the appeal were moot, it would be appropriate for the Court to exercise its discretion in order to decide these important issues. The social cost of leaving this matter undecided would be significant."[130] The problem with this statement is that, in two important senses, the matter *had not* been left undecided in Ontario. First, the previous government, under the leadership of NDP premier Bob Rae, had unsuccessfully attempted to amend the statutory definition of spouse.[131] Second, the Ontario Court of Appeal had decided that the unamended definition violated the constitution. Where the matter was undecided was at the national level, and while the Court's intervention was unnecessary to correct inadequate consideration of a controversial question, it was necessary to establish a national standard for the definition of spouse.

If Cory's brief discussion (two paragraphs) of mootness was necessary because the original parties' direct interests were no longer implicated, his much longer discussion (thirty paragraphs) of the section 15 question would seem to have been redundant given that Ontario had conceded this point. However, although Cory thought that Ontario was "correct in taking this position," he asserted that "it would not be appropriate in this appeal to undertake only a s. 1 analysis without considering whether s. 15 has in fact been violated."[132] Cory began his analysis by summarizing the Court's recent judgment in *Law* v. *Canada* (1999).[133] Although the equality rights claim failed in *Law*, the judgment represented a consolidated restatement of the Court's approach to equality and discrimination. First, the justices definitively agreed on the following purpose of section 15(1): "to prevent the violation of essential human dignity and freedom through the imposition of disadvantage, stereotyping, or political or social prejudice, and to promote a society in which all persons enjoy equal recognition at law as human beings or as members of Canadian society, equally capable and equally deserving of concern, respect and consideration."[134] Second, they agreed that three broad inquiries should guide the judicial determination of discrimination:[135]

First, does the impugned law (a) draw a formal distinction between the claimant and others on the basis of one or more personal characteristics, or (b) fail to take into account the claimant's already disadvantaged position within Canadian society resulting in substantively differential treatment between the claimant and others on the basis of one or more personal characteristics? If so, there is differential treatment for the purpose of s. 15(1). Second, was the claimant subject to differential treatment on the basis of one or more of the enumerated and analogous grounds? And third, does the differential treatment discriminate in a substantive sense, bringing into play the *purpose* of s. 15(1) of the *Charter* in remedying such ills as prejudice, stereotyping, and historical disadvantage?

The *Law* approach largely followed the approach to equality rights that Justice L'Heureux-Dubé had been urging on the Court in a series of cases, including *Egan* and *Vriend*, and it is significant that she did not write separate judgments in *Law* or *M.* v. *H.*

Applying this approach to the FLA's spousal definition, Cory found that it denied certain individuals a legal benefit (a dedicated process for protecting their economic interests in the event of relationship breakdown) solely on the basis of an analogous personal characteristic (sexual orientation). Consequently, the impugned provision of the FLA stereotyped gays and lesbians as incapable of forming long-term conjugal relationships, which promoted the view that "individuals in same-sex relationships ... are less worthy of recognition and protection"; perpetuated "the disadvantages suffered by individuals in same-sex relationships"; and contributed to "the erasure of their existence."[136] All this indicated that "the human dignity of individuals in same-sex relationships is violated by the impugned legislation," leading Cory to conclude "that the definition of 'spouse' in s. 29 of the *FLA* violates s. 15(1)."[137]

With this violation established, Iacobucci took up the section 1 analysis. Although he accepted as pressing and substantial objectives "the equitable resolution of economic disputes when intimate relationships between financially interdependent individuals break down" and "alleviating the burden on the public purse to provide for dependent spouses," he could find no rational connection between those objectives and the exclusion of same-sex relationships from the FLA's definition of spouse. Moreover, even if such a connection could be established, for the reasons discussed above (drawn from LEAF's factum) Iacobucci did not find any of the common law alternatives to the FLA's support determination process adequate to achieve those objectives. Therefore, over the sole dissent of Justice Gonthier, the Court nullified the definition of "spouse" in the FLA, but suspended the constitutional remedy for six months to allow for an appropriate legislative response.

Although the Court gave the feminist and lesbian and gay rights movements overwhelming victories in both *Vriend* and *M. v. H.*, it was not entirely unconcerned with potential political opposition to the judgments. For example, fifteen of the fifty-one paragraphs that Justice Iacobucci devoted to remedial issues in *Vriend* dealt with the relationship between legislatures and courts under the Charter. In defending the decision to read sexual orientation into Alberta's human rights statute and order Alberta to act consistently with that remedy immediately, Justice Iacobucci took direct aim at critics who "allege" that judicial review is "illegitimate because it is antidemocratic."[138] Dismissing these concerns, Iacobucci defended the Court's relatively new role in the political process as being the product of a "deliberate choice of our provincial and federal legislatures" that "promotes democratic values." According to Iacobucci, the Court's function is simply to serve as the "trustee" of the Charter and "scrutinize the work of the legislature and the executive not in the name of the courts, but in the interests of the new social contract that was democratically chosen." "Judges," Iacobucci continued, "are not acting undemocratically by intervening when there are indications that a legislative or executive decision was not reached in accordance with the democratic principles mandated by the *Charter*." Instead,

Charter review creates "a more dynamic interaction among the branches of governance."

Similarly, despite their conclusion and relatively strong endorsement of LEAF's arguments in *M. v. H.*, Justices Cory and Iacobucci nevertheless emphasized that the appeal had "nothing to do with marriage *per se.*"[139] As Iacobucci stressed, the appeal "does not challenge traditional conceptions of marriage." Nor did he want "to be understood as making any comment on marriage or indeed on related issues."[140] By qualifying their judgment in this way, Cory and Iacobucci tacitly acknowledged that changing the definition of spouse was only part of the overall strategic objective of the social movements that mobilized around the *M. v. H.* litigation. Indeed, these movements launched more or less simultaneous constitutional challenges to the traditional definition of marriage in British Columbia, Ontario, and Quebec. Cory and Iacobucci were well aware, however, of the social and political limitations on the Court's institutional capacity to alter the definition of marriage even as it changed the definition of "spouse." Confirmation of these obstacles came from the province of Alberta, where the legislature passed the Marriage Amendment Act in March 2000. The Act added a preamble to the province's Marriage Act declaring that marriage is between a man and a woman, as well as a section declaring that the Marriage Act operates notwithstanding the Charter.[141]

Political considerations may also provide a partial answer to two puzzling questions raised by *M. v. H.* First, why did the Court take fifteen months to render its judgment, and second, after such a long delay, why did the Court release its judgment in the midst of an Ontario election campaign rather than wait an additional two weeks until the election's conclusion? One possible answer to the first question is that the Court was engaged in an internal reevaluation of its approach to section 15 in the context of the *Law* case, which it heard in January of 1998, reheard in December of 1998, and finally decided in March of 1999. However, this answer is not entirely persuasive, given Ontario's concession on the question of discrimination and the Court's unanimous judgment in *Vriend* one month after oral argument in *M. v. H.* The precise approach to section 15, in other words, was irrelevant to deciding one of the case's principal issues. As to the second question, neither M nor H had anything directly at stake in the actual decision because they had resolved their financial dispute. Even for Ontario there was little need for a resolution because it was already operating under an appellate court decision that the impugned provision was unconstitutional. There was thus no urgency to release a judgment that had already been on the Court's docket for so long. One might speculate that the Court released its judgment in the midst of the campaign to minimize the possibility of political fallout on the assumption that the incumbent Conservative government would want to avoid making the rights of gays and lesbians a campaign issue. If this was strategic, then it was effective. The incumbent premier, Mike Harris, immediately declared his intention to comply with the judgment. "It is not my definition of family," Harris told the media, "but it is of others. And the courts have ruled that it is constitutional."[142] To be sure, it would have been equally "political" for the Court to have delayed releasing the judgment, but that option would not have served its institutional interests as well.

The achievements of the gay and lesbian rights movement in the Supreme Court over a short period of time is one of the remarkable stories of legal mobilization under the Charter. From its uncontested addition of sexual orientation to the list of analogous categories protected under section 15 to its near unanimous redefinition of spouse, the Court has been the source of significant policy change. Indeed, as Justice L'Heureux-Dubé told a London conference on the legal recognition of same-sex partnerships shortly after the *M. v. H.* judgment, "courts are taking the lead in changing society's attitudes to same-sex partnerships."[143] Although the recognition of same-sex partnerships was not the primary focus of LEAF's campaign, the women's movement played an important part in this success. Particularly in *M. v. H.*, where its arguments on section 1 issues appear to have influenced the Court, LEAF's intervention in these cases made a difference. By lending its credibility, built on almost a decade of Charter interventions, to another movement's campaign, LEAF also advanced its own agenda in significant ways.

Conclusion

The three policy areas discussed in this chapter pitted six sets of social movements against each other: pro-choice versus pro-life, civil libertarians versus antipornography activists, same-sex activists versus traditionalist family defenders. In each case, the movement either led or supported by LEAF prevailed. LEAF's success is particularly striking in the expression cases, where both civil libertarians and antipornography activists could claim to speak on behalf of historically disadvantaged groups: civil libertarians for holders of unconventional opinions and aesthetic tastes, and antipornography activists for the largely female victims of violence and sexual oppression. Given a choice between these two groups, the Court sided with LEAF. However, as *Little Sisters* indicated, there were limits to how far the Court was willing to take this support.

4
Family Matters:
Breakdowns and Benefits

From 1988 to 2000, LEAF participated in six cases that dealt with various aspects of family and social policy. Like *M*. v. *H*., three of these cases – *Moge* v. *Moge* (1992), *Thibaudeau* v. *Canada* (1995), and *Gordon* v. *Goertz* (1996) – dealt with the consequences of relationship breakdown.[1] Three cases – *Schachter* v. *Canada* (1992), *Eldridge* v. *British Columbia* (1997), and *New Brunswick (Minister of Health and Community Services)* v. *G.(J.)* (1999) – involved the provision of social benefits such as parental leave, health care, and legal aid. For the most part, LEAF was on the winning side in these cases. The Court agreed with LEAF's position on five of seven substantive issues (*Schachter* encompassed two separate issues), reached the outcome favoured by LEAF in five of six cases, and cast 76 percent of its individual votes (thirty-eight of fifty) for the position advocated by LEAF. Despite this cumulative success, LEAF did suffer two important losses in these cases. First, in *Schachter* the Court disagreed with LEAF on the issue of extending financial benefits where social legislation is underinclusive. Second, in *Thibaudeau* the Court refused to amend the Income Tax Act's treatment of child support payments in the manner suggested by LEAF. However, these legal defeats became political victories when Parliament subsequently enacted the changes that LEAF had advocated.

Breakdowns

As I discussed in earlier chapters, two Supreme Court decisions – *Bliss* and *Lavell* – galvanized feminist legal mobilization in Canada. To these decisions should be added *Murdoch* v. *Murdoch* (1975).[2] In this case the Supreme Court denied an Alberta woman's claim that her contributions – "haying, raking, swathing, mowing, driving trucks and tractors and teams, quietening horses, taking cattle back and forth to the reserve, dehorning, vaccinating, and branding" – entitled her to a share in the family ranch when her marriage broke down. Despite a "vigorous dissent" by Bora Laskin, the Court described these contributions as the work of "any ranch wife" and held that they did not amount to "a claim in partnership." The *Murdoch* decision spurred a movement for family property reform and provided an additional focal point for feminist litigation. Not surprisingly, LEAF intervened in three cases involving spousal support, child support taxation policies, and child custody rules.

The first of these cases was *Moge*. The Moges married in Poland in the mid-1950s and immigrated to Canada in 1960. They separated in 1973 and divorced in 1980, with Zofia Moge acquiring custody of the children and receiving monthly child and spousal support. In 1989 her husband, Andrzej Moge, obtained a court order terminating support, but the Manitoba Court of Appeal set aside that judgment and awarded Mrs. Moge spousal support for an indefinite period. Andrzej Moge appealed to the Supreme Court, where LEAF intervened to support dismissal of the appeal.

Moge was essentially a case of statutory interpretation involving two provisions of the federal Divorce Act, but LEAF intervened to ensure that Charter equality principles informed that interpretation. More than one-third of the factum aimed at establishing that the "gender-based division of labour within marriage" placed women at an economic disadvantage, and that this disadvantage should be viewed as a sex equality issue. The argumentation and evidence in this section of the factum was almost exclusively extralegal, with only a single legal citation – to *Brooks* v. *Canada Safeway* (1989) – appearing in the factum's first thirty-one paragraphs. When LEAF did turn its attention to largely legal arguments, it repeated its misleading declaration that the Charter is the "supreme law of Canada."[3] It followed this with three citations of *Andrews* (1989) on the idea of equality as "one of the fundamental values ... against which the objects of all legislation must be measured."[4] It followed from this, LEAF argued, "that principles for the determination of spousal support must not impose a detrimental burden on women as compared with men by virtue of the division of labour within marriage."[5]

From LEAF's perspective, the interpretation of the Divorce Act had to recognize, contrary to existing case law, that marriage is an inherent cause of women's economic disadvantage, and that marital breakdown exacerbates that disadvantage. LEAF thus rejected the existing classification of marriages as either "traditional" or "nontraditional," with the former providing a stronger basis for support claims. This approach shifted "the focus away from a concrete examination of the economic disadvantages and advantages arising from all varieties of marriage."[6] According to LEAF, the more appropriate "gauge for determining economic disadvantage is the extent to which the marriage is characterized by a differential and/or inequitable division of labour."[7] However, since every marriage is characterized by "a gender-based division of labour" that has "significant economic consequences for women,"[8] it would be difficult to imagine a situation in which a woman would not be entitled to spousal support following marital break-down. But how long should support continue? On this point LEAF attacked the existing doctrine of economic self-sufficiency, arguing that, in order "to be consistent with and further section 15 of the Charter," any "assessment of the ability of women to achieve economic self-sufficiency following marriage breakdown must take account of the ongoing nature of the economic disadvantage arising from the marriage."[9]

The extralegal material cited in LEAF's factum also found its way into the Court's unanimous judgment dismissing Andrzej Moge's appeal. Justice L'Heureux-Dubé, writing for herself and four other justices, began her substantive discussion of the issues with three observations.[10] First, she expressed concern "about making a spouse's entitlement to support contingent on the degree to which he or she is able to fit within a mythological stereotype" based on the distinction between traditional and nontraditional marriages.[11] Second, she observed that, "in determining spousal support it is important not to lose sight of the fact that the support provisions of the Act are intended to deal with the *economic* consequences, for both parties, of the marriage or its breakdown."[12] Finally, although she conceded that her "analysis applies equally to both spouses, depending on how the division of labour is exercised in a particular marriage," L'Heureux-Dubé acknowledged "the reality is that in many if not most marriages, the wife still remains the economically disadvantaged partner."[13]

All of these observations, of course, were consistent with LEAF's argument. In particular, L'Heureux-Dubé relied extensively on material found in LEAF's factum in building a case for dissatisfaction with existing norms for determining support.[14] From this material she identified compensation for lost opportunities and nonmonetary contributions to the family unit as an emerging principle of spousal support. This principle, which L'Heureux-Dubé also referred to as the "doctrine of equitable sharing," was based on the recognition that "each spouse is an equal economic and social partner in marriage, regardless of function."[15] Finding support for this doctrine in the broad scope of the relevant sections of the Divorce Act, L'Heureux-Dubé argued that it "recognizes that work within the home has undeniable value and transforms the notion of equality from the rhetorical status to which it was relegated under a deemed self-sufficiency model, to a substantive imperative."[16] Spousal support, therefore, might be best understood as a form of compensatory remedy for the economic disadvantages suffered by the spouse claiming support. That this spouse is generally the wife was sufficiently well documented in the social science literature, according to L'Heureux-Dubé, that it was "amenable to judicial notice."[17] Judges should not terminate support, she concluded, until there has been full compensation for the negative economic consequences flowing from marriage and marital breakdown.

In all but one respect, the *Moge* judgment fully incorporated LEAF's perspective on spousal support and interpretation of the Divorce Act. The missing component was the Court's failure to link its interpretation of the Act directly to section 15 of the Charter. Indeed, the Charter does not appear on the list of statutes and regulations cited by the Court. As Justice McLachlin wrote in her concurring judgment, *Moge* was, "first and last, a case of statutory interpretation." Perhaps indicating some impatience with Justice L'Heureux-Dubé's fondness for extralegal material, McLachlin noted that, while it might be "interesting and useful to consider how different theories of support yield different answers to the question of how support should be determined ... in the end the judge must return to what Parliament has said on the subject."[18]

Justice L'Heureux-Dubé's comments about the gendered division of labour and female responsibility for child care in *Moge* played a prominent role in LEAF's factum in *Gordon*.[19] As in *Moge*, LEAF devoted a significant portion of its factum (twenty-four of sixty paragraphs) to the broader social and Charter context in which the custodial provisions of the Divorce Act should be interpreted.[20] In particular, LEAF argued that relocation of custodial parents, which was the issue in dispute in *Gordon*, be resolved with recognition that "the legal treatment of women following separation has a significant impact on the social and economic status of women and their children, and as such, their substantive equality."[21] The argument linked the substantive equality of female custodial parents to the best interests of the child by asserting that custodial parents are in the best position to determine those interests, and that a custodial parent's well-being is essential to the child's best interests.[22] All this meant that

> the inextricable link between the well-being of the child and the custodial mother, requires a recognition of the realities and interests of the custodial mother. Promoting women's substantive equality is fundamental to the well-being of women and the children in their care. Accordingly, it is submitted that the concept of the best interests of the child should be interpreted in a manner consistent with the constitutional goal of promoting women's substantive equality.[23]

From this argument it followed that an interpretation of the relevant provisions of the Divorce Act consistent with section 15 of the Charter required the following test:

> Where a parent with sole custody seeks to relocate, the move, in and of itself, is a material change in circumstances with respect to access only, but not with respect to custody. Accordingly, a sole custodial parent's decision

to relocate is not subject to the court's review, as the relocation decision is an incident of custody. However, access may be restructured by the court.[24]

According to this test, Janet Gordon had the right to relocate to Australia with her child, and LEAF urged the Court to dismiss Robin Goertz's appeal of the lower court decisions permitting the move.

In terms of outcome, the Court's judgment was mostly consistent with LEAF's objectives. The lower courts had permitted relocation and given the father liberal access rights to be exercised exclusively in Australia. While the Court dismissed his appeal on the relocation issue, it did vary the access order so that it could be exercised in Canada. Although all nine members of the Court supported this outcome, they did generate three separate reasons for judgment by Justices McLachlin (for six justices), Gonthier (alone), and L'Heureux-Dubé (for two justices). Noting that this was the first time the issue had come before the Court, McLachlin acknowledged that LEAF had invited the Court "to consider the principles which should guide judges" in considering "the effect of a custodial parent's move on custody and access."[25] However, although she conceded that "the views of the custodial parent ... are entitled to great respect and the most serious consideration," McLachlin rejected LEAF's submission that a custodial parent's decision is not subject to a court's review.[26] Thus, in terms of doctrine, *Gordon* gave LEAF less than it would have preferred. Indeed, at no point in any of the reasons for judgment did the justices refer to LEAF's equality arguments.

The final case in this "family breakdown" trilogy is *Thibaudeau*. At issue was the constitutionality of a provision of the Income Tax Act (ITA) under which recipient custodial parents declared child support payments as income while support providers deducted those payments from their income. The gist of the constitutional complaint was that the impugned provision of the ITA imposed a burden on separated and divorced custodial parents, and that this group constituted an analogous ground of discrimination under section 15. The rationale for including this group as an analogous ground, according to the claim, was that it had been historically subjected to disadvantageous treatment and was linked to an enumerated ground of prohibited discrimination (sex) because most custodial parents are women. As in the *Symes* case (discussed in Chapter 1), the Court divided along gender lines, with five male justices rejecting Suzanne Thibaudeau's claim, and Justices McLachlin and L'Heureux-Dubé dissenting to support it.

The purpose of LEAF's submission, which began by noting the economic disadvantage of women relative to men,[27] was to ensure recognition of the gendered nature of the distinctions made in the impugned provisions of the ITA. According to LEAF, these distinctions were twofold.[28] First, the Act distinguished between separated custodial parents and parents who were not separated; and second, it distinguished between separated custodial and noncustodial parents. Although these distinctions were on their face gender neutral, LEAF argued that "in the larger social and economic context, it becomes clear that the vast majority of the affected groups are women."[29] It was therefore an overly narrow approach to characterize the source of discrimination in the relevant section of the ITA as "family status" (i.e., imposition of a burden on separated custodial parents). It was preferable, the factum argued, to view the impugned provision as imposing "a tax liability on those performing the traditionally female role of primary care giver for children after separation of the two-parent family," which therefore affected "the group concerned on the basis of a socially gendered role related to sex and family status."[30]

For LEAF, *Thibaudeau* was not exclusively a case of direct discrimination against a group defined by the analogous characteristic of "family status." Nor, despite its coalition with the Charter Committee on Poverty Issues and the Federated Anti-Poverty Groups of BC, was LEAF willing to view *Thibaudeau* as primarily a case of direct discrimination on the basis of poverty (although it supported "poverty" as an analogous ground).[31] To LEAF this was a clear case of indirect discrimination against a group defined by an enumerated characteristic (sex), since it reinforced the economic disadvantages experienced by women and stereotyped child-rearing as a predominantly female activity.[32] Although understandable given LEAF's organizational imperatives, it is questionable whether, in retrospect, this was the best strategy to achieve the immediate legal objective. By 1997 only one of six indirect/enumerated discrimination cases had been successful in the Supreme Court. By contrast, as *Vriend* and *M. v. H.* suggest, the Court was much more receptive to direct/analogous discrimination claims.[33] Even direct/enumerated discrimination cases were slightly more successful than indirect/enumerated cases.[34] In other words, indirect discrimination claims have proved to be relatively unsuccessful in the Supreme Court.

The outcome in *Thibaudeau* was consistent with this general pattern in equality rights cases. However, although the Court rejected Suzanne Thibaudeau's constitutional claim by a five-to-two margin, a majority actually endorsed an approach to equality rights analysis that was closer to the method proposed by counsel for LEAF than to the approach advanced by the government. At one end of the analytical spectrum were Justices La Forest, Sopinka, and Gonthier, all of whom took a relatively narrow approach to equality rights and subsequently found no inconsistency between this provision of the ITA and section 15. Writing on behalf of this group, Justice Gonthier focused his section 15 analysis on the relevance of the legislative distinction to the overall purpose and context of the legislative scheme.[35] At the other end of the spectrum were Justices L'Heureux-Dubé and McLachlin, who took a broader approach to equality rights and found a violation of section 15. L'Heureux-Dubé accused Gonthier of "watering down" the Court's analysis of legislative distinctions,[36] and argued that any

> distinction will be discriminatory within the meaning of s. 15 where it is capable of either promoting or perpetuating the view that the individual adversely affected by this distinction is less capable, or less worthy of recognition or value as a human being or as a member of Canadian society, equally deserving of concern, respect, and consideration.[37]

L'Heureux-Dubé had articulated the same approach to equality in the parallel ITA case of *Symes*. She began her dissenting judgment in that case by noting that the ITA could serve as a "powerful tool" for preventing "the attainment of substantive equality for women."[38] After arguing that the ITA should be interpreted to reflect the changing social reality of increased female participation in the workforce, particularly in business and the professions, L'Heureux-Dubé stressed that the goal of section 15 with respect to gender "is the attainment of true substantive equality between men and women."[39] In her view, the majority's approach did not promote substantive equality because its interpretation of the ITA failed to compensate for the disproportionate child-care burden borne by women. A contextual approach to equality, L'Heureux-Dubé argued, leads to the conclusion that "s. 15 of the Charter demands that the experience of both women and men shape the definition of business expense."[40] To her, it was not the ITA itself that violated the Charter, but the majority's traditional, "male-centric" interpretation of it. Although she joined L'Heureux-Dubé's dissent in *Thibaudeau*, Justice McLachlin also decided to write separately. Like L'Heureux-Dubé, she focused on the adverse impact of "irrelevant distinctions" on "human dignity," especially where the affected group "constitutes a discrete and insular minority" and where "the distinction is based on an immutable personal characteristic rather than on an individual's merit, capacities or circumstances."[41]

As a group, the "family breakdown" cases provided LEAF with mixed results. One case – *Thibaudeau* – was a loss both in terms of issue and outcome. Both *Moge* and *Gordon* can be seen as issue and outcome wins, although in neither case did the Court explicitly link its interpretation of the Divorce Act to section 15 of the Charter, as LEAF would have liked. Nevertheless, the social science evidence LEAF introduced in *Moge* became an important part of Justice L'Heureux-Dubé's judgment, and in this sense the Court adopted LEAF's understanding of the economic consequences of marriage and marital breakdown. Moreover, the loss in *Thibaudeau* provided the focal point for extrajudicial legal mobilization to change the ITA, and in 1997 Parliament amended the Act to provide that child support payments are no longer deductible by noncustodial parents nor taxed as income of custodial parents.[42]

Thus, by the end of the 1990s, through a combination of litigation and lobbying, the Canadian women's movement had established a favourable policy regime governing important issues of family breakdown.

Benefits

The Unemployment Insurance Act (UIA) has been the focus of litigation by the women's movement on two important occasions. The first was obviously the *Bliss* case in the late 1970s; the second was *Schachter* about a decade later. *Schachter* is the one post-Charter case where LEAF came to the Supreme Court as something other than an intervener. In 1985, after his wife gave birth to their second child, Shalom Schachter applied for benefits under two sections of the UIA: section 30, which provided fifteen weeks of maternity benefits to biological mothers, and section 32, which provided fifteen weeks of child care benefits to adoptive parents (to be taken by one parent or shared between parents). Both of Schachter's applications were rejected on the grounds that neither of the provisions applied to him. After losing an internal administrative appeal, he announced his intention to raise constitutional issues and filed an action in the Federal Court, Trial Division, to challenge the constitutionality of the relevant UIA provisions under section 15 of the Charter. Although the Act clearly did not provide a benefit to Schachter, the exact nature of any discrimination against him was unclear. On the one hand, he argued that the Act treated natural and adoptive parents differently, but this distinction was not obviously prohibited by section 15. On the other hand, he also argued that the Act unconstitutionally distinguished between biological fathers and mothers, which was discrimination on the basis of sex. In fact, Schachter's original statement of claim asked to have maternal benefits either nullified or shared with biological fathers. With this argument and claim on the table, LEAF successfully applied to be added as a party to the case, giving it the ability to introduce evidence, call witnesses of its own, and cross-examine witnesses for the other parties.[43] With Mary Eberts at the helm, LEAF thus had its greatest opportunity to shape the structure and arguments of a case to suit its own purposes.

This opportunity was completely realized in the Federal Court proceedings. At trial, Justice Barry Strayer held that section 32 of the UIA denied equal benefit of the law with discrimination on the basis of "parental status."[44] Given that the Supreme Court had not yet articulated the concept of "analogous grounds" in *Andrews*, Strayer's finding that section 15 encompassed "parental status" was judicially creative. However, his creativity would not stop there. His finding that the benefit scheme violated the right to equality led to a delicate remedial task: either nullify the existing provisions or order the extension of benefits to natural fathers. Relying on section 24(1) of the Charter, Strayer concluded that the impugned provisions of the

Act were "underinclusive" and declared that the appropriate remedy was to extend to natural parents the same benefits available to adoptive parents until Parliament amended the Act to bring it into conformity with the Charter.[45] The Federal Court of Appeal subsequently agreed with Strayer's determination that section 24(1) empowers "a court to extend benefits to groups aggrieved by an exclusion of benefits."[46] For LEAF these outcomes were doubly positive. First, it succeeded in protecting the benefits for biological mothers in section 30 of the UIA. Second, the Federal Court judgments endorsed a broad set of remedial principles in circumstances where benefit regimes were found to be underinclusive.

By the time the federal government's appeal in *Schachter* reached the Supreme Court for oral argument in December 1991, two important things had happened. First, Parliament had amended the UIA to equalize access to parental leave benefits, although at a lower level than the original provisions. Second, the government had conceded the unconstitutionality of those previous provisions. Thus, the only real issue on appeal to the Supreme Court was the trial court's remedial order under section 24(1) of the Charter.

This did not, however, diminish the case's importance. Legal scholars have long recognized that the value of rights depends on the availability of effective remedial instruments. In this sense, one of the principal weaknesses of the 1960 Canadian Bill of Rights was its failure to articulate how courts should enforce its substantive provisions. At most, the Bill of Rights instructed courts to "construe and apply" federal legislation in a manner that did not "abridge or infringe" the rights and freedoms it recognized. Courts had no explicit power to nullify legislation on Bill of Rights grounds, let alone to formulate more creative remedies for rights violations.

The anemic enforcement provisions of the 1960 document limited its political utility and motivated the drafters of the 1982 constitution to provide courts with *three* remedial alternatives for enforcing rights. First, section 52(1) of the Constitution Act, 1982, establishes the doctrine of constitutional supremacy and authorizes courts to nullify federal and provincial legislation that conflicts with the constitution, including the Charter. Section 24(2) of the Charter articulates a qualified rule for excluding evidence from criminal trials, thereby establishing a distinctive remedy for violations of constitutional rights in the context of the criminal justice process. Finally, section 24(1) of the Charter grants courts a broad power to redress Charter infringements by crafting whatever remedies they consider "appropriate and just in the circumstances."

Although the use of any of these remedies can alter public policy, the unique nature of section 24(1) of the Charter distinguishes its potential impact from that of sections 52(1) and 24(2). The principal difference is that the policy impact of the latter two provisions is largely prohibitive in nature, since they allow judges to proscribe certain types of legislation or

official conduct. To be sure, the negative judicial pronouncements associated with nullification of legislation or exclusion of evidence may guide
future policy development, but this impact is largely indirect. Section 24(1),
by contrast, provides judges with an opportunity to impose new social policy
directly through prescriptive remedies. Nowhere was this more evident than
in Justice Strayer's *Schachter* decision. The federal government, supported
by seven intervening provinces (Ontario, Quebec, New Brunswick, British
Columbia, Saskatchewan, Alberta, and Newfoundland), appealed to the
Supreme Court to constrain judicial remedial powers under the Charter.

Despite the appeal's singular focus on remedies, LEAF's factum (at 113
paragraphs, the second longest it has submitted to the Court) nevertheless
devoted several paragraphs to the issues of equality and discrimination.
The purpose of these paragraphs was to stress to the Court that biological
fathers and mothers *were not* similarly situated with respect to childbirth,
even if this were an appropriate way of understanding equality. "Although
the mother and father have in common that they are biological parents,"
LEAF argued, "they experience pregnancy and birth very differently."[47]
Moreover, the factum argued, whatever commonalities exist between biological fathers and adoptive parents, "none of these three undergoes the
particular experience of childbearing, childbirth, and recovery from childbirth, or establishment of breast feeding, which is the domain of the biological mother."[48] LEAF clearly wanted to ensure that, in the competition for scarce
financial resources, the interests of biological mothers took precedence.

Most of the factum (seventy-seven paragraphs), however, defended the
lower courts' remedial decision to extend benefits. The organizing principle
of this argument was that "positive rights, including political and egalitarian rights, call for positive remedies."[49] According to LEAF, remedies, such
as the meaning of substantive Charter rights, should be determined purpo-
sively. In the case of section 15, the purpose of any remedy should be "to
promote equality and to alleviate the effects of disadvantage, not merely to
create sameness or to eliminate distinctions."[50] Indeed, to pursue the latter
two objectives would be "punitive," a kind of "equality with a vengeance."[51]
LEAF criticized the tradition of judicial deference in circumstances where
legislatures balance interests and allocate resources because, although "popu-
larly elected," legislatures are not "representative in other important ways."[52]
Citing John Hart Ely's "trenchant criticism" of "the representativeness of
the modern democratic state," LEAF cautioned the Court against selecting
"a remedy that would leave the disadvantaged dependent on the actions of
a majoritarian legislature to restore to them benefits that fulfil a constitutional purpose and are deficient only in that they are underinclusive."[53]

LEAF's reliance on Ely in this context was problematic in several ways. To
begin with, his theory of judicial review was a direct product of his negative
reaction to the US Supreme Court's abortion decision, *Roe* v. *Wade* (1973).

His theory itself is process, rather than outcome, oriented. According to Ely, judicial intervention is legitimate to reinforce the representative nature of democratic politics, but not to reverse the substantive policy choices generated by that process.[54] As alluded to in LEAF's argument, Ely's "representation-reinforcing" approach to judicial review is particularly solicitous of the interests of "discrete and insular" minorities.[55] However, Ely was skeptical about including women in this category. At most, he argued that gender-based classifications enacted before women received the right to vote in the United States be summarily nullified by courts, but he was more cautious about whether his theory of judicial review justified interference with more contemporary laws.[56] Finally, the absence of benefits for biological fathers in the UIA cannot easily be explained by their lack of representation in the federal government or Parliament. Ely's theory of judicial review, therefore, provided weak support for a remedy that extended benefits to a group that was perfectly capable of advancing its own interests in the legislative arena.

To be sure, LEAF recognized that a "biological father is not usually considered a disadvantaged person."[57] It dealt with this inconvenient fact by turning Schachter's constitutional claim on its head, asserting that it was, in fact, "challenging the stereotype that the mother should be the primary, if not exclusive, caregiver to infants and young children." From this perspective, the remedy fashioned in the lower courts became an instrument for promoting "the equality of women (a disadvantaged group) by promoting the participation of fathers in childcare without sacrificing measures aimed at benefiting the adoptive parents."[58] Yet even this argument was problematic. If Parliament had been insensitive to, or ignorant of, the possibility that fathers might participate in child care, then why did it extend leave benefits to adoptive fathers? Surely a legislature completely blinded by stereotypes about gender and child care would have provided leave benefits exclusively to adoptive mothers. In the context of Ely's theory, therefore, it was difficult to argue that the absence of benefits for biological fathers was the product of either hostility toward the excluded group by an institution made up largely of other biological fathers,[59] or a desire to keep a disadvantaged group in a subordinate position.[60] In all likelihood, Parliament did not provide benefits to biological fathers because it decided, probably incorrectly, that there was little need for them. Biological fathers did not have the same need for physiological recuperation as biological mothers, nor did natural parents face the same integration demands as adoptive parents.

LEAF's factum was unpersuasive that the trial court's remedy was uniquely consistent with the purposes of section 15 in a second way. It argued that, unlike nullification, a remedy of extension "affords Parliament an opportunity to act in accordance with the constitutional principles laid down in the judgment." In so doing, courts avoid creating "a legislative vacuum" where benefits are concerned.[61] What the factum failed to explain adequately, however, was why the alternative of suspended nullification would not accomplish the same objective. To be sure, this alternative would not automatically bring excluded groups within benefit schemes, but neither would it eliminate benefits to those already receiving them. While it might be true, as LEAF did argue, that legislatures could ignore the constitutional decision and refuse to act, the political pressure to respond would be substantial.

Despite LEAF's argument that the trial court's remedy represented the "best possible solution" to the constitutional deficiencies of the UIA,[62] the Supreme Court narrowed the scope of the remedial power under section 24(1) and reversed the lower court decisions in *Schachter*. Chief Justice Lamer began his judgment by registering "the Court's dissatisfaction with the state in which this case came to us." He criticized the federal government for conceding the section 15 violation and for choosing "not to attempt a justification under s. 1 at trial." According to Lamer, the constitutional concession precluded the Court "from examining the s. 15 issue on its merits," and the absence of a section 1 justification left it "in a factual vacuum with respect to the nature and extent of the violation, and certainly with respect to the legislative objective embodied in the impugned provision." The combined effect was to put "the Court in a difficult position in attempting to determine what remedy is appropriate in the present context."[63]

None of these difficulties, however, prevented Lamer from embarking on a broad discussion of remedial principles under the Charter. Beginning first with section 52, Lamer noted that it permitted courts to declare a law "of no force or effect" only "to the extent of the inconsistency" between the law and the constitution. He argued that this was consistent with pre-Charter principles of constitutional law, which allowed courts to "sever," or "read down," unconstitutional elements of statutes in order to preserve "as much of the legislative purpose as possible."[64] In Lamer's view, this "preservation of purpose" principle also provided a rationale for the analogous, but novel, remedy of "reading in" under section 52. Where "the inconsistency can be defined as what is left out" of the law, then the missing words can be inserted into the statute by a court.[65] Referring explicitly to LEAF's "equality with a vengeance" formula, Lamer indicated that this approach might be especially appropriate in the context of laws that confer benefits on disadvantaged groups.[66]

Lamer next turned to section 24(1), deployed both independently and in conjunction with section 52. On the first point, he held that section 24(1) can be used independently only where a constitutional violation results from action taken under a statute rather than from the statute itself.[67] In this circumstance, an individual victim of unconstitutional action – presumably unauthorized by a statute – is entitled to redress under section 24(1). On the second point, Lamer averred that an individual remedy under s. 24(1) of the *Charter* will rarely be available in conjunction with action under s. 52 of the *Constitution Act, 1982*. Ordinarily, where a provision is declared unconstitutional and immediately struck down pursuant to s. 52, that will be the end of the matter. No retroactive s. 24 remedy will be available. It follows that where the declaration of invalidity is temporarily suspended, a s. 24 remedy will not often be available either. To allow for s. 24 remedies during the period of suspension would be tantamount to giving the declaration of invalidity retroactive effect. Finally, if a court takes the course of reading down or in, a s. 24 remedy would probably only duplicate the relief flowing from the action that court has already taken.[68]

In sum, Lamer clearly disagreed with LEAF's submission that section 24(1) "grants to the courts a wide and unfettered discretion to fashion remedies."[69] Applying these principles to the case before him, Lamer reached a conclusion completely at odds with the order sought by LEAF. Expressing concern about the relationship between the UIA's overall objective and the budgetary implications of reading the excluded group (biological fathers) into the benefit regime,[70] the Chief Justice held that the lower court should have chosen suspended nullification as the appropriate remedy. However, given that Parliament had already repealed and replaced the impugned provision of the UIA, such a declaration from the Court itself was unnecessary. All of this led Justice La Forest, joined by Justice L'Heureux-Dubé, to wonder why the Court had engaged in more than the most minimal analysis.[71] La Forest expressed dissatisfaction at how the case had come to the Court, as well as doubt about whether there was even a violation of the Charter.

For LEAF, the outcome in *Schachter* was largely negative. Although the Court accepted reading in as a legitimate remedy under section 52, it completely rejected the approach to section 24(1) that LEAF had been instrumental in establishing at trial and in the first appeal. Moreover, while Lamer demonstrated sensitivity to LEAF's "equality with a vengeance" argument, its specific arguments about the purposes of section 32 of the UIA fell on deaf ears. Indeed, Lamer found himself without any "mandate based on a clear legislative objective,"[72] and he was unwilling to fill the gap with LEAF's interpretation. Thus, despite successfully exploiting its most direct opportunity to implement law reform in the lower courts, LEAF saw those efforts reversed in the Supreme Court.

This loss was not permanent, however. By 1997, the relatively restrained remedial principles articulated in *Schachter* appeared to have been superseded as LEAF ventured into arguably Canada's most crucial field of public policy: health care. At issue in *Eldridge* v. *British Columbia* (1997) was the manner in which the British Columbia Medical Services Commission and individual hospitals exercised their spending discretion under the province's Hospital Insurance Act.[73] Although provinces must respect the five fundamental principles of the Canada Health Act in order to qualify for federal funding, they are otherwise free to design their health care systems to address the specific needs of their residents by regulating health care delivery and financing.[74] Hospitals have remained for the most part self-governing, nonprofit institutions rather than government-operated facilities. Nevertheless, they depend on public funds and are subject to government budgetary decisions. In 1977, when hospital budgeting became the sole responsibility of provincial health ministries, the provinces adopted fixed annual budgets to control hospital expenditures. Hospitals are not permitted to run deficits in most provinces and must be creative in matching available funds to patient and staff demands. Typical control measures include closing beds and operating rooms, establishing waiting lists for nonemergency surgery, reducing staff availability, and outsourcing nonmedical services.[75] In *Eldridge*, LEAF intervened in association with the DisAbled Women's Network (DAWN) to support the claim that a decision *not* to provide a comprehensive system of publicly funded sign language interpretation for deaf patients denied those patients equal benefit of the law by limiting their ability to communicate effectively with health care practitioners.

LEAF's factum not only challenged the specific policy decision, but the very distinction between "abled" and "disabled." Beginning with the observation that the "history of people with disabilities in Canada is a history of exclusion, marginalization and social devaluation," LEAF attributed this history to the "fundamentally ableist notion of disability as a defect and of disabled persons as unfortunate victims."[76] Indeed, the factum noted that "many Deaf persons object to the notion that deafness is an impairment; they identify as members of the Deaf community which has its own language and culture."[77] In taking this approach, LEAF began to develop the theory of equality and accommodation that would form the basis of its argument in *British Columbia (Public Service Employee Relations Commission) v. BCGSEU* (1999).[78] At the core of this theory was a rejection of the principle that equality could be achieved through accommodation. Since "substantive equality challenges the very existence of mainstream structural and institutional barriers," it requires "much more than simply 'accommodating' persons with disabilities into existing societal norms and structures leaving unscrutinized those norms and structures themselves."[79] The problem with the "duty to accommodate" as it had developed under human rights law was that it did not impose "an obligation on those responsible for the discrimination to effect proactive institutional change in order to root out and remedy the underlying causes of systemic discrimination."[80] Accommodation, in other words, assumed that existing practices were essentially acceptable and required only small adjustments to increase access at the margins.

LEAF and its coalition partner used this theory to criticize existing attempts to accommodate the communication needs of deaf patients. Noting the general importance of "effective communication" in the contemporary health care environment,[81] LEAF highlighted the shortcomings of various alternatives, including lip-reading, written exchanges, and interpretation by friends and family.[82] The inability of most physicians to communicate through American Sign Language, combined with the inadequacies of existing alternatives, increased the risk of poor health care, particularly for deaf women and their children.[83] The only solution, LEAF implied, was to reconceptualize the idea of effective communication in the provision of health care services to include the needs of deaf patients. More precisely, LEAF argued that effective communication is a distinctive type of health care service, one unrecognized by hearing persons because it is so routinely available to them.[84] Consequently, sign language interpretation should be understood as a "medically required service" being denied to an enumerated group in a discriminatory fashion.

Although the Supreme Court refused to declare that the absence of sign language interpretation from the list of medically required services rendered British Columbia's Hospital Insurance Act and Medical and Health Care Services Act in violation of section 15, it nevertheless supported Robin Eldridge's claim that hospitals have a constitutional obligation to provide deaf patients with sign language interpretation. According to the Court's unanimous judgment, the failure of subordinate entities – hospitals and the Medical Services Commission – to provide such services denied the appellants the equal benefit of the two laws. The Court directed British Columbia to administer its statutes in a manner consistent with section 15 of the Charter within six months of the judgment, but it stopped short of issuing detailed instructions as to how the province should implement this policy change.

Two-thirds (sixty-five paragraphs) of the Court's ninety-seven paragraph judgment was devoted to two key legal issues: whether the Charter applies to the decision to deny funding for sign language interpreters (thirty-four paragraphs) and whether this denial violates equality rights (thirty-one paragraphs). The Court's legal judgment had three central components. First, it stipulated that the objectives underlying the Charter's equality rights provisions – which are to promote the equal worth and dignity of all persons, and to prevent and remedy discrimination against particular groups – cannot be achieved simply by granting formally equal access to benefits. Second, the Court determined that effective communication between patients and practitioners is an integral component of adequate health care, and that deaf patients must rely on sign language interpretation to communicate effectively. Finally, it concluded that the absence of public funding for sign language interpretation denies deaf persons the equal benefit of British Columbia's health care regime, since it results in inferior medical service relative to the general population by diminishing their ability to communicate effectively.

Having declared a constitutional right to "effective communication" in the provision of health care, and extending that right to encompass sign language interpretation, the Supreme Court in *Eldridge* did not devote any serious attention to the costs of providing this service. It took at face value the claim that the annual cost of providing province-wide sign language interpretation would be only $150,000, or .0025 percent of the total provincial health care budget.[85] Nor did it take seriously the province's concerns about the broader implications of the decision. Like LEAF, the Court dismissed as mere "speculation"[86] the argument that a positive decision for the claimants might generate additional claims on behalf of the hearing impaired and other disabled groups, as well as analogous claims to language interpretation services by linguistic minorities.[87] However, while British Columbia may have exaggerated the likelihood of additional or analogous claims, its concern was not entirely unreasonable. Including LEAF and DAWN, six nongovernmental advocacy groups intervened in the case,[88] and it is unlikely that they would have deployed scarce resources to support a rights claim solely intended to generate a benefit worth only $150,000 to a relatively small and circumscribed group. Their broader interest was in acquiring a legal resource that might be mobilized to achieve additional policy gains.

The Court based its $150,000 estimate on an informal examination of the costs incurred by a private institute in providing interpretation services in Victoria and the lower mainland of British Columbia.[89] This examination appeared in a briefing note prepared for the Executive Committee of the Ministry of Health, and it simply extrapolated the costs of providing eight hundred hours of interpretation services to four hundred clients to the total estimated population of the hearing impaired in the province (approximately four to five thousand). There were at least two problems with this cost determination. First, the institute's interpreters provided services on a voluntary basis, and there was no serious analysis at any stage of the proceedings of whether this would be an adequate basis for supplying the more extensive services implicit in the appellants' claim. Second, neither the Court nor any of the parties analyzed whether these services could be provided at the same cost in more remote regions of the province as in the densely populated urban areas of Victoria and Vancouver.

Finally, the Court downplayed the federalism issues raised by the litigation. Given the case's potential impact on policy developments in other provinces, it is not surprising that three provinces (Ontario, Manitoba, and

Newfoundland) intervened to support British Columbia's position. As Manitoba argued, the appellants' claim "has potentially enormous implications, not just in this area, but in respect of every benefit program implemented by government and every statutory right to receive public services."[90] Ontario argued that rights analysis must "take into account the finite nature of resources available to address the satisfaction of competing demands made by different groups in society."[91] Newfoundland suggested five options for payment of interpretation services, along with five factors that should be considered in choosing among those options.[92] Even the Government of Canada, which has overall responsibility for administering the Canada Health Act, intervened to support the denial of some benefits as consistent with a province's duty to "provide reasonable access to a fiscally sustainable health care system."[93]

The Court made only a single reference to the interveners' arguments, describing their claim that section 15 of the Charter "does not oblige governments to implement programs to alleviate disadvantages that exist independently of state action" as a "thin and impoverished" vision of equality.[94] It also ignored entirely the federal government's support for provincial autonomy on this issue, instead declaring almost in passing that the federal government's "inherent spending power" permits it to set "national standards for provincial medicare programs."[95] Together, these two elements of the judgment imply significant constraints on provincial policy discretion in an area that the Court ironically described as "within the exclusive jurisdiction of the provinces."[96] Indeed, the Court seemed to view *itself* as having the responsibility for imposing national standards for the accommodation of at least this type of physical disability in the provision of health care services.

Two points are especially worth noting about *Eldridge*. First, LEAF appeared to have learned something from *Schachter*, as it moderated its remedial claims. It neither asked for an extension of benefits to deaf persons nor a declaration of unconstitutionality. It simply asked the Court to declare that the relevant statutes and regulations "be interpreted, applied and administered in a way that would include funding of sign language interpretation for Deaf persons."[97] Second, *Eldridge* provides suggestive evidence of the Court's receptivity to nongovernmental litigants. Despite the arguments of five governments, the Court *reversed* a court of appeal decision and vindicated a rights claim advanced by three individuals and supported by nongovernmental organizations. While three of these organizations (the Canadian Association of the Deaf, the Canadian Hearing Society, and the Council of Canadians with Disabilities) might be considered "traditional," the other three (LEAF, DAWN, and the Charter Committee on Poverty Issues) were part of the new, post-Charter equality-seeking movement. In this respect, *Eldridge* was an important vindication of this movement's legal mobilization activities.

Access to government-funded professional services was also at issue in *New Brunswick (Minister of Health and Community Services)* v. *G.(J.)* (hereafter *NBMHCS*). In this case, Jeannine Godin found herself ineligible for legal aid in a proceeding to place her three children in the temporary custody (wardship) of the health and community services ministry. LEAF intervened to support her argument that she had a constitutional right to legal aid under sections 7, 15, and 28 of the Charter. Its coalition partners in this intervention were NAWL and DAWN, with the Canadian Bar Association, the Charter Committee on Poverty Issues, and the Watch Tower Bible and Tract Society (Jehovah's Witnesses) also intervening to support Godin's position. Family law legal aid had been on LEAF's agenda since at least 1997, when British Columbia placed restrictions on access to legal services. In 1998, led by West Coast LEAF, the Women's Access to Legal Services Coalition submitted a brief to the BC Legal Services Society on the impact of these restrictions on women in the province. The coalition subsequently secured a grant from Status of Women Canada to pursue the issue, and West Coast LEAF began actively recruiting women who had been rejected for legal aid in order to launch a case for judicial review of the cutbacks. Its intervention in *NBMHCS* can thus be viewed as part of a broader law reform agenda with relatively deep roots in Canadian feminist legal scholarship.[98]

After setting out the structure of family law legal aid in Canada and New Brunswick, LEAF's factum turned to the nature of its clients and the type of proceedings in which they typically find themselves. LEAF characterized the clients of family law legal aid as poor women who "already have experienced a disproportionate amount of state involvement in and documentation of" their lives, as well as "a life of violence and abuse by fathers, husbands and lovers."[99] Wardship proceedings, it argued, are adversarial in nature and based on the "disputed" notion of the "best interests of the child."[100] According to LEAF, the reason for the dispute is that the state relies on "models of acceptable child care based on dominant culture and middle class norms," constructed by "professionals whose life experiences differ dramatically from those of the care-giving parent."[101] In other words, the women least likely to fit these models were the ones most likely to be subject to adversarial wardship proceedings.[102]

LEAF next turned to its section 7 argument, where it faced two burdens: (1) demonstrating that wardship proceedings implicate "life, liberty or security of the person"; and (2) demonstrating that the absence of legal aid for temporary wardship proceedings violates the principles of fundamental justice. On the first point, LEAF relied on the Supreme Court's adoption of a "dignity enhancement" approach to interpreting the procedural guarantees of section 7.[103] From this perspective, a proceeding that might lead to the removal of a child from its mother undermines the mother's "personal autonomy" and jeopardizes "her sense of human dignity and personhood."[104]

On the second point, LEAF conceded that the state has a right to interfere in the family as long as "the care-giving parent has the right to participate in and contribute to decisions which will have a fundamental effect on the family."[105] Moreover, when viewed through the equality lens, fundamental justice "means the right to have actual and equal participation in decision-making processes which affect your life, that is, your autonomy, dignity, essential social relationships, and status."[106] Given the complexity of wardship proceedings, LEAF continued, this right could not be made effective without legal representation. Therefore, the "denial of state funded legal representation in these circumstances is discriminatory in that it has a disproportionate impact on women."[107]

Although the Court conceded that Jeannine Godin's case was moot for several reasons,[108] it determined that the circumstances satisfied the 1989 *Borowski* criteria for exercising its discretion to decide otherwise moot cases. Thus, the Court proceeded to determine "whether s. 7 would likely have been infringed had the custody hearing proceeded with the appellant unrepresented and, if so, what the appropriate remedy should have been."[109] Chief Justice Lamer wrote for himself and Justices Gonthier, Cory, McLachlin, Major, and Binnie. In addition, Justices McLachlin and Gonthier joined a concurring judgment by Justice L'Heureux-Dubé. While Lamer's judgment focused exclusively on section 7 issues, L'Heureux-Dubé included a discussion of gender equality. Indeed, her reasons constituted a strong endorsement of LEAF's position.[110]

Although Godin had advanced both liberty and security of the person arguments under section 7, in Lamer's view, her appeal could be resolved exclusively with reference to security of the person. Noting the psychological dimension of this right recognized in earlier cases, he concluded that "state removal of a child from parental custody pursuant to the state's *parens patriae* jurisdiction constitutes a serious interference with the psychological integrity of the parent."[111] Moreover, he asserted that section 7 applies to the justice system and the administration of justice broadly understood, not simply to the administration of criminal justice. Given the requirement of a judicial hearing to sever parental custody rights, Lamer found it relatively easy to declare that a provincial application for custody restricts security of the person under section 7.

Turning his attention to the principles of fundamental justice, Lamer found that child custody proceedings involved both procedural and substantive principles.[112] Thus, parents can be relieved of custody only if a "neutral and impartial arbiter" determines after a "fair hearing" that it is in the best interests of the child for the state to take custody. A "fair hearing" requires that parents have an opportunity to participate effectively in the substantive discussion of the child's best interests. In Lamer's view, whether this required that parents be entitled to government-funded representation by counsel depended on "the seriousness of the interests at stake, the complexity of the proceedings, and the capacities of the appellant."[113] In the circumstances of Jeannine Godin's case, Lamer found that her right to a fair hearing required that she be represented by counsel. He thus concluded that New Brunswick had failed to meet its constitutional obligations in this case, and ordered the province to pay the costs Godin had incurred in both the Supreme Court and the lower courts.

Significantly, neither judgment declared an absolute constitutional right to state-funded representation in the family law context. Indeed, Chief Justice Lamer referred three times to the particular circumstances of Jeannine Godin's case, even describing them at one point as "unusual."[114] He found it "unnecessary to direct the Government of New Brunswick to rectify the policy's constitutional infirmities through the adoption of a new policy."[115] Instead, he outlined a procedure that should be followed in future similar cases that revolved around the three criteria of seriousness, complexity, and capacity. Moreover, he confined his ruling to child protection proceedings without implying any obligations for other types of family law proceedings. In fact, he stated explicitly that "s. 7 should not be interpreted as providing an *absolute* right to state-funded counsel at all hearings where an individual's life, liberty, and security is at stake and the individual cannot afford a lawyer."[116] Although Justice L'Heureux-Dubé was willing to go so far as to assert that "the situations in which counsel will be required will not necessarily be rare," she followed the Chief Justice in not imposing a new policy regime on provinces.[117]

This was less than LEAF had asked for, which was an order that New Brunswick provide "effective legal representation to care-giving parents throughout temporary wardship proceedings, from the beginning of the individual's involvement with the state."[118] In practice, of course, the difference between the Court's judgment and the order sought by LEAF was potentially small. As the experience with the Court's 1990 judgment on criminal trial court delays suggested,[119] when faced with a choice between a complex case-by-case analysis (e.g., determine eligibility for legal aid according to seriousness, complexity, and capacity) and application of an unambiguous rule (e.g., state-funded counsel must be provided to indigent parents in wardship proceedings), lower courts tend to follow the latter. Given high workloads and resource constraints, the rational decision for judges on these courts is to err on the side of caution and follow that aspect of the Court's judgment with which it is easiest to comply. Of course, this was precisely the choice New Brunswick made. Rather than contest applications for legal aid in temporary wardship proceedings on a case-by-case basis, it changed its policy after the provincial court of appeal's decision in *Godin* to provide legal aid for a first temporary wardship proceeding. As in *Schachter*, it was easy for the Supreme Court to avoid imposing a new policy regime on the government in question because the change had already been implemented.

Conclusion

With the exception of *Eldridge*, the cases discussed in this chapter dealt with the relationship of women to their families. In examining LEAF's factums in these cases, at least two characteristics stand out. First, in substantive terms, they contain an implicitly negative view of marriage as reducing the life chances of women. This view is perhaps most obvious in *Moge*, where LEAF rejected the emerging distinction in family law between traditional and nontraditional marriages. In LEAF's view, regardless of appearances, *all* marriages are traditional in the sense that women disproportionately bear the domestic burdens of the family and therefore sacrifice their present and future economic opportunities. From this perspective, family policy – whether dealing with the aftermath of marital breakdown or the consequences of childbirth – must serve to compensate women for the damages they suffer as a result of marriage.

The second characteristic, which is related to the first, is the extent to which sociological arguments take precedence over legal arguments. In most of these cases, LEAF was not arguing about the proper interpretation of statutes or the application of existing case law, but about the state of the world in which women find themselves. This was most evident in *Moge*, where LEAF devoted the first thirty-one of eighty-six paragraphs to social context without a single traditional legal reference. LEAF's *Eldridge* (twenty-two of sixty-four paragraphs) and *Gordon* (eighteen of sixty paragraphs) factums were also deeply infused with extralegal evidence and argumentation. Even *Schachter*, where the issue was a strictly legal one about appropriate remedies, contained an important theoretical discussion of the role of the courts in democratic government. None of this should be surprising, however, since LEAF's very purpose was to challenge the conventions on which existing law was based.

Although successful by many measures, LEAF's interventions in these cases failed in one important respect. Again with the exception of *Eldridge*, the Court refused to constitutionalize LEAF's policy preferences. The significance of this failure, however, should not be overstated. In *Schachter*, *Thibaudeau*, and *NBMHCS*, those preferences prevailed in the legislative arena even without a constitutional mandate from the Supreme Court. In this sense, feminist legal mobilization succeeded at the level of outcome, doctrine, and policy. Whether it succeeded in changing the state of the world documented by LEAF is a separate question, of course.

5
A Difficult Dialogue

In November 1999, and then again in October 2000, the Supreme Court delivered two positive judgments for LEAF in the area of sexual assault trial procedures. At issue in *R. v. Mills* (1999) was the constitutionality of so-called "privacy shield" amendments to the Criminal Code, which control defendants' access to the medical and therapeutic records of sexual assault complainants. In *R. v. Darrach* (2000) the Court considered a revised set of "rape shield" provisions that govern the process and content of questions concerning sexual assault complainants' past sexual conduct. In both judgments the Court upheld legislative provisions that Parliament had enacted in response to earlier judgments *(R. v. O'Connor and R. v. Seaboyer)*[1] expanding the rights of defendants in sexual assault trials. In *Mills* the Court characterized Parliament's apparent reversal of the *O'Connor* judgment as evidence that "courts do not hold a monopoly on the protection and promotion of rights and freedoms."[2] It also stressed that it would not insist on "slavish conformity" to judicial pronouncements, because to do so "would belie the mutual respect that underpins the relationship" between courts and legislatures.[3] The Court repeated this principle in *Darrach*, where it upheld legislation that followed the spirit, if not the exact wording, of guidelines articulated in *Seaboyer.*[4]

In both popular and scholarly accounts, *Mills* and *Darrach* have become symbols of the idea that judicial review under the Charter establishes a "dialogue" between courts and legislatures.[5] The principle source for this metaphor is a 1997 article by Peter Hogg and Allison Bushell in the *Osgoode Hall Law Journal*.[6] According to Hogg and Bushell, the functional essence of dialogue is the ability of legislatures to reverse, modify, or avoid judicial nullification through the enactment of alternative statutes. Two features of the Charter, in particular, facilitate dialogue.[7] First, section 33 gives legislatures the ultimate power of reversal through the notwithstanding mechanism. Second, section 1 allows legislatures to explore alternative means of achieving important objectives. Taken as a whole, these features of the

Charter mean that it "can act as a catalyst for a two-way exchange between the judiciary and legislature on the topic of human rights and freedoms, but it rarely raises an absolute barrier to the wishes of the democratic institutions."[8] Hogg and Bushell supported this argument with an empirical analysis of "legislative sequels" to judicial nullification, in which they found a legislative response to judicial nullification in 80 percent of the cases they examined.[9]

If there has been a dialogue between the Court and other political actors about sexual assault law, the Canadian women's movement has been one of its primary participants. Nine of LEAF's thirty-six interventions before the Supreme Court between 1988 and 2000 came in sexual assault cases. In the legislative arena, both LEAF and its close ally, the National Association of Women and the Law (NAWL), have played key roles in the development of legislative responses to judgments such as *Seaboyer* and *O'Connor*. However, the dialogue between LEAF and the Court, in particular, has been a difficult one. Indeed, three of LEAF's eleven issue "losses" came in sexual assault cases, and until *Mills* and *Darrach* it was on the losing side of every sexual assault trial procedure case decided by the Court. On the other hand, LEAF's record in cases involving the definition of consent is much better. This chapter examines the sexual assault dialogue between LEAF and the Court in an effort to understand several phenomena. Why has the dialogue been more difficult in procedural cases than in consent cases? How did the women's movement transform its legal defeats into political victories? Does the persuasive effect of dialogue explain why the Court became more deferential in procedural cases?

Setting the Context

A strong case can be made that no issue is more salient to the Canadian women's movement than violence, especially in the form of sexual assault. From 1993 to 2000, Canada averaged more than 27,000 reported cases of sexual assault per year, with women as the victims in approximately 85 percent of those assaults.[10] However, if the results of the 1999 General Social Survey are accurate, almost 80 percent of sexual assaults go unreported to the police, which means that the actual number of cases may be closer to 140,000 per year.[11] Indeed, the impact of procedural rules on the sexual assault reporting rate has been one of the key points of dispute in the sexual assault dialogue.

The crime of sexual assault is itself the relatively recent product of an extensive project of criminal law reform. For most of Canada's history, the criminal law prohibited rape, which was defined as "unlawful intercourse between persons not married to each other accomplished through the use of force by the man and implying lack of consent and resistance by the woman."[12] In 1983 the federal government repealed the crime of rape and replaced it with sexual assault. Although the absence of consent remained a key element of the offence, the crime of sexual assault eliminated the spousal exemption, broadened its coverage beyond intercourse, and reduced the emphasis on the use of force. Instead, the Criminal Code identifies three levels of sexual assault, ranging from simple (or Level 1) to aggravated (or Level 3). At no level is intercourse (or penetration) a required element of the crime; nor does Level 1 sexual assault require the use of force. The use and amount of force is relevant only for determining the severity of, and maximum punishment for, the crime. Whereas Level 1 sexual assault can be a summary or indictable offence, carrying a maximum penalty of ten years' imprisonment (as an indictable offence), Levels 2 and 3 are indictable offences that carry maximum penalties of fourteen years' and life imprisonment, respectively.

In addition to these substantive changes to the law, Parliament also completed a set of evidentiary changes it had begun in 1976. Common law rules of evidence had treated complainants' sexual history and reputation as relevant indicators of their credibility and propensity to consent to sexual intercourse. In 1976, Parliament amended the Criminal Code to protect complainants from certain types of cross-examination, but courts interpreted the new provisions as actually broadening the scope of permissible inquiry about past sexual conduct.[13] Consequently, the comprehensive package of amendments that became law in 1983 restricted the admissibility of two types of sexual conduct evidence. First, section 276 of the Criminal Code narrowed the circumstances under which defendants could lead evidence about a complainant's sexual activity with third parties. Second, section 277 categorically prohibited the use of evidence about a complainant's general sexual reputation to challenge her credibility. The purpose of these pre-Charter amendments to the Code was to correct a perceived imbalance in the law that favoured defendants over complainants. The subsequent post-Charter "dialogue" about sexual assault law is whether this balance has now shifted too far in the opposite direction.

Between 1982 and 2000, the Supreme Court of Canada decided thirty-three cases involving sexual assault.[14] These thirty-three cases raised thirty-four separate procedural and substantive issues (see Table 5.1).[15] The pro-complainant argument, advocated either explicitly or implicitly by the women's movement, prevailed on twenty-four of these issues. These pro-complainant victories were not distributed randomly, however. The Court issued pro-complainant decisions on nine of thirteen substantive issues, in contrast to pro-complainant decisions on twelve of twenty-one procedural issues. However, were it not for a remarkable run of pro-complainant success from 1998 to 2000 (ten consecutive substantive and procedural issue victories), the substance-procedure "gap" would be almost 30 percentage points.

Table 5.1

Sexual assault cases in the Supreme Court, 1986-2000

Case	Year	Legal source	Issue	LEAF present	Winner
A.G.	2000	Criminal law	Appeal standard		Complainant
Beharriel	1995	Charter	Fair trial	Yes	Defendant
Bernard	1988	Charter	*Mens rea*		Complainant
Carosella	1997	Charter	Fair trial		Defendant
Cook	1997	Criminal Code	Fair trial		Complainant
Darrach	2000	Charter	Fair trial	Yes	Complainant
Daviault	1994	Charter	*Mens rea*		Defendant
Davis	1999	Criminal law	Consent		Complainant
Esau	1997	Common law	Consent		Defendant
Ewanchuk	1999	Criminal Code	Consent	Yes	Complainant
Hess/Nguyen	1990	Charter	*Mens rea*		Complainant
Heywood	1994	Charter	*Mens rea*		Complainant
Hodgson	1998	Criminal law	Evidence		Complainant
J.-L.J.	2000	Criminal law	Evidence		Complainant
Jones	1994	Charter	Self-incrimination		Defendant
L. (D.O.)	1993	Charter	Fair trial		Complainant
L. (W.K.)	1991	Charter	Fair trial		Complainant
La	1997	Charter	Fair trial		Complainant
Levogiannis	1993	Charter	Fair trial		Complainant
M. (M.L.)	1994	Criminal Code	Consent	Yes	Complainant
Mannion	1986	Charter	Self-incrimination		Defendant
McDonnell	1997	Criminal Code	Sentencing		Defendant
Mills	1999	Charter	Fair trial	Yes	Complainant
Norberg	1992	Common law	Consent	Yes	Complainant
O'Connor	1995	Charter	Fair trial	Yes	Defendant
Osolin	1993	Criminal Code	Consent		Complainant
Osolin	1993	Charter	Fair trial		Defendant
Park	1995	Criminal Code	Consent		Complainant
R.A.R.	2000	Criminal Code	Sentencing		Complainant
R.N.S.	2000	Criminal Code	Sentencing		Complainant
Robertson	1987	Common law	Consent		Complainant
Seaboyer/ Gayme	1991	Charter	Fair trial	Yes	Defendant
Wells	2000	Criminal Code	Sentencing		Complainant
Whitley	1994	Criminal Code	Consent	Yes	Complainant

In more general terms, the Supreme Court's sexual assault jurisprudence is emblematic of one of the most important developments of the post-Charter era: enhanced judicial review of criminal law and procedure.[16] In exercising this function, the Court has sought to equalize the balance of power between the criminally accused and the state by constraining police powers and increasing the procedural and substantive hurdles the Crown faces in achieving convictions.[17] One of the key components in this development has been the articulation of a new principle of fundamental justice: the right to make full answer and defence.

The Court fully articulated this principle in *R. v. Stinchcombe* (1991).[18] At issue was the extent of the Crown's disclosure obligation in criminal proceedings. Unlike civil proceedings, which are governed by a formal requirement of full discovery rights for both parties, criminal proceedings traditionally followed an informal rule of voluntary disclosure by the Crown. Canadian prosecutors have opposed the establishment of comprehensive mandatory disclosure rules on the grounds that there should be reciprocal obligations placed on the defence. In *Stinchcombe*, however, the Court determined that one of the "principles of fundamental justice" protected by section 7 of the Charter is the right to make "full answer and defence," and that this right cannot be exercised properly without obliging the Crown to disclose all "relevant information" in its possession to the defence. Although the Court attempted to moderate the impact of its decision by giving the Crown discretion to determine what constitutes "relevant information" (subject to review by the trial judge), *Stinchcombe* imposed significant costs and administrative burdens on Crown prosecutors and police agencies.[19] Moreover, the internal logic of the *Stinchcombe* rule has generated even broader disclosure obligations, especially in the area of sexual assault.

In this context, therefore, it is unremarkable that sexual assault law would come within the Court's increased scrutiny over the last two decades. However, two things distinguish the developments in sexual assault from those in other areas of the criminal law. One is that this was an area of the criminal law where legal rules already seemed to favour defendants' interests. Second, the Court has expanded defendants' rights in this area *despite* the opposition of a well-organized social movement. Unlike victims of other crimes, sexual assault complainants have strong advocates able to intervene before the Supreme Court in order to defend the social importance and fairness of rules that ease some of the difficulties the Crown faces in securing sexual assault convictions. Indeed, given the Charter-induced legal battles that followed the 1983 reforms, some Canadian feminists came to regret the shift from rape to the gender-neutral crime of sexual assault.[20] The reforms, they suggested, were inherently apolitical and missed the vital character of "feminist work unpacking sexualized violence as an abuse of institutionalized power." "Charter-backed discourses about and court-defined elements of 'fair trial' rights," they argued, "do not differ meaning-fully from long-standing discourses of male right."[21] Use of the term "com-plainant," rather than "victim" (or, more radically, "survivor") epitomized the depoliticization of sexual assault discourse. Thus, while "dialogue" has become the term used to characterize the development of constitutional jurisprudence in this area, for the women's movement it might also be de-scribed as a play in three acts: legal failure, political success, and (perhaps) judicial retrenchment. Before considering these three moments in the de-velopment of sexual assault law, however, it is worthwhile to consider one area where the Supreme Court and the women's movement have supported similar principles.

Speaking the Same Language: The Law of Consent

One area of sexual assault law in which LEAF and the Court have moved more or less consistently in the same direction is the definition of consent. Four of LEAF's sexual assault interventions occurred in consent cases, and in each one the Court adopted a progressively narrower definition of con-sent. LEAF's first consent case, *Norberg* v. *Wynrib* (1992), involved a private action for damages against a physician on the grounds of sexual assault, professional negligence, and breach of fiduciary duty. Laura Norberg had become addicted to the painkiller Fiorinal and was finding it increasingly difficult to locate physicians willing to prescribe the amount necessary to satisfy her growing dependence. Dr. Morris Wynrib, who had treated her once before, eventually agreed to write the prescription in exchange for sexual contact. After more than a year, Ms. Norberg asked Dr. Wynrib for medical help in overcoming her addiction, but he simply advised her to "just quit." She sued Dr. Wynrib for sexual assault under the rubric of the tort of battery. With Ms. Norberg conceding that no physical force had ever occurred, Dr. Wynrib successfully tendered the defence of consent in both lower courts.

At issue on appeal to the Supreme Court, therefore, was the meaning of consent in the context of "power-dependency" relationships. As the sole intervener, LEAF's factum focused on three broad issues: (1) the importance of developing common law principles in a manner consistent with the Char-ter, (2) the role of sexual assault in symbolizing and perpetuating gender inequality, and (3) the meaning of consent.[22] The last of these issues occu-pied twenty-four of the factum's fifty-seven paragraphs, with LEAF's princi-pal argument being that "the legal standard set for consent to batteries termed 'sexual assault' should restrain abuses of power." Failure to adopt such a standard, LEAF continued, would deny "women the equal protection and benefit of tort law."[23] Citing Catherine MacKinnon's *Toward a Feminist Theory of the State*, LEAF criticized the lower courts for adopting "an unduly broad definition of consent which did not address the distinction between consent and coerced submission in the context of unequal power."[24] While conceding that a broader definition might be appropriate in criminal sexual assault law,[25] LEAF urged the Court to place the interests of disadvantaged groups over "those in a position to exploit [such groups'] relative powerlessness."[26] In sum, LEAF concluded that "courts should find that consent to sex does not exist where the defendant occupies a position of such power, trust or authority that the plaintiff is left no free choice to decline to have sex."[27]

The Supreme Court unanimously (six to zero) decided the appeal in Laura Norberg's favour. In addition, five of the six justices agreed with LEAF on the consent issue, although they took slightly different paths to that agreement. The plurality judgment by Justice La Forest (with Justices Gonthier and Cory) focused on the battery claim and criticized the lower courts' approach to consent as "too limited." According to La Forest, a "position of relative weakness can, in some circumstances, interfere with the freedom of a person's will."[28] "Our notion of consent," he continued, "must be modified to appreciate the power relationships between the parties."[29] Justice McLachlin and L'Heureux-Dubé, by contrast, focused on the fiduciary nature of the physician-patient relationship. Referring to the report of the Ontario College of Physicians and Surgeons' Task Force on Sexual Abuse of Patients, chaired by one of LEAF's founders, Marilou McPhedran, and cited in LEAF's factum,[30] they pointed out that women are particularly vulnerable to exploitation and abuse of this trust relationship. Treating the relationship as a fiduciary one carried three consequences. First, it elevated the standard of care expected from physicians in their personal relationship with patients. Second, it made consent to sexual relations in the physician-patient context difficult to prove. Finally, it allowed for adequate compensation for women exploited sexually by their physicians.

Only Justice Sopinka accepted the lower court findings on consent. Rather than "establishing categories of individuals or relationships with respect to which apparent consent will never or rarely be considered valid," Sopinka expressed his preference for a case-by-case approach in which the "question of consent ... is ultimately a factual one that must be determined on the basis of all the circumstances of a particular case."[31] Although conceding that these determinations must be made carefully where there is an imbalance of power or high degree of trust, Justice Sopinka maintained that this did not negate the presumptive capacity of individuals to consent. Consequently, he was unwilling to overturn the trial court's finding that Ms. Norberg had consented to a sexual relationship with Dr. Wynrib. However, Sopinka did find that Dr. Wynrib had breached his professional duty to Laura Norberg by promoting her addiction rather than assisting her in overcoming it. For this reason, he, like his colleagues, decided the appeal in Norberg's favour.

LEAF was able to build on the La Forest and McLachlin judgments in its second intervention in *R. v. M. (M.L.)* (1994). At issue was whether "submission or lack of resistance must be equated with consent" in criminal sexual assault proceedings.[32] Citing La Forest's judgment in *Norberg*, LEAF reminded the Court that it had "recognized that the relative power and powerlessness of the parties will affect consent," at least in the context of civil sexual assault cases.[33] As in all its sexual assault interventions, LEAF devoted a significant part of its factum to the negative impact of sexual assault on women's equality rights under the Charter (twenty-four of sixty-seven paragraphs). In particular, it characterized the equation of nonresistance with consent as one of the rape myths that undermine gender equality.[34] Linking these two points was the idea that consent should be defined in a way that promotes equality by respecting "the principles of individual autonomy and agency of the person whose lack of consent is at issue."[35] In a single-paragraph oral judgment, a unanimous Supreme Court held that the Nova Scotia Court of Appeal had erred "in holding that a victim is required to offer some minimal word or gesture of objection and that lack of resistance must be equated with consent."[36]

Seven months later, LEAF was before the Court in another criminal consent case, *R. v. Whitley* (1994). At issue was the defence of "mistaken belief in consent," which the two appellants in *Whitley* had unsuccessfully tendered at trial and in the Ontario Court of Appeal. Inaccurately describing the Charter as "the supreme law of the land,"[37] LEAF once again rehearsed its argument that sexual assault is a sex inequality practice. The factum added to this generic argument three paragraphs about particularly vulnerable women, including young women like the complainant in *Whitley*.[38] The bulk of the factum, however, dealt with the law of consent in general terms and with the distinction between mistakes of law and of fact. Relying in part on *M. (M.L.)*, LEAF stressed that consent requires an explicit "expression of voluntary agreement."[39] In this sense, the appellants' in *Whitley* had made a mistake of law, rather than of fact, by interpreting the complainant's lack of resistance as consent.[40] Once again, in a unanimous oral judgment delivered after hearing arguments, the Court dismissed the appeals and upheld the conviction. However, it did so without offering any substantive comments about the honest but mistaken belief in consent defence. The Court simply interpreted the jury's conviction as having negated that defence, and it did not find any miscarriage of justice or errors in the lower court proceedings.

LEAF's interventions concerning consent reached their apex in *R. v. Ewanchuk* (1999).[41] At issue was the application by lower courts of a relatively new set of Criminal Code provisions about consent in sexual assault. Passed in 1992 under circumstances detailed later in this chapter, these provisions defined "consent" as "the voluntary agreement of the complainant to engage in the sexual activity in question" (Criminal Code, section 273.1[1]) and identified five specific circumstances under which consent could not be obtained (section 273.1[2]). Steven Ewanchuk had been acquitted at trial of sexually assaulting a seventeen-year-old woman who had come to see him about possible employment. Although the complainant told Ewanchuk "no" when he first attempted to touch her breasts, she remained silent and did not try to leave his trailer as the sexual touching continued. She did not, however, communicate consent in any positive or explicit manner, and she later testified that she felt afraid of Ewanchuk. Both the trial court judge and a majority of the Alberta Court of Appeal concluded that she had nevertheless implicitly consented to the sexual activity.

LEAF intervened in the Supreme Court to support the Alberta government's argument that the trial judge had erred in his interpretation of the legal meaning of consent. Its fifty-seven-paragraph factum consisted of three substantive sections dealing with consent and equality (eight paragraphs), *actus reus* and the absence of consent (twenty-seven paragraphs), and *mens rea* (twelve paragraphs). The first section laid out LEAF's basic argument that the legal definition of consent must comply with Charter equality guarantees. According to this argument, sexual assault "is inextricably linked with women's inequality because women experience an unequal and disproportionate burden of sexual victimization."[42] Indeed, the entire evolution of sexual assault law is driven by the belated recognition of this fact. In particular, according to LEAF, "current sexual assault law is premised primarily on recognizing and protecting women's sexual autonomy."[43] Consequently, "the interpretation of consent must be one that respects the principles of autonomy and the agency of the person whose consent is at issue" by confronting "sexual assault as a practice of inequality."[44]

The second major section of LEAF's factum encompassed four separate arguments. First, it argued that consent is "communicative conduct," in the sense that it must consist of "a word, gesture or other action that communicates voluntary agreement to the specific sexual activity in question."[45] It cannot exist simply in the "private mental state of the complainant," nor be inferred from silence, nonresistance, or a failure to attempt to escape.[46] Second, it follows from this notion of consent that it must be "something a person actually does" and cannot be assumed or intuited by the accused.[47] Where a woman's actions are equivocal, the accused runs a high risk of making a mistake as to consent and should therefore err on the side of caution by presuming that equivocation means lack of consent.[48] Third, there can be no consent where the complainant "fears the application of force," which must be ascertained from the subjective perspective of the complainant rather than according to any objective test.[49] On this point, the factum relied on the holding in *Norberg* that "the relative power and powerlessness of the aggressor and the victim will affect consent."[50] Finally,

LEAF stressed that the concept of consent is meaningless unless both verbal and nonverbal expressions of a lack of agreement are given legal effect by courts. At a minimum, recognition of "the sexual autonomy and liberty of women as independent agents with legal rights must ... acknowledge that to say 'No' is to communicate non-agreement, and such an expression must have an enforceable legal effect."[51] This meant that any sexual activity following any expression of disagreement, regardless of when it occurs, must be considered nonconsensual.

In the final section of the factum, LEAF reiterated the point it had made in *M. (M.L.)*, that most "mistaken" beliefs in consent are mistakes of law rather than of fact. More precisely, LEAF argued that the accused were usually simply misinterpreting the legal significance of facts such as silence and failure to resist (among others) rather than mistakenly interpreting those facts as signs of consent. In other words, if silence is not equated with consent, for example, then relying on silence as a sign of consent is a mistake of law rather than of fact. That is, the accused's mistaken belief would be that "non-resistance indicates consent," rather than that consent had been given.[52] Implicit in this argument is that there is only one legitimate indicator of consent – namely, explicit agreement to sexual activity – and that it would be difficult for any individual to be mistaken as to the absence of this indicator. In any event, the accused may not rely on his belief in consent where he has failed to take "reasonable steps to ascertain consent."[53]

The Supreme Court unanimously reversed the trial and appellate court decisions, entered a conviction for sexual assault, and remanded the case to the trial judge for sentencing. The majority judgment by Justice John Major (of Alberta) began by characterizing the point on appeal as one of law rather than of fact. This was crucial because only the former gives the Crown a right to appeal in criminal cases, and both judges at the intermediate appellate court level had dismissed the appeal on the grounds that it was a "fact-driven acquittal."[54] Justice Major, by contrast, sided with the dissenting judge and declared that "if the trial judge misdirected himself as to the legal meaning or definition of consent, then his conclusion is one of law, and is reviewable."[55] With this preliminary matter out of the way, Justice Major turned to the elements of *actus reus* and *mens rea* that define a sexual assault.

With respect to *actus reus*, Major identified three elements: (1) touching, (2) the sexual nature of the contact, and (3) the absence of consent.[56] Major characterized the first two of these elements as objective but described the absence of consent as "subjective and determined by reference to the complainant's subjective internal state of mind towards the touching, at the time it occurred."[57] This led Major to reject to a large degree the idea that consent requires some active behaviour. In his view, this was less important than the complainant's state of mind, and the most direct evidence of this state is the complainant's own testimony. According to Major, and the five justices who joined his judgment, if the complainant offers credible, uncontradicted testimony that, in her own mind, she did not welcome being touched, the "absence of consent" element of *actus reus* is proven.[58] Major concluded this part of his judgment by explicitly rejecting the existence of a defence of "implied consent" in Canadian sexual assault law. There is either actual consent or no consent at all. Moreover, Major agreed with LEAF that fear of harm, honestly believed by the complainant, negates any indicator of consent and satisfies the third element of *actus reus*.[59] Applying all these principles to the case before him, Justice Major found that the trial judge erred in rejecting the Crown's case for *actus reus*.

At this point, Major turned to the question of *mens rea*, which contains two elements: (1) whether the accused intended to touch the complainant, and (2) whether he did so regardless of the absence of consent.[60] At this point, the question before the Court is whether the accused "believed that the complainant effectively said 'yes' through her words and/or actions."[61] Demonstrating consistency with LEAF's position, Major affirmed that a "belief that silence, passivity or ambiguous conduct constitutes consent is a mistake of law, and provides no defence." In addition, Major rejected the idea that the accused could interpret express lack of consent to some touching as an "invitation to more persistent or aggressive contact."[62] In short, "no means no" and "only yes means yes." In particular, where lack of agreement to engage in sexual activity has once been communicated, the accused bears a heavy burden of pointing to some reasonable indication that consent had been subsequently given.[63]

While the majority focused its discussion rather narrowly on the immediate issues of the case, Justice L'Heureux-Dubé (joined by Justice Gonthier) provided a concurring judgment that ranged over much wider territory. Indeed, her discussion began by noting the general problem of violence against women as documented by Statistics Canada's 1993 survey of the subject. "Violence against women," she noted in her introductory remarks, "is as much a matter of equality as it is an offence against human dignity and a violation of human rights."[64] The international community recognized this in 1979 when it adopted the Convention on the Elimination of All Forms of Discrimination Against Women, and, as a signatory to this convention, Canada undertook an obligation to give it domestic effect through the Charter of Rights and Freedoms. In practice, this meant, among other things, revamping Canada's sexual assault law in a manner consistent with the Charter's equality rights and general protection for life, liberty, and security of the person.[65] For L'Heureux-Dubé, this was the larger context in which the legal issues raised in *Ewanchuk* needed to be analyzed.

In the final analysis, however, very little of Justice L'Heureux-Dubé's judgment concerns the legal issues, on which she mostly agreed with Justice Major. Instead, she characterized the case differently, asserting that it was not really about consent but about "myths and stereotypes." Referencing an important list of extralegal material, including Catherine MacKinnon's *Toward a Feminist Theory of the State* and Susan Esterich's well-known *Yale Law Review* article entitled "Rape," she catalogued these myths by citing yet another author's summary:

> Myths of rape include the view that women fantasise about being rape victims; that women mean 'yes' even when they say 'no'; that any woman could successfully resist a rapist if she really wished to; that the sexually experienced do not suffer harms when raped (or at least suffer lesser harms than the sexually 'innocent'); that women often deserve to be raped on account of their conduct, dress, and demeanour; that rape by a stranger is worse than one by an acquaintance.[66]

Although L'Heureux-Dubé criticized the trial judge for acting on the second of these myths (that "no" does not really indicate lack of consent),[67] she reserved her harshest criticism for Justice John McClung of the Alberta Court of Appeal. In six paragraphs she outlined how McClung had "compounded" the trial judge's error by denigrating the complainant's character and minimizing the nature of Ewanchuk's actions.[68] According to L'Heureux-Dubé, McClung had improperly focused on the complainant's appearance, lifestyle, and lack of physical resistance. In her view, the Court's role was not only to resolve the legal issues in the appeal but to "denounce" the type of language used by Justice McClung that "not only perpetuates archaic myths and stereotypes about the nature of sexual assaults but also ignores the law."[69]

The final reasons for judgment in the case came from Justice Beverley McLachlin, who contributed two short paragraphs stating her agreement with Justice Major's reasons and with Justice L'Heureux-Dubé's assertion that "stereotypical assumptions lie at the heart of what went wrong in this case."[70] Given that she brought nothing extra to the Court's final decision, one might wonder why Justice McLachlin bothered to write separately rather than simply join her colleagues' reasons. One explanation might be her association with the Court's decision in *R. v. Seaboyer* (1991) eight years earlier, a decision that Justice L'Heureux-Dubé had also criticized as relying on rape myths and stereotypes.[71] By condemning those myths and stereotypes explicitly in her own name, rather than as part of a group, Justice McLachlin may have been attempting to distance herself from her majority judgment in *Seaboyer*, a judgment that represented one of LEAF's most significant legal defeats.

Although *Ewanchuk* was widely described and celebrated as vindication of the principle that "no means no," it actually represents the culmination of a much more successful effort by the women's movement to enshrine the principle that "only yes means yes." By defining consent as communicative conduct that cannot be inferred from silence or passivity, LEAF's arguments shifted the focus away from expressions of nonconsent to affirmations of agreement to participate in sexual activity. Moreover, LEAF laid the groundwork for later legislative changes that defined certain circumstances – such as the existence of power-dependency relationships – under which even positive affirmations of consent might not be valid. In this respect, however, the line of argument that ties *Ewanchuk* to *Norberg* conceals an underlying paradox involving the relationship among equality, autonomy, and consent. The essence of the paradox is that the increasingly narrow circumstances under which women can be said to have consented to sexual activity is to some degree inconsistent with the stated purpose of sexual assault law to promote the equal dignity and autonomy of women. Implicit in LEAF's approach, in other words, is the idea that women have so little autonomy under current conditions that true consent is quite rare. That this should be the case is hardly surprising, given the strand of feminist theory from which LEAF's approach to consent is drawn. For example, Catherine MacKinnon's book *Toward a Feminist Theory of the State* appears in LEAF's *Norberg* factum and L'Heureux-Dubé's *Ewanchuk* judgment.[72] One of MacKinnon's core arguments is that the unequal power relationship between men and women makes consensual heterosexual relationships virtually impossible.

In any event, LEAF and the Supreme Court ended the 1990s by speaking the same language with respect to the meaning of consent. This was not so much the product of a dialogue as it was of an educational process led by LEAF's interventions in a series of appeals to the Court, as well as the broader women's movement's mobilization in the legislative arena. Ironically, that mobilization was in large measure the reaction to a series of legal defeats on the question of sexual assault trial procedures. It is to those defeats which I now turn.

Legal Failure

Seaboyer/Gayme

Seaboyer and Gayme[73] came to the Supreme Court as a result of two separate sexual assault prosecutions in Ontario. In the first case, the Crown charged Steven Seaboyer with sexual assault and supported its charge with evidence of bruises and other physical injuries suffered by the complainant. Seaboyer's counsel argued during a preliminary inquiry that he should be permitted to cross-examine the complainant about other acts of sexual intercourse that might have caused the bruising. In the second prosecution, the Crown charged eighteen-year-old Nigel Gayme with sexual assault of a fifteen-year-old acquaintance. Gayme's counsel raised the defences of consent and honest belief in consent, and argued that the complainant had been the sexual aggressor. To support this defence, he proposed to cross-examine and present evidence of the girl's prior and subsequent sexual conduct. In both cases, the preliminary inquiry judges ruled that the Criminal Code prohibited the defence from pursuing these lines of inquiry. Both defendants appealed the respective rulings.

LEAF intervened in both the Ontario Court of Appeal and the Supreme Court to support the constitutionality of the Criminal Code provisions limiting the ability of defendants to introduce evidence about complainants' previous sexual conduct and general reputation. In the Supreme Court it was the lead intervener for a coalition of groups "dedicated to protecting and advancing the equality and security of women and children under Canadian law."[74] The emergence of this coalition, and the precise content of LEAF's factum, reflected the organization's response to criticism that its appellate court intervention was too conventionally liberal.[75] According to LEAF, the impugned provisions of the Code constituted a necessary response to multiple deficiencies in the common law of rape. The source of these deficiencies was the failure of rape law, like the common law generally, to recognize women and men as equally autonomous agents. This fundamental flaw gave to the law of rape several unique characteristics, including skepticism about the veracity of rape complaints, unique corroboration requirements, and nonapplicability to the marriage relationship. These characteristics were the underlying reason for evidentiary rules that permitted cross-examination of complainants about their previous sexual history and reputation. Indeed, citing the 1970 edition of a classic treatise on evidence, LEAF argued that such cross-examination was not only permitted, but practically required.[76]

LEAF constructed its factum's argument around the central proposition that violence and inequality are mutually reinforcing realities for women. The argument itself consisted of two broad components. First, LEAF asserted that sections 276 and 277 of the Criminal Code – which narrowed the circumstances under which defendants could lead evidence about a complainant's sexual activity with third parties (section 276) and prohibited the use of evidence about a complainant's general sexual reputation (section 277) – promoted the right to equality (section 15) and security of the person (section 7) of women and children. This part of the argument unfolded in three steps. Relying on the Court's previous equality rights jurisprudence, LEAF characterized the purpose of section 15 as the promotion of substantive equality for socially, legally, and politically disadvantaged groups.[77] Next, LEAF characterized sexual assault as a social practice that discriminates on the basis of age and sex because it disproportionately victimizes women and children.[78] Finally, the factum argued that the admission of sexual reputation and conduct evidence is prejudicial to complainants because it reduces the probability of conviction and lowers sentences even where conviction does occur.[79] From these assertions, LEAF concluded that sections 276 and 277 constituted remedial legislation to mitigate this prejudice and promote the equality of sexual assault victims against an insidious social practice.[80]

The second component of the argument concerned the impact of excluding sexual conduct and reputation evidence on the constitutional rights of defendants. This part of the argument revolved around the legal concept of relevance, with LEAF averring that "constitutional guarantees of fair trial rights do not include the right to present irrelevant evidence." Moreover, according to LEAF, even relevant evidence could be excluded where its "probative value is outweighed by its prejudicial effect."[81] From this perspective, sections 276 and 277 simply applied ordinary rules of evidence to sexual assault cases by excluding evidence that could not meet criminal standards of admissibility. This interpretation depended on a crucial principle of feminism: female and male experiences of sex and sexual relationships differ in fundamental ways.[82] According to LEAF, the fatal error at the heart of common law rules of evidence in sexual assault cases was the failure to recognize this difference, and the subsequent application of male standards of relevance and probative value to conduct and reputation evidence. Sections 276 and 277 corrected this error by reorienting the concepts of relevance and probative value to reflect the experiences of the mostly female victims of sexual assault. From this perspective, conduct and reputation evidence fell outside the range of ordinarily admissible evidence, and therefore its exclusion could not infringe a defendant's constitutional rights.

LEAF's use of extralegal material was one of the most striking aspects of these elements of the factum, which encompassed slightly more than half of the document (thirty-nine of seventy-seven paragraphs). Indeed, of the fifty citations of authority contained in these paragraphs, only nineteen (38 percent) are citations of traditional legal sources such as case law and legal textbooks. The remaining thirty-one citations encompass references to work in the social sciences (nineteen citations), law reform scholarship (ten citations), and government reports (two citations). Moreover, at least six of these works were the product of strategic post-Charter feminist legal scholarship, including two articles in the *Canadian Journal of Women and the Law*.[83] Eighteen of these citations eventually found their way into the Court's judgments in *Seaboyer/Gayme*, albeit mostly in the dissenting judgment of Justice L'Heureux-Dubé. In fact, the majority judgment used one of LEAF's citations to highlight weaknesses in the approach to sexual conduct evidence exemplified by section 276 of the Code.[84] In the final analysis, the impact of LEAF's authorities on the Court majority's ultimate disposition of the constitutional questions at issue in *Seaboyer/Gayme* was mixed.

Although the Court unanimously upheld the prohibition against sexual reputation evidence contained in section 277, a seven-justice majority led by Justice Beverley McLachlin declared that section 276 constituted an unjustified infringement of an accused's right to a fair trial guaranteed by sections 7 and 11(d) of the Charter. According to Justice McLachlin, section 277 survived constitutional scrutiny because the evidence it prohibited had no probative value. She agreed, in other words, with Parliament's judgment (and LEAF's factum) that there was no relationship between a complainant's sexual reputation and her capacity to provide credible testimony. By contrast, McLachlin concluded that section 276 might "exclude evidence which is relevant to the defence and the probative value of which is not substantially outweighed by the potential prejudice to the trial process."[85] Moreover, she was unimpressed by the three exceptions built into section 276's rule of admissibility, which covered rebuttal evidence, identity evidence, and evidence about consent to other sexual activity on the same occasion as the alleged assault.

In McLachlin's judgment, section 276 contradicted a crucial principle of fundamental justice guaranteed by section 7 of the Charter: the general right of an accused to give full answer and defence to criminal charges. By limiting this right, she continued, section 276 also limited the more specific right to a fair trial guaranteed by section 11(d). McLachlin conceded that section 276 was a rational means of advancing a pressing and substantial legislative objective but declared that it did not represent the least restrictive means of achieving that objective. Indeed, she argued that Parliament had implicitly recognized circumstances where sexual activity evidence might be relevant when it had provided for exceptions to the general inadmissibility of such evidence. Section 276 failed to survive constitutional review precisely because it did not carry the logic of those exceptions far enough.

According to McLachlin, the following principles should apply in determining the admissibility of sexual history evidence:[86]

1 On a trial for a sexual offence, evidence that the complainant has engaged in consensual sexual conduct on other occasions (including past sexual conduct with the accused) is not admissible solely to support the inference that the complainant is by reason of such conduct:
   (a) more likely to have consented to the sexual conduct at issue in the trial;
   (b) less worthy of belief as a witness.
2 Evidence of consensual sexual conduct on the part of the complainant may be admissible for purposes other than an inference relating to the consent or credibility of the complainant where it possesses probative

value on an issue in the trial and where that probative value is not substantially outweighed by the danger of unfair prejudice flowing from
the evidence.

By way of illustration only, and not by way of limitation, the following are examples of admissible evidence:

(A) Evidence of specific instances of sexual conduct tending to prove
that a person other than the accused caused the physical consequences
of the rape alleged by the prosecution;

(B) Evidence of sexual conduct tending to prove bias or motive to fabri-
cate on the part of the complainant;

(C) Evidence of prior sexual conduct, known to the accused at the time
of the act charged, tending to prove that the accused believed that
the complainant was consenting to the act charged (without laying
down absolute rules, normally one would expect some proximity in
time between the conduct that is alleged to have given rise to an
honest belief and the conduct charged);

(D) Evidence of prior sexual conduct which meets the requirements for
the reception of similar act evidence, bearing in mind that such evidence cannot be used illegitimately merely to show that the complainant consented or is an unreliable witness;

(E) Evidence tending to rebut proof introduced by the prosecution regarding the complainant's sexual conduct.

3 Before evidence of consensual sexual conduct on the part of a victim is
received, it must be established on a voir dire (which may be held in
camera) by affidavit or the testimony of the accused or third parties, that
the proposed use of the evidence of other sexual conduct is legitimate.

4 Where evidence that the complainant has engaged in sexual conduct on
other occasions is admitted on a jury trial, the judge should warn the
jury against inferring from the evidence of the conduct itself, either that
the complainant might have consented to the act alleged, or that the
complainant is less worthy of credit.

The importance of judicial discretion in Justice McLachlin's judgment is
evident in her equal disdain for the preexisting categorical rules of the common law and for legislative codification of the principles underlying her
decision. "Striking down s.276 does not imply reversion to the old common law rules," she stressed, "which permitted evidence of the complainant's
sexual conduct even though it might have no probative value to the issues
on the case and, on the contrary, might mislead the jury." The courts, she
continued, must rely "on the basic principles that actuate our law of evidence" and "seek a middle way that offers the maximum protection to the
complainant compatible with the maintenance of the accused's fundamental right to a fair trial."[87] Finding this middle way was simply too complex a

process for the blunt instrument of legislation.[88] Instead, according to McLachlin, the Charter requires that the decision to admit such evidence be left to judicial discretion on a case-by-case basis according to rules set down by the Supreme Court.

Although LEAF's arguments had apparently little impact on Justice McLachlin, they were crucial to Justice L'Heureux-Dubé's dissent. Along with Justice Gonthier, she described the *Seaboyer/Gayme* appeals as being "about relevance, myths and stereotypes in the context of sexual assault." In her view, "meaningful constitutional analysis" of the issues on appeal could be achieved only by examining them "in their broader political, social and historical context."[89] In undertaking this particular type of analysis, L'Heureux-Dubé used much of the material contained in LEAF's factum. Indeed, her dissent contains twenty-six citations of material referred to in the factum. Reflecting on this material, L'Heureux-Dubé concluded that "social science research findings contradict assertions that sexual conduct evidence assists the fact-finding process or the test for 'judicial truth.' Far from being relevant to ensuring a 'fair' hearing or a full defence, the introduction of sexual history evidence may advantage the accused in a way that is not related to innocence."[90] Although rhetorically powerful, this conclusion is problematic on at least two related grounds. First, the research findings to which Justice L'Heureux-Dubé refers do not represent a comprehensive survey of the relevant literature but are those explicitly selected by LEAF to support a particular argument. Second, the social science evidence had not been introduced or developed in the adversarial context of a trial proceeding. To draw a firm conclusion from such material is to stretch the utility of social science in the courtroom.

Nevertheless, L'Heureux-Dubé was so persuaded by LEAF's argument that she took the rare step of quoting directly from the factum:

> I also heartily concur in the submissions at p.17 of the intervener Women's Legal Education and Action Fund et al on this point: "in all of the hypothetical situations outlined in the Appellants' factums, evidence of sexual history and/or sexual reputation is either totally irrelevant, admissible pursuant to the exceptions provided for in s.276, or, in the alternative, of very low probative value and highly prejudicial to the interests of the administration of justice."[91]

In both tone and substance, therefore, L'Heureux-Dubé's dissent captured the essence of LEAF's intervention. In so doing it enhanced LEAF's credibility as a contributor to the sexual assault policy debate.

O'Connor

L'Heureux-Dubé would also find herself in the minority in *R. v. O'Connor*

(1995),[92] which was the logical outgrowth of the Court's 1991 decision in *Stinchcombe*.[93] At issue in *O'Connor* was the right of sexual assault defendants under the *Stinchcombe* principle to secure production of complainants' therapeutic records held by third parties, as well as the process that might govern the production of such records. In addition, although the issue was not raised directly in the case, five judges considered it appropriate to comment on the Crown's duty to disclose to the defence therapeutic records of sexual assault complainants in its possession.

Hubert O'Connor was a Roman Catholic bishop in British Columbia, accused in 1991 of sexually assaulting four Aboriginal women during his tenure as principal of a residential school twenty-five years earlier. Although Bishop O'Connor admitted engaging in sexual intercourse with two of the women, he claimed it had occurred with their consent. His counsel obtained a court order requiring the Crown to disclose the complainants' medical, therapeutic, education, and employment records, and when the Crown delayed its compliance with the order, the trial court stayed the proceedings against O'Connor. The Crown appealed both the stay and the original disclosure order.

Not surprisingly, a coalition of women's groups, including LEAF, the Aboriginal Women's Council, the Canadian Association of Sexual Assault Centres, and the DisAbled Women's Network Canada, intervened to oppose the extension of *Stinchcombe* to therapeutic records. As in *Seaboyer and Gayme*, however, the effort largely failed. The Court was unanimous in holding that defendants have a right to request production of records held by third parties, and there was no opposition to the declaration by five justices that therapeutic records in possession of the Crown must be disclosed according to the rule set down in *Stinchcombe*.[94] The Court was divided only on the question of process, with four justices supporting strict access to third-party therapeutic records.

LEAF's factum on behalf of the coalition framed the central issue in *O'Connor* as follows:

> The constitutional rights of the victims of sexual violence to security of the person without discrimination based on sex, race or disability and to equal protection and benefit of the law cannot be fully recognized or vindicated ... unless courts take cognizance of the social, historical, political and legal conditions of inequality in which sexual violence occurs; out of which legal principles and legal practices emerge; and under which records sought to be disclosed are generated.[95]

To make this link among record disclosure, violence, and inequality, LEAF devoted most of its factum to a discussion of the application of equality guarantees to disclosure principles and practice (twenty-nine of sixty-six paragraphs) and the oppressive nature of the specific disclosure order in *O'Connor* (twenty-five of sixty-six paragraphs). Underlying the entire discussion, and consistent with the facts of the case and the interests of one of its coalition partners, was an explicit criticism of Canadian policy toward Aboriginal people.

The argument began with the charge that "evolving contemporary disclosure jurisprudence reinforces ... discriminatory stereotypes about women, children and their sexuality" because it completely ignores complainants' equality rights under section 15.[96] LEAF criticized this jurisprudence on the grounds that it gave a higher status to the fair trial rights of accused persons than to the section 7 and 15 rights of complainants. Citing the Court's own words in *Dagenais* v. *Canadian Broadcasting Corp.* (1994), LEAF asserted that "a hierarchical approach to rights ... must be avoided ... when interpreting the Charter."[97] The factum undermined the force of this criticism a few paragraphs later, however, by implicitly urging the Court to do precisely what LEAF had just praised it for rejecting: elevate one Charter right (equality) over another (fair trial). The factum argued that disclosure rules had been framed under conditions of systematic inequality of women generally – and disabled and Aboriginal women in particular – and they therefore perpetuated this inequality and undermined the integrity of the justice system.[98] The remedy was for the Court to reassert the primacy of section 15 and subordinate disclosure requirements that might flow from fair trial rights to the equality rights of complainants. While this would not eliminate all disclosure requirements, it would certainly prohibit disclosure of therapeutic records. As the factum put it, a "justice system animated by equality principles" would view complainants' "history of mental health treatment or of sexual violence not as justification for extra-invasive disclosure, but as reason for caution, sensitivity, and heightened vigilance about the purpose and effects of records disclosure."[99] Instead, LEAF argued, contemporary arguments in favour of disclosure, based on fair trial concerns, were simply a new version of older arguments based on what LEAF described as "discredited science" about the nature of sexual assault and sexual assault complaints.[100]

In contrast to its *Seaboyer/Gayme* factum, LEAF's citations of authority in the key equality rights component of its argument (paragraphs seven to thirty-five) were almost equally divided between legal (twenty-four of fifty) and extralegal (twenty-six of fifty) sources. The extralegal sources included eleven social science citations, eight law reform citations, and seven citations of government reports. Included among the last group of sources were several citations of material from the *Report of the Aboriginal Justice Inquiry of Manitoba,* which dealt with the particular vulnerability of Aboriginal women to sexual violence. Indeed, LEAF devoted part of its factum (nine of sixty-six paragraphs) to the specific issues raised by a disclosure order made in the context of Aboriginal complainants and a non-Aboriginal accused.[101] LEAF cited social science evidence to support arguments about the general prevalence of sexual assault victimization against women, the particular vulnerabilities of disabled and visible minority women, and the "mythological" nature of common law presumptions about rape.[102] These citations apparently had little influence on the Court, however, since its judgments referred to only two of the extralegal sources cited by LEAF.[103]

LEAF's factum miscalculated the Court's willingness to use the *O'Connor* appeal as an opportunity to undertake a comprehensive review of racism and sexism in the administration of sexual assault law. The factum's emphasis on the mistreatment of sexual assault complainants "doubly disadvantaged" by sex and race or disability took the focus away from the principal issue: whether access to therapeutic records is necessary to a fair trial. Indeed, unlike in *Seaboyer and Gayme,* LEAF made no attempt to rebut the fair trial argument. To be sure, this was an important element of the government's argument, but by ignoring it, LEAF made its factum irrelevant to a Court concerned primarily with the technical rules governing disclosure. In fact, LEAF marginalized its position by advocating an approach that would prohibit *any* disclosure of personal records in sexual offence proceedings.[104] Given the Court's decisions in *Stinchcombe* and *Seaboyer/Gayme,* it is difficult to imagine why LEAF would expect this argument to persuade a Court that had experienced only one personnel change during the intervening years.

As in *Seaboyer/Gayme,* the Court's judgment concerning records held by third parties derived from the constitutional right "to make full answer and defence" protected under section 7 of the Charter. For all nine justices, this right provided the defence with at least some claim to the production of third-party records. Where the Court divided was on the competing claims against which this right should be balanced. Speaking for a five-justice majority, Chief Justice Lamer argued that the only competing claim was a "constitutional right to privacy."[105] The minority, led by Justice L'Heureux-Dubé, added "right to equality without discrimination" to the equation.[106] The two approaches led to different assessments of the "likely relevance" of therapeutic records to the accused's right to make full answer and defence. Indeed, Lamer expressly disagreed with L'Heureux-Dubé's assertion that third-party therapeutic records would be rarely relevant. In Lamer's view, therapeutic records might be relevant in determining "the competence of a witness to testify" or "the use of a therapy which influenced the complainant's memory of the alleged events."[107] For L'Heureux-Dubé, assumptions such as these reflected the historically "pernicious role" played by "discriminatory" evidentiary rules in sexual assault proceedings.[108] Thus, while Lamer and L'Heureux-Dubé agreed that the relevance criterion should impose a "significant" burden on the defence,[109] they differed on how high the barrier to production should be. As in *Seaboyer/Gayme*, L'Heureux-Dubé demonstrated more openness to equality-based arguments for limiting defendants' rights.

Table 5.2 summarizes the main differences between the procedures set out by Lamer and L'Heureux-Dubé. Although both justices envisioned a two-step process in which the "likely relevance" of third-party records played a crucial role, the similarities mostly end there. Chief Justice Lamer's process stressed that the accused should not bear an "onerous burden" in demonstrating likely relevance, while Justice L'Heureux-Dubé described this burden as "a significant one." In addition, the L'Heureux-Dubé process specified five circumstances as insufficient for meeting the relevance standard. Similarly, her process for making the actual production order was much more stringent. Whereas Lamer focused on the impact of a *non-production* order on the accused's right to make full answer and defence, L'Heureux-Dubé emphasized the impact of production on the witness's privacy rights. She also directed judges to consider seven, rather than Lamer's five, factors before ordering production of third-party records.

The key difference between the approaches of Lamer and L'Heureux-Dubé was the degree of judicial discretion involved in the production decision. In Lamer's process, judges would be relatively unconstrained in determining the likely relevance of therapeutic records and in balancing the competing constitutional rights of privacy and full answer and defence. A fair trial, Lamer implied, requires that judges have enough discretionary authority to equalize the position of the Crown and the accused with respect to the production of third-party records. By contrast, L'Heureux-Dubé attempted to specify certain considerations, such as the mere fact that a complainant has a medical record or sought therapy, which could not be used to meet the relevance criterion. In addition, unlike Lamer, she would have trial judges consider society's interest in encouraging the reporting of sexual offences and the effect of production on the integrity of the trial process in balancing the competing constitutional claims. Indeed, L'Heureux-Dubé explicitly mentioned the necessity of providing rules for lower courts in the absence of legislation.

The Court pushed the *O'Connor* ruling further in a case that did not involve LEAF: *R. v. Carosella* (1997).[110] *Carosella* arose as a result of practices implemented by some sexual assault centres in reaction to their lack of success in opposing post-*O'Connor* production orders. The particular centre involved in *Carosella* had instructed its staff to take notes in a way that would reduce their utility to defence lawyers, and had instituted a policy of destroying client records that might lead to judicial proceedings (unless the records had already been subpoenaed or were the subject of a production application). At issue in *Carosella* was whether the centre's failure to produce notes of its interview with a sexual assault complainant, which had been destroyed pursuant to the centre's policy, violated the defendant's Charter rights.

In his judgment for the majority, Justice Sopinka expressed something close to outrage that the actions of even a private party might interfere with a trial judge's discretionary authority to construct a fair trial for the accused. Referring to *Stinchcombe* and *O'Connor*, Sopinka declared at the outset that

Table 5.2

O'Connor regimes: Lamer and L'Heureux-Dubé compared

Topic	Lamer	L'Heureux-Dubé
Basic structure	Onus of proof on accused.	Onus of proof on accused.
	Two-step procedure: • Written application, supported by affidavit, that "information likely to be relevant." • Judicial determination that records should be produced or not.	Two-step procedure: • Accused serves subpoena on third party and makes written application, supported by affidavit, that "information likely to be relevant." • Two-part judicial determination concerning production: – Production to court – Production to accused.
Standards for step one	Likely relevance means "reasonable possibility that the information is logically probative to an issue at trial or the competence of a witness to testify."	No assumption that records are likely to be relevant. "Burden on an accused to demonstrate likely relevance is a significant one."
	Should not be interpreted as an onerous burden on the accused.	Five circumstances specified as insufficient to establish "likely relevance."
Standards for step two	Judicial balance of "the salutary and deleterious effects of a production order and determine whether a non-production order would constitute a reasonable limit on the ability of the accused to make full answer and defence."	Production should be ordered only where "significant probative value ... is not substantially outweighed by the danger of prejudice to the proper administration of justice or by the harm to the privacy rights of the witness or to the privileged relation."
	Five factors to consider.	Seven factors to consider.

the "entitlement of an accused person to production either from the Crown or third parties is a constitutional right," the foundation of which is the more general right to make full answer and defence.[111] "It is immaterial," Sopinka continued, that neither the rights to disclosure nor full answer and defence are "explicitly listed as one of the components of the principles of fundamental justice."[112] Describing the centre's policy as "high-handed," Sopinka averred that in a system "governed by the rule of law, decisions as to which evidence is to be produced or admitted is [sic] for the courts."[113] Consequently, it was simply impossible for the administration of justice to condone "conduct designed to defeat the processes of the court."[114] Finding the violation of the accused's rights too extensive to justify a lesser remedy, the majority ordered a stay of proceedings.

Justice L'Heureux-Dubé criticized almost every aspect of the majority judgment, beginning with the observation that the case had "nothing to do with disclosure" which, she felt compelled to remind Sopinka, "is a concept ... binding solely on the Crown."[115] L'Heureux-Dubé also questioned the relevance of *O'Connor,* which she characterized as dealing with the process for producing third-party therapeutic records rather than circumstances where the records were no longer available.[116] She took Sopinka to task for suggesting that an accused has a right to "every piece of potentially relevant evidence in the world," arguing instead that the Charter "does not entitle an accused to a perfect trial."[117] In her view, the threshold for determining unfairness must be set relatively high, which in the disclosure context meant that missing evidence would violate the Charter only if the accused could demonstrate a "*real* likelihood of prejudice to the right to full answer and defence."[118] Mere speculation that the evidence might assist the accused was insufficient.

Summary
In both *Seaboyer/Gayme* and *O'Connor,* LEAF mobilized to preserve the legal status quo as established in one case by legislation *(Seaboyer/Gayme)* and in the other by common law *(O'Connor).* In both instances, however, the status quo could not survive the Court's heightened understanding of the constitutional right to a fair trial, which majorities in both cases said encompassed the principle of fundamental justice of full answer and defence. Nevertheless, LEAF's interventions persuaded some justices in important ways. Most obviously, Justice L'Heureux-Dubé showed herself to be a strong advocate of LEAF's position, bringing its argument and evidence to the pages of the Supreme Court Reports. In *O'Connor,* Beverley McLachlin retreated somewhat from her position in *Seaboyer/Gayme* and supported a less extensive fair trial right. Finally these two losses in the legal arena provided new opportunities for the women's movement in the legislative process.

Political Success

Rather than retreat after its losses in *Seaboyer* and *O'Connor*, the women's movement intensified its legal mobilization around the issue of sexual assault and moved it to a new field of battle. Two weeks after *Seaboyer*, Minister of Justice Kim Campbell announced that she would introduce legislation to mitigate the effects of the decision by October of 1991. The justice minister's initiation of a consultation process with various stakeholders, including women's groups, highlighted a gulf between her government and feminist activists, as well as divisions among feminists themselves. Feminist groups were skeptical about how much trust they should place in a Conservative government, and activists among women additionally marginalized by race, class, and sexual orientation had little confidence in the "white/ professional/academic feminism" they perceived LEAF to practice.[119] LEAF's *Seaboyer* factum did not help in alleviating this perception, since it characterized sexual assault as "discrimination on the basis of sex and age."[120] LEAF's failure to acknowledge other forms of discrimination undoubtedly served to heighten the sense of alienation among other constituencies within the women's movement.

Initial estimates by federal and provincial officials of the policy space still open after *Seaboyer* were pessimistic. According to Sheila McIntyre, Justice minister Campbell defined the task as one of articulating appropriate procedures for admitting sexual history evidence rather than challenging *Seaboyer*'s core holding as inconsistent with gender equality. For provincial justice ministers, the solution was better judicial education.[121] Feminist groups, led by NAC, LEAF, and NAWL, pressed for a delay in ministerial action in order to construct a more comprehensive response. In late October, "LEAF's national legal committee reached a consensus in support of pursuing substantive (rather than simply evidentiary) amendments to sexual assault law."[122] These substantive amendments would focus on the *mens rea* of sexual assault by narrowing the definition of consent.

The Justice Department's view that *Seaboyer* represented the minimally acceptable constitutional starting point for policy discussion was a source of tension with women's groups. Indeed, the LEAF-led coalition decided that it would oppose any reform less than an entire overhaul of sexual assault law consistent with Charter equality rights.[123] This strategy proved successful when the minister announced in November that she was considering broader changes than those minimally necessary to respond specifically to *Seaboyer*. In particular, she signalled her willingness to define consent in a manner consistent with the coalition's position.[124] One week later, a joint consultation meeting between coalition representatives and Justice Department lawyers (which the minister briefly attended) produced the text that would be tabled as Bill C-49 in mid-December. Despite initial skepticism about Campbell's motivations and political will, at least some equality rights activists described her consultations in the aftermath of *Seaboyer* as her "finest hour."[125]

The Bill contained four parts: a preamble, new consent definitions, clarification of the "mistake" defence, and new evidentiary and procedural guidelines. Sheila McIntyre, Renate Mohr, and Joanne St. Lewis testified for LEAF before the House of Commons committee on Bill C-49 on 19 May 1992. McIntyre told the committee that the Bill's "most important feature ... is that it doesn't address itself solely to admissibility of sexual history evidence." Instead, the Justice Department had accepted the recommendation of LEAF's coalition "to expand its review and amendments of sexual assault law in a more systematic fashion so that the one piece that was evidence is integrated with a broader constitutional responsive law."[126] Although obviously supportive of the Bill, LEAF did argue that its preamble should be incorporated into the Criminal Code itself. LEAF saw the preamble as having an important educational function, especially with respect to judges. Indeed, both LEAF and the Canadian Association of Sexual Assault Centres expressed concern about the remaining degree of "judicial discretion ... to make foolish decisions."[127] Although LEAF failed to have the preamble become part of the Criminal Code, the federal government certainly recognized its importance in defending the Bill C-49 amendments against future constitutional challenges that it correctly foresaw as inevitable.[128] Thus, while the preamble might not be explicitly available to educate trial court judges in specific disputes about the admissibility of sexual history evidence, it would at least be available to educate the Supreme Court about the constitutional balancing underlying Parliament's amendments to the Criminal Code.

In fact, Janet Hiebert has described Bill C-49's preamble as "representing a stage in a conversation between elected and judicial officials on how the Charter should be interpreted and applied to the particular case at hand."[129] Five years later, as Hiebert reports, the process repeated itself in the debate surrounding Bill C-46, the federal government's response to *O'Connor*.[130] However, unlike for *Seaboyer*, the Justice Department began preparing its response even prior to the Court's decision. Before the Court heard oral argument in *O'Connor* on 1 February 1995, the Justice Department had begun consultations with a variety of stakeholders, including women's groups and equality-seeking organizations, to discuss legislative alternatives in the event of a negative judicial decision.[131] Consequently, by November 1995 (one month before the Court's judgment in *O'Connor*), the department had already produced a discussion paper on access to records in sexual assault cases.[132] In this sense, although Bill C-46 was motivated by the *O'Connor* litigation, it was not exclusively a response to the judgment.[133]

Canadian feminists mobilized against *O'Connor* on two fronts. The Court had reached its judgment in a factual vacuum in the sense that there had been no general information presented at trial or any level of appeal about the use of complainants' medical and therapeutic records by defence counsel in sexual assault cases. Consequently, LEAF commissioned Karen Busby of the University of Manitoba (and a member of its national legal committee) to undertake the first comprehensive study of the subject. Busby completed the study, which she would eventually publish in the *Canadian Journal of Women and the Law*, in time for its use during committee hearings on Bill C-46.[134] The second front was in the legislative arena. Both LEAF and NAWL submitted briefs on Bill C-46 to the Standing Committee on Justice and Legal Affairs, and representatives of both groups appeared before the committee on 6 March 1997.

NAWL's written brief began by stating its unequivocal position "that personal records should never be produced in sexual assault proceedings," a position it repeated in its appearance before the committee.[135] Nevertheless both NAWL and LEAF supported Bill C-46 as a good "second best" response to *O'Connor*, largely because it corrected the Supreme Court's singular focus on the right to a fair trial by promoting privacy and equality considerations. However, both organizations recommended amendments to the proposed legislation, including the addition to the Criminal Code of "a strong, gender specific Declaration of Principles which will explicitly guide judicial interpretation of the amendments and outline the social facts which Parliament intends to address."[136] Despite these recommendations for amendment, Sheila McIntyre of LEAF praised the Justice Department for having "done an extraordinary piece of drafting at the end of a very demanding process." McIntyre rejected the notion that Bill C-46 represented a one-sided victory for the interests of complainants over those of defendants. In her view, the process had been "brutally, legally demanding, where every single argument that could be made, had been made."[137]

Given the length (two and a half years) and apparent intensity of the process, it is noteworthy that Bill C-46 so closely resembles the guidelines set out in Justice L'Heureux-Dubé's *O'Connor* dissent. Indeed, as Table 5.3 demonstrates, section 278.5(2) of the Criminal Code repeats virtually word for word the seven factors that Justice L'Heureux-Dubé indicated judges should follow before granting access to third-party medical and therapeutic records. Thus, although Bill C-46 rejected the majority's approach, it adhered to a policy that had the support of at least four justices. Nevertheless, the government's decision to follow the minority rendered the amendments vulnerable to constitutional attack, and within five months of Bill C-46's becoming law, courts in Alberta and Ontario declared its provisions unconstitutional.[138] Some commentators had expected this, and had even provided partial blueprints for judicial reversal of the two bills.[139] These outcomes obviously meant that LEAF had to shift its legal mobilization back to the courtroom to preserve the political successes it had salvaged from the legal setbacks in *Seaboyer* and *O'Connor*.

Table 5.3

Comparison of the Criminal Code "privacy shield" and the alternative *O'Connor* regime

Alternative *O'Connor* regime (L'Heureux-Dubé, La Forest, Gonthier, McLachlin)	Criminal Code, section 278.5(2)
The extent to which the record is necessary for the accused to make full answer and defence;	(a) the extent to which the record is necessary for the accused to make a full answer and defence;
The probative value of the record in question;	(b) the probative value of the record;
The nature and extent of the reasonable expectation of privacy vested in that record;	(c) the nature and extent of the reasonable expectation of privacy with respect to the record;
Whether production of the record would be premised upon any discriminatory belief or bias;	(d) whether production of the record is based on a discriminatory belief or bias;
The potential prejudice to the complainant's dignity, privacy or security of the person that would be occasioned by production of the record in question;	(e) the potential prejudice to the personal dignity and right to privacy of any person to whom the record relates;
The extent to which production of records of this nature would frustrate society's interest in encouraging the reporting of sexual offences and the acquisition of treatment by victims; and	(f) society's interest in encouraging the reporting of sexual offences; (g) society's interest in encouraging the obtaining of treatment by complainants of sexual offences; and
The effect on the integrity of the trial process of producing, or failing to produce, the record, having in mind the need to maintain consideration in the outcome.	(h) the effect of the determination on the integrity of the trial process.

Judicial Retrenchment?

R. v. Mills (1999)

The majority judgment in *Mills*, coauthored by Justices Beverley McLachlin and Frank Iacobucci, identified several issues underlying the broader question of Bill C-46's constitutionality. In substantive terms, the majority defined the task as one of balancing the right to make full answer and defence against the right to privacy, with neither right negating the other and with both rights "informed by the equality rights at play in this context." In process terms, and undoubtedly influenced by Justice Iacobucci's personal attachment to the dialogue metaphor, the judgment focused on "the relationship between the courts and Parliament."[140] Reflecting on the *O'Connor* precedent, the judgment noted that "it is important to keep in mind that the decision in *O'Connor* is not necessarily the last word on the subject," since "law develops through dialogue between courts and legislatures." "Against the backdrop of *O'Connor*," the majority continued, "Parliament was free to craft its own solution to the problem consistent with the Charter."[141]

The *Mills* majority characterized the *O'Connor* regime as a set of constitutionally mandated common law rules for the production of therapeutic records held by third parties. In this sense, Bill C-46 represented a statutory alteration of the common law rules, and the question before the Court was whether this alternative nevertheless complied with the constitutional principles articulated in *O'Connor*. In the majority's view, the principal differences between the two production regimes were the following:

- Bill C-46 was more specific about both the type of record and offence to which the production regime applies.
- The *O'Connor* regime essentially treated therapeutic records in the Crown's possession like any other type of evidence, and thus subject to the discovery rules articulated in *Stinchcombe*. Bill C-46, by contrast, included these records within its production regime.
- Both regimes mandated a two-stage process (production to the court, followed by production to the accused), but the accused faced a higher burden during the first stage of the C-46 regime. Bill C-46 required the accused to establish a record's relevance at this stage and made the privacy rights of complainants a specific factor in determining relevance.

Not surprisingly, defence lawyers found these distinctions between the two regimes problematic in several different ways. For example, they argued that it was virtually impossible for the defence to meet its burden of establishing relevance without some access to the records in order to know what they might contain. More generally, the fact that the Crown could access privately held therapeutic records without following the C-46 rules, with no obligation to surrender those records to the defence, created an imbalance of power. In other words, the Crown could possess information unavailable to the defence, which was clearly contrary to at least the spirit of *Stinchcombe*.

Having acknowledged the differences between C-46 and the *O'Connor* regime, the majority devoted five paragraphs to the judicial-legislative relationship. At the core of this discussion were two notions. The first was that no dialogue can exist between the two branches of governance if "the common law were to be taken as establishing the only possible constitutional regime."[142] Second, Parliament can be an "ally for vulnerable groups," and the Court therefore has an obligation to consider Parliament's "attempt to respond" to "the voices of those vulnerable to being overlooked by the majority."[143]

This last point was consistent with the Court's development of the idea that it "must be cautious to ensure that [the Charter] does not simply become an instrument of better situated individuals to roll back legislation which has as its object the improvement of the condition of less advantaged persons." The Court thus drew an explicit distinction between policies where legislatures are mediating the claims of competing groups and those where government "is best characterized as the singular antagonist of an individual."[144] For policies of the first type, Chief Justice Dickson had suggested, the Court should be circumspect in assessing legislative objectives and means. By contrast, the second type of policy frees the Court to exercise its review function more aggressively.

The most obvious example of the second policy type, according to Dickson, is infringement on legal rights. In this context,

the state, on behalf of the whole community, typically will assert its responsibility for prosecuting crime whereas the individual will assert the paramountcy of principles of fundamental justice. There might not be any further competing claims among different groups. In such circumstances, and indeed whenever the government's purpose relates to maintaining the authority and impartiality of the judicial system, the courts can assess with some certainty whether the "least drastic means" for achieving the purpose has been chosen, especially given their accumulated experience in dealing with such questions.[145]

The justification for judicial activism, or at least a lesser degree of deference, in the legal rights field rests, therefore, on a general distinction between socioeconomic policy and criminal justice policy. Where legislatures have sought to balance competing claims in complex areas of socioeconomic policy, in other words, the Court should exercise restraint. Only in procedural matters, where courts have an important responsibility to protect individuals from state coercion, and possess unique expertise, is judicial activism un-equivocally legitimate.

In this earlier context, therefore, the Court anticipated that one of the groups most "vulnerable to being overlooked by the majority" was the crimi-nally accused. However, in the *Mills* context, the Court identified the women and children victimized by sexual offences as the vulnerable voices to which Parliament was responding. In contrast to the earlier decisions in *Seaboyer* and *O'Connor*, the *Mills* decision reconceptualized sexual assault law as be-ing closer in substance to social policy than to criminal justice policy. In the unique context of sexual assault law, the Court implied, the state was not "the singular antagonist of the individual" but the champion of groups even more vulnerable than accused criminals.

Justices McLachlin's and Iacobucci's focus on the vulnerability of sexual assault complainants instead of the criminally accused at least partially re-flected LEAF's intervention. The majority judgment contained three favourable references to material cited in LEAF's factum, including the pub-lished version of Karen Busby's report and another report she had prepared for the Justice Department.[146] In addition, the judgment is sprinkled with conclusions drawn from LEAF's factum. For example, it accepted LEAF's sub-mission that therapeutic records are often used to "whack the complain-ant."[147] Indeed, both the *Mills* majority and LEAF stressed the "routine" use of defence requests for private records as a way of attacking "the complain-ants' credibility, motives and character."[148] The judgment also referred to LEAF's argument that "heavily documented" women and children, already likely to be suffering inequality based on poverty, race, class, and mental health, would be further discriminated against by a porous boundary be-tween privacy and the right to full answer and defence.[149] Finally, following LEAF, the majority questioned the utility of such records in promoting the "search for truth" underlying every criminal trial. The majority based this skepticism on its general concern about the myths, stereotypes, and assump-tions commonly held about sexual assault complainants, as well as on a specific concern that therapeutic records are not prepared with criminal proceedings in mind.[150] This last point was crucial in evaluating the pre-sumption of irrelevance on which the entire C-46 regime rested.

The actual analysis of the legislative provisions generated by Bill C-46 occupied 50 paragraphs of the majority's 130-paragraph judgment (Chief Justice Lamer's partial dissent occupied 16 paragraphs of the entire 146 para-graphs written by the Court in *Mills*). Three potential constitutional defi-ciencies of the C-46 regime dominated the analysis. The first deficiency concerned the definition of the records subject to the regime, which critics argued was too broad and protected records that should be accessible with-out any judicial oversight. Second, the Court considered the argument that Crown-held records should not be included within the C-46 regime.

Finally, critics of the regime averred that the procedures governing production to the trial judge imposed an unreasonable standard of relevance by adding the additional criterion that production must be "necessary in the interests of justice."

The majority rejected all these claims. With respect to the first deficiency it held that the regime applied only to records "for which there is a reasonable expectation of privacy." Consequently, the C-46 regime did not protect records that fell outside this category. The majority's response to the second claim was that, since the *O'Connor* majority had not addressed the procedures applicable to Crown-held records, Parliament had significant leeway to fill this void legislatively. Moreover, Parliament's decision to impose greater restrictions on defence access to private records than on the Crown's access was justified by "the fact that unlike the Crown, the accused bears no responsibility to protect the rights of others."[151] Finally, the majority held that Bill C-46's relevance standard was the product of a lengthy consultation process that supported Parliament's reasonable conclusion that "trial judges have sufficient evidence to engage in an informed balancing process" in determining likely relevance.[152]

Indeed, in the final analysis what seemed to impress the majority most was the "wide discretion" that C-46 gave to trial judges. This discretion, according to McLachlin and Iacobucci, allowed judges "to consider a variety of factors" and to "make whatever order is necessary in the interest of justice at both stages of an application for production." In so doing, C-46 "created a scheme that permits judges not only to preserve the complainant's privacy and equality rights to the maximum extent possible, but also to ensure that the accused has access to the documents required to make full answer and defence."[153] In other words, by avoiding a categorical rule in one direction or the other, Parliament satisfied the Court's emerging principle that trial judges are best situated to determine fairness to both the accused and complainants.

Darrach

After the *Mills* decision, the Court's unanimous judgment in *Darrach* was almost anticlimactic. In contrast to that of *Mills,* the *Darrach* Court did not find it necessary to devote any of its judgment to the legislative-judicial relationship. In fact, in three different places, the Court stressed the similarities between the legislative provisions generated by Bill C-49 and the guidelines articulated in *Seaboyer*.[154] Writing for his colleagues, Justice Charles Gonthier described the provisions as a "codification" of the *Seaboyer* guidelines, which followed "the Court's suggestions very closely." The Court thus began its analysis from the standpoint that the "ultimate justification" for the provisions in the new section 276 was that "they are found in some form in the *Seaboyer* guidelines."

The Court focused on four alleged constitutional deficiencies in section 276: two substantive provisions defining the type of evidence excluded from sexual assault trials, and two procedural provisions designed to enforce the exclusion. Darrach's counsel argued that the substantive provisions constituted a "blanket exclusion" of sexual history evidence, a claim rejected by the Court. According to Justice Gonthier, section 276 excluded such evidence only if its intent is to support either of the "twin myths" about sexual assault, namely that the complainant's past sexual activity suggests a propensity to consent or a lack of credibility.[155] In addition, the Court affirmed the requirement under section 276 that only sexual history evidence with "significant probative value" should be admitted. Parliament's addition of the qualifying term "significant" to the *Seaboyer* guidelines, Gonthier concluded, simply reflected the reality that the highly prejudicial nature of sexual history evidence requires a high threshold of protection against its use.[156]

The two procedural provisions dealt with the process by which defendants established the relevance, and hence admissibility, of sexual history evidence. Section 276 requires that anyone seeking to introduce such evidence "must present an affidavit and establish on a voir dire that the evidence is admissible in accordance with" the Criminal Code's criteria.[157] Counsel for Darrach argued that this procedure infringed the principle against self-incrimination in two distinct ways. First, the affidavit requirement forced defendants to reveal their defence and disclose evidence they planned to use at trial. Second, the voir dire requirement compelled defendants to testify at their own trial.[158] The Court rejected this argument due to the absence of a *legal* compulsion to testify. According to Justice Gonthier, sexual history evidence "is most often used in attempts to substantiate claims of an honest but mistaken belief in consent."[159] The purpose of the impugned procedures was precisely to establish the connection between this defence and the sexual history evidence the defendant wished to introduce. The affidavit provides the basic connection, and the voir dire allows the Crown to cross-examine the accused on the facts in the affidavit.

Most of these points are also contained in LEAF's factum, although the degree of overlap between the *Darrach* judgment and LEAF's submission is not as striking as in *Mills*. Within the general context of its characterization of sexual assault as "one of the clearest expressions of women's subjugation and oppression on the basis of sex," LEAF defended section 276 for promoting equality by shifting the focus of sexual assault trials away from "discriminatory myths and stereotypes which distort the trial process."[160] Moreover, the Court's conclusion that section 276 did not depart "from the conventional rules of evidence" mirrors the position articulated by LEAF.[161] Finally, there is substantial congruence between the Court's treatment of the probative value-prejudice balance and the discussion of this point in LEAF's factum.[162]

On one interpretation, *Darrach* represents the final move in a process of convergence between Parliament's desire to shield sexual assault complainants from intrusive inquiries into their past and the Court's desire to safeguard the rights of defendants. As a crucial intervener in this process in both its judicial and legislative components, LEAF played a key role in the apparent judicial-legislative dialogue that produced this convergence. It did so by continuously pressing two related points: that sexual assault is an ingrained social practice the purpose of which is to perpetuate the subordinate position of women, and that limitations on defendants' rights are justified by the Charter's equality provisions as a means of eradicating this practice. By mobilizing in the distinctive legal arenas of litigation and legislation, LEAF apparently succeeded in persuading both institutions to view sexual assault substantially – if not completely – from its point of view.

Yet several aspects of the sexual assault story caution against characterizing it as an unqualified success for either judicial-legislative dialogue or feminist legal mobilization. Indeed, some of the evidence in favour of a cautious interpretation is found in *Darrach* itself, where the Court located the ultimate constitutional justification for Bill C-49's provisions in their similarity to the judicially crafted guidelines of *Seaboyer*. The question raised by this observation, of course, is whether the dialogue converged at a common point because the Court accepted the merits of the approach agreed on by LEAF and Parliament, or because Parliament told the Court what it wanted to hear. Similarly, although Bill C-46 departed from the guidelines articulated by the *O'Connor* majority, the *Mills* Court did not have to look very hard in that earlier judgment to find judicial support for the provisions of the C-46 records disclosure regime.

The Difficulties of Dialogue

Since the early 1970s, Canada has experienced two waves of comprehensive sexual assault law reform, each in varying degrees a response to judicial policy making. The first wave, which produced Criminal Code amendments in 1976 and 1983, was in part a reaction against judicially created common law rules of evidence – some with an extremely long history – that critics blamed for suppressing reporting and conviction rates. When these reforms reached the Supreme Court for review in the post-Charter era, they did not fare well, as the Court used the Charter to reassert some of the procedural rights of defendants diluted in 1976 and 1983. The second wave of sexual assault law reform, which produced Criminal Code amendments in 1992 and 1997, was a direct reaction to these judicially created constitutional rules of evidence that arguably negated some of the first-wave reforms. This time, however, the Court responded differently to the legislative reaction, affirming the essential elements of the second-wave reforms in three decisions: *Ewanchuk* (consent), *Mills* (access to medical and therapeutic records), and *Darrach* (sexual history evidence). The Canadian women's movement, primarily through LEAF (but also through NAWL) played a major role in the 1990s by stressing to both the Court and government that the Charter contains rights and values beyond those that simply protect defendants from unjustified conviction.

In this sense, the interaction among the Court, Parliament, and LEAF might be considered a paradigmatic instance of what Peter Hogg, Allison Bushell, and Kent Roach call democratic dialogue. To repeat the point made in this chapter's introduction, the idea of dialogue is offered to counter the claim of judicial supremacy in Charter-based policy development. Judicial supremacy is nonexistent, or at least extremely rare, because the Charter itself gives legislatures the ability to "reverse, modify or avoid" judicial nullification.[163] The most obvious way in which legislatures can *avoid* nullification is to persuade courts that no constitutional violation exists. The Charter facilitates this in two ways, by qualifying some rights (e.g., "*unreasonable* searches and seizures") and by allowing legislatures to justify even *prima facie* rights violations as "reasonable limits" under section 1. Section 1 also facilitates legislative *modification* of negative judicial decisions by allowing legislatures to take a second crack at pursuing their policy objectives through different means than those initially found wanting by courts. Finally, section 33 gives legislatures the ultimate authority in some policy areas to *reverse* judicial nullification by declaring that a law shall operate "notwithstanding" certain provisions of the Charter (sections 2, and 7 to 14). Preemptive uses of section 33 (which have been the norm) might also be described as a way to avoid judicial nullification by foreclosing the possibility of judicial review altogether.

There is no doubt that this dialogue metaphor constitutes a powerful account of judicial review as an instrument of democratic governance – so powerful, in fact, that it was quickly adopted by the Supreme Court. Citing the Hogg and Bushell article in *Vriend* v. *Alberta* (1998), Justice Frank Iacobucci argued that the Charter establishes "a more dynamic interaction among the branches of governance."[164] For Justice Iacobucci and the rest of the *Vriend* Court, the growth of this interactive dynamic demands more active participation by the judiciary in a dialogue with legislatures and executives about the proper balance between individual rights and the common good. From this perspective, Charter-based judicial review is an integral component of a more comprehensive and sophisticated democratic discourse. Justice Iacobucci continued to champion the dialogue metaphor even when his colleagues appeared to distance themselves from it. In his partial dissent in *Little Sisters Book and Art Emporium* v. *Canada*, Iacobucci noted that the Court "has frequently recognized the importance of fostering a dialogue between courts and legislatures," and he urged his colleagues to strike down the impugned customs regulations to "encourage much needed changes."[165]

How well does the development of sexual assault law in the 1990s fit the dialogue metaphor? Having failed to avoid judicial nullification of section 276 of the Criminal Code in *Seaboyer*, the government responded with a comprehensive reform of sexual assault law (Bill C-49) that incorporated both evidentiary/procedural changes and a substantive redefinition of consent. In *Ewanchuk*, the Court applied the new definition of consent to reverse lower court sexual assault acquittals, thereby sending a strong signal to lower courts to implement the new policy change. However, because this redefinition was not directly a response to *Seaboyer* or the object of constitutional challenge, it is difficult to evaluate it within the dialogue theory. Indeed, Roach's study does not mention the *Ewanchuk* decision. The decision that does attract the attention of dialogue theorists, of course, is *Darrach*. The argument here is that the government's response modified the *Seaboyer* holding, and that the Court's deference to that modification blunts any claim of judicial supremacy. Recall, however, that Justice Gonthier, who joined the dissent in *Seaboyer* and wrote the *Darrach* judgment, considered Bill C-49 more a codification than modification of the *Seaboyer* guidelines. Although Roach argues that the *Darrach* Court overstated the degree of similarity between C-49 and the *Seaboyer* guidelines,[166] the differences are arguably so marginal as to stretch the definition of "modification." In the final analysis, while C-49 introduced broader reforms than were absolutely required by *Seaboyer*, it adopted the 1991 judgment's core policy holding virtually unchanged.

A similar argument might be made about the *O'Connor*, C-46, *Mills* sequence.[167] As with *Seaboyer*, in *O'Connor* the federal government failed to avoid a constitutional interpretation that mandated a policy on defendants' access to records inconsistent with its preferences. It responded, of course, by enacting, for the first time in Canadian history, a set of legislative guidelines for production of such records. Furthermore, these guidelines rejected the approach of the majority judgment in *O'Connor* in favour of the minority's approach. To Roach, this constituted an "in your face" reply that was tantamount to reversal rather than modification of the Court. According to Roach, the constitutionally proper way for the government to have proceeded in this instance was to invoke section 33. In his view, the Court's deference to Parliament in *Mills* was an abdication of its responsibility that actually foreclosed democratic dialogue about the policy issue in question.[168] Another interpretation, however, is that C-46 was neither a modification nor reversal of *O'Connor*. It was simply the product of a legislative choice between two judicially crafted policies that commanded almost equal support of the Court (five justices versus four). From this perspective, C-46 was not the product of an independent legislative assessment of what might constitute optimal public policy within the broad constraints of previously unknown constitutional principles, but of the government's best guess about which policy might withstand future judicial scrutiny. The Court did not defer to legislative judgment in *Mills* but merely affirmed a policy constructed by four of its own members. If any dialogue occurred, it was among the justices themselves about which *O'Connor* regime should ultimately prevail.

If the dialogue metaphor does not capture the essence of sexual assault reform and LEAF's involvement in it during the 1990s, then how might it be understood? One interpretation is that LEAF found itself enmeshed in a struggle over the location of institutional authority to define the elements of a fair trial. The Court saw this as a purely judicial matter, as a matter of both principle and application. Indeed, the theme running through the judgments in LEAF's two losses is the importance of judicial discretion to ensure defendants a fair trial consistent with the principles of fundamental justice. Since nothing in Bills C-49 or C-46 challenged that notion, it was relatively easy for the Court to defer to Parliament in *Darrach* and *Mills*. To some degree, LEAF's legal defence of C-49 and C-46 gave the Court a more principled justification for that deference.

The difficulty with dialogue lies in overcoming the presumption in favour of judicial supremacy of constitutional *interpretation*. This presumption is evident throughout the major statements of the dialogue metaphor. In four places in their original article on the dialogue metaphor, Hogg and Bushell identify courts as the sole author of "Charter values" and "the requirements of the Charter."[169] Kent Roach argues that "conventional understandings of the rule of law ... suggest that the legislature should respect the Court's interpretation of the constitution."[170] In other words, whatever reasonable disagreement supporters of the dialogue metaphor allow legislatures to have with respect to courts, the one subject on which it is not reasonable for them to disagree is with judicial interpretation of rights themselves. Although LEAF was able to support the federal government in its response to the policy implications of the Supreme Court's interpretation of defendants' rights in the context of sexual assault, it could not persuade the government to challenge the essence of that interpretation.

6
Making a Difference: The Policy Consequences of Legal Mobilization

In her introduction to the 1996 compendium of LEAF's Supreme Court factums, Carissima Mathen identified three principles underlying the organization's litigation activity:

1 Women as a group, compared with men as a group, experience widespread and pervasive discrimination.
2 Women who are oppressed on the basis of, for example, their race, class, sexual orientation, religion or disability, experience inequality different in degree and/or kind, in various contexts.
3 Law can be an effective tool for egalitarian social change.[1]

The first two of these principles are abundantly evident in LEAF's factums themselves. LEAF continually stressed the social, economic, and political inequalities between men and women. In addition, especially in later cases when LEAF joined coalitions with other equality-seeking groups, its factums highlighted the multiple disadvantages experienced by certain women. That LEAF invested the resources necessary to intervene in almost forty Supreme Court cases is also evidence of at least its *belief* in the third principle. By engaging in litigation to bring the first two principles to the Court's attention, LEAF expected to affect the law in ways that would reduce women's inequality. In essence, by fully realizing the third principle, LEAF hoped to render the first two principles moot.

In this chapter I focus my attention on LEAF's third principle by examining whether legal mobilization has been an effective strategy for the Canadian feminist movement. Although LEAF's principles understand effectiveness in terms of policy consequences (law generating egalitarian social change), at least two other measures of effectiveness should not be ignored. One measure is the effect on legal rules: Did legal mobilization change (or preserve) legal rules in the manner desired? The second measure is the organizational effect on social movements: Did legal mobilization

strengthen the movement? In an ideal world, these measures of effectiveness would be causally connected. Legal mobilization would establish desired legal rules; desired legal rules would generate positive policy
consequences; success would strengthen the movement. In the real world,
however, these measures are often mutually exclusive. Legal mobilization
may fail to establish desired legal rules, but positive policy consequences
follow anyway; desired rules emerge from the legal process, but have no
impact on policy or social conditions; unsuccessful legal mobilization may
nevertheless strengthen a movement by energizing members around
particular causes; successful mobilization, by contrast, may enervate a movement or energize a counter movement. Superimposed over all these considerations is whether any particular group's activity makes a difference. In
other words, would law and policy have developed as they did even in the
absence of legal mobilization by a social movement? This chapter addresses
each of these questions.

The LEAF Difference
In a comparative study of the impact of women's groups on judicial decision making in Canada and the United States, Lori Hausegger used multi-
variate regression analysis to measure the difference these groups made in
litigation. The results, at least with respect to LEAF, were mixed. According
to Hausegger, LEAF's presence did matter in terms of outcome, increasing
the likelihood of a favourable outcome by 33 percentage points and leading
Hausegger to conclude that LEAF was "a very valuable ally" in litigation.[2]
Indeed, Justice L'Heureux-Dubé was likely the swing vote in the Court's
four-to-three decision to uphold the Criminal Code's hate propaganda provisions in *Keegstra*, and she may have been persuaded by LEAF's arguments.

By contrast, Hausegger found that LEAF's interventions did not necessarily increase the likelihood of generating favourable doctrine. Although
Hausegger found that LEAF had a significant influence on doctrine in the
areas of general equality principles and pornography, its influence was less
evident in the areas of abortion, family law, and sexual assault.[3] In fact, she
found that legal considerations had a more significant impact in all five
issue areas than any other variable, including women's interest-group
participation.

In broader terms, however, one might argue that LEAF made a difference
through the type of evidence it brought to the Court's attention. The use of
legal scholarship and other extralegal documents to communicate new legal theories and policy information to courts came of age in the United
States in the 1940s, when US Supreme Court justices such as Felix Frankfurter, Charles Evans Hughes, and Robert Jackson explicitly acknowledged
their utility and legitimacy as sources of information.[4] Historically rooted
in the sociological and economic studies first introduced into American

constitutional jurisprudence by Louis Brandeis, the strategic and tactical use of law review and other nonlegal publications was perfected by the NAACP in its constitutional struggle against racially restrictive covenants and segregated education.[5]

While the US Court began to consider extrinsic evidence early in the twentieth century, the Canadian Supreme Court remained hostile to its use until the 1970s. Moreover, even after becoming more accepting of such evidence, the Court was still able to dismiss it as irrelevant in resolving the legal questions at issue in important cases. Indeed, although he pioneered the use of extrinsic evidence in Canadian constitutional adjudication, Chief Justice Bora Laskin did precisely that in the *Anti-Inflation Reference* (1976) when he dismissed as irrelevant a technical submission by several economists that the law in question would have little impact on inflation. In his view,

> the wisdom or expediency or likely success of a particular policy expressed in legislation is not subject to judicial review. Hence, it is not for the Court to say in this case that because the means adopted to realize a desirable end, i.e., the containment and reduction of inflation in Canada, may not be effectual, those means are beyond the legislative power of Parliament.[6]

The use of extrinsic evidence is unavoidable, however, under section 1 of the Charter and the criteria established for its application in *Oakes*. Indeed, it is precisely the "expediency or likely success of a particular policy" that is reviewed under the proportionality element of the *Oakes* test.

As Table 6.1 demonstrates, the use of extrinsic evidence in the form of legal scholarship, government reports, and other documents was a central feature of LEAF's factums. In eight cases, LEAF cited more than twenty separate pieces of legal scholarship, ranging from 22 citations in *Mills* to 36 citations in *Seaboyer*. The use of reports and documents was less frequent, but there were still three cases in which LEAF cited more than 10 such sources (*Gordon*: 15; *Moge*: 13; *Canadian Council of Churches*: 12). One of the distinguishing features of all eleven of these cases is that, in each one, LEAF's argument challenged prevailing doctrine. For example, according to Colleen Sheppard, *Moge* "arose at a particular juncture in societal and legal debates regarding the post-marriage economic obligations of former spouses."[7] In 1987, the Supreme Court had abandoned the model of lifetime alimony in favour of a self-sufficiency model.[8] Although the self-sufficiency model was authored by Justice Bertha Wilson, feminists criticized its assumption of equality between the parties at the time of marital breakdown.[9] Much of LEAF's argument in its *Moge* factum, therefore, challenged the nonlegal assumptions on which this new legal rule had been based. Similarly, in *Canadian Council of Churches*, LEAF found itself in the position of seeking a novel expansion of the doctrine of standing.

Table 6.1

Extrinsic evidence cited by LEAF

Case	Scholarship	Reports/Documents
Canadian Newspapers	4	7
Andrews	16	6
Janzen	4	1
Brooks	16	7
Borowski	13	2
Daigle	4	0
Keegstra/Andrews (90)	4	6
Taylor	0	9
Sullivan	14	4
Seaboyer	36	3
Canadian Council of Churches	7	12
Norberg	24	5
Moge	10	13
Schachter	8	1
Butler	24	8
M.(K.) v. M.(H.)	14	3
Weatherall	7	5
M. (M.L.)	3	2
Whitley	10	4
O'Connor	17	9
Beharriel	15	4
Thibaudeau	9	8
Gordon	28	15
R. v. S.	5	4
Eldridge	26	6
Winnipeg Child and Family Services	29	8
Vriend	14	1
Ewanchuk	12	1
M. v. H.	10	2
BC (Public Service Employee Relations Commission)	5	0
NB (Minister of Health and Community Services) v. G.(J.)	14	9
Mills	22	1
Blencoe	4	1
Darrach	3	0
Little Sisters	23	0

Extrinsic evidence was also important in LEAF's defence of legislative changes to sexual assault trial procedures in *Seaboyer* and *Mills*. In *Seaboyer*, LEAF cited 36 items of legal and other scholarship to support its causal argument linking the defence's right to question women about their sexual history and reputation to low reporting rates. In *Mills*, LEAF marshalled 22 items of scholarship to defend the federal government's legislative response to the *O'Connor* judgment on access to third-party medical and therapeutic records. LEAF also relied extensively on extrinsic evidence in *Butler* to establish its harm-based justification for pornography regulation (24 items), a tactic on which it also had to rely in *Little Sisters* (23 items) when it appeared to reverse its absolutist position about the harmful consequences of pornography. Finally, extrinsic evidence was highly visible in LEAF's *Eldridge* factum (26 items), where it was arguing to establish a new right (effective communication, operationalized as government-funded sign language interpretation) in the context of health care provision.

One exception to this pattern is *Winnipeg Child and Family Services*, where LEAF used extrinsic evidence (29 items) and other reports and documents (8 items) to warn the Court about the historical antecedents and future consequences of expanding *parens patriae* doctrine to include forcible confinement of pregnant women to protect their unborn children. This material aimed at two objectives. First, it drew an analogy between the social service agency's contemporary action and widely criticized past practices such as the removal of Aboriginal children to residential schools. Second, it indicated that confinement orders would most likely be made against poor women already caught up in the social welfare network. Thus, LEAF used extrinsic evidence to suggest that this expansion of *parens patriae* would not only discriminate directly against women but would also *indirectly* discriminate on the basis of poverty and race.

Table 6.2 expands this discussion of LEAF's impact on the Court by detailing the Court's use of extrinsic evidence cited by LEAF, as well as explicit references by the Court to LEAF arguments. In twenty-three of LEAF's thirty-six interventions, the Court referred to material contained in its factums, and in six of those twenty-three cases the Court made explicit reference to LEAF arguments.

In total, the Court made 108 references to extralegal material cited in LEAF factums. Some of this material was the product of scholars associated with LEAF, or connected in some other way with LEAF's initiatives to increase the amount of feminist legal scholarship in circulation. For example, books by Catherine MacKinnon – a frequent consultant to LEAF – on sexual harassment *(Sexual Harassment of Working Women: A Case of Sex Discrimination)* and general feminist theory *(Toward a Feminist Theory of the State)* found their way into judgments via LEAF's factums in *Janzen* and *Seaboyer*. Similarly, material published in the *Canadian Journal of Women and the Law* – founded specifically to promote scholarship that could support feminist litigation – also came to the Court's attention through LEAF factums. Scholars associated with LEAF, such as Elizabeth Sheehy, Dianne Pothier, Shelagh Day, and Gwen Brodsky, also saw their work get to the Court via LEAF. While most of the references to LEAF factum material were in majority judgments, one important exception to this rule should be noted. In *Seaboyer*, all but one of the twenty-six references to LEAF factum material were made

Table 6.2

Supreme Court use of LEAF material and arguments

Case	LEAF material cited	References to LEAF arguments
Andrews	• European Convention on Human Rights • Tarnopolsky and Pentney, *Discrimination and the Law,* 2nd ed.	
Janzen	• *Report of the Commission on Equality in Employment* • Aggarwal, *Sexual Harassment in the Workplace* • Backhouse and Cohen, *The Secret Oppression: Sexual Harassment of Working Women* • Hickling, "Employer's Liability for Sexual Harassment," *Man. L. J.* • MacKinnon, *Sexual Harassment of Working Women: A Case of Sex Discrimination*	• As the LEAF factum puts it, "sexual harassment is a form of sex discrimination because it denies women equality of opportunity in employment because of their sex" (Section v, para. 48).
Taylor	• Canada, Special Committee on the Participation of Visible Minorities in Canadian Society, *Equality Now!* • Law Reform Commission, Working Paper 50, *Hate Propaganda* • Special Committee on Hate Propaganda in Canada, *Report of the Special Committee on Hate Propaganda in Canada* • CBA, *Report of the Special Committee on Racial and Religious Hatred* • McAlpine, *Report Arising out of the Activities of the Ku Klux Klan in British Columbia*	
Keegstra	• Canada, Special Committee on the Participation of Visible Minorities in Canadian Society, *Equality Now!* • Law Reform Commission, Working Paper 50, *Hate Propaganda* • Special Committee on Hate Propaganda in Canada, *Report of the Special Committee on Hate Propaganda in Canada*	

▶

◄ *Table 6.2*

Case	LEAF material cited	References to LEAF arguments
	• CBA, *Report of the Special Committee on Racial and Religious Hatred* • Delgado, "Words that Wound: A Tort Action for Racial Insults, Epithets, and Name-Calling," *Harv. C.R.-C.L. L. Rev.* • Matsuda, "Public Response to Racist Speech: Considering the Victim's Story," *Mich. L. Rev.* • McAlpine, *Report Arising out of the Activities of the Ku Klux Klan in British Columbia*	
Andrews (90)	• Special Committee on Hate Propaganda in Canada, *Report of the Special Committee on Hate Propaganda in Canada*	
Seaboyer	• Adler, "The Relevance of Sexual History Evidence in Rape," *Crim. L. R.* (in dissent) • Backhouse and Schoenroth, "A Comparative Survey of Canadian and American Rape Law," *Can.-U.S. L. J.* (in dissent) • Berger, "Man's Trial, Woman's Tribulation," *Colum. L. Rev.* (in majority) • Brickman and Briere, "Incidence of Rape and Sexual Assault in an Urban Canadian Population," *Int'l. J. of Women's Stud.* (in dissent) • Borginda and White, "Social Perception of Rape Victims," *Law and Hum. Behav.* (in dissent) • House of Commons, Standing Committee on Justice and Legal Affairs, *Minutes of Proceedings and Evidence* (22 April 1982) (in dissent) • Committee on Sexual Offences Against Children and Youth, *Sexual Offences Against Children* (in dissent) • Solicitor General, *Canadian Urban Victimization Survey: Female Victims of Crime* (in dissent)	• "I also heartily concur in the submissions at p.17 of the factum of the intervener [LEAF] on this point: 'in all of the hypothetical situations outlined in the Appellants' factums, evidence of sexual history and/or sexual reputation is either totally irrelevant, admissible pursuant to the exceptions provided for in s.276, or, in the alternative, of very low probative value and highly prejudicial to the interests of the administration of justice'" (p.684, paras. 3-4, by L'Heureux-Dubé, J., dissenting).

►

◀ *Table 6.2*

Case	LEAF material cited	References to LEAF arguments
Seaboyer	• Catton, "Evidence Regarding the Prior Sexual History of an Alleged Rape Victim: Its Effect on the Perceived Guilt of the Accused," *U.T. Fac. L. Rev.* (in dissent) • Check and Malamuth, "Sex Role Stereotyping and Reactions to Depictions of Stranger Versus Acquaintance Rape," *J. of Pers. and Soc. Psych.* (in dissent) • Clark and Lewis, *Rape: The Price of Coercive Sexuality* (in dissent) • Cross and Tapper, *Cross on Evidence* (in dissent) • Dawson, "Sexual Assault Law and Past Sexual Conduct of the Primary Witness," *C.J.W.L.* (in dissent) • Galvin, "Shielding Rape Victims in the State and Federal Courts," *Minn. L. Rev.* (in majority and dissent) • Gordon and Riger, *The Female Fear* (in dissent) • Holmstrom and Burgess, *The Victim of Rape* (in dissent) • Inorma Inc., "Sexual Assault: Measuring the Impact of the Launch Campaign" (in dissent) • La Free, "Variables Affecting Guilty Pleas and Convictions in Rape Cases," *Soc. Forces* (in dissent) • La Free, Reskin, and Visher, "Jurors' Responses to Victims' Behavior and Legal Issues in Sexual Assault Trials," *Soc. Prob.* (in dissent) • MacKinnon, *Toward a Feminist Theory of the State* (in dissent) • Marshall, "Sexual Assault, the Charter and Sentencing Reform," *C.R.* (in dissent) • Renner and Sahjpaul, "The New Sexual Assault Law," *Can. J. Crim.* (in dissent) • Sheehy, "Canadian Judges and the Law of Rape," *Ottawa L. Rev.* (in dissent)	

▶

◄ *Table 6.2*

Case	LEAF material cited	References to LEAF arguments
	• Vandervort, "Mistake of Law and Sexual Assault," *C.J.W.L.* (in dissent) • Wigmore, *Evidence in Trials at Common Law (1970)* (in dissent) • Williams, *The Prosecution of Sexual Assaults* (in dissent)	
Norberg	• College of Physicians and Surgeons of Ontario, Task Force on Sexual Abuse of Patients, *Final Report* • Feldman-Summers, "Sexual Contact in Fiduciary Relationships," in Gabbard, ed., *Sexual Exploitation in Professional Relationships* • Fleming, *The Law of Torts,* 7th ed.	
Schachter	• Rogerson, "The Judicial Search for Appropriate Remedies Under the Charter," in Sharpe, ed., *Charter Litigation*	
Moge	• Department of Justice, *Evaluation of the Divorce Act, Phase II (1990)* • Law Reform Commission, Working Paper 12, *Maintenance on Divorce* • National Council on Welfare, *Women and Poverty Revisited* • Statistics Canada, *Family History Project* • Statistics Canada, *Women in Canada: A Statistical Report,* 2nd ed. • Grassby, "Women in their Forties," *R.F.L.* • Gunderson, Muszynski, and Keck, *Women and Labour Market Poverty* • Pask and McCall, "How Much and Why?," *C.F.L.Q.* • Rogerson, "The Causal Connection Test in Spousal Support Law," *Can. J. Fam. L.* • Rogerson, "Judicial Interpretation of the Spousal and Child Support Provisions of the Divorce Act, 1985," *Can. Fam. L. Q.* • Weitzman, *The Divorce Revolution*	

►

◀ *Table 6.2*

Case	LEAF material cited	References to LEAF arguments
M.(K.) v. *M.(H.)*	• Allen, "Tort Remedies for Incestuous Abuse," *Golden Gate U. L. Rev.* • DeRose, "Adult Incest Survivors and the Statute of Limitations," *Santa Clara L. Rev.* • Finkelhor and Browne, "The Traumatic Impact of Child Sexual Abuse," *American Orthopsychiatric Association* • Gelinas, "The Persisting Negative Effects of Incest," *Psychiatry* • Handler, "Civil Claims of Adults Molested as Children," *Fordham Urb. L. J.* • Hartnett, "Use of a Massachusetts Discovery Rule by Adult Survivors of Father-Daughter Incest," *New Eng. L. Rev.* • Lamm, "Easing Access to the Courts for Incest Victims," *Yale L. J.* • Ontario, Attorney General, *Recommendations for a New Limitations Act* • Rosenfeld, "The Statute of Limitations Barrier in Childhood Sexual Abuse Cases," *Harvard Women's L. J.* • Salten, "Statutes of Limitations in Civil Incest Suits," *Harvard Women's L. J.* • Shepherd, *The Law of Fiduciaries* • Summit, "The Child Sexual Abuse Accommodation Syndrome," *Child Abuse & Neglect*	• "The intervener, LEAF, argued that the Limitations Act, in so far as its provisions bar incest claims, violates s.15 of the [Charter]. It submits that the provisions bar claims of women in a disproportionate fashion and so constitutes discrimination on the basis of sex. Alternatively, it submits that the Limitations Act should be interpreted in a manner consistent with the Charter in effecting a liberal application of the limitations provisions as they affect incest victims. In view of the result I have arrived at, it is unnecessary to pursue these constitutional arguments" (pp.24-25).
O'Connor	• Committee on Sexual Offences Against Children and Youth, *Sexual Offences Against Children* • Firsten, "An Exploration of the Role of Physical and Sexual Abuse for Psychiatrically Institutionalized Women," unpublished, available from Ontario Women's directorate (in dissent) • Wigmore, *Evidence in Trials at Common Law*, 3rd ed. (1970)	

▶

◀ *Table 6.2*

Case	LEAF material cited	References to LEAF arguments
Beharriel	• Canadian Panel on Violence Against Women, *Changing the Landscape: Ending Violence – Achieving Equality* • MacCrimmon, "Developments in the Law of Evidence: The 1991-92 Term," *Sup. Ct. L. Rev. (2d)* • Roberts, "Criminal Justice Processing of Sexual Assault Cases," *Juristat*	
Gordon	• Department of Justice, *Custody and Access: Public Discussion Paper* • Furstenberg and Cherlin, *Divided Families* • Maccoby and Mnookin, *Dividing the Child*	• "This appeal raises only one issue: did the trial and appellate court err in permitting the child to move to Australia with her mother, the custodial parent? This is the first time this Court has considered the effect of a custodial parent's move on custody and access. Accordingly, both the parties and the two interveners, [LEAF] and the Children's Lawyer for Ontario invited us to consider the principles which should guide judges in dealing with such applications in the future" (para. 8).
R. v. S.	• Devlin, "We Can't Go On Together with Suspicious Minds," *Dalhousie L. J.* • Nova Scotia, *Royal Commission on the Donald Marshall, Jr. Prosecution*	
Eldridge	• Minister of Human Resources Development, *Improving Social Security in Canada: Persons with Disabilities* • Statistics Canada, *A Portrait of Persons with Disabilities*	

▶

◄ *Table 6.2*

Case	LEAF material cited	References to LEAF arguments
	• Chilton, "Ensuring Effective Communication," *Hastings L. J.* • Goundry and Peters, *Litigating for Disability Equality Rights* (Canadian Disability Rights Council, 1994) • Lepofsky, "A Report Card on the Charter's Guarantee of Equality to Persons with Disability after 10 Years," *N.J.C.L.* • Pothier, "M'Aider, Mayday," *N.J.C.L.*	
Winnipeg Child and Family Services	• Royal Commission on Aboriginal Peoples, *Report* • Royal Commission on New Reproductive Technologies, *Final Report* • Johnsen, "The Creation of Fetal Rights," *Yale L. J.*	
Vriend	• Pothier, "The Sounds of Silence," *Constitutional Forum*	
Ewanchuk	• Estrich, "Rape," *Yale L. J.* • McInnes and Boyle, "Judging Sexual Assault Law Against a Standard of Equality," *U.B.C. L. Rev.* • Sheehy, "Canadian Judges and the Law of Rape," *Ottawa L. Rev.*	
M. v. H.	• Cossman and Ryder, *Gay, Lesbian and Unmarried Heterosexual Couples and the Family Law Act* (Ontario Law Reform Commission, 1993) • Ontario Law Reform Commission, *Report on the Rights and Responsibilities of Cohabitants Under the Family Law Act* • Ontario Legislative Debates, 26 Oct. 1976; 18 Nov. 1976; 22 Nov. 1976; 18 Oct. 1977	• "As submitted by LEAF, the infrequency with which members of same-sex relationships find themselves in circumstances resembling those of many heterosexual women is no different from heterosexual men who, notwithstanding that they tend to benefit from the gender-based division of labour and inequality of earning power, have as much

►

◀ *Table 6.2*

Case	LEAF material cited	References to LEAF arguments
		right to apply for support as their female partners" (para. 110). • "Indeed, as submitted by LEAF, the FLA expressly recognizes that entitlement to the division of property is in addition to, and not in lieu of entitlement to support. Thus, it seems to me that compared to awards of spousal support, the equitable remedies are less flexible, impose more onerous requirements on claimants, and are available under far narrower circumstances. I do not accept that they provide an adequate alternative to spousal support under the FLA" (para. 120).
BC (Public Service Employee Relations Commission)	• Day and Brodsky, "The Duty to Accommodate," *Can. Bar. Rev.* • Messing, *One-Eyed Science* • Watkin, "The Justification of Discrimination Under Canadian Human Rights Legislation and the Charter," *N.J.C.L.*	
New Brunswick (Minister of Health and Community Services) v. G.(J.)	• Cossman and Rogerson, "Case Study in the Provision of Legal Aid: Family Law," *Ontario Legal Aid Review* • Hughes, "New Brunswick's Domestic Legal Aid System," *Windsor Y.B. Access Just.* • Thomson, "Judging Judiciously in Child Protection Cases," in Abella and L'Heureux-Dubé, eds., *Family Law*	

▶

◄ *Table 6.2*

Case	LEAF material cited	References to LEAF arguments
Blencoe	• Bryden, "Blencoe v. British Columbia: A Case Comment," *U.B.C. L. Rev.*	
Little Sisters	• Lepofsky, "Towards a Purposive Approach to Freedom of Expression and its Limitation," in McArdle, ed., *The Cambridge Lectures 1989*	• "The appellants, supported by the interveners LEAF and EGALE, contend that homosexual erotica plays an important role in providing a positive self-image to gays and lesbians, who may feel isolated and rejected in the heterosexual mainstream" (para. 53). • "The intervener LEAF took the position that sado-masochism performs an emancipatory role in gay and lesbian culture and should therefore be judged by a different standard from that applicable to heterosexual culture. In support of this position LEAF points out that, by definition, gender discrimination is not an issue in 'same-sex erotica'" (para. 63). • "LEAF's argument seems to presuppose that the *Butler* test is exclusively gender-based. Violence against women was only one of several concerns, albeit an important one, that led to the formulation of the *Butler* harm-based test, which itself is gender neutral. While it would be quite open to the appellants to argue that a particular publication does not exceed the general community's tolerance of harm for various reasons, gay and lesbian culture as such does not constitute a general exemption from the *Butler* test" (para. 64).

by Justice L'Heureux-Dubé in dissent. Thus, while LEAF did not affect the outcome in this case, the voice it found in the dissenting judgment laid the groundwork for mobilization around a political response to the decision.

L'Heureux-Dubé's *Seaboyer* dissent also took the rare step of expressly referring to LEAF's argument by quoting directly from its factum. She concurred with LEAF's submission that the type of evidence allegedly excluded under section 276 was "either totally irrelevant, admissible pursuant to the exceptions provided for in s.276, or, in the alternative, of very low probative value and highly prejudicial to the interests of the administration of justice." Short references to LEAF's arguments also occurred in *Janzen*, where the majority adopted LEAF's position that "sexual harassment is a form of sex discrimination"; in *M.(K.)* v. *M.(H.)*, where the majority noted LEAF's equality argument but did not pursue its constitutional arguments; and in *Gordon*, where the Court credited LEAF with inviting it to "consider the principles which should guide judges in dealing with applications" by custodial parents to move. More extensive references to LEAF's arguments are found in *M. v. H.*, where the Court adopted two aspects of LEAF's submissions. First, the Court adopted LEAF's counter-argument to Ontario's claim that same-sex partners were not in a comparable position to the heterosexual women targeted by the Family Law Act. The gravamen of this counterargument was that the same could be said about heterosexual men, who were nevertheless entitled to apply for support under the FLA. Second, the Court accepted LEAF's position about the inadequacy of equitable remedies as an alternative to the FLA's support provisions. Citing LEAF, the Court rejected these remedies because they are "less flexible, impose more onerous requirements on claimants, and are available under far narrower circumstances."

Although these cases were typified by positive uses of LEAF material and references to its argument, the last case in the period covered by this book – *Little Sisters* – may signal a change in the relationship between LEAF and the Court. Although LEAF cited twenty-three scholarly articles, only one made it into the list of references cited by the Supreme Court. More significantly, the Court made three explicit references to LEAF's arguments concerning the unique nature of gay and lesbian erotica. The first reference concerned the claim that "homo-sexual erotica plays an important role in providing a positive self-image to gays and lesbians," while the second concerned the idea that "sado-masochism performs an emancipatory role in gay and lesbian culture and should therefore be judged by a difference standard." The Court cited both of these arguments in order to reject them, holding that "gay and lesbian culture as such does not constitute a general exemption from the *Butler* test." Such direct repudiation of an *intervener's* argument is unusual, and the *Little Sisters* majority, which included Chief Justice McLachlin and Justice L'Heureux-Dubé, may have been indicating its displeasure with the apparent contradiction between LEAF's positions in *Butler* and *Little Sisters*. Although too soon to draw any firm conclusions, it is worth noting in this context that LEAF experienced two consecutive outcome losses after *Little Sisters*.[10]

Another indicator of LEAF's influence is the importance of the cases in which it has been involved. Given the role of precedent in common law adjudication, one rough measure of such importance is the citation of these cases in subsequent Supreme Court decisions. In addition, importance can also be approximated by a case's impact on legal literature, also measured by citation frequency. Table 6.3 provides the citation frequencies for all of LEAF's cases (as of 31 October 2002), as well as the results of those cases by both outcome and issue.[11]

Interestingly, the two most cited LEAF cases – *O'Connor* and *Seaboyer* – are both issue losses (although outcome wins). *O'Connor* ranks second in both Supreme Court and legal literature citations, and the large number of citations is noteworthy given that *O'Connor* was not one of LEAF's earliest cases (one would expect citations, especially by the Supreme Court, to be lower for cases decided later in the period studied). Both *O'Connor* and *Seaboyer* generated critical comments in the legal literature, which may have played a role in the development of legislative responses.

Vriend, *M. v. H.*, and *Butler* have relatively low levels of Supreme Court citations (although *Vriend* and *M. v. H.* were also decided late in the period) but high levels of legal literature citations. This is not surprising, given that each decision rested on novel legal interpretations. *Butler*'s innovation was to recognize a harm-based, rather than public morality, justification for anti-obscenity laws, while *Vriend* and *M. v. H.* both advanced gay and lesbian rights in new ways. *Vriend* was the first victory for the gay rights movement. It recognized that Charter violations can take the form of "sins of omission" and imposed an intrusive remedy for the violation. *M. v. H.* redefined "spouse" in Canadian law, which affected dozens of statutes at the provincial and federal levels. As the principal source of the harm-based analysis in *Butler*, LEAF can thus claim an important influence on the development of freedom of expression jurisprudence in Canada. While not all the commentators, including some feminists, were pleased with the result in *Butler*, there was general recognition that it changed the terms of debate in this area.

Legal novelty can also account for the high ratio of legal literature to Supreme Court citations in cases such as *Winnipeg Child and Family Services*, *R. v. S.*, *G.(J.)*, and *Gordon*. In *R. v. S.* the Court elaborated on the definition of judicial bias in a manner influenced by LEAF; in *G.(J.)* it established a constitutional right to legal aid in a new context; in *Gordon* it backed off from a recently developed principle governing spousal support. *Winnipeg Child and Family Services* is slightly different because the Court actually rejected a novel

Table 6.3

Citation frequencies for LEAF cases

Case	Supreme Court	Legal literature	Total	Outcome	Issue
O'Connor	29	30	59	Win	Loss
Seaboyer	34	16	50	Win	Loss
Vriend	15	27	42	Win	Win
M. v. H.	10	32	42	Win	Win
Keegstra	23	17	40	Win	Win
Butler	13	24	37	Loss	Win
Eldridge	17	14	31	Win	Win
Moge	11	19	30	Win	Win
Thibaudeau	8	19	27	Loss	Loss
Andrews	19	8	27	Win	Win
WCFS	6	17	23	Win	Win
Schachter	21	1	22	Loss	Loss
Mills	11	9	20	Win	Win
R. v. S.	2	14	16	Win	Win
Ewanchuk	7	8	15	Win	Win
G.(J.)	4	11	15	Win	Win
Brooks	11	2	13	Win	Win
Borowski	7	6	13	Win	Win
M.(K.) v. M.(H.)	8	4	12	Win	Win
Gordon	1	10	11	Loss	Win
Norberg	8	2	10	Win	Win
Weatherall	6	2	8	Win	Win
Daigle	4	4	8	Win	Win
Little Sisters	2	6	8	Win	Loss
Janzen	3	4	7	Win	Win
Taylor	7	0	7	Win	Win
Beharriel	7	0	7	Win	Loss
Blencoe	2	5	7	Win	Win
Sullivan	4	1	5	Win/Loss	Win
Darrach	0	5	5	Win	Win
Canadian Council of Churches	1	3	4	Loss	Loss
Canadian Newspapers	4	0	4	Win	Win
BC (Public Service Employee Relations Commission)	3	0	3	Win	Win
Andrews (90)	0	0	0	Win	Win
M. (M.L.)	0	0	0	Win	Win
Whitley	0	0	0	Win	Win

interpretation of *parens patriae* power. However, the Court's comments about fetal rights, and their implications for reproductive autonomy, captured most commentators' attention.

LEAF's first intervention, *Andrews*, ranks tenth in terms of citations, despite its obvious importance in setting the initial parameters for equality rights adjudication. Surprisingly, the number of citations in the legal literature is relatively small for what might be considered a landmark decision. It has had more influence, however, on the development of section 15 jurisprudence. As Table 6.4 indicates, references to *Andrews* can be found in several other important equality rights cases, including *Vriend, Eldridge, M. v. H., Corbiere, Lovelace, Benner,* and *Law*. While some of these cases also involved LEAF, others did not.

One of the most important cases that cites *Andrews* and several other LEAF cases *(Vriend, Eldridge, Thibaudeau, Brooks)* is *Law* v. *Canada* (1999).[12] At issue in *Law* was a provision of the Canada Pension Plan that excludes able-bodied claimants under the age of thirty-five and without dependent children from survivor's benefits. The appellant, Nancy Law, argued that the provision discriminated on the basis of age. Heard by a seven-justice panel in January 1998, and reheard by a nine-justice panel ten months later, Ms. Law's appeal was dismissed by the Court on 25 March 1999. The Court took the opportunity presented by *Law* to consolidate the various strands of its equality rights jurisprudence in order to provide better guidance to lower courts in evaluating discrimination claims.

Justice Iacobucci's analysis of section 15 began with eight paragraphs "revisiting" *Andrews*. He followed these with nine paragraphs on post-*Andrews* jurisprudence. Combining the *Andrews* approach with these later developments, Iacobucci articulated "three broad inquiries" that courts should undertake in discrimination claims:[13]

First, does the impugned law (a) draw a formal distinction between the claimant and others on the basis of one or more personal characteristics, or (b) fail to take into account the claimant's already disadvantaged position within Canadian society resulting in substantively differential treatment between the claimant and others on the basis of one or more personal characteristics? If so, there is differential treatment for the purpose of s. 15(1). Second, was the claimant subject to differential treatment on the basis of one or more of the enumerated and analogous grounds? And third, does the differential treatment discriminate in a substantive sense, bringing into play the purpose of s. 15(1) of the Charter in remedying such ills as prejudice, stereotyping, and historical disadvantage?

At the heart of these inquiries was the concept of human dignity, which Iacobucci defined in the following way:[14]

Table 6.4

Supreme Court citation of LEAF cases

Case	Year	Supreme Court citations
Canadian Newspapers	1988	• *Hill* v. *Church of Scientology*, [1995] 2 S.C.R. 1130 • *A. (L.L.)* v. *B. (A.)*, [1995] 4 S.C.R. 536 • *R.* v. *Adams*, [1995] 4 S.C.R. 707 • *Canadian Broadcasting Corp.* v. *New Brunswick*, [1996] 3 S.C.R. 480
Andrews	1989	• *Adler* v. *Ontario*, [1996] 3 S.C.R. 609 • *Vriend* v. *Alberta*, [1998] 1 S.C.R. 493 • *R.* v. *Sullivan*, [1991] 1 S.C.R. 489 • *Newfoundland Association of Public Employees* v. *Newfoundland*, [1996] 2 S.C.R. 3 • *Battlefords and District Co-Operative* v. *Gibbs*, [1996] 3 S.C.R. 566 • *Eaton* v. *Brant County Board of Education*, [1997] 1 S.C.R. 241 • *Eldridge* v. *British Columbia*, [1997] 3 S.C.R. 624 • *M.* v. *H.*, [1999] 2 S.C.R. 3 • *Corbiere* v. *Canada*, [1999] 2 S.C.R. 203 • *Winko* v. *British Columbia*, [1999] 2 S.C.R. 625 • *British Columbia (Public Service Employee Relations Commission)* v. *BCGSEU*, [1999] 3 S.C.R. 3 • *New Brunswick (Minister of Health and Community Services)* v. *G.(J.)*, [1999] 3 S.C.R. 46 • *Quebec (Commission des droits de la personne et des droits de la jeunesse)* v. *Montréal (City) Quebec (Commission des droits de la personne et des droits de la jeunesse)* v. *Boisbriand (City)*, [2000] 1 S.C.R. 665 • *Lovelace* v. *Ontario*, [2000] 1 S.C.R. 950 • *Fortin* v. *Chrétien*, [2001] 2 S.C.R. 500 • *Law Society of British Columbia* v. *Mangat*, [2001] 3 S.C.R. 113 • *Granovsky* v. *Canada*, [2000] 1 S.C.R. 703 • *Benner* v. *Canada*, [1997] 1 S.C.R. 358 • *Law* v. *Canada*, [1999] 1 S.C.R. 497
Borowski	1989	• *St. Marys Paper Inc. (Re)*, [1996] 1 S.C.R. 3 • *R.* v. *Adams*, [1995] 4 S.C.R. 707 • *Ontario Home Builders' Association* v. *York Region Board of Education*, [1996] 2 S.C.R. 929 • *M.* v. *H.*, [1999] 2 S.C.R. 3 • *Winko* v. *British Columbia (Forensic Psychiatric Institute)*, [1999] 2 S.C.R. 625 • *Bese* v. *British Columbia (Forensic Psychiatric Institute)*, [1999] 2 S.C.R. 722

▶

168 *Making a Difference*

◄ *Table 6.4*

Case	Year	Supreme Court citations
		• *New Brunswick (Minister of Health and Community Services)* v. *G.(J.)*, [1999] 3 S.C.R. 46
Brooks	1989	• *Battlefords and District Co-operative Ltd.* v. *Gibbs*, [1996] 3 S.C.R. 566 • *Janzen* v. *Platy Enterprises Ltd.*, [1989] 1 S.C.R. 1252 • *R.* v. *Sullivan*, [1991] 1 S.C.R. 489 • *Eldridge* v. *British Columbia (Attorney General)*, [1997] 3 S.C.R. 624 • *Vriend* v. *Alberta*, [1998] 1 S.C.R. 493 • *Law* v. *Canada (Minister of Employment and Immigration)*, [1999] 1 S.C.R. 497 • *M.* v. *H.*, [1999] 2 S.C.R. 3 • *R.* v. *Stone*, [1999] 2 S.C.R. 290 • *Dobson (Litigation Guardian of)* v. *Dobson*, [1999] 2 S.C.R. 753 • *Quebec (Commission des droits de la personne et des droits de la jeunesse)* v. *Montréal (City) Quebec (Commission des droits de la personne et des droits de la jeunesse)* v. *Boisbriand (City)*, [2000] 1 S.C.R. 665 • *Lovelace* v. *Ontario*, [2000] 1 S.C.R. 950
Daigle	1989	• *Winnipeg Child and Family Services (Northwest Area)* v. *G. (D.F.)*, [1997] 3 S.C.R. 925 • *Dobson (Litigation Guardian of)* v. *Dobson*, [1999] 2 S.C.R. 753 • *R.* v. *Sullivan*, [1991] 1 S.C.R. 489 • *Vriend* v. *Alberta*, [1998] 1 S.C.R. 493
Janzen	1989	• *Battlefords and District Co-operative Ltd.* v. *Gibbs*, [1996] 3 S.C.R. 566 • *R.* v. *R.A.R.*, [2000], 1 S.C.R. 163 • *Quebec (Commission des droits de la personne et des droits de la jeunesse)* v. *Montréal (City) Quebec (Commission des droits de la personne et des droits de la jeunesse)* v. *Boisbriand (City)*, [2000] 1 S.C.R. 665
Andrews (90)	1990	
Keegstra	1990	• *RJR-MacDonald Inc.* v. *Canada (Attorney General)*, [1995] 3 S.C.R. 199 • *R.* v. *Keegstra*, [1996] 1 S.C.R. 458 • *Thomson Newspapers Co.* v. *Canada (Attorney General)*, [1998] 1 S.C.R. 877

►

◄ *Table 6.4*

Case	Year	Supreme Court citations
		• *R. v. Chartrand*, [1994] 2 S.C.R. 864
		• *Hill* v. *Church of Scientology of Toronto*, [1995] 2 S.C.R. 1130
		• *Ross* v. *New Brunswick School District No. 15*, [1996] 1 S.C.R. 825
		• *R. v. Van der Peet*, [1996] 2 S.C.R. 507
		• *Harvey* v. *New Brunswick (Attorney General)*, [1996] 2 S.C.R. 876
		• *Canadian Broadcasting Corp.* v. *New Brunswick (Attorney General)*, [1996] 3 S.C.R. 480
		• *Eldridge* v. *British Columbia (Attorney General)*, [1997] 3 S.C.R. 624
		• *R. v. Lucas*, [1998] 1 S.C.R. 439
		• *Vriend* v. *Alberta*, [1998] 1 S.C.R. 493
		• *Aubry* v. *Éditions Vice-Versa Inc.*, [1998] 1 S.C.R. 591
		• *Canada (Human Rights Commission)* v. *Canadian Liberty Net*, [1998] 1 S.C.R. 626
		• *R. v. Ewanchuk*, [1999] 1 S.C.R. 330
		• *M. v. H.*, [1999] 2 S.C.R. 3
		• *Baker* v. *Canada (Minister of Citizenship and Immigration)*, [1999] 2 S.C.R. 817
		• *Delisle* v. *Canada (Deputy Attorney General)*, [1999] 2 S.C.R. 989
		• *U.F.C.W., Local 1518,* v. *KMart Canada Ltd.*, [1999] 2 S.C.R. 1083
		• *R. v. Mills*, [1999] 3 S.C.R. 668
		• *Little Sisters Book and Art Emporium* v. *Canada (Minister of Justice)*, [2000] 2 S.C.R. 1120
		• *R. v. Sharpe*, [2001] 1 S.C.R. 45
		• *United States* v. *Burns*, [2001] 1 S.C.R. 283
Taylor	1990	• *Canada (Human Rights Commission)* v. *Canadian Liberty Net*, [1998] 1 S.C.R. 626
		• *R. v. Sharpe*, [2001] 1 S.C.R. 45
		• *R. v. Litchfield*, [1993] 4 S.C.R. 333
		• *Ross* v. *New Brunswick School District No. 15*, [1996] 1 S.C.R. 825
		• *Cooper* v. *Canada (Human Rights Commission)*, [1996] 3 S.C.R. 854
		• *Blencoe* v. *British Columbia (Human Rights Commission)*, [2000] 2 S.C.R. 307
		• *Little Sisters Book and Art Emporium* v. *Canada (Minister of Justice)*, [2000] 2 S.C.R. 1120
Seaboyer	1991	• *R. v. O'Connor*, [1995] 4 S.C.R. 411

►

◄ *Table 6.4*

Case	Year	Supreme Court citations
		• *R. v. G.(S.G.)*, [1997] 2 S.C.R. 716 • *R. v. Starr*, [2000] 2 S.C.R. 144 • *R. v. Marquard*, [1993] 4 S.C.R. 223 • *R. v. Arcangioli*, [1994] 1 S.C.R. 129 • *R. v. Crosby*, [1995] 2 S.C.R. 912 • *R. v. Harrer*, [1995] 3 S.C.R. 562 • *A. (L.L.)* v. *B. (A.)*, [1995] 4 S.C.R. 536 • *Mooring* v. *Canada (National Parole Board)*, [1996] 1 S.C.R. 75 • *R. v. R.(D.)*, [1996] 2 S.C.R. 291 • *Michaud* v. *Quebec (Attorney General)*, [1996] 3 S.C.R. 3 • *R. v. Hawkins*, [1996] 3 S.C.R. 1043 • *R. v. Carosella*, [1997] 1 S.C.R. 80 • *R. v. Leipert*, [1997] 1 S.C.R. 281 • *Canada (Minister of Citizenship and Immigration)* v. *Tobiass*, [1997] 3 S.C.R. 391 • *R. v. Cuerrier*, [1998] 2 S.C.R. 371 • *R. v. Hodgson*, [1998] 2 S.C.R. 449 • *R. v. Rose*, [1998] 3 S.C.R. 262 • *R. v. Ewanchuk*, [1999] 1 S.C.R. 330 • *Smith* v. *Jones*, [1999] 1 S.C.R. 455 • *R. v. Campbell*, [1999] 1 S.C.R. 565 • *R. v. Stone*, [1999] 2 S.C.R. 290 • *R. v. White*, [1999] 2 S.C.R. 417 • *R. v. W.(G.)*, [1999] 3 S.C.R. 597 • *R. v. Mills*, [1999] 3 S.C.R. 668 • *R. v. A.G.*, [2000] 1 S.C.R. 439 • *Non-Marine Underwriters, Lloyd's of London* v. *Scalera*, [2000] 1 S.C.R. 551 • *R. v. Darrach*, [2000] 2 S.C.R. 443 • *R. v. J.-L.J.*, [2000] 2 S.C.R. 600 • *R. v. Sharpe*, [2001] 1 S.C.R. 45 • *R. v. McClure*, [2001] 1 S.C.R. 445 • *R. v. Ruzic*, [2001] 1 S.C.R. 687 • *R. v. Find*, [2001] 1 S.C.R. 863 • *R. v. Pan R.* v. *Sawyer*, [2001] 2 S.C.R. 344
Sullivan	1991	• *R. v. Hanes*, [1995] 4 S.C.R. 597 • *Finlay* v. *Canada (Minister of Finance)*, [1993] 1 S.C.R. 1080 • *Winnipeg Child and Family Services (Northwest Area)* v. *G. (D.F.)*, [1997] 3 S.C.R. 925 • *Dobson (Litigation Guardian of)* v. *Dobson*, [1999] 2 S.C.R. 753

►

◄ *Table 6.4*

Case	Year	Supreme Court citations
Butler	1992	• *R.* v. *Tremblay,* [1993] 2 S.C.R. 932 • *RJR-MacDonald Inc.* v. *Canada (Attorney General)*, [1995] 3 S.C.R. 199 • *Thomson Newspapers Co.* v. *Canada (Attorney General)*, [1998] 1 S.C.R. 877 • *M.* v. *H.,* [1999] 2 S.C.R. 3 • *Little Sisters Book and Art Emporium* v. *Canada (Minister of Justice)*, [2000] 2 S.C.R. 1120 • *R.* v. *Sharpe,* [2001] 1 S.C.R. 45 • *Hill* v. *Church of Scientology of Toronto,* [1995] 2 S.C.R. 1130 • *R.* v. *Jorgensen,* [1995] 4 S.C.R. 55 • *Ross* v. *New Brunswick School District No. 15,* [1996] 1 S.C.R. 825 • *R.* v. *Gladstone,* [1996] 2 S.C.R. 723 • *R.* v. *Mara,* [1997] 2 S.C.R. 630 • *Libman* v. *Quebec (Attorney General)*, [1997] 3 S.C.R. 569 • *Aubry* v. *Éditions Vice-Versa Inc.*, [1998] 1 S.C.R. 591
Canadian Council of Churches	1992	• *Vriend* v. *Alberta,* [1998] 1 S.C.R. 493
M.(K.) v. *M.(H.)*	1992	• *Non-Marine Underwriters, Lloyd's of London* v. *Scalera,* [2000] 1 S.C.R. 551 • *Murphy* v. *Welsh Stoddard* v. *Watson,* [1993] 2 S.C.R. 1069 • *Hodgkinson* v. *Simms,* [1994] 3 S.C.R. 377 • *Blueberry River Indian Band* v. *Canada (Department of Indian Affairs and Northern Development)*, [1995] 4 S.C.R. 344 • *Peixeiro* v. *Haberman,* [1997] 3 S.C.R. 549 • *Cadbury Schweppes Inc.* v. *FBI Foods Ltd.*, [1999] 1 S.C.R. 142 • *Novak* v. *Bond,* [1999] 1 S.C.R. 808 • *R.* v. *Sharpe,* [2001] 1 S.C.R. 45
Moge	1992	• *M.* v. *H.,* [1999] 2 S.C.R. 3 • *Peter* v. *Beblow,* [1993] 1 S.C.R. 980 • *Marzetti* v. *Marzetti,* [1994] 2 S.C.R. 765 • *Tataryn* v. *Tataryn Estate,* [1994] 2 S.C.R. 807 • *G.(L.)* v. *B.(G.)*, [1995] 3 S.C.R. 370 • *R.* v. *S. (R.D.)*, [1997] 3 S.C.R. 484 • *Bracklow* v. *Bracklow,* [1999] 1 S.C.R. 420

►

◄ *Table 6.4*

Case	Year	Supreme Court citations
		• *Law* v. *Canada (Minister of Employment and Immigration)*, [1999] 1 S.C.R. 497 • *Hickey* v. *Hickey*, [1999] 2 S.C.R. 518 • *New Brunswick (Minister of Health and Community Services)* v. *G.(J.)*, [1999] 3 S.C.R. 46 • *Boston* v. *Boston*, [2001] 2 S.C.R. 413
Norberg	1992	• *Hall* v. *Hebert*, [1993] 2 S.C.R. 159 • *Non-Marine Underwriters, Lloyd's of London* v. *Scalera*, [2000] 1 S.C.R. 551 • *R.* v. *Litchfield*, [1993] 4 S.C.R. 333 • *Hodgkinson* v. *Simms*, [1994] 3 S.C.R. 377 • *Blueberry River Indian Band* v. *Canada (Department of Indian Affairs and Northern Development)*, [1995] 4 S.C.R. 344 • *R.* v. *Audet*, [1996] 2 S.C.R. 171 • *Arndt* v. *Smith*, [1997] 2 S.C.R. 539 • *R.* v. *Cuerrier*, [1998] 2 S.C.R. 371
Schachter	1992	• *R.* v. *Nikal*, [1996] 1 S.C.R. 1013 • *Vriend* v. *Alberta*, [1998] 1 S.C.R. 493 • *Corbiere* v. *Canada (Minister of Indian and Northern Affairs)*, [1999] 2 S.C.R. 203 • *Winnipeg Child and Family Services* v. *K.L.W.*, [2000] 2 S.C.R. 519 • *Harvey* v. *New Brunswick (Attorney General)*, [1996] 2 S.C.R. 876 • *Michaud* v. *Quebec (Attorney General)*, [1996] 3 S.C.R. 3 • *R.* v. *Adams*, [1996] 3 S.C.R. 101 • *Guimond* v. *Quebec (Attorney General)*, [1996] 3 S.C.R. 347 • *Adler* v. *Ontario*, [1996] 3 S.C.R. 609 • *Benner* v. *Canada (Secretary of State)*, [1997] 1 S.C.R. 358 • *Ref re Remuneration of Judges of the Prov. Court of P.E.I. Ref re Independence and Impartiality of Judges of the Prov. Court of P.E.I.*, [1997] 3 S.C.R. 3 • *Libman* v. *Quebec (Attorney General)*, [1997] 3 S.C.R. 569 • *Eldridge* v. *British Columbia (Attorney General)*, [1997] 3 S.C.R. 624 • *R.* v. *Lucas*, [1998] 1 S.C.R. 439 • *R.* v. *Cuerrier*, [1998] 2 S.C.R. 371 • *M.* v. *H.*, [1999] 2 S.C.R. 3 • *Delisle* v. *Canada (Deputy Attorney General)*, [1999] 2 S.C.R. 989 • *U.F.C.W., Local 1518*, v. *KMart Canada Ltd.*, [1999] 2 S.C.R. 1083

►

◄ *Table 6.4*

Case	Year	Supreme Court citations
		• *Blencoe* v. *British Columbia (Human Rights Commission)*, [2000] 2 S.C.R. 307
		• *Little Sisters Book and Art Emporium* v. *Canada (Minister of Justice)*, [2000] 2 S.C.R. 1120
		• *R.* v. *Sharpe*, [2001] 1 S.C.R. 45
Weatherall	1993	• *Mooring* v. *Canada (National Parole Board)*, [1996] 1 S.C.R. 75
		• *Benner* v. *Canada (Secretary of State)*, [1997] 1 S.C.R. 358
		• *Law* v. *Canada (Minister of Employment and Immigration)*, [1999] 1 S.C.R. 497
		• *R.* v. *Stone*, [1999] 2 S.C.R. 290
		• *Lovelace* v. *Ontario*, [2000] 1 S.C.R. 950
		• *Miron* v. *Trudel*, [1995] 2 S.C.R. 418
M. (M.L.)	1994	
Whitley	1994	
Beharriel	1995	• *R.* v. *O'Connor*, [1995] 4 S.C.R. 411
		• *M.(A.)* v. *Ryan*, [1997] 1 S.C.R. 157
		• *R.* v. *Leipert*, [1997] 1 S.C.R. 281
		• *Smith* v. *Jones*, [1999] 1 S.C.R. 455
		• *R.* v. *Campbell*, [1999] 1 S.C.R. 565
		• *R.* v. *Mills*, [1999] 3 S.C.R. 668
		• *Therrien (Re)*, [2001] 2 S.C.R. 3
O'Connor	1995	• *R.* v. *Wickstead*, [1997] 1 S.C.R. 307
		• *A. (L.L.)* v. *B. (A.)*, [1995] 4 S.C.R. 536
		• *R.* v. *Carosella*, [1997] 1 S.C.R. 80
		• *M.(A.)* v. *Ryan*, [1997] 1 S.C.R. 157
		• *R.* v. *La*, [1997] 2 S.C.R. 680
		• *R.* v. *Mills*, [1999] 3 S.C.R. 668
		• *Blencoe* v. *British Columbia (Human Rights Commission)*, [2000] 2 S.C.R. 307
		• *R.* v. *Hinse*, [1995] 4 S.C.R. 597
		• *R.* v. *Robinson*, [1996] 1 S.C.R. 683
		• *R.* v. *Sarson*, [1996] 2 S.C.R. 223
		• *Michaud* v. *Quebec (Attorney General)*, [1996] 3 S.C.R. 3
		• *Canadian Broadcasting Corp.* v. *New Brunswick (Attorney General)*, [1996] 3 S.C.R. 480
		• *R.* v. *Leipert*, [1997] 1 S.C.R. 281
		• *R.* v. *Curragh Inc.*, [1997] 1 S.C.R. 537
		• *R.* v. *Cook*, [1997] 1 S.C.R. 1113
		• *United States of America* v. *Dynar*, [1997] 2 S.C.R. 462

►

◄ *Table 6.4*

Case	Year	Supreme Court citations
		• *Canada (Minister of Citizenship and Immigration)* v. *Tobiass*, [1997] 3 S.C.R. 391 • *Schreiber* v. *Canada (Attorney General)*, [1998] 1 S.C.R. 841 • *R.* v. *Thomas*, [1998] 3 S.C.R. 535 • *R.* v. *Pearson*, [1998] 3 S.C.R. 620 • *R.* v. *Campbell*, [1999] 1 S.C.R. 565 • *R.* v. *Biniaris*, [2000] 1 S.C.R. 381 • *R.* v. *Jolivet*, [2000] 1 S.C.R. 751 • *R.* v. *Darrach*, [2000] 2 S.C.R. 443 • *Winnipeg Child and Family Services* v. *K.L.W.*, [2000] 2 S.C.R. 519 • *R.* v. *McClure*, [2001] 1 S.C.R. 445 • *United States of America* v. *Cobb*, [2001] 1 S.C.R. 587 • *R.* v. *Find*, [2001] 1 S.C.R. 863 • *R.* v. *Pan R.* v. *Sawyer*, [2001] 2 S.C.R. 344
Thibaudeau	1995	• *M.* v. *H.*, [1999] 2 S.C.R. 3 • *Schwartz* v. *Canada*, [1996] 1 S.C.R. 254 • *Benner* v. *Canada (Secretary of State)*, [1997] 1 S.C.R. 358 • *Eldridge* v. *British Columbia (Attorney General)*, [1997] 3 S.C.R. 624 • *Vriend* v. *Alberta*, [1998] 1 S.C.R. 493 • *Law* v. *Canada (Minister of Employment and Immigration)*, [1999] 1 S.C.R. 497 • *Quebec (Commission des droits de la personne et des droits de la jeunesse)* v. *Montréal (City) Quebec (Commission des droits de la personne et des droits de la jeunesse)* v. *Boisbriand (City)*, [2000] 1 S.C.R. 665 • *Will-Kare Paving & Contracting Ltd.* v. *Canada*, [2000] 1 S.C.R. 915
Gordon	1996	• *W.(V.)* v. *S.(D.)*, [1996] 2 S.C.R. 108
Eldridge	1997	• *M.* v. *H.*, [1999] 2 S.C.R. 3 • *Vriend* v. *Alberta*, [1998] 1 S.C.R. 493 • *Canadian Egg Marketing Agency* v. *Richardson*, [1998] 3 S.C.R. 157 • *R.* v. *M.(M.R.)*, [1998] 3 S.C.R. 393 • *Law* v. *Canada (Minister of Employment and Immigration)*, [1999] 1 S.C.R. 497 • *R.* v. *Beaulac*, [1999] 1 S.C.R. 768 • *Corbiere* v. *Canada (Minister of Indian and Northern Affairs)*, [1999] 2 S.C.R. 203

►

◀ *Table 6.4*

Case	Year	Supreme Court citations
		• *Winko* v. *British Columbia (Forensic Psychiatric Institute),* [1999] 2 S.C.R. 625
		• *Delisle* v. *Canada (Deputy Attorney General),* [1999] 2 S.C.R. 989
		• *U.F.C.W., Local 1518,* v. *KMart Canada Ltd.,* [1999] 2 S.C.R. 1083
		• *New Brunswick (Minister of Health and Community Services)* v. *G.(J.),* [1999] 3 S.C.R. 46
		• *British Columbia (Superintendent of Motor Vehicles)* v. *British Columbia (Council of Human Rights),* [1999] 3 S.C.R. 868
		• *Quebec (Commission des droits de la personne et des droits de la jeunesse)* v. *Montréal (City) Quebec (Commission des droits de la personne et des droits de la jeunesse)* v. *Boisbriand (City),* [2000] 1 S.C.R. 665
		• *Granovsky* v. *Canada (Minister of Employment and Immigration),* [2000] 1 S.C.R. 703
		• *Lovelace* v. *Ontario,* [2000] 1 S.C.R. 950
		• *Blencoe* v. *British Columbia (Human Rights Commission),* [2000] 2 S.C.R. 307
		• *Little Sisters Book and Art Emporium* v. *Canada (Minister of Justice),* [2000] 2 S.C.R. 1120
R. v. S.	1997	• *Arsenault-Cameron* v. *Prince Edward Island,* [1999] 3 S.C.R. 851
		• *R.* v. *A.G.,* [2000] 1 S.C.R. 439
Winnipeg Child and Family Services	1997	• *Dobson (Litigation Guardian of)* v. *Dobson,* [1999] 2 S.C.R. 753
		• *Winnipeg Child and Family Services* v. *K.L.W.,* [2000] 2 S.C.R. 519
		• *Porto Seguro Companhia De Seguros Gerais* v. *Belcan S.A.,* [1997] 3 S.C.R. 1278
		• *R.* v. *Cuerrier,* [1998] 2 S.C.R. 371
		• *R.* v. *Hodgson,* [1998] 2 S.C.R. 449
		• *M.* v. *H.,* [1999] 2 S.C.R. 3
Vriend	1998	• *M.* v. *H.,* [1999] 2 S.C.R. 3
		• *Little Sisters Book and Art Emporium* v. *Canada (Minister of Justice),* [2000] 2 S.C.R. 1120
		• *Thomson Newspapers Co.* v. *Canada (Attorney General),* [1998] 1 S.C.R. 877
		• *Law* v. *Canada (Minister of Employment and Immigration),* [1999] 1 S.C.R. 497

▶

◄ *Table 6.4*

Case	Year	Supreme Court citations
		• *Corbiere* v. *Canada (Minister of Indian and Northern Affairs)*, [1999] 2 S.C.R. 203 • *Winko* v. *British Columbia (Forensic Psychiatric Institute)*, [1999] 2 S.C.R. 625 • *Delisle* v. *Canada (Deputy Attorney General)*, [1999] 2 S.C.R. 989 • *U.F.C.W., Local 1518*, v. *KMart Canada Ltd.*, [1999] 2 S.C.R. 1083 • *R.* v. *Mills*, [1999] 3 S.C.R. 668 • *Quebec (Commission des droits de la personne et des droits de la jeunesse)* v. *Montréal (City) Quebec (Commission des droits de la personne et des droits de la jeunesse)* v. *Boisbriand (City)*, [2000] 1 S.C.R. 665 • *Granovsky* v. *Canada (Minister of Employment and Immigration)*, [2000] 1 S.C.R. 703 • *Lovelace* v. *Ontario*, [2000] 1 S.C.R. 950 • *R.* v. *Sharpe*, [2001] 1 S.C.R. 45 • *R.* v. *Ruzic*, [2001] 1 S.C.R. 687 • *Trinity Western University* v. *British Columbia College of Teachers*, [2001] 1 S.C.R. 772
BC (Public Service Employee Relations Commission)	1999	• *Quebec (Commission des droits de la personne et des droits de la jeunesse)* v. *Montréal (City) Quebec (Commission des droits de la personne et des droits de la jeunesse)* v. *Boisbriand (City)*, [2000] 1 S.C.R. 665 • *Granovsky* v. *Canada (Minister of Employment and Immigration)*, [2000] 1 S.C.R. 703 • *McKinley* v. *BC Tel*, [2001] 2 S.C.R. 161
Ewanchuk	1999	• *R.* v. *W.(G.)*, [1999] 3 S.C.R. 597 • *R.* v. *Davis*, [1999] 3 S.C.R. 759 • *R.* v. *R.A.R.*, [2000] 1 S.C.R. 163 • *R.* v. *A.G.*, [2000] 1 S.C.R. 439 • *R.* v. *Darrach*, [2000] 2 S.C.R. 443 • *R.* v. *Araujo*, [2000] 2 S.C.R. 992 • *R.* v. *Find*, [2001] 1 S.C.R. 863
NB (Minister of Health and Community Services) v. G.(J.)	1999	• *R.* v. *Mills*, [1999] 3 S.C.R. 668 • *Winnipeg Child and Family Services* v. *K.L.W.*, [2000] 2 S.C.R. 519 • *Blencoe* v. *British Columbia (Human Rights Commission)*, [2000] 2 S.C.R. 307 • *R.* v. *Ruzic*, [2001] 1 S.C.R. 687

►

◄ *Table 6.4*

Case	Year	Supreme Court citations
M. v. H.	1999	• *Little Sisters Book and Art Emporium* v. *Canada (Minister of Justice)*, [2000] 2 S.C.R. 1120 • *R.* v. *Sharpe*, [2001] 1 S.C.R. 45 • *Trinity Western University* v. *British Columbia College of Teachers*, [2001] 1 S.C.R. 772 • *Corbiere* v. *Canada (Minister of Indian and Northern Affairs)*, [1999] 2 S.C.R. 203 • *Winko* v. *British Columbia (Forensic Psychiatric Institute)*, [1999] 2 S.C.R. 625 • *Delisle* v. *Canada (Deputy Attorney General)*, [1999] 2 S.C.R. 989 • *R.* v. *Marshall*, [1999] 3 S.C.R. 533 • *R.* v. *Mills*, [1999] 3 S.C.R. 668 • *Lovelace* v. *Ontario*, [2000] 1 S.C.R. 950 • *Ocean Port Hotel Ltd.* v. *British Columbia (General Manager, Liquor Control and Licensing Branch)*, [2001] 2 S.C.R. 781
Mills	1999	• *Non-Marine Underwriters, Lloyd's of London* v. *Scalera*, [2000] 1 S.C.R. 551 • *R.* v. *Oickle*, [2000] 2 S.C.R. 3 • *R.* v. *Starr*, [2000] 2 S.C.R. 144 • *Blencoe* v. *British Columbia (Human Rights Commission)*, [2000] 2 S.C.R. 307 • *R.* v. *Darrach*, [2000] 2 S.C.R. 443 • *Winnipeg Child and Family Services* v. *K.L.W.*, [2000] 2 S.C.R. 519 • *Little Sisters Book and Art Emporium* v. *Canada (Minister of Justice)*, [2000] 2 S.C.R. 1120 • *R.* v. *Sharpe*, [2001] 1 S.C.R. 45 • *R.* v. *McClure*, [2001] 1 S.C.R. 445 • *United States of America* v. *Kwok*, [2001] 1 S.C.R. 532 • *R.* v. *Ruzic*, [2001] 1 S.C.R. 687
Blencoe	2000	• *Winnipeg Child and Family Services* v. *K.L.W.*, [2000] 2 S.C.R. 519 • *United States of America* v. *Cobb*, [2001] 1 S.C.R. 587
Darrach	2000	
Little Sisters	2000	• *R.* v. *Sharpe*, [2001] 1 S.C.R. 45 • *Trinity Western University* v. *British Columbia College of Teachers*, [2001] 1 S.C.R. 772

Human dignity means that an individual or group feels self-respect and self-worth. It is concerned with physical and psychological integrity and empowerment ... Human dignity is harmed when individuals and groups are marginalized, ignored, or devalued, and is enhanced when laws recognize the full place of all individuals and groups within Canadian society.

The emphasis on human dignity as defined in this way reflected the influence of Justice L'Heureux-Dubé's separate judgments in *Thibaudeau, Egan,* and *Vriend,* two of which came in LEAF cases and reflected LEAF's own equality analysis. In these judgments, status and recognition became more important than tangible material disadvantage in determining discrimination. In fact, Iacobucci's judgment contains ten separate references to L'Heureux-Dubé, and unlike for other equality rights cases she did not write a separate judgment in *Law.*

LEAF's opportunity to introduce new types of evidence and arguments concerning a wide range of issues never before dealt with by the Court, as well as the "percolation" of that evidence and those arguments through citations in subsequent decisions and the legal literature, represents an important accomplishment of legal mobilization. In some sense, LEAF's interventions have affected the legal culture in which Charter litigation is embedded. While this might not always translate into obvious doctrinal or policy change, it must nevertheless be seen as a positive consequence by the movement.

Consequences:
Rule Changes, Movement Dynamics, and Social Conditions

In this section, I trace through various consequences of the cases in which LEAF intervened in four key issue areas: abortion, violence, family policy, and sexual orientation. The focus of this analysis is on how rules changed through litigation, how legal mobilization affected LEAF and the women's movement more generally, and how social conditions varied in the aftermath of legal mobilization.

Abortion

In 1988, without LEAF's participation, the Supreme Court of Canada removed national-level rules governing access to legal abortions. As Flanagan argues, the judicial nullification of section 251 of the Criminal Code created a new policy status quo, favourable to feminist interests, which LEAF was in a position to defend.[15] The likely necessity of defensive action was the result of three factors. First, the Court did not declare a constitutional right to abortion, which left the future development of access rules squarely in the hands of legislatures. Second, the *Morgentaler 2* Court expressly invited Parliament to make another attempt at abortion regulation in light of its judgment. Finally, pro-choice advocates faced an active pro-life counter movement, symbolized by Joe Borowski, which actually predated the 1988 judgment. The existence of this counter movement, in combination with the Court's reluctance to declare a constitutional right to abortion and its invitation to enact new federal legislation, placed the post-1988 status quo at risk. Although *Morgentaler 2* did not create the pro-life movement, as some would argue *Roe* v. *Wade* did in the United States,[16] the judgment gave that counter movement a new urgency. It worked legislatively at both the federal and provincial levels, and intervened in relevant litigation.

For LEAF, therefore, post-1988 legal mobilization in the abortion field consisted of opposition to proposed legal rules that would have changed the status of fetuses in a manner threatening to abortion access. It mobilized in *Borowski* to block the establishment of a constitutionally entrenched right to fetal life, and in *Daigle* to oppose civil and common law rules giving fathers input into the abortion decision. In *Winnipeg Child and Family Services*, LEAF mobilized against a common law *(parens patriae)* rule allowing state interference with maternal liberty in the name of fetal interests, and in *Sullivan* it fought the interpretation of a criminal law rule that would extend personhood to fetuses. In sum, although feminist legal mobilization itself was not directly responsible for changing the legal framework governing abortion policy, it played a role in preserving the post-1988 status quo. At the level of legal rules, the cases in which LEAF participated achieved the feminist movement's objective of protecting the gain represented by *Morgentaler 2*.

But did the post-1988 legal framework, which LEAF mobilized to preserve, have its intended policy impact? Policy impact was certainly at the heart of the Supreme Court's nullification of the Criminal Code's abortion provisions in *Morgentaler 2*. Indeed, the Court relied extensively on the *Report of the Committee on the Operation of the Abortion Law* (the Badgley Report)[17] in determining whether the structure and decision-making criteria of section 251 of the Criminal Code violated the security of the person of women in a manner contrary to the principles of fundamental justice. Among the committee's several findings, the Court found two especially relevant to its evaluation of section 251 under section 7 of the Charter. One finding was that, under the existing therapeutic abortion regulations, there was an average interval of eight weeks between a woman's first medical consultation and the performance of an induced abortion. Since women waited on average about three weeks after the first indications of pregnancy before consulting a physician, therapeutic abortions were most often performed between the ninth and twelfth weeks of gestation.[18] What caught the Supreme Court's attention was the relationship between these delays and the complication rates of therapeutic abortions. According to data compiled in the Badgley Report, abortions performed between eight and twelve weeks of pregnancy were almost one and a half times more dangerous for women than those performed at less than nine weeks of gestation. This risk factor increased dramatically after the thirteenth week of pregnancy, with abortions performed between thirteen and sixteen weeks almost six times more dangerous than those performed at less than nine weeks.[19] In the view of the majority, therefore, the decision-making delays attributable to section 251 posed a real risk to the physical health of women seeking therapeutic abortions. This led the Court to find an infringement of security of the person.

The second important finding of the Badgley Report on which the Court relied concerned the committee's investigation of the impact of provincial requirements and hospital practices on the distribution and availability of therapeutic abortions. The committee found that 271 hospitals in Canada had established therapeutic abortion committees by 1976. This represented only one-fifth of all hospitals, and less than half of all the hospitals that met the basic provincial standards necessary for establishing a committee. As a result, according to the report, 45 percent of the Canadian population was not served by hospitals with therapeutic abortion committees. Moreover, access to "committee hospitals" varied among provinces and regions. In Newfoundland, for example, only 23 percent of the population was served by a committee hospital. By contrast, fully 65 percent of the Ontario population had access to such hospitals. Similarly, the ratio of women between fifteen and forty-four years of age to committee hospitals in Quebec was four times higher than the national ratio.[20] Little wonder, then, that Chapter 6 of the Badgley Report provided Chief Justice Dickson with his principal conclusion that "the procedure provided in the Criminal Code for obtaining therapeutic abortion is in practice illusory for many Canadian women."[21]

As Figure 6.1 and Tables 6.5, 6.6, and 6.7 show, the data available from Statistics Canada on therapeutic abortions suggest that this changed in the post-1988 policy world. Although the total number and rate of therapeutic abortions per thousand women aged between fifteen and forty-four years increased by 5.0 and 2.7 percent respectively from 1985 to 1988, there was a significant increase in both measures after 1988. Between 1988 and 1989, the number of abortions increased by 9.1 percent (from 72,693 to 79,315), while the rate per thousand women increased by 8.6 percent (from 11.6 to 12.6). In the first full year of decriminalization (1989-90), the number of abortions increased by 17.1 percent (from 79,315 to 92,901), and the rate per thousand women increased by 15.9 percent (12.6 to 14.6). Indeed, from 1988 to 1998, which covers the entire period of LEAF's Supreme Court activity in this policy field, the number of therapeutic abortions increased by 52.0 percent (72,693 to 110,520), and the rate per thousand women increased by 35.3 percent (11.6 to 15.7).

Figure 6.1

Therapeutic abortions, 1978-98

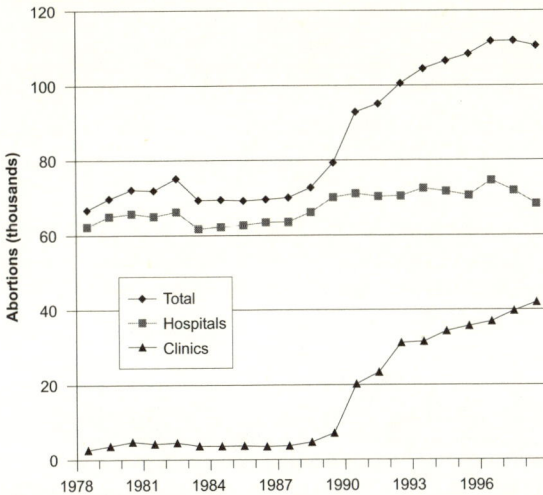

The growth in the number of abortions is primarily a function of an increase in the number of abortions performed in clinics rather than hospitals, a development directly traceable to *Morgentaler 2*. Prior to 1988, abortion clinics operated only in Quebec, but within six years of the decision, every jurisdiction except Prince Edward Island, Saskatchewan, and the two territories had private abortion clinics. While the number of abortions performed in hospitals increased by only 387 from 1989 to 1990, the number performed in clinics increased by 13,177. Indeed, the number of abortions performed in hospitals was actually less in 1995 (70,549) than in 1989 (70,705), while the number performed in clinics increased by 405 percent. Between 1978 and 1989, clinics performed only 5.8 percent of all abortions, but between 1990 and 1995 they accounted for 35.4 percent.

In this sense the removal of a legal rule – that therapeutic abortions must be performed in accredited hospitals – affected access by legitimating a new venue for the procedure. The rate of legal abortions per thousand women across the provinces to some degree confirms this conclusion. In 1999, the two provinces without private clinics, Prince Edward Island and Saskatchewan, ranked ninth (4.8) and sixth (8.7) respectively.[22] Quebec, which has the longest tradition of private clinics, ranked first (18.9) in this category. Among the other provinces, all of which have private clinics, the rate varied from 6.1 in New Brunswick to 16.2 in British Columbia. In other words, it is not entirely clear whether decriminalization and greater access to private clinics solved the second problem identified by the Court in 1988 – unequal access across provinces. In retrospect, a simple change in legal

Table 6.5

Therapeutic abortions among Canadian women, 1978-98

Year	Total abortions*	Hospitals	Clinics	Rate per 1,000 women
1978	66,710	62,290	2,618	
1979	69,745	65,043	3,629	
1980	72,099	65,751	4,704	
1981	71,911	65,053	4,207	
1982	75,071	66,254	4,506	
1983	69,368	61,750	3,635	
1984	69,449	62,247	3,571	
1985	69,216	62,712	3,706	11.3
1986	69,572	63,462	3,498	11.2
1987	70,023	63,585	3,681	11.3
1988	72,693	66,137	4,617	11.6
1989	79,315	70,705	7,059	12.6
1990	92,901	71,092	20,236	14.6
1991	95,059	70,277	23,343	14.7
1992	100,497	70,408	31,151	14.9
1993	104,400	72,434	31,508	15.0
1994	106,517	71,630	34,287	15.3
1995	108,329	70,549	35,650	15.5
1996	111,757	74,579	36,877	15.9
1997	111,819	71,845	39,681	15.9
1998	110,520	68,290	41,933	15.7

* The total number of abortions also includes abortions performed in selected US states (Canadian women visiting the states along the Canada-US border). It thus exceeds the combined total of abortions performed in Canadian hospitals and clinics.
Sources: 1978-92, Statistics Canada, "Therapeutic Abortions, 1992," Cat. No. 82-219; 1993, Statistics Canada Yearbook 1997; 1994-98, Statistics Canada Website

Table 6.6

Abortion rates per 100 live births (selected years, by province)

Jurisdiction	1990	1994	1995
Canada	17.5	18.6	18.7
Newfoundland	6.1	7.6	9.0
Prince Edward Island	2.5	0.4	0.5
Nova Scotia	14.5	16.4	16.8
New Brunswick	5.5	6.9	7.3
Quebec	14.7	19.3	20.8
Ontario	20.7	20.2	19.9
Manitoba	14.6	17.3	17.6
Saskatchewan	8.3	12.4	13.6
Alberta	15.4	16.9	17.0
British Columbia	25.2	20.7	18.3

Source: Statistics Canada, *The Daily*, 5 November 1997.

Table 6.7

Abortion rates per 1,000 women (15-44), 1998-99 (by province)

Province	1998	1999
Newfoundland	6.3	6.7
Prince Edward Island	4.9	4.8
Nova Scotia	9.7	9.1
New Brunswick	6.5	6.1
Quebec	19.4	18.9
Manitoba	14.0	14.3
Saskatchewan	9.1	8.7
Alberta	15.1	14.7
British Columbia	17.1	16.2

Note: Ontario is excluded because of incomplete reporting by the province for 1999.
Source: Statistics Canada, *The Daily*, 18 January 2002.

rules should not have been expected to resolve this issue. As the Badgley Report itself noted, it was not the law itself that produced operational disparities in obtaining therapeutic abortions but rather "the Canadian people, their health institutions and the medical profession."[23] These factors were evident in the diverse provincial response to *Morgentaler 2*, which ranged from restrictions on abortion clinics and the establishment of low fees to discourage physicians from performing the procedure (especially in Alberta) to Ontario's almost immediate decision to pay for abortions performed in private clinics. Although LEAF prevented two *nonlegislative* attempts to fill the policy vacuum (in *Borowski* and *Daigle*), nothing in its post-*Morgentaler 2* mobilization around abortion and fetal rights affected the ability of provinces to enact restrictive measures, although the Canadian Abortion Rights Action League's success in *Morgentaler 3* prevented the prohibition of private clinics.

These policy developments are consistent with Rosenberg's argument regarding the conditions under which courts can bring about social change. According to him, one such condition is the emergence of parallel institutions willing to implement the policy change ordered or implied by a judicial decision.[24] In this case, the removal of barriers to the establishment of private abortion clinics, and the willingness of key actors to establish such clinics, compensated for the absence of change in the behaviour of hospitals. In essence, hospitals became largely irrelevant to the implementation of judicially mandated social change.

Reducing Violence: Sexual Assault and Pornography

In 1983 the federal government redesigned the law of sexual assault both procedurally and substantively. These changes were "complainant friendly" in the sense that they removed key elements of the old crime of rape and sought to protect complainants from certain lines of defence questioning. Not surprisingly, these changes came under attack from defence lawyers and rights organizations such as the Canadian Civil Liberties Association. The main line of attack was that the changes violated the legal rights entrenched contemporaneously in the Charter. LEAF intervened to support the government's defence of its rules, largely by arguing that an emphasis on procedural concerns without considering equality issues would undermine efforts to reduce violence against women.

As Chapter 5 details, the success of feminist legal mobilization at this level is mixed. From 1991 to 1995, LEAF found itself on the losing side of three key judgments involving the balance between legal rights and equality concerns. However, the federal government did not accept these losses as final, and worked with the feminist movement – led by LEAF – to construct legislative responses to the judgments. Thus, within a year of *Seaboyer*, and two years of *O'Connor*, the federal government had responded legislatively to the Court's judgment. LEAF mobilized its litigation resources once again to support the government's position, this time successfully in 1999 (twice) and 2000. Although it might be easy to conclude that legal mobilization ultimately produced a set of legal rules desired by the feminist movement, this conclusion would not be entirely accurate. With the exception of Bill C-49's consent provisions, effectively approved by the Court in *Ewanchuk*, the rules sanctioned in *Mills* and *Darrach* did not reflect LEAF's preferred position. Equality rights moderated, but did not trump, legal rights claims. The Court was simply unwilling to defer unconditionally to Parliament's understanding of the right to a fair trial in this context.

Tracing the actual policy consequences of these various legislative and judicial reforms is exceedingly difficult. The theory underlying LEAF's arguments throughout its sexual assault interventions was that any dilution of the protective measures found in the 1983 reforms would discourage women from reporting sexual assaults, reduce conviction rates, and ultimately, increase the incidence of sexual assault. Unfortunately, the readily available data on crime in Canada do not lend themselves easily to measuring changes in these variables. Table 6.8 provides the rate of reported sexual assaults per 100,000 population from 1983 to 2001. According to these data the rate increased steadily from 1983 to 1993, and then began to drop until stabilizing from 1999 to 2001. Interestingly, rates peaked just after *Seaboyer* in 1991, but continued to drop even after *O'Connor* in 1995.

Although it is difficult to draw conclusions from these data, some speculative remarks are nevertheless possible. First, the rapid increase in reporting rates immediately following the 1983 reforms might appear to undermine LEAF's estimation of their value. This conclusion, however, is probably not warranted. Recall that the 1983 reforms broadened the range of behaviour classified as sexual assault. Indeed, almost all of the rate increase occurred

Table 6.8

Sexual assault rates per 100,000 population, 1983-2001

Year	Total reported	Combined rate	Level 1 assaults	Level 2 and 3 assaults
1983	13,851	46	41	5
1984	17,323	57	52	5
1985	21,264	70	65	5
1986	24,114	78	73	5
1987	26,443	85	79	6
1988	29,114	93	88	5
1989	31,756	97	93	4
1990	32,908	99	95	4
1991	35,577	108	103	5
1992	39,858	120	116	4
1993	39,947	120	116	4
1994	36,489	108	104	4
1995	32,522	97	92	5
1996	30,369	90	87	3
1997	30,735	89	86	3
1998	25,553	84	81	3
1999	23,872	78	76	2
2000	24,049	78	76	2
2001	24,419	79	78	1

Source: 1983-97, Statistics Canada, "A Graphical Overview of Crime and the Administration of Justice in Canada, 1997," Cat. No. 85F0018XIE, p. 17; 1997-2001, Statistics Canada, Crimes by Type of Offence, at <www.statcam.ca/english/Pgdb/State/Justice/legal02.htm>, accessed 25 September 2002.

in Level 1 sexual assaults, with the rate of Level 2 and 3 incidents low and varying within only a small range over the nineteen-year period. In other words, the increase may simply reflect the criminalization of types of behaviour that the pre-1983 regime did not consider serious enough to warrant the criminal justice system's intervention. Moreover, if the new rules had their intended impact of increasing reporting rates, one would expect an increase in the rate of reported incidents. From these perspectives, the data would be a positive sign for feminists. LEAF might also find some support for its arguments in the 1992-94 data. An 11 percent increase in sexual assaults in the years immediately after *Seaboyer* would, on the surface, confirm the worst fears of the decision's harshest critics. Similarly, the 10 percent decrease from 1993 to 1994 might vindicate the supporters of Bill C-49 who argued for a vigorous legislative response. However, these conclusions require extremely strong assumptions about knowledge of, and sensitivity to, changes in legal rules among potential violators of sexual assault laws.

The General Social Survey (GSS), conducted by Statistics Canada, offers additional insights into the incidence of sexual assault. In 1988, 1993, and

1999, the GSS surveyed Canadians (approximately 26,000 in 1999) about their crime victimization experiences and perceptions of crime and the justice system. Among the eight offence types included in the survey of Canadians over the age of fifteen is sexual assault. Perhaps the most striking result of the survey is the generally low rate at which Canadians report *any* criminal victimization to the police. In 1999, for example, the overall reporting rate for Canada was 37 percent, with break and enter (62 percent) and motor vehicle theft (60 percent) having the highest reporting rates, likely because of insurance requirements. Personal crimes, including theft of personal property, sexual assault, robbery, and general assault had a combined reporting rate of 32 percent. Significantly, the number of sexual assaults that victims said they reported to the police was too small to be expressed in 1999.

The GSS did find a 78 percent non-report rate and a further 14 percent of victims who either did not know or refused to state whether they reported the incident to the police. Consequently, the 1999 GSS suggests a reporting rate for sexual assaults that may range from a low of 8 percent to a high of 22 percent. In fact, while Table 6.8 indicates 23,872 sexual assaults reported to the police in 1999, the respondents to the GSS reported 499,000 such incidents, suggesting an even lower reporting rate of 4.8 percent. Whether because or in spite of the various rule changes throughout the 1990s, by the end of the decade sexual assault remained an infrequently reported crime.

Nevertheless, the GSS suggests relative stability in the incidence of sexual assault over time. The reported rate of sexual assaults increased from 16 per 1,000 in 1993 to 21 per 1,000 in 1999, a difference that Statistics Canada did not find statistically significant. However, given that the "official" rate reported to police was 35 percent lower in 1999 than in 1993, one might conclude that the reporting rate dropped precipitously during this period. As Table 6.9 indicates, sexual assault also appears to differ from other Criminal Code offences in two other ways, one negative and the other positive. On the one hand, a larger proportion of sexual assaults are declared by police to be "unfounded." On the other hand, the rate at which sexual assault cases are cleared by charge is much higher than it is for all other Criminal Code offences. This second comparison is particularly important because it suggests an emphasis by police on sexual assault. While the overall clearance rate varied only slightly between approximately 22 and 24 percent from 1983 to 1995, the clearance rate for sexual assault increased steadily from 41.6 percent, reaching a high of 52.8 percent in 1993 before levelling off at 48 percent. Quite apart from the rules governing sexual assault trial procedures, police behaviour in sexual assault cases appears to have changed in a "pro-feminist" direction over this period. Even the proportion of sexual assault reports declared "unfounded" decreased from a high of 15.6 percent in 1989 to 13.2 percent in 1995.

Table 6.9

Unfounded incidents and clearance rates, 1983-95 (sexual assault and all Criminal Code offences)

Year	Criminal Code unfounded	Sexual assault unfounded	Criminal Code cleared	Sexual assault cleared
1983	5.0	13.9	21.7	41.6
1984	4.8	14.6	22.3	43.9
1985	4.8	14.2	22.6	47.2
1986	4.7	14.9	23.2	47.1
1987	4.6	15.4	23.8	48.0
1988	4.5	14.5	24.0	48.6
1989	4.7	15.6	24.5	48.6
1990	4.6	15.4	23.8	50.9
1991	4.3	14.7	23.5	51.8
1992	4.1	13.8	22.8	49.7
1993	4.1	13.0	23.2	52.8
1994	4.0	13.1	22.7	50.1
1995	3.9	13.2	22.3	48.0

A similarly mixed message is provided by the data in Table 6.10. Although conviction rates, acquittal rates, and the proportion of cases withdrawn or resulting in stays are higher for sexual assault than other crimes against the person, a much larger proportion of sexual assaults produced prison terms of more than two years. In addition, the data indicate improvement in all areas. The conviction rate increased, the acquittal rate decreased, and the proportion of stays and withdrawn charges decreased. On the whole, therefore, these data suggest that courts are taking sexual assault seriously.

Anecdotal evidence suggests that the judicial setbacks of the 1990s *(Seaboyer, O'Connor)* allowed some individuals to avoid conviction for sexual assault, but there is no strong aggregate data to support the claim that the risk of sexual assault increased for women as a result of these setbacks. Similarly, the legislative responses to those judgments, and subsequent judicial acceptance of the responses, do not appear to have lowered the risk. In all

Table 6.10

Sexual assault conviction rates, acquittal rates, and sentences

Year	Conviction rate	Acquittal rate	Stays/ Withdrawn	Prison terms more than two years
1998/99	34.7 (52.0)	6.8 (4.2)	40.8 (38.2)	12.4 (3.5)
1999/2000	37.8 (51.7)	6.1 (4.3)	38.8 (38.5)	12.7 (3.4)

Note: Figures in parentheses are for all crimes against the person.

likelihood, the impact of the changing rules for sexual assault trials during the 1990s was a strictly microlevel phenomenon. The probability of conviction may have changed in varying ways for some accused, but the changes were likely too technical and short-lived to make a significant difference at the macrolevel.

Whatever its actual policy consequences, LEAF's sexual assault dialogue with the Supreme Court and the federal government generated organizational benefits for the feminist movement. In particular, according to Sheila McIntyre, "the coalition formed to circumvent *Seaboyer* remained intact and expanded in the succeeding five years."[25] The coalition was an important participant in consultations by the Department of Justice on violence against women, held annually from 1994 to 1997.[26] Funded by the government, these consultations had broad representation from various constituencies within the women's movement. Most importantly, according to McIntyre, non-lawyers outnumbered lawyers by about a six-to-one ratio. Legal mobilization around sexual assault law provided both the necessity and opportunity for building an effective coalition that was far more inclusive than LEAF alone.[27]

The same cannot be said for LEAF's interventions in cases involving government regulation of pornography. As I discuss in Chapter 3, the decision to support the federal government's defence of the Criminal Code's obscenity provisions exacerbated, to the breaking point, existing tensions within the feminist movement. According to Lise Gotell, LEAF's unequivocal position that pornography is inherently violent and degrading to women "produced an intensification of the feminist porn wars in Canada as artists, academics, writers, lesbians, bookstore and media workers, and sex trade workers, reacted with outrage to the presentation of antipornography feminism as feminist orthodoxy."[28] Beyond the procedural issue of LEAF's lack of consultation with movement stakeholders, critics objected in particular to LEAF's singular portrayal of women as "passive, silent victim[s]" rather than "agents with voice."[29] Nor did LEAF's response – to defend its *Butler* factum, attribute negative consequences to faulty interpretations of the "degrading and dehumanizing standard," and to intervene in *Little Sisters* to attack those interpretations – completely satisfy these critics. At the same time, the decision to intervene in *Little Sisters* managed to alienate supporters of the position LEAF originally took in *Butler*.[30] From a movement-building standpoint, therefore, LEAF's attempt to attack pornography as a source of violence against women was problematic.

This result might have been acceptable if the practical consequences of pornography regulation were less ambiguous. Statistics Canada provides data only on "offences against public morals," which is the category in which the Criminal Code's anti-obscenity provisions (section 163) fall. Very few charges are laid under this category – a total of only 607 from 1997 to 2000, or about 150 per year. Even if all these charges were laid under section 163, they would still represent a tiny fraction of Criminal Code charges. Moreover, given the small annual variation in the number of charges – from a low of 138 in 1999 to a high of 166 in 1998 – these data do not suggest a "crackdown" on such activity in the wake of *Butler*. The absence of strong enforcement raises questions about the impact of section 163 on the supply of pornography and hence its impact on what LEAF deemed to be an important factor contributing to violence against women (and women's equality more generally).

Family Policy
Chapter 4 discusses a series of LEAF interventions in the general area of "family policy." On two issues – child support and maternity and parental leave – significant policy change occurred despite LEAF's failure to persuade the Supreme Court to change the relevant legal rules. In the first issue, a majority of the Court in *Thibaudeau* rejected the claim supported by LEAF that the existing income inclusion and deduction rules in the Income Tax Act infringed section 15. Although the federal government prevailed in court on this issue, the constitutional challenge inspired the development of a new approach to child support. The package of changes introduced in the 1996 budget affected four key areas:[31]

- Child support paid under orders made or varied after 30 April 1997 would no longer be taxed as income by recipients, or deducted from income by payers.
- Federal child support guidelines were introduced to establish "fair and consistent" child support awards.
- New enforcement measures were introduced.
- The Working Income Supplement of the Federal Child Tax Benefit was doubled in two stages.

The changes were the product of consultations with the intergovernmental Family Law Committee and the Task Group on the Taxation of Child Support. The federal government provided several reasons for changing the inclusion and deduction rules: public opinion that it was neither appropriate to tax child support nor to provide a tax break to support payers; failure of existing tax benefits to target children who need it most; impact of complex tax calculations on child support negotiations; the rules made financial planning more difficult for both payers and recipients of child support.

Another factor underlying the change was that the pre-1996 inclusion and deduction tax rules generated a *net loss* in tax revenues. For fiscal year 1996-97, this loss was estimated to be $410 million, with the federal portion estimated to be $240 million. The new rules were expected eventually to generate revenue gains of $120 million for the federal government by the third year of implementation. Lest it be accused of acting simply to enhance its bottom line, the federal government committed these revenue gains to fund the other elements of the 1996 changes, namely to fund the implementation costs of the federal child support guidelines and the new enforcement measures, as well as increases to the Working Income Supplement.

Although women's rights activists were dissatisfied that the elimination of the inclusion and deduction rules did not apply retroactively, the change still marked political victory in the aftermath of legal defeat. The same characterization applies to changes in the maternity and parental leave regime following the defeat in *Schachter*. Even before the Court's decision, the federal government had extended parental leave benefits (first introduced in 1990) to natural fathers. Consequently, natural parents had access to a total of twenty-five weeks of benefits: fifteen weeks of maternity benefits and ten weeks of parental benefits (which could be claimed entirely by one parent or shared by both parents). By 1998, 93 percent of women who took maternity leave from paid employment received monetary compensation (up from 77 percent in 1980), mostly in the form of employment insurance benefits.[32] The availability of benefits is an important predictor of when women return to work, with those receiving benefits returning to work later than those who do not.[33] In 1999-2000, almost 350,000 parents claimed more than $1 billion in combined maternity and parental leave benefits.[34] On 1 January 2001, the federal government further enhanced parental leave benefits to thirty-five weeks. This change also reduced the qualifying criterion from 700 to 600 hours of insurable earnings, eliminated the waiting period for the second benefit claim when parents shared benefits, and allowed some additional earnings without reducing parental benefits.

In short, there can be little doubt that the current child support and maternity and parental leave benefits schemes are more generous now than they were when LEAF intervened in *Schachter* and *Thibaudeau*. Thus, even without directly affecting rules through litigation, legal mobilization appears to have had an effect in these areas of public policy. At a minimum, it raised issues to a position on the policy agenda that they might not have reached, or reached as quickly, without the visibility of Supreme Court decisions.

Sexual Orientation
There is little doubt that the sexual orientation cases in which LEAF intervened resulted in favourable rule changes. By imposing a constitutional obligation on provinces to include sexual orientation in their human rights statutes, *Vriend* essentially nationalized a policy that seven provinces had already adopted legislatively. More dramatically, *M. v. H.* established a new, more inclusive definition of spouse that effectively changed public policy in every province and territory, as well as at the federal level. The most

immediate effects were evident in Ontario: in October of 1999, the province passed An Act to Amend Certain Statutes Because of the Supreme Court of Canada Decision in M. v. H. This Act amended sixty-six statutes (from the Absentees Act to the Workplace Safety and Insurance Act) by, for example, replacing all references to "spouse" with "spouse or same-sex partner." In June 2000, the federal government's Bill C-23, An Act to Modernize the Statutes of Canada in Relation to Benefits and Obligations, received royal assent. This Act amended sixty-eight federal laws by extending benefits and obligations to *all* couples who have been cohabiting in a conjugal relationship for at least one year. However, the interpretation section of the Act made it clear that "the amendments made by this Act do not affect the meaning of the word 'marriage', that is, the lawful union of one man and one woman to the exclusion of all others."

As this last point suggests, the rule changes initiated in *Vriend* and *M. v. H.* are not yet complete. The legal and legislative battle over the definition of marriage progressed rapidly over the summer of 2003. After decisions of the British Columbia and Ontario courts of appeal that the federal definition of marriage as exclusively heterosexual is unconstitutional, the government decided not to appeal and drafted new legislation that would define marriage, for civil purposes, as the "lawful union between two persons to the exclusion of all others." In addition, the legislation would exempt religious organizations from performing same-sex marriages if they wished not to do so. The government referred the draft legislation to the Supreme Court, which scheduled hearings for April 2004. The legislation's fate in Parliament is not at all certain, with the official opposition and a large number of government MPs opposed to changing the definition. Clearly, legal mobilization in this policy area, partly supported by LEAF, has initiated a process that may have broad social consequences.

Conclusion

The cases in which LEAF has intervened changed legal rules either directly – as in *Gordon, Eldridge, Vriend, M. v. H.,* and *G.(J.)* – or indirectly – as in *Thibaudeau* and *Schachter*. In other cases, particularly in the area of sexual assault, LEAF's interventions were part of a broader policy debate about the proper balance between collective interests and individual rights. In these cases LEAF brought the perspective of feminist theory to bear on the debate and affected both legislative responses to judicial decisions and the judicial response to those legislative adjustments. At times, however, these achievements came at the cost of dividing the feminist movement, especially in the area of pornography. Indeed, LEAF's attempt to repair that division in *Little Sisters* may have had some impact on its credibility with the Court, at least in the short term.

As the literature on legal mobilization stresses, however, there is often a great distance between changes in legal rules and practical achievements.

By far the most successful area for feminist legal mobilization has been abortion. The number of legal abortions performed in Canada increased significantly after 1988. Moreover, almost all of that increase can be traced to the elimination of the legal rule that only hospitals may perform abortions. Although LEAF did not participate directly in the removal of that rule, it has participated in litigation to help prevent its reestablishment. LEAF also helped in ushering in new maternity and parental leave policies and a new federal child support regime through its attack on existing rules. While those attacks failed in the Court, they resonated with the public and policy makers, resulting in political victories in the aftermath of legal defeat. Finally, to the extent that LEAF has contributed to the normalization of same-sex relationships, it has influenced the implementation of rule changes that will undoubtedly have a far-reaching effect on Canadian society.

Conclusion

The Canadian feminist movement's initial reason for participating in the politics of constitutional amendment and Supreme Court litigation after 1980 was to leverage legal rules to improve the status and social conditions of women. There is no doubt that the movement succeeded completely in one respect: it established the constitutional and jurisprudential basis for a comprehensive theory of substantive equality in Canadian law. Unlike its counterparts in the United States, LEAF never viewed its objective as the attainment of "same treatment" for women and men. Although it obviously sought to eliminate gender-based distinctions that disadvantage women, it also sought to preserve or establish such distinctions where they benefited women. Consequently, LEAF did not intervene to support just *any* equality rights or sex discrimination claim. Nowhere is this more apparent than in Brodsky and Day's 1989 study for the Canadian Advisory Council on the Status of Women and LEAF's intervention in *Weatherall*. In the former, Brodsky and Day lamented the number of sex discrimination claims then being brought on behalf of men; in the latter, LEAF intervened specifically to avoid a formal equality outcome that would extend the same privacy rights to male inmates as female inmates enjoyed.

LEAF was also largely, if not completely, successful in mobilizing the substantive equality principles emanating from cases such as *Andrews* to affect rule development in other areas of the law. Among its successes are the areas of antidiscrimination policy *(Janzen, Brooks, Weatherall, BCPSERC,* and *Blencoe),* reproductive rights *(Borowski, Daigle, Sullivan,* and *WCFS),* family law *(Moge, G.(J.),* and *Gordon),* the provision of benefits *(Eldridge),* and sexual orientation *(Vriend, M. v. H.).* LEAF was also able to turn some legal defeats into political victories *(Schachter, Thibaudeau).* As well, it successfully introduced substantive equality principles into the discussion of expressive freedom in cases such as *Keegstra, Andrews (90), Taylor,* and *Butler.* However, as *Little Sisters* and the events surrounding it indicate, this success came at a price. It fractured the feminist movement and apparently alienated a previously friendly institution.

The principles of substantive equality had their weakest affect when they conflicted with equally powerful principles of due process. This was most apparent in the area of sexual assault trial procedures, where LEAF failed in three consecutive cases *(Seaboyer, O'Connor, Beharriel)*. Although there were legislative responses to these decisions that were subsequently upheld in later cases *(Ewanchuk, Darrach, Mills)*, it would be difficult to describe this outcome as fully satisfactory to LEAF. The federal government never invoked substantive equality principles to challenge the core definition of the right to fair trial articulated in *Seaboyer* and *O'Connor*. Indeed, one could argue that the Supreme Court upheld Bills C-49 and C-46 in *Darrach* and *Mills* precisely because those laws did not challenge the Court's institutional authority in this respect. The Court decided *Darrach* and *Mills* differently from *Seaboyer* and *O'Connor* not because it reconsidered the evidence and arguments presented by LEAF in these earlier cases but because the government had introduced greater sensitivity to due process rights into sexual assault trial procedures.

In developing the arguments in all its factums, LEAF began to construct a uniquely feminist theory of the Charter grounded in its perception of the social distribution of power. At the core of this theory was the systemic subordination of women. LEAF tended to view social and political power as distributed almost exclusively along gender lines, with women obviously in a subordinate position. This approach was unproblematic for almost the first five years of LEAF's activity in the Supreme Court, as the issues on which it intervened (e.g., reproductive rights in *Borowski, Daigle,* and *Sullivan*; antidiscrimination in *Janzen* and *Brooks*; violence in *Seaboyer* and *Norberg*) were ones on which a feminist coalition could easily be built. However, as the issues became more complicated in cases such as *Butler*, LEAF found itself open to the criticism of "essentialism." As Lise Gotell argues, this "universalized and abstracted description of 'women's experience'" ignored nongender-based distributions of power.[1] After 1992, Gotell argues, LEAF began to pay much closer attention to the *particular* experiences of the women involved in the cases in which it intervened. Thus, while there is not a single reference to the complainant or the circumstances of her victimization in LEAF's *Seaboyer* factum, its factum in *O'Connor* emphasizes the complainants' status as Aboriginal women who attended a residential school. Similarly, race plays a central role in *WCFS* and *R. v. S.*; disability in *Eldridge*; and the specificity of lesbianism in *Vriend, M. v. H.,* and *Little Sisters*.

This debate within the movement between essentialism and particularism highlights a central dilemma that LEAF faced: whether its litigation strategy would be driven by the demands of its constituency, or whether it would be driven by the demands of the institutions in which this strategy is deployed. In many ways, this is the general dilemma of legal mobilization. Are the objectives internal or external? How should trade-offs between these two sets of objectives be made? Should success be measured by the outputs of litigation or by its impact on the movement itself? Having suffered three consecutive losses in the Supreme Court from 2000 to 2002, LEAF may have broadened its constituency appeal while reducing its persuasive effectiveness.

Does LEAF's activity in the Supreme Court from 1988 to 2000 shed any light on the debate about the utility of legal mobilization? Recall that the subtitle of Gerald Rosenberg's book is "Can Courts Bring About Social Change?" Although the analysis is court-centric, the clear implication of this subtitle is that if courts cannot generate social change, then legal mobilization is to a large degree a waste of resources. Two issues are buried within this implication, one empirical and the other theoretical. The empirical issue is whether policy-oriented litigation does, in fact, lead to social change, or whether courts are so constrained that litigation-driven change is rare. LEAF's experience speaks to this issue in two conflicting ways. On the one hand, legal rules did change as either a direct or indirect result of legal mobilization in the policy areas where LEAF was involved, and these rule changes do appear to have had an impact on social conditions. The most obvious example is abortion, where LEAF mobilized to preserve a rule change accomplished in 1988. The data are relatively unambiguous that the number and rate of legal abortions increased after 1988, and that this increase is almost entirely attributable to the removal of legal barriers to the establishment of private abortion clinics. Similarly, although unsuccessful in purely legal terms, legal mobilization around issues of parental leave benefits and child support acted as a catalyst for rule changes that established improved policy regimes.

On the other hand, legal mobilization by LEAF did not prevent the introduction of due process values into the construction of sexual assault trial procedures. Although the Court allowed the federal government to deviate slightly from its preferred position, it did so only because those deviations were broadly consistent with, and did not contradict, the Court's understanding of the right to a fair trial. In fact, one can argue that feminist legal mobilization could not prevent adverse rule changes. However, it is unclear whether these rule changes had much impact on the level of violence against women or the actual processing of sexual assault cases. The rate of reported sexual assaults did increase immediately after the *Seaboyer* decision in 1991, but they began to drop as the Court decided *O'Connor* and continued to drop afterward. In retrospect, as I argue in Chapter 5, it seems highly unlikely that complex technical changes in trial procedures would affect micro-level individual behaviour in a way that would strongly influence the aggregate level of sexual assault.

The theoretical issue is whether, as Stuart Scheingold and Michael McCann might argue, there are noninstrumental reasons to litigate. Given that one of the criteria LEAF uses to select cases is "winnability," instrumental factors are clearly important in its internal decision-making process (and given LEAF's track record, it has been successful in selecting "winnable" cases). It is also clear, however, that noninstrumental factors played a role in the decision to intervene in *Little Sisters*. In view of the unanimity of the *Butler* decision, and LEAF's own role in that case, there was little chance that the Court would enact the social change LEAF supported in *Little Sisters* (exempting gay and lesbian pornography, including sado-masochistic material, from the Criminal Code's obscenity provisions). Nevertheless, there was significant pressure within the movement to intervene. Thus, while LEAF did not litigate "lost causes" in the same way as Canada's early gay rights movement,[2] it demonstrated a willingness to ignore winnability, or at least to interpret it broadly, where there were movement imperatives to do so.

One of the difficulties in evaluating legal mobilization derives from a disagreement about how to define the phrase "bring about" in Rosenberg's subtitle. Rosenberg's own definition is relatively narrow: he wants to see a direct causal link from legal arguments to changes in legal rules and social conditions. Unless these links are apparent, Rosenberg declines to attribute change to legal mobilization. Although it is difficult to draw a direct causal line from LEAF's legal arguments to specific decisions, the Supreme Court *did* change legal rules in many of the cases in which LEAF intervened, and in the direction advocated by LEAF. With the possible exceptions of access to abortion and benefits for same-sex partners, it is equally difficult to draw a line from these changes to changes in social conditions.

McCann, by contrast, offers a broader definition, one that sees legal mobilization as a catalyst rather than a necessarily causal agent. From this perspective it is part of a constellation of social forces that contribute to the achievement of social movement objectives. Thus, even where LEAF cases failed to change rules (e.g., *Schachter*, *Thibaudeau*) litigation created a climate for policy change. Moreover, even in the difficult area of sexual assault law, LEAF's participation enhanced sensitivity to sexual assault law (evident in changes in "unfounded" and clearance rates). Whether women as a group are better off as a result of twenty years of LEAF participation in Supreme Court litigation is an open question, although it would be demanding a great deal from legal mobilization to expect that this activity alone would have made a difference.

Courts, especially final courts of appeal, are political institutions. They make policy not as an accidental by-product of performing their adjudicative function but because a majority of their members concludes that one set of legal rules is more socially beneficial than another. However, relative to other political institutions, courts have a limited capacity to set their own agenda. They rely on litigants to select issues, present evidence, and frame arguments. Although the Women's Legal Education and Action Fund did not play as large a role in selecting issues as it had originally planned, it contributed both evidence and arguments to the Supreme Court's consideration of issues of importance to Canadian feminists. That it did so effectively is evident at the level of both case outcome and issue resolution. Moreover, there is evidence that the cases in which LEAF participated had the desired policy impact, at least to some degree. LEAF may not have captured the Court, but by the end of 2000, its imprint on constitutional principles of equality was clearly visible.

Notes

Introduction

1 For a history of the movement in the United States and Britain, see Olive Banks, *Faces of Feminism: A Study of Feminism as a Social Movement* (New York: St. Martin's Press, 1981). A summary of key developments in Canada can be found in Jill Vickers, Pauline Rankin, and Christine Appelle, *Politics as if Women Mattered: A Political Analysis of the National Action Committee on the Status of Women* (Toronto: University of Toronto Press, 1993), 19-22.

2 *Edwards* v. *A.-G. Canada*, [1930] A.C. 124, at 136.

3 Government of Canada, *Report of the Royal Commission on the Status of Women in Canada* (Ottawa: Queen's Printer, 1970).

4 Susan D. Phillips, "Meaning and Structure in Social Movements: Mapping the Network of National Canadian Women's Organizations," *Canadian Journal of Political Science* 24 (1991): 763.

5 Ibid., 765.

6 Sylvia Bashevkin, *Women on the Defensive: Living Through Conservative Times* (Toronto: University of Toronto Press, 1998), 39-40.

7 Ibid., 5.

8 *Lavell* v. *A.-G. Canada*, [1974] S.C.R. 1349; *Murdoch* v. *Murdoch*, [1975] 1 S.C.R. 423; *Leatherdale* v. *Leatherdale*, [1982] 2 S.C.R. 743; *Morgentaler* v. *The Queen*, [1976] 1 S.C.R. 616; *Pappajohn* v. *The Queen*, [1980] 2 S.C.R. 120; *Bliss* v. *A.-G. Canada*, [1979] 1 S.C.R. 183.

9 *Roe* v. *Wade*, 410 U.S. 113 (1973).

10 [1976] 1 S.C.R. 616, at 671.

11 [1979] 1 S.C.R. 183, at 190.

12 Christopher P. Manfredi, "Institutional Design and the Politics of Constitutional Modification: Understanding Amendment Failure in the United States and Canada," *Law and Society Review* 31 (1997): 127.

13 Bashevkin, *Women on the Defensive*, 249-56. These rates are based on Bashevkin's own measure of success, which was simply to look at whether pro-women's movement legislative proposals were enacted and whether arguments supported by the movement were successful in the Supreme Court.

14 Ibid., 252. See, for example, *Reed* v. *Reed*, 404 U.S. 71 (1971); *Orr* v. *Orr*, 440 U.S. 268 (1979); *Roe* v. *Wade*, 410 U.S. 113 (1973); *Pittsburgh Press* v. *Pittsburgh Commission on Human Relations*, 413 U.S. 376 (1973); *Cleveland Board of Education* v. *LaFleur*, 414 U.S. 632 (1974).

15 Karen O'Connor, *Women's Organizations' Use of the Courts* (Lexington, MA: Lexington Books, 1980); Laurence Tribe, *American Constitutional Law* (Mineola, NY: Foundation Press, 1978), 1975. "Strict scrutiny" requires that a classification be necessary to achieve a compelling state interest in order to survive constitutional review. It applies whenever legislation involves a "fundamental right" or a "suspect category." The assumption was that the ERA would make "sex" a suspect category (something the Supreme Court had been unwilling to do) and therefore bring it within a type of analysis described as "strict in theory, fatal in fact."

16 Some version of the ERA had enjoyed the support of every president from Truman to Carter. It was broadly consistent with the Fourteenth Amendment's equal protection clause and Title VII of the 1964 Civil Rights Act (prohibiting sex discrimination). Finally, the House approved the ERA by a vote of 354 to 23, while the Senate vote was 84 to 8 in favour.
17 Jane Mansbridge, *Why We Lost the ERA* (Chicago: University of Chicago Press, 1986), 29, 27-28.
18 Gwen Brodsky and Shelagh Day, *Canadian Charter Equality Rights for Women: One Step Forward or Two Steps Back?* (Ottawa: Canadian Advisory Council on the Status of Women, 1989); Sherene Razack, *Canadian Feminism and the Law: The Women's Legal Education and Action Fund and the Pursuit of Equality* (Toronto: Second Story Press, 1993).
19 William A. Bogart, *Courts and Country: The Limits of Litigation and the Social and Political Life of Canada* (Toronto: Oxford University Press, 1994), 134-64; F.L. Morton and Avril Allen, "Feminists and the Courts: Measuring Success in Interest Group Litigation in Canada," *Canadian Journal of Political Science* 34 (2001): 55-84.
20 See Brodsky and Day, *Canadian Charter Equality Rights for Women*. Section 15 is the equality rights section of the Charter. It did not become effective until 1985, to allow governments to assess legislation in light of its requirements.
21 Ibid., 3.
22 Ibid., 119.
23 Razack, *Canadian Feminism and the Law*, 51.
24 Ibid., 53, 57-58.
25 Ibid., 58.
26 Ibid., 127.
27 Radha Jhappan, ed., *Women's Legal Strategies in Canada* (Toronto: University of Toronto Press, 2002), 13.
28 Ibid., 175-218.
29 Bogart, *Courts and Country*, 135.
30 Morton and Allen, "Feminists and the Courts," 63-67.
31 Ibid., 73. Morton and Allen examined all Charter and non-Charter appellate court rulings concerning feminist issues.
32 Ibid., 75-76.
33 Alexandra Dobrowolsky, *The Politics of Pragmatism: Women, Representation and Constitutionalism in Canada* (Toronto: Oxford University Press, 2000); Peter Russell, *Constitutional Odyssey: Can Canadians Be a Sovereign People?* (Toronto: University of Toronto Press, 1992), 75.
34 Dobrowolsky, *The Politics of Pragmatism*, 3.
35 Ibid., 195.
36 Ibid., 26.
37 Manfredi, "Institutional Design"; Christopher P. Manfredi and Michael Lusztig, "Why Do Formal Amendments Fail? An Institutional Design Analysis," *World Politics* 50 (1998): 377-400.
38 George Tsebelis, *Nested Games: Rational Choice in Comparative Politics* (Berkeley: University of California Press, 1990), 98.
39 For an elaboration of this model of constitutional politics, see Manfredi and Lusztig, "Why Do Formal Amendments Fail?" 379-86.
40 For an exception, see Miriam Smith, *Lesbian and Gay Rights in Canada: Social Movements and Equality-Seeking, 1971-1995* (Toronto: University of Toronto Press, 1999).
41 Michael W. McCann, *Rights at Work: Pay Equity Reform and the Politics of Legal Mobilization* (Chicago: University of Chicago Press, 1994), 7.
42 Lee Epstein and Joseph Kobylka, *The Supreme Court and Legal Change: Abortion and the Death Penalty* (Chapel Hill, NC: University of North Carolina Press, 1992), 8. Emphasis in original.

Chapter 1: Legal Doctrine, Legal Mobilization, and LEAF
1 [1989] 1 S.C.R. 1219.
2 Ibid., 1243.
3 Ibid., 1244.
4 LEAF Factum, *Brooks* v. *Canada Safeway*, paras. 11, 16.

5 Ibid., paras. 39-41.
6 Leslie Pal and F.L. Morton, "*Bliss* v. *Attorney General of Canada*: From Legal Defeat to Political Victory," *Osgoode Hall Law Journal* 24 (1986): 141-60.
7 Rainer Knopff, *Human Rights and Social Technology: The New War on* Discrimination (Ottawa: Carleton University Press, 1989), 74.
8 *Action Travail des Femmes* v. *Canadian National Railway* (1987), 40 D.L.R. (4th) 193, at 205-9.
9 These included *R.* v. *Drybones*, [1970] S.C.R. 282; *Lavell* v. *A.-G. Canada*, [1974] S.C.R. 1349; *Bliss* v. *A.-G. Canada*, [1979] 1 S.C.R. 183.
10 Lee Epstein and Joseph Kobylka, *The Supreme Court and Legal Change: Abortion and the Death Penalty* (Chapel Hill, NC: University of North Carolina Press, 1992), 9.
11 Jeffrey A. Segal and Harold J. Spaeth, *The Supreme Court and the Attitudinal Model* (New York: Cambridge University Press, 1993).
12 C. Herman Pritchett, *The Roosevelt Court: A Study in Judicial Politics and Values* (New York: Macmillan, 1948).
13 Ibid., 240-41.
14 C.L. Ostberg and Matthew Wetstein, "Dimensions of Attitudes Underlying Search and Seizure Decisions of the Supreme Court of Canada," *Canadian Journal of Political Science* 31 (1998): 786. See also Donald E. Fouts, "Policy-Making in the Supreme Court of Canada, 1950-1960," in *Comparative Judicial Behavior: Cross-Cultural Study of Decision-Making in the East and West,* ed. Glendon Schubert and David Danelski (New York: Oxford University Press, 1969), 257-91; Sidney Peck, "A Scalogram Analysis of the Supreme Court of Canada, 1958-1967," in *Comparative Judicial Behavior,* ed. Schubert and Danelski, 293-324; C. Neil Tate and Panu Sittiwong, "Decision-Making in the Canadian Supreme Court: Extending the Personal Attributes Model Across Nations," *Journal of Politics* 51 (1989): 900-16.
15 James B. Kelly, "Judging the Judges: The Decline of Dissent in the Supreme Court's Charter Decisions," in *Law, Politics and the Judicial Process in Canada,* 3rd ed., ed. F.L. Morton (Calgary: University of Calgary Press, 2001), 560-69.
16 The origin of this distinction is the "Court Party" index developed in F.L. Morton, Peter H. Russell, and Troy Riddell, "The Canadian Charter of Rights and Freedoms: A Descriptive Analysis of the First Decade, 1982-1992," *National Journal of Constitutional Law* 1 (1994): 45-46. The index measures judicial support for post-material interests.
17 Interestingly, Ostberg and Wetstein found that social background had a strong impact on Justice L'Heureux-Dubé's decision making, at least in search and seizure cases. Ostberg and Wetstein, "Dimensions of Attitudes," 782.
18 [1995] 2 S.C.R. 513.
19 *Vriend* v. *Alberta*, [1998] 1 S.C.R. 493; *M.* v. *H.*, [1999] 2 S.C.R. 3. There was also an apparent attitude shift by Chief Justice Lamer and Justice Major.
20 Bertha Wilson, "Will Women Judges Really Make a Difference?" *Osgoode Hall Law Journal* 28 (1990): 507-22.
21 Carol Gilligan, *In a Different Voice: Psychological Theory and Women's Development* (Cambridge, MA: Harvard University Press, 1982). See Wilson, "Will Women Judges Really Make a Difference?" 519-20.
22 Sherene Razack, *Canadian Feminism and the Law: The Women's Legal Education and Action Fund and the Pursuit of Equality* (Toronto: Second Story Press, 1991), 73-97.
23 Peter McCormick, *Supreme at Last: The Evolution of the Supreme Court of Canada* (Toronto: Lorimer, 2000), 138.
24 *Little Sisters Book and Art Emporium* v. *Canada*, [2000] 2 S.C.R. 1120.
25 *R.* v. *Seaboyer*, [1991] 2 S.C.R. 577.
26 Although the data are limited – five votes in three cases – McLachlin's support for LEAF has decreased since she became chief justice (60.0 versus 75.7 percent). Moreover, her support for LEAF in 2000 came in unanimous judgments.
27 James L. Gibson, "Decision Making in Appellate Courts," in *The American Courts: A Critical Assessment,* ed. John B. Gates and Charles A. Johnson (Washington, DC: CQ Press, 1991), 256.

28 James Gibson, "Judges' Role Orientations, Attitudes, and Decisions: An Interactive Model," *American Political Science Review* 72 (1978): 918.
29 Jeffrey A. Segal, "Supreme Court Justices as Human Decision Makers: An Individual-Level Analysis of the Search and Seizure Cases," *Journal of Politics* 48 (1986): 938-55.
30 Lee Epstein, Thomas G. Walker, and William J. Dixon, "The Supreme Court and Criminal Justice Disputes: A Neo-Institutional Perspective," *American Journal of Political Science* 33 (1989): 825-41.
31 Lee Epstein and Jack Knight, *The Choices Justices Make* (Washington, DC: CQ Press, 1998), xiii.
32 Ibid., 59-107. Attention to the strategic elements of judicial choice dates from at least the mid-1960s. See Walter F. Murphy, *Elements of Judicial Strategy* (Chicago: University of Chicago Press, 1964). The relative explanatory power of pure attitudinal and strategic models of judicial decision making is the subject of some debate. See Jeffrey Segal, "Separation-of-Powers Games in the Positive Theory of Congress and Courts," *American Political Science Review* 91 (1997): 28-44.
33 *Re Ontario Human Rights Commission et al. and Simpsons-Sears Ltd.*, [1985] 2 S.C.R. 536; *Re Bhinder et al. and Canadian National Railways*, [1985] 2 S.C.R. 561; *Action Travail des Femmes v. Canadian National Railway*, [1987] 1 S.C.R. 1114.
34 Lawrence Baum, *The Puzzle of Judicial Behavior* (Ann Arbor, MI: University of Michigan Press, 1997), 123.
35 Christopher P. Manfredi, *Judicial Power and the Charter: Canada and the Paradox of Liberal Constitutionalism*, 2nd ed. (Toronto: Oxford University Press, 2001), 186-88.
36 [1988] 2 S.C.R. 712.
37 Patrick Monahan, *Meech Lake: The Inside Story* (Toronto: University of Toronto Press, 1991), 165.
38 House of Commons, *Debates*, 6 April 1989, p. 153 (Brian Mulroney).
39 Patrick Monahan, *Politics and the Constitution: The Charter, Federalism and the Supreme Court of Canada* (Toronto: Carswell/Methuen, 1987), 118-19.
40 Monahan, *Meech Lake*, 169.
41 Andrew Heard, *Canadian Constitutional Conventions: The Marriage of Law and Politics* (Toronto: Oxford University Press, 1991), 147. In the spring of 2000 a private member's bill passed the Alberta legislature that defined marriage as an act between persons of the opposite sex and included a notwithstanding clause. The bill is probably unconstitutional on federalism grounds, since "marriage" is a federal legislative responsibility.
42 Chris Schwarz, "New Hope for 'Forgotten' Victims," *Edmonton Journal*, 12 March 1998, A1.
43 Joseph F. Fletcher and Paul Howe, "Public Opinion and the Courts," *Choices* 6: 3 (Institute for Research on Public Policy, May 2000).
44 Kent Roach, "The People versus the Supreme Court," *Literary Review of Canada* (June 2001): 16.
45 Kent Roach, *The Supreme Court on Trial: Judicial Activism or Democratic Dialogue* (Toronto: Irwin Law, 2001), 90, 94.
46 Charles Epp, *The Rights Revolution: Lawyers, Activists, and Supreme Courts in Comparative Perspective* (Chicago: University of Chicago Press, 1998), 17-20.
47 Robert O. Lempert, "Mobilizing Private Law: An Introductory Essay," *Law and Society Review* 2 (1976): 173.
48 Frances Kahn Zemens, "Legal Mobilization: The Neglected Role of the Law in the Political System," *American Political Science Review* 77 (1983): 700.
49 Susan E. Lawrence, *The Poor in Court: The Legal Services Program and Supreme Court Decision Making* (Princeton, NJ: Princeton University Press, 1990), 40.
50 Karen O'Connor and Lee Epstein, "Rebalancing the Scales of Justice: Assessment of Public Interest Law," *Harvard Journal of Law and Public Policy* 7 (1984): 483.
51 See J.R. Mallory, *Social Credit and the Federal Power in Canada* (Toronto: University of Toronto Press, 1954).
52 Stuart Scheingold, *The Politics of Rights* (New Haven, CT: Yale University Press, 1974), 173.
53 Robert L. Rabin, "Perspectives on Public Interest Law," *Stanford Law Review* 28 (1976): 221.

54   Ibid., 216.
55   See *United States* v. *Carolene Products*, 304 U.S. 144, 152-53 n. 4 (1938). A discrete and insular minority is any group that is identifiably different from the majority of citizens and is denied the power to defend its interests through ordinary political action.
56   Clement E. Vose, *Caucasians Only: The Supreme Court, the NAACP, and the Restrictive Covenant Cases* (Berkeley: University of California Press, 1959), 39, 44.
57   *Shelley* v. *Kraemer*, 334 U.S. 1 (1948) (restrictive covenants); *Brown* v. *Board of Education*, 347 U.S. 483 (1954) (segregated education); *Smith* v. *Allwright*, 321 U.S. 659 (1944) (Jim Crow voting restrictions); *Reynolds* v. *Sims*, 377 U.S. 533 (1964) (malapportionment).
58   Robert M. Cover, "The Origins of Judicial Activism in the Protection of Minorities," *Yale Law Journal* 91 (1982): 1287-1316.
59   Alan D. Gold, "The Legal Rights Provisions – A New Vision or Déjà Vu?" *Supreme Court Law Review* 4 (1982): 108.
60   Marc Galanter, "Why the 'Haves' Come Out Ahead: Speculations on the Limits of Legal Change," *Law and Society Review* 9 (1974): 95-160.
61   Kim Lane Scheppele and Jack L. Walker, Jr., "The Litigation Strategies of Interest Groups," in Jack L. Walker, Jr., *Mobilizing Interest Groups in America: Patrons, Professions and Social Movements* (Ann Arbor, MI: University of Michigan Press, 1991), 161-68.
62   Susan Olson, "Interest Group Litigation in Federal District Courts: Beyond the Political Disadvantage Theory," *Journal of Politics* 52 (1990): 854-82.
63   Mark V. Tushnet, *The NAACP's Legal Strategy Against Segregated Education, 1925-1950* (Chapel Hill, NC: University of North Carolina Press, 1987), 2; Richard Kluger, *Simple Justice* (New York: Vintage Books, 1975), 388-90.
64   This argument is pursued at length in Ian Brodie, *Friends of the Court: The Privileging of Interest Group Litigants in Canada* (Albany: State University of New York Press, 2002).
65   Scheingold, *The Politics of Rights*, 95.
66   Ibid., 131.
67   Gerald Rosenberg, *The Hollow Hope: Can Courts Bring About Social Change?* (Chicago: University of Chicago Press, 1991).
68   Ibid., 10. Rosenberg is not entirely pessimistic, however. Litigation can be effective, he argues, when certain conditions are met. First, incentives must exist for key actors to implement changes. Second, there must be costs associated with resisting change. Third, compliance is more likely where the possibility exists that social change can be implemented by parallel institutions. Finally, success will be higher where court orders can be used as leverage to extract additional resources. Ibid., 33-35.
69   Michael McCann, "Reform Litigation on Trial," *Law and Social Inquiry* 17 (1992): 720-21.
70   Ibid., 733. For Rosenberg's response to McCann, see Gerald N. Rosenberg, "Hollow Hopes and Other Aspirations," *Law and Social Inquiry* 17 (1992): 761-78.
71   Michael W. McCann, *Rights at Work: Pay Equity Reform and the Politics of Legal Mobilization* (Chicago: University of Chicago Press, 1994).
72   McCann, *Rights at Work*, 4.
73   Ibid., 292.
74   Gerald N. Rosenberg, "Positivism, Interpretivism, and the Study of Law," *Law and Social Inquiry* 21 (1996): 448.
75   Ibid., 454.
76   Interveners are legal persons who are not direct parties to a case but are allowed to present arguments in it. See Ian Brodie, "Lobbying the Court," in *Political Dispute and Judicial Review*, ed. M.W. Westmacott and H. Mellon (Toronto: Nelson, 1999), 195-203.
77   Lori Joanne Hausegger, "The Impact of Interest Groups on Judicial Decision Making: A Comparison of Women's Groups in the U.S. and Canada" (PhD diss., Ohio State University, 2000), Chapter 2.
78   LEAF, *Annual Report, 2000-2001*, 6.
79   For a list of cases sponsored by LEAF during its first ten years, see Women's Legal Education and Action Fund, *Equality and the Charter: Ten Years of Feminist Advocacy Before the Supreme Court of Canada* (Toronto: Emond Montgomery, 1996), 515-17. In 2000 the following notice appeared on West Coast LEAF's website:

West Coast LEAF, in conjunction with the Legal Aid Lawyers Association of BC, is seeking two clients, one who the Legal Services Society has rejected for family law legal aid because she is slightly over the financial eligibility cut off, and one who requires legal aid for a serious family law problem not currently covered by legal aid, preferably a problem related to abuse or potential abuse by a former partner.

The purpose is to bring an application for judicial review of the Legal Services Society's interpretation of its statutory responsibility to provide legal aid to applicants with family law problems. When the provincial government severely restricted LSS funding in 1997, thousands of women requiring family law legal services were denied legal aid.

In 1999, with a grant from Status of Women Canada, the Women's Access to Legal Services (WALS) Coalition ... interviewed women and women's advocates in four BC communities to document the impact of the cuts. The report ... recommends that the LSS revise its financial eligibility guidelines and family law coverage rules to comply with its statute. A successful judicial review will require the LSS to carry out those recommendations.

See <http://www.westcoastleaf.org/legal.html> (16 August 2000).

80 Brodie, *Friends of the Court*, Chapter 2. The Canadian Civil Liberties Association was also active in the pro-intervention lobbying campaign. The leading academic criticism of pre-Charter intervention rules was Jillian Welch, "No Room at the Top: Interest Group Interveners and Charter Litigation in the Supreme Court of Canada," *University of Toronto Faculty of Law Review* 43 (1985): 204-31.

81 Brodie, *Friends of the Court*, Tables 2.1, 2.2.

82 James B. Kelly, "The Charter of Rights and Freedoms and the Rebalancing of Liberal Constitutionalism in Canada, 1982-1997," *Osgoode Hall Law Journal* 37 (1999): 641.

83 Hausegger, "The Impact of Interest Groups," Chapter 3. Hausegger's study also found that LEAF participation had an important impact on case outcome, as the probability of a favourable outcome was 33 percentage points higher when LEAF participated in a case than when it was absent.

84 F.L. Morton and Avril Allen, "Feminists and the Courts: Measuring Success in Interest Group Litigation in Canada," *Canadian Journal of Political Science* 34 (2001): 71.

85 The subtitle of LEAF's tenth anniversary compilation of Supreme Court facta is "Ten Years of Feminist Advocacy Before the Supreme Court of Canada." Sherene Razack's "authorized" history of LEAF is entitled *Canadian Feminism and the Law*.

86 *Morgentaler, Smoling and Scott* v. *The Queen*, [1988] 1 S.C.R. 30; *R.* v. *Morgentaler*, [1993] 3 S.C.R. 463; *Symes* v. *Canada*, [1993] 4 S.C.R. 695; *R.* v. *Daviault*, [1994] 3 S.C.R. 63.

87 F.L. Morton, *Morgentaler v. Borowski: Abortion, the Charter, and the Courts* (Toronto: McClelland and Stewart, 1992), 163.

88 [1988] 1 S.C.R. at 51.

89 *Symes* v. *Canada*, [1993] 4 S.C.R. 695, 786.

90 The same could be said of another case, *Gould* v. *Yukon Order of Pioneers*, [1996] 1 S.C.R. 571. At issue was the Yukon Order of Pioneers' restriction of membership to men. Mary Eberts served as counsel for Gould, and Gwen Brodsky represented the intervener Yukon Status of Women Council.

91 Razack, *Canadian Feminism and the Law*, 58.

92 Conversely, there is also an argument that a decision in Symes's favour would have forced the federal government "to respond with new policy because it would have been politically intolerable to allow full deductions of the cost of child care for self-employed parents, but not for salaried ones." Susan D. Phillips, "Legal as Political Strategies in the Canadian Women's Movement: Who's Speaking? Who's Listening?," in *Women's Legal Strategies in Canada*, ed. Radha Jhappan (Toronto: University of Toronto Press, 2002), 396.

93 Daiva Stasiulis and Abigail Bakan, "Negotiating the Citizenship Divide: Foreign Domestic Worker Policy and Legal Jurisprudence," in *Women's Legal Strategies*, ed. Jhappan, 238-39.

94 Joanne St. Lewis, "Beyond the Confinement of Gender: Locating the Space of Legal Existence for Racialized Women," in *Women's Legal Strategies*, ed. Jhappan, 309-10.

95   For a summary, see Christopher P. Manfredi and Scott Lemieux, "Judicial Discretion and Fundamental Justice: Sexual Assault in the Supreme Court of Canada," *American Journal of Comparative Law* 47 (1999): 504-6.
96   Sandra Rubin, "Supreme Court's Burden 'Critical'," *National Post,* 13 August 2001, A1.
97   Women's Legal Education and Action Fund, *Equality and the Charter,* 499-503, 505, 515-17. The women's movements in Quebec and the rest of Canada had also become alienated over the Meech Lake Accord.
98   Radha Jhappan, "Feminist Adventures in Law," in *Women's Legal Strategies,* ed. Jhappan, 40 n. 87.
99   M. Elizabeth Atcheson, Mary Eberts, and Beth Symes, *Women and Legal Action: Precedents, Resources and Strategies for the Future* (Ottawa: Canadian Advisory Council on the Status of Women, 1984). I discuss this report in more detail in the next chapter.
100   LEAF, *Annual Report, 1999/2000* (Toronto, 2000), 3.
101   Ian Brodie, "Interest Group Litigation and the Embedded State: Canada's Court Challenges Program," *Canadian Journal of Political Science* 34 (2001): 365-71.
102   Ibid., 375.
103   Women's Legal Education and Action Fund, *Equality and the Charter,* xix.

Chapter 2: The Path to Substantive Equality
1   Gwen Brodsky and Shelagh Day, *Canadian Charter Equality Rights for Women: One Step Forward or Two Steps Back?* (Ottawa: Canadian Advisory Council on the Status of Women, 1989), 14-15.
2   For an interesting discussion of different modes of constitutional modification and their consequences, see Donald S. Lutz, "Toward a Theory of Constitutional Amendment," *American Political Science Review* 88 (1994): 355-70.
3   See Christopher P. Manfredi, "Institutional Design and the Politics of Constitutional Modification: Understanding Amendment Failure in the United States and Canada," *Law and Society Review* 31 (1997): 113-16.
4   Lutz, "Toward a Theory of Constitutional Amendment," 364.
5   Stephen M. Griffin, "Constitutionalism in the United States: From Theory to Politics," in *Responding to Imperfection: The Theory and Practice of Constitutional Amendment,* ed. Sanford Levinson (Princeton, NJ: Princeton University Press, 1995), 40.
6   Jane Mansbridge, *Why We Lost the ERA* (Chicago: University of Chicago Press, 1986), 29.
7   The story of the ERA in this section relies on Mansbridge, *Why We Lost the ERA;* Mary Frances Berry, *Why ERA Failed: Politics, Women's Rights, and the Amending Process of the Constitution* (Bloomington, IN: Indiana University Press, 1986); Janet K. Boles, *The Politics of the Equal Rights Amendment: Conflict and the Decision Process* (New York: Longman, 1979); and Gilbert Y. Steiner, *Constitutional Inequality: The Political Fortunes of the Equal Rights Amendment* (Washington, DC: Brookings Institution, 1985).
8   Steiner, *Constitutional Inequality,* 63-66.
9   Roy Romanow, John Whyte, and Howard Leeson, *Canada Notwithstanding: The Making of the Constitution, 1976-1982* (Toronto: Carswell/Methuen, 1984).
10   Patrick Monahan, *Meech Lake: The Inside Story* (Toronto: University of Toronto Press, 1991), 290-92.
11   Voters in seven of twelve provinces and territories rejected the accord. Overall, 55.1 percent of voters rejected the accord.
12   *Reference re Legislative Authority of Parliament to Alter or Replace the Senate,* [1980] 1 S.C.R. 54; *A.-G. Manitoba et al. v. A.-G. Canada et al. (Patriation Reference),* [1981] 1 S.C.R. 753; *A.-G. Quebec v. A.-G. Canada (Quebec Veto Reference),* [1982] 2 S.C.R. 793.
13   Christopher P. Manfredi and Michael Lusztig, "Why Do Formal Amendments Fail? An Institutional Design Analysis," *World Politics* 50 (1998): 387.
14   Andrew Heard, *Canadian Constitutional Conventions: The Marriage of Law and Politics* (Toronto: Oxford University Press, 1991).
15   *Edwards v. A.-G. Canada,* [1930] A.C. 124, at 136.

16 Peter W. Hogg, *Constitutional Law of Canada*, 3rd ed. (Toronto: Carswell, 1992), 774-77.
17 Patrick Monahan, *Politics and the Constitution: The Charter, Federalism and the Supreme Court of Canada* (Toronto: Carswell/Methuen, 1987), 221-44.
18 Ibid., 21.
19 Peter H. Russell, *The Judiciary in Canada: The Third Branch of Government* (Toronto: McGraw-Hill Ryerson, 1987), 343.
20 Christopher P. Manfredi, *Judicial Power and the Charter: Canada and the Paradox of Liberal Constitutionalism*, 2nd ed. (Toronto: Oxford University Press, 2001), 17.
21 Romanow, Whyte, and Leeson, *Canada Notwithstanding*, 248.
22 That rule is contained in section 33 of the Charter, which allows the federal and provincial governments to declare that legislation shall operate "notwithstanding" the fundamental freedoms, legal rights, and equality rights entrenched through the Charter.
23 Jill Vickers, Pauline Rankin, and Christine Appelle, *Politics as if Women Mattered: A Political Analysis of the National Action Committee on the Status of Women* (Toronto: University of Toronto Press, 1993), 104-19; Leslie A. Pal, *Interests of State: The Politics of Language, Multiculturalism, and Feminism in Canada* (Montreal and Kingston: McGill-Queen's University Press, 1993), 231.
24 *Joint Committee Proceedings*, 17:64 (2 December 1980).
25 Ibid., 24:61, 79 (11 December 1980).
26 Ibid., 9:57 (20 November 1980).
27 Ibid., 9:58-61 (20 November 1980).
28 This recommendation was repeated by NAWL. See ibid., 22:53 (9 December 1980).
29 NAWL also argued for expanding the list of prohibited grounds of discrimination to include marital status, physical or mental handicaps, political belief, sexual orientation, and previous conviction. Ibid., 22:58 (9 December 1980).
30 Once again, this recommendation can be found in NAWL's testimony. Ibid., 22:53 (9 December 1980).
31 Ibid., 9:66 (20 November 1980).
32 Ibid., 9:124 (20 November 1980). Emphasis added.
33 Ibid., 9:127 (20 November 1980).
34 I use the term "sex" rather than "gender" here because it is the ground of distinction actually listed in section 15, and it is the term that CAC used in its submission.
35 *Joint Committee Proceedings*, 9:151 (20 November 1980).
36 Ibid., 22:58 (9 December 1980).
37 Gerald Gunther, "The Supreme Court, 1971 Term – Forward: In Search of Evolving Doctrine on a Changing Court: A Model for Newer Equal Protection," *Harvard Law Review* 86 (1972): 8.
38 The rational basis test simply requires that statutory classifications be reasonable in view of their purposes. Intermediate or heightened scrutiny requires that classifications be substantially related to achieving important governmental objectives.
39 Like NAC, NAWL also objected to this clause. See *Joint Committee Proceedings*, 22:53 (9 December 1980).
40 Ibid., 22:62-63 (9 December 1980).
41 I am grateful to Lori Hausegger for bringing this point to my attention.
42 See ibid., 22:56 (9 December 1980).
43 This recommendation was contained in NAWL's evidence. See ibid., 22:55 (9 December 1980).
44 The full text of section 28 is, "Notwithstanding anything in this Charter, the rights and freedoms referred to in it are guaranteed equally to male and female persons."
45 See Penney Kome, *The Taking of Twenty-Eight: Women Challenge the Constitutional* (Toronto: Women's Press, 1983). The statements of Joe Clark and Ed Broadbent in the House of Commons Debates on section 28 are significant. *See House of Commons Debates*, 20 November 1981, pp. 13050, 13056.
46 Pal, *Interests of State*, 143.

47 Mary Eberts, "The Constitution, the Charter, and the Distinct Society Clause: Why Are Women Being Ignored?" in Michael D. Behiels, *The Meech Lake Primer: Conflicting Views of the 1987 Constitutional Accord* (Ottawa: University of Ottawa Press, 1989), 313.
48 *Toronto Star*, 9 April 1988. Quoted in Behiels, *The Meech Lake Primer*, 283.
49 Eberts, "The Constitution, the Charter, and the Distinct Society Clause," 304.
50 Vickers, Rankin, and Appelle, *Politics as if Women Mattered*, 276.
51 Monahan, *Meech Lake*, 146, 157, 181.
52 Kenneth McRoberts and Patrick Monahan, eds., *The Charlottetown Accord, the Referendum, and the Future of Canada* (Toronto: University of Toronto Press, 1993), 104.
53 Ibid., 106, 58.
54 Vickers, Rankin, and Appelle, *Politics As If Women Mattered*, 277-78.
55 Michael Lusztig, "Constitutional Paralysis: Why Canadian Constitutional Initiatives Are Doomed to Fail," *Canadian Journal of Political Science* 27 (1994): 767.
56 Vickers, Rankin, and Appelle, *Politics as if Women Mattered*, 275.
57 It should be noted that the Meech Lake Accord also remained controversial from the perspective of Aboriginal Canadians.
58 *Joint Committee Proceedings*, 22:50 (9 December 1980).
59 M. Elizabeth Atcheson, Mary Eberts, and Beth Symes, *Women and Legal Action: Precedents, Resources and Strategies for the Future* (Ottawa: Canadian Advisory Council on the Status of Women, 1984). Atcheson had appeared before the Joint Committee for NAWL, while Eberts had appeared for CAC.
60 Sherene Razack, *Canadian Feminism and the Law: The Women's Legal Education and Action Fund and the Pursuit of Equality* (Toronto: Second Story Press, 1991), 47.
61 Atcheson, Eberts, and Symes, *Women and Legal Action*, 172.
62 Gayle Noble, *Legal Literature and S. 15 Charter Litigation: An Interest Group Strategy* (MA research essay, Department of Political Science, McGill University, 1993), 12-13.
63 Ibid., 19.
64 Ibid., 23, 49.
65 [1989] 1 S.C.R. 143. Andrews, a British subject with the status of permanent resident in Canada, brought the original dispute before the British Columbia Supreme Court in 1985. The Supreme Court of Canada added Kinersly, a US citizen permanently resident in Canada and articling in British Columbia, as a co-respondent on 28 January 1987. The Court apparently took this step to avoid the problem of mootness, since Andrews acquired Canadian citizenship before the case was resolved.
66 For a discussion and defence of judicial minimalism, see Cass Sunstein, *One Case at a Time: Judicial Minimalism on the Supreme Court* (Cambridge, MA: Harvard University Press, 1999).
67 Factum of the Women's Legal Education and Action Fund, *Andrews* v. *Law Society of British Columbia*, paras. 1-2.
68 Ibid., paras. 4, 3.
69 *Hunter* v. *Southam* (1984), 11 D.L.R. (4th) 641, at 650.
70 *Law Society of Upper Canada* v. *Skapinker* (1984), 9 D.L.R. (4th) 161, at 169. See *Marbury* v. *Madison*, 1 Cranch (5 U.S.) 137 (1803) and *McCulloch* v. *Maryland*, 17 U.S. 316 (1819).
71 *Reference re s.94(2) of the Motor Vehicle Act (B.C.)* (1985), 24 D.L.R. (4th) 536, at 554-55.
72 LEAF Factum, *Andrews*, para. 7.
73 Ibid., para. 8; *R.* v. *Oakes*, [1986] 1 S.C.R. 103, at 136.
74 *R.* v. *Edwards Books and Art* (1986), 35 D.L.R. (4th) 1. See Janet Hiebert, *Limiting Rights: The Dilemma of Judicial Review* (Montreal and Kingston: McGill-Queen's University Press, 1996), 64, 76.
75 To be sure, Andrews was also an immigrant, which made him a member of a historically disadvantaged group. However, he was also different from the types of immigrants who had been discriminated against in the past.
76 LEAF Factum, *Andrews*, para. 13.
77 Ibid., paras. 14-15.
78 Ibid., paras. 21, 24.
79 [1989] 1 S.C.R. at 163-64.
80 Ibid., 163-69.

81 Ibid., 170-71.
82 Ibid., 174.
83 LEAF Factum, *Andrews,* para. 41.
84 [1989] 1 S.C.R. at 183. Discrete and insular minorities differ from other social groups in that their members share a common characteristic that sets them apart from the majority *and* imposes obstacles that render them incapable of defending or advancing their commonly shared interests through ordinary political action. Since noncitizens lack political power, including the basic right to vote, it is understandable that McIntyre would describe them as discrete and insular.
85 See Rainer Knopff, *Human Rights and Social Technology: The New War on Discrimination* (Ottawa: Carleton University Press, 1989), 224.
86 LEAF Factum, *Andrews,* para. 37.
87 Factum of the Women's Legal Education and Action Fund, *Janzen* v. *Platy Enterprises,* para. 11.
88 Catharine MacKinnon, *Sexual Harassment of Working Women* (New Haven, CT, and London: Yale University Press, 1979) and Constance Backhouse and Leah Cohen, *The Secret Oppression: Sexual Harassment of Working Women* (Toronto: Macmillan of Canada, 1978).
89 LEAF Factum, *Janzen,* para. 10.
90 Ibid., paras. 13-15.
91 Ibid., para. 40.
92 M.A. Hickling, "Employer's Liability for Sexual Harassment," *Manitoba Law Journal* 17 (1988): 127. See LEAF Factum, *Janzen,* para. 18.
93 Arjun P. Aggarwal, *Sexual Harassment in the Workplace* (Toronto: Butterworths, 1987).
94 LEAF Factum, *Janzen,* para. 6, quoted in *Janzen* v. *Platy Enterprises,* [1989] 1 S.C.R. 1252, section v, para. 48.
95 Factum of the Women's Legal Education and Action Fund, *Weatherall* v. *Canada,* paras. 17-20.
96 Joanne St. Lewis, "Beyond the Confinement of Gender: Locating the Space of Legal Existence for Racialized Women," in *Women's Legal Strategies in Canada,* ed. Radha Jhappan (Toronto: University of Toronto Press, 2002), 315-16.
97 LEAF Factum, *Weatherall,* para. 37.
98 Ibid., para. 38.
99 Ibid., para. 28.
100 *Gould* v. *Yukon Order of Pioneers,* [1996] 1 S.C.R. 571.
101 This component of the test required that firefighters be able to run two and a half kilometres in eleven minutes.
102 Factum of the Women's Legal Education and Action Fund, *BCPSERC,* paras. 68, 73.
103 Ibid., paras. 22-23.
104 Ibid., para. 17.
105 Ibid., para. 25.
106 Ibid., para. 26.
107 *British Columbia (Public Service Employee Relations Commission)* v. *BCGSEU,* [1999] 3 S.C.R. 3, para. 41, citing Shelagh Day and Gwen Brodsky, "The Duty to Accommodate: Who Will Benefit?" *Canadian Bar Review* 75 (1996): 462. LEAF's factum made extensive reference to this article, and Gwen Brodsky served as counsel for the appellant in the case.
108 Ibid., para. 41.
109 Ibid., para. 50.
110 Ibid., para. 54.
111 Ibid., para. 64.
112 Not surprisingly, the Court held that the occupational fitness test failed this three-pronged assessment of bona fide occupational requirements. The Court thus reversed the Court of Appeal and reinstated the arbitrator's judgment.
113 Section 7 states that "Everyone has the right to life, liberty and security of the person and the right not to be deprived thereof except in accordance with the principles of fundamental justice." For a commentary on its application, see Manfredi, *Judicial Power and the Charter,* 75-102.

114   Ian Brodie, "The Market for Political Status," *Comparative Politics* 28 (1996): 253.
115   *Minutes and Proceedings of the Special Joint Committee*, 48:28, 33 (29 January 1981).
116   *Andrews* v. *Law Society of British Columbia*, [1989] 1 S.C.R. 143 (citizenship); *Egan* v. *Canada*, [1995] 2 S.C.R. 513 (sexual orientation).
117   *Reference re workers' compensation act, 1983 (Nfld.)*, [1989] 1 S.C.R. 922 (workers' compensation claimants challenging lack of access to courts); *Weatherall* v. *Canada (Attorney General)*, [1993] 2 S.C.R. 872 (male prisoners seeking relief from cross-gender personal searches).
118   Several states actually revoked their initial ratification of the ERA, and the province of Newfoundland revoked its ratification of the Meech Lake Accord.

Chapter 3: Gaining Ground

1   *Borowski* v. *Canada*, [1989] 1 S.C.R. 342; *Tremblay* v. *Daigle*, [1989] 2 S.C.R. 530; *R.* v. *Sullivan*, [1991] 1 S.C.R. 489; *Winnipeg Child and Family Services* v. *G. (D.F.)*, [1997] 3 S.C.R. 925. A note on spelling is in order here. The Canadian Supreme Court generally uses the spelling "foetal" and "foetus." I have opted for "fetal" and "fetus," except where I am quoting the Court directly.
2   *R.* v. *Keegstra*, [1990] 3 S.C.R. 697; *R.* v. *Andrews and Smith*, [1990] 3 S.C.R. 870; *Canada* v. *Taylor*, [1990] 3 S.C.R. 892; *R.* v. *Butler*, [1992] 1 S.C.R. 452; *Little Sisters Book and Art Emporium* v. *Canada*, [2000] 2 S.C.R. 1120.
3   *Vriend* v. *Alberta*, [1998] 1 S.C.R. 493; *M.* v. *H.*, [1999] 2 S.C.R. 3.
4   To remind readers, I count as an "issue" any general point of law or policy on which LEAF made an argument in its factum.
5   Other defining issues include pay equity and violence against women.
6   *Griswold* v. *Connecticut*, 381 U.S. 479 (1965); *Eisenstadt* v. *Baird*, 405 U.S. 438 (1972); *Roe* v. *Wade*, 410 U.S. 113 (1973).
7   These amendments included the First (freedom of speech and religion), Third (prohibition on the quartering of soldiers in private homes during peacetime), Fourth (prohibition against unwarranted searches and seizures), Fifth (right against self-incrimination) and Ninth (unenumerated rights).
8   *Stenberg* v. *Carhart*, 530 U.S. 914 (2000). A majority of the Court finally accepted the undue burden test, long championed by Justice Sandra Day O'Connor, in *Planned Parenthood of Southeastern Pa.* v. *Casey*, 505 U.S. 833 (1992).
9   See F.L. Morton, *Morgentaler v. Borowski: Abortion, the Charter and the Courts* (Toronto: McClelland and Stewart, 1992).
10   *Morgentaler* v. *The Queen*, [1976] 1 S.C.R. 616, 671.
11   *Min. of Justice (Canada)* v. *Borowski*, [1981] 2 S.C.R. 575, 598.
12   [1988] 1 S.C.R. 30.
13   *Morgentaler, Smoling and Scott* v. *The Queen*, [1988] 1 S.C.R. 30, 46.
14   Lorne Bozinoff and André Turcotte, "Support for Legalization of Abortion Is Increasing," *The Gallup Report*, 19 October 1992.
15   As noted above, the *Roe* decision granted women an unconditional right to abortion during the first trimester of pregnancy but allowed states to impose health-related regulations during the second trimester and to prohibit third trimester abortions altogether. However, the right to abortion did not include an obligation for public funding of the procedure.
16   *Morgentaler, Smoling and Scott* v. *The Queen*, [1988] 1 S.C.R. 30, 143.
17   Ibid., 172.
18   Ibid., 63.
19   Government of Canada, Committee on the Operation of the Abortion Law, *Report of the Committee on the Operation of the Abortion Law* (Ottawa: Supply and Services, 1977).
20   Factum of the Women's Legal Education and Action Fund, *Borowski* v. *Canada*, para. 6.
21   *Morgentaler, Smoling and Scott* v. *The Queen*, [1988] 1 S.C.R. 30, at 51 (Dickson), 141 (McIntyre). See LEAF Factum, *Borowski*, paras. 8, 11.
22   Robert H. Bork, *Coercing Virtue: The Worldwide Rule of Judges* (Toronto: Vintage Canada, 2002), 75.
23   LEAF Factum, *Borowski*, para. 12.

24 Cass Sunstein, *One Case at a Time: Judicial Minimalism on the Supreme Court* (Cambridge, MA: Harvard University Press, 1999), 9.
25 Ibid., 46, 53.
26 Interestingly, three years later LEAF would argue for an even broader rule of "public-interest standing" than the one granted to Joe Borowski. See Factum of the Women's Legal Education and Action Fund, *Canadian Council of Churches* v. *Canada*, [1992] 1 S.C.R. 236, paras. 81-84.
27 LEAF Factum, *Borowski*, para. 23.
28 Ibid., para. 54.
29 Ibid., para. 60.
30 The narrative in this paragraph is drawn from Morton, *Morgentaler* v. *Borowski*, 275-80.
31 Factum of the Women's Legal Education and Action Fund, *Daigle* v. *Tremblay*, paras. 3-24.
32 Ibid., para. 36.
33 Ibid., para. 38.
34 Ibid., para. 44. Compare this to LEAF Factum, *Borowski*, para. 54.
35 Morton, *Morgentaler* v. *Borowski*, 282.
36 Factum of the Women's Legal Education and Action Fund, *R.* v. *Sullivan and Lemay*, para. 34.
37 Ibid., para. 41.
38 Ibid., paras. 42-43, 50.
39 *R.* v. *Sullivan*, [1991] 1 S.C.R. 489.
40 Factum of the Women's Legal Education and Action Fund, *Winnipeg Child and Family Services* v. *G. (D.F.)*, para. 7.
41 Ibid., para. 14.
42 Ibid., para. 19.
43 Ibid., para. 22.
44 LEAF Factum, *Borowski*, para. 18. In this paragraph LEAF contrasted birth to the moment of conception and the point of fetal viability, arguing that these vary from case to case and according to changes in medical technology.
45 LEAF Factum, *Winnipeg Child and Family Services*, para. 24.
46 Ibid., para. 34. As an Aboriginal woman with a substance addiction problem, G arguably fell under three of section 15's enumerated categories: race, sex, and disability. Without citing any legal authority, LEAF also listed poverty as a characteristic protected under section 15. However, poverty is not enumerated in section 15, nor has the Court ever recognized it as an analogous ground of discrimination.
47 [1997] 3 S.C.R. 925, para. 4.
48 Ibid., para. 15.
49 Ibid., para. 12.
50 John Hart Ely, "The Wages of Crying Wolf: A Comment on *Roe* v. *Wade*," *Yale Law Journal* 82 (1973): 926.
51 See, for example, *Friends of Point Pleasant Park* v. *A.-G. Canada*, Docket T-1235-00 (F.C.T.D., 21 August 2000), in which a Federal Court judge issued an interlocutory injunction against the destruction of trees in a Halifax park. The injunction was later dissolved.
52 [1997] 3 S.C.R. 925, para. 18.
53 Ibid., para. 20. The changes included, (1) overturning the rule that rights accrue to a person only at birth; (2) recognizing a fetal right to sue the mother carrying the fetus; (3) recognizing a cause of action for lifestyle choices which may adversely affect others; and (4) recognizing an injunctive remedy which deprives a defendant of important liberties, including her involuntary confinement.
54 Ibid., paras. 30-45. The reference is to Dawn E. Johnsen, "The Creation of Fetal Rights: Conflicts with Women's Constitutional Rights to Liberty, Privacy and Equal Protection," *Yale Law Journal* 95 (1986): 606-7.
55 [1997] 3 S.C.R. 925, para. 47.
56 Ibid., para. 58.
57 John Stuart Mill, *On Liberty*, ed. C.V. Shields (Indianapolis: Bobbs-Merrill, 1956 [1859]), 19.

58   Stephen Holmes, *Passions and Constraints: On the Theory of Liberal Democracy* (Chicago: University of Chicago Press, 1995), 183, 171.
59   Ibid., 169.
60   Ibid., 179.
61   This language is borrowed from *The Federalist Papers*. See Alexander Hamilton, James Madison, and John Jay, *The Federalist Papers*, ed. C. Rossiter (New York: New American Library, 1961), no. 1, 33.
62   Holmes, *Passions and Constraints*, 182.
63   John Rawls, *Political Liberalism* (New York: Columbia University Press, 1993), 303.
64   Mill, *On Liberty*, 85.
65   Ibid., 42.
66   "Congress shall make no law ... abridging the freedom of speech."
67   *Roth* v. *United States*, 354 U.S. 476 (1957).
68   *Miller* v. *California*, 413 U.S. 15 (1973).
69   *Stanley* v. *Georgia*, 394 U.S. 561 (1969).
70   *Taylor* v. *The Canadian Human Rights Commission*, [1990] 3 S.C.R. 892; *R.* v. *Andrews and Smith*, [1990] 3 S.C.R. 870; *R.* v. *Keegstra*, [1990] 3 S.C.R. 697.
71   *R.* v. *Keegstra*, [1990] 3 S.C.R. 733, 755-57, 833-35, 847.
72   Kathleen Mahoney, "*R.* v. *Keegstra*: A Rationale for Regulating Pornography?" *McGill Law Journal* 37 (1992): 242-69.
73   *R.* v. *Butler*, [1992] 1 S.C.R. 452.
74   Factum of the Women's Legal Education and Action Fund, *R.* v. *Butler*, para. 7.
75   Ibid.
76   These harms included "dehumanization, humiliation, sexual exploitation, forced sex, forced prostitution, physical injury, child sexual abuse, and sexual harassment." More generally, according to LEAF, "pornography also diminishes the reputation of women as a group, deprives women of their credibility and social and self worth, and undermines women's equal access to protected rights." See LEAF Factum, *Butler*, para. 23.
77   *Irwin Toy* v. *A.-G. Quebec*, [1989] 1 S.C.R. 927. In this case, the Court defined expression as any activity that attempts to convey meaning, with the exception of actual violence.
78   LEAF Factum, *Butler*, para. 30.
79   Ibid., para. 34.
80   Ibid., para. 35.
81   Ibid., para. 65.
82   [1992] 1 S.C.R. 452, at 491-92.
83   Ibid., 502.
84   Ibid., 501.
85   Ibid., at 507.
86   Ibid., 503-4.
87   Ibid., 509.
88   Although obscenity is not protected by the First Amendment's "free speech" clause, US feminists have been unable to persuade the courts to recognize the constitutionality of antipornography regulations similar to the one upheld in *Butler*. For example, an Indianapolis municipal ordinance similar to the Canadian regulation was declared unconstitutional in *American Booksellers' Association* v. *Hudnut*, 771 F.2d. 323 (7th Cir. 1975), a decision subsequently affirmed by the US Supreme Court, 475 U.S. 1001 (1986). For a discussion, see David Bryden, "Between Two Constitutions: Feminism and Pornography," *Constitutional Commentary* 2 (1985), 147-89.
89   Nancy Pollack, "Business as Usual," *Ms.* (May/June 1995), 12.
90   See, e.g., Brenda Cossman, ed., *Bad Attitudes on Trial: Pornography, Feminism and the Butler Decision* (Toronto: University of Toronto Press, 1997).
91   Statement by Catherine A. MacKinnon and Andrea Dworkin Regarding Canadian Customs and Legal Approaches to Pornography, 26 August 1994. Available at <http://www.igc.org/Womensnet/dworkin/OrdinanceCanada.html> (23 August 2001).
92   [2000] 2 S.C.R. 1120.

93   Factum of the Women's Legal Education and Action Fund, *Little Sisters Book and Art Emporium* v. *Canada*, para. 2.
94   Ibid., para. 8.
95   Ibid., para. 11.
96   Ibid., para. 24.
97   Ibid., para. 29.
98   Ibid., paras. 44-46.
99   LEAF Factum, *Butler*, para. 5.
100 *Little Sisters Book and Art Emporium* v. *Canada*, [2000] 2 S.C.R. 1120, at paras. 63-64. One should note that LEAF's factum does not explicitly link sado-masochism (S&M) to gay and lesbian culture, although it does argue that the harmfulness of gay and lesbian S&M must be evaluated differently than heterosexual S&M. See LEAF Factum, *Little Sisters*, para. 34.
101 [2000] 2 S.C.R. 1120, at para. 165.
102 Ibid., para. 268.
103 Miriam Smith, *Lesbian and Gay Rights in Canada: Social Movements and Equality-Seeking, 1971-1995* (Toronto: University of Toronto Press, 1999), 41.
104 See Equality Now's website at <http://www.equalitynow.org> (31 July 2002).
105 Janine Benedet, "*Little Sisters Book and Art Emporium* v. *Minister of Justice:* Sex Equality and the Attack on *R.* v. *Butler*," *Osgoode Hall Law Journal* 39 (2001): 187-204. In direct contradiction to LEAF's claim, Benedet argues that "gay and lesbian pornography is a threat to sex equality."
106 Ibid., 189, 191, 204. Benedet points out, for example, that Little Sisters was not a lesbian or women's bookstore but was owned by two gay men who had named it after their cat. She also points out that the long court battle was the result of the bookstore's appealing the trial court's remedy.
107 [1993] 1 S.C.R. 554.
108 Ibid., 579.
109 [1995] 2 S.C.R. 513.
110 Ibid., 528.
111 [1998] 1 S.C.R. 493.
112 Factum of the Women's Legal Education and Action Fund, *Vriend* v. *Alberta*, para. 4.
113 Ibid., paras. 25-36.
114 [1998] 1 S.C.R. 493, paras. 102, 104.
115 Ibid., para. 116.
116 Ibid., para. 77: "the fact that a lesbian and a heterosexual woman are both entitled to bring a complaint of discrimination on the basis of gender does not mean that they have *equal* protection under the Act" (emphasis in original).
117 LEAF Factum, *Vriend*, para. 32.
118 *M.* v. *H.*, [1999] 2 S.C.R. 3.
119 Factum of the Women's Legal Education and Action Fund, *M.* v. *H.*, paras. 4-18. The factum did not ignore the section 15 issue entirely, however. Inaccurately describing the Charter as "the supreme law of Canada" for the second time in five years, LEAF lifted two paragraphs almost verbatim from its *Vriend* factum to characterize the fundamental purposes of section 15. This factum continued by describing the discriminatory effects of the distinction between "heterosexual common law relationships and intimate lesbian relationships" as consisting in "promoting and preserving the view that lesbians are less worthy, less capable and less valuable as human beings and as members of Canadian society and therefore not equally deserving of concern, respect and consideration."
120 LEAF Factum, *M.* v. *H.*, para. 22.
121 Ibid., paras. 31-33.
122 Ibid., para. 51. There is some irony in this assertion since the M and H relationship did in fact resemble a "normal" heterosexual relationship. H was the couple's principal "breadwinner," while M undertook most of the domestic responsibilities. H apparently precipitated the breakdown because of dissatisfaction with M's unequal financial contribution to the relationship. When H presented M with a draft agreement to end the relationship, M

took some personal belongings and left their common residence. H responded by changing the locks on the house. That M and H's relationship, like Egan's forty-year relationship with his partner, did not exceptionally deviate from the heterosexual "norm" is consistent with one of the strategic demands of legal mobilization: select sympathetic parties and fact situations that do not require courts to venture into completely uncharted terrain.

123 Ibid., para. 49.
124 Ibid., para. 56.
125 Ibid., paras. 60-61.
126 Ibid., para. 62.
127 [1999] 2 S.C.R. 3, at para. 110. Compare this with the following from LEAF's factum, para. 39: "The infrequency with which members of same-sex couples find themselves in situations akin to those of many heterosexual women is thus no different from heterosexual men who – notwithstanding the fact that they generally profit from the gendered division of labour – are entitled to support when their individual circumstances warrant."
128 [1999] 2 S.C.R. 3, at para. 120. "Indeed, as submitted by LEAF, the *FLA* expressly recognizes that entitlement to the division of property is in addition to, and not in lieu of entitlement to support. Thus, it seems to me that compared to awards of spousal support, the equitable remedies are less flexible, impose more onerous requirements on claimants, and are available under far narrower circumstances. I do not accept that they provide an adequate alternative to spousal support under the *FLA*." This submission can be found in LEAF's factum, paras. 60-61.
129 [1999] 2 S.C.R. 3, at para. 43.
130 Ibid., para. 44.
131 The amendment was the subject of a vigorous public and legislative debate, in which gay and lesbian rights activists enjoyed the support of the premier and his cabinet. Nevertheless, the Ontario legislature defeated the amendment in a free vote.
132 [1999] 2 S.C.R. 3, at para. 45.
133 *Law* v. *Canada (Minister of Employment and Immigration)*, [1999] 1 S.C.R. 497. The Court issued this judgment two months before its judgment in *M.* v. *H.*
134 Ibid., para. 51.
135 Ibid., para. 39.
136 [1999] 2 S.C.R. 3, para. 73.
137 Ibid., para. 74.
138 *Vriend* v. *Alberta*, [1998] 1 S.C.R. 493, paras. 129-43. Iacobucci cited the following examples of these critics: Anthony Peacock, ed., *Rethinking the Constitution: Perspectives on Canadian Constitutional Reform, Interpretation, and Theory* (Toronto: Oxford University Press, 1996); Rainer Knopff and F.L. Morton, *Charter Politics* (Scarborough, ON: Nelson Canada, 1992); and Michael Mandel, *The Charter of Rights and the Legalization of Politics in Canada*, rev. ed. (Toronto: Thompson Educational Publishing, 1994). Iacobucci also referred to Alexander Bickel, *The Least Dangerous Branch: The Supreme Court at the Bar of Politics*, 2nd ed. (New Haven, CT: Yale University Press, 1986). While Iacobucci described Bickel's book as "eloquent" and "outstanding," he was silent about the quality of the other volumes. One might speculate that this was done intentionally to denigrate the Canadian critics. My own bias may be discerned from the fact that I am the author of one of the chapters in the Peacock volume.
139 [1999] 2 S.C.R. 3, para. 52.
140 Ibid., para. 134.
141 The legal, as opposed to symbolic, value of this amendment is highly questionable because the definition of marriage is within federal jurisdiction under the Constitution Act, 1867.
142 Kirk Makin, "Gay Couples Win Rights," *Globe and Mail*, 21 May 1999, A1.
143 Justice Claire L'Heureux-Dubé, "Opening Remarks to the Panel Discussion: Same-Sex Partnerships in Canada," Conference on the Legal Recognition of Same-Sex Partnerships, London, UK, 1 July 1999.

Chapter 4: Family Matters
  1 [1992] 3 S.C.R. 813; [1995] 2 S.C.R. 627; [1996] 2 S.C.R. 27.

2 [1975] 1 S.C.R. 423. See W.A. Bogart, *Courts and Country: The Limits of Litigation and the Social and Political Life of Canada* (Toronto: Oxford University Press, 1994), 137-38.
3 Factum of the Women's Legal Education and Action Fund, *Moge v. Moge*, para. 32.
4 Ibid., paras. 33-35.
5 Ibid., para. 41.
6 Ibid., para. 64.
7 Ibid., para. 66.
8 Ibid., para. 67.
9 Ibid., paras. 71, 73.
10 Six justices decided the appeal. Justice McLachlin wrote a concurring judgment.
11 [1992] 3 S.C.R. 813, para. 41.
12 Ibid., para. 42. Emphasis in original.
13 Ibid., para. 47.
14 This material included Law Reform Commission of Canada, *Maintenance on Divorce: Working Paper 12* (Ottawa: Information Canada, 1975); Miriam Grassby, "Women in Their Forties: The Extent of Their Rights to Alimentary Support," *Review of Family Law 3d* 30 (1991): 369-403; E. Diane Pask and M.L. McCall, "How Much and Why? An Overview," *Canadian Family Law Quarterly* 5 (1989): 129-50; Carol J. Rogerson, "Judicial Interpretation of the Spousal and Child Support Provisions of the *Divorce Act, 1985* (Part I)," *Canadian Family Law Quarterly* 7 (1990-91): 155-314; Carol J. Rogerson, "The Causal Connection Test in Spousal Support Law," *Canadian Journal of Family Law* 8 (1989): 95-132.
15 [1992] 3 S.C.R. 813, para. 73.
16 Ibid.
17 Ibid., para. 91.
18 Ibid., para. 102.
19 This section of the factum contains seven references to L'Heureux-Dubé's *Moge* judgment.
20 The LEAF factum again referred to the Charter as the supreme law of Canada. See Factum of the Women's Legal Education and Action Fund, *Gordon v. Goertz*, para. 19.
21 Ibid., para. 23.
22 Ibid., paras. 34, 36.
23 Ibid., para. 40.
24 Ibid., para. 49.
25 [1996] 2 S.C.R. 27, para. 8.
26 Ibid., para. 48.
27 Factum of the Women's Legal Education and Action Fund, *Thibaudeau v. Canada*, para. 2.
28 Ibid., paras. 22-23.
29 Ibid., para. 30.
30 Ibid., para. 37.
31 Ibid., para. 44.
32 Ibid., paras. 36, 46.
33 Christopher P. Manfredi, *Judicial Power and the Charter: Canada and the Paradox of Liberal Constitutionalism,* 2nd ed. (Toronto: Oxford University Press, 2001), 127, 130.
34 Ibid., 126-27. Two of five such cases were successful through 1999.
35 *Thibaudeau v. Canada*, paras. 103-19 (*per* Gonthier, J.).
36 Ibid., para. 6 (*per* L'Heureux-Dubé, J.).
37 Ibid., para. 42 (*per* L'Heureux-Dubé, J.).
38 *Symes v. Canada,* [1993] 4 S.C.R. 695, 786 (*per* L'Heureux-Dubé, J.).
39 Ibid., 826.
40 Ibid., 828.
41 *Thibaudeau v. Canada,* para. 205 (*per* McLachlin, J.).
42 Income Tax Budget Amendments Act, 1996, S.C. 1997, c. 25. The amendments were not retroactive, however.
43 See Sherene Razack, *Canadian Feminism and the Law: The Women's Legal Education and Action Fund and the Pursuit of Equality* (Toronto: Second Story Press, 1991), 89-94.
44 *Schachter v. The Queen* (1988) 52 D.L.R. (4th) 525 (F.C.T.D.).
45 Ibid., 548.

46 *Schachter* v. *The Queen* (1990), 66 D.L.R. (4th) 635, 652 (F.C.A).
47 Factum of the Women's Legal Education and Action Fund, *R.* v. *Schachter*, para. 3.
48 Ibid., para. 4.
49 Ibid., para. 38.
50 Ibid., para. 39.
51 Ibid., para. 42.
52 Ibid., para. 47.
53 Ibid., paras. 48-49. Citing John Hart Ely, *Democracy and Distrust* (Cambridge, MA: Harvard University Press, 1980), 78.
54 Ely, *Democracy and Distrust*, 11-41, 92, 102.
55 See LEAF Factum, *Schachter*, para. 51.
56 Ely, *Democracy and Distrust*, 166-67.
57 LEAF Factum, *Schachter*, para. 56.
58 Ibid.
59 Even if this were the case, it is unclear that it would be unconstitutional according to Ely's theory. In a discussion of affirmative action, Ely allows that there is "nothing constitutionally suspicious about a majority's discriminating against itself." See Ely, *Democracy and Distrust*, 172.
60 Otherwise, why provide adoptive fathers with benefits that would allow adoptive mothers to continue their employment during an adopted child's integration into the family?
61 LEAF Factum, *Schachter*, para. 64.
62 Ibid., para. 76.
63 [1992] 2 S.C.R. 679, 695. Note that the Court did not express the same concerns about constitutional concessions in *Egan* or *M.* v. *H.* Indeed, in contrast to Chief Justice Lamer in *Schachter*, Justice Cory did not find any difficulty in considering the nature of the section 15 violation in *M.* v. *H.*, despite Ontario's constitutional concession on this point.
64 Ibid., 697.
65 Ibid., 699.
66 Ibid., 702.
67 Ibid., 719.
68 Ibid., 720.
69 LEAF Factum, *Schachter*, 75.
70 [1992] 2 S.C.R. 679, 723.
71 Ibid., 726-29.
72 Ibid., 723.
73 [1997] 3 S.C.R. 624.
74 The five principles of the Canada Health Act are public administration, comprehensiveness, universality, portability, and equal access.
75 Peggy Leatt and A. Paul Williams, "The Health Systems of Canada," in *Health Care and Reform in Industrialized Countries*, ed. M. Raffel (University Park, PA: Pennsylvania State University Press, 1997), 12-15.
76 Factum of the Women's Legal Education and Action Fund, *Eldridge* v. *British Columbia*, paras. 5-6.
77 Ibid., para. 10.
78 [1999] 3 S.C.R. 3. See the discussion of this case *(BCPSERC)* in Chapter 2, above.
79 LEAF Factum, *Eldridge*, para. 35. The source of this argument was Shelagh Day and Gwen Brodsky, "The Duty to Accommodate: Who Will Benefit?" *Canadian Bar Review* 7 (1996): 462-63. Although the Court would not refer to this article in *Eldridge*, it would list it among the authors cited in *BCPSERC* two years later.
80 LEAF Factum, *Eldridge*, para. 36.
81 Ibid., paras. 11, 14.
82 Ibid., paras. 21-23.
83 Ibid., paras. 19, 25.
84 Ibid., para. 47.
85 [1999] 3 S.C.R. 3, para. 87.
86 Ibid., para. 89. See LEAF Factum, *Eldridge*, para. 61.

87 Factum of the Province of British Columbia, *Eldridge* v. *British Columbia*, paras. 125-26.
88 The others were the Charter Committee on Poverty Issues, the Canadian Association of the Deaf, the Canadian Hearing Society, and the Council of Canadians with Disabilities.
89 Factum of the Appellants, *Eldridge* v. *British Columbia*, paras. 48-50.
90 Factum of the Intervener the Attorney General of Manitoba, *Eldridge*, para. 6.
91 Factum of the Intervener the Attorney General of Ontario, *Eldridge*, para. 34.
92 Factum of the Intervener the Attorney General of Newfoundland, *Eldridge*, paras. 19-20.
93 Factum of the Attorney General of Canada, *Eldridge*, para. 41.
94 [1997] 3 S.C.R. 3, paras. 72-73.
95 Ibid., para. 25.
96 Ibid., para. 24.
97 LEAF Factum, *Eldridge*, para. 64.
98 A key figure in this regard is Mary Jane Mossman of Osgoode Hall Law School. LEAF referred to two of her articles in its factum: "Gender Equality and Legal Services: A Research Agenda for Institutional Change," *Sydney Law Review* 15 (1993): 30-58 and "Gender Equality, Family Law and Access to Justice," *International Journal of Law and the Family* 8 (1994): 357-73. See also Mary Jane Mossman, "The Charter and Access to Justice in Canada," in *Charting the Consequences: The Impact of Charter Rights on Canadian Law and Politics,* ed. David Schneiderman and Kate Sutherland (Toronto: University of Toronto Press, 1997), 279-81.
99 Factum of the Women's Legal Education and Action Fund, *New Brunswick (Minister of Health and Community Services)* v. *G.(J.)*, paras. 15, 20, 21. To some degree this characterization echoed LEAF's description in *Winnipeg Child and Family Services* of the type of women likely to experience state intervention in their pregnancies under an expanded *parens patriae* doctrine.
100 Ibid., paras. 28, 23.
101 Ibid., paras. 25, 24.
102 This argument had also been used in *Winnipeg Child and Family Services* regarding Aboriginal women. In fact, LEAF's *NBMHCS* factum repeated the argument from its *WCFS* factum that the child welfare system had replaced the residential school system as the instrument for removing Aboriginal children from their homes.
103 LEAF Factum, *NBMHCS*, paras. 40, 42. For a discussion of the "dignity enhancement" approach to section 7, see Manfredi, *Judicial Power and the Charter*, 85-87.
104 LEAF Factum, *NBMHCS*, para. 43.
105 Ibid., para. 45.
106 Ibid., para. 47.
107 Ibid., para. 60.
108 [1999] 3 S.C.R. 46, para. 42. Godin had been represented by counsel, the custody order had expired, and she had regained custody of her children.
109 Ibid., para. 52.
110 Ibid., paras. 112-15. According to L'Heureux-Dubé, the case "raises issues of gender equality because women, and especially single mothers, are disproportionately and particularly affected by child protection proceedings." Consequently, "in considering the s. 7 rights at issue, and the principles of fundamental justice that apply in this situation, it is important to ensure that the analysis takes into account the principles and purposes of the equality guarantee in promoting the equal benefit of the law and ensuring that the law responds to the needs of those disadvantaged individuals and groups whose protection is at the heart of s. 15. The rights in s. 7 must be interpreted through the lens of ss. 15 and 28, to recognize the importance of ensuring that our interpretation of the Constitution responds to the realities and needs of all members of society." In making this argument, L'Heureux-Dubé cited extralegal material from LEAF's factum.
111 Ibid., para. 61.
112 Ibid., para. 70. For a discussion of how the Court came to define "fundamental justice" in both procedural and substantive terms, see Manfredi, *Judicial Power and the Charter*, 35-38.
113 Ibid., para. 75.
114 Ibid., paras. 75, 83, 100.

115 Ibid., para. 102.
116 Ibid., para. 107.
117 Ibid., para. 125.
118 LEAF Factum, *NBMHCS*, para. 67.
119 *R. v. Askov*, [1990] 2 S.C.R. 199. For a discussion, see Manfredi, *Judicial Power and the Charter*, 159-60, 162-63.

Chapter 5: A Difficult Dialogue

 1 *R. v. O'Connor*, [1995] 4 S.C.R. 411; *R. v. Seaboyer*, [1991] 2 S.C.R. 577.
 2 *R. v. Mills*, [1999] 3 S.C.R. 668, at para. 58.
 3 Ibid., para. 55.
 4 *R. v. Darrach*, [2000] 2 S.C.R. 443, at para. 34.
 5 Kirk Makin, "Top Court Bows to Will of Parliament," *Globe and Mail*, 26 November 1999, A1; Kent Roach, *The Supreme Court on Trial: Judicial Activism or Democratic Dialogue* (Toronto: Irwin Law, 2001), 271-73, 277-81.
 6 Peter W. Hogg and Allison A. Bushell, "The Charter Dialogue Between Courts and Legislatures," *Osgoode Hall Law Journal* 35 (1997): 75-124.
 7 Ibid., 82-91.
 8 Ibid., 81.
 9 Ibid., 82, 97.
10 Statistics Canada, <http://www.statcan.ca/english/Pgdb/State/Justice/legal02.htm> (31 January 2002); Canadian Center for Judicial Statistics, *The Juristat Reader: A Statistical Overview of the Canadian Justice System* (Toronto: Thompson Educational, 1999), 134.
11 Fourteen percent of the General Social Survey respondents who reported being victimized by a sexual assault also indicated that they did not know, or refused to state, whether the incident was reported to the police. Consequently, the actual reporting rate may range from a low of 8 percent to a high of 22 percent.
12 John A. Yogis, *Canadian Law Dictionary* (Toronto: Barron's Educational Series, 1983), 175.
13 See, e.g., *Forsythe v. The Queen*, [1980] 2 S.C.R. 268.
14 Matthew A. Hennigar, "Value Hierarchy on the Supreme Court of Canada: Explaining *Seaboyer* and *O'Connor*" (Unpublished manuscript on file with the author, 1997). Hennigar's study, which included all Supreme Court decisions concerning sexual assault and a due process value during pretrial, trial, and sentencing phases, covers nineteen cases decided between 1986 and 1996. I have used Hennigar's criteria to add fifteen cases decided from 1997 to 2000.
15 For the purposes of this analysis, substantive cases are those involving the definition of sexual assault, while procedural cases are those involving the rules for investigating and trying sexual assault charges.
16 In 1987, F.L. Morton concluded that criminal law enforcement was the area of public policy most affected by the Charter, and nothing has changed during the intervening fifteen years. F.L. Morton, "The Political Impact of the Canadian Charter of Rights and Freedoms," *Canadian Journal of Political Science* 20 (1987): 37.
17 Christopher P. Manfredi, *Judicial Power and the Charter: Canada and the Paradox of Liberal Constitutionalism*, 2nd ed. (Toronto: Oxford University Press, 2001), 83-90.
18 *R. v. Stinchcombe*, [1991] 3 S.C.R. 326.
19 Gerald Owen, "Disclosure After Stinchcombe," in *Rethinking the Constitution: Perspectives on Canadian Constitutional Reform, Interpretation, and Theory*, ed. Anthony Peacock (Toronto: Oxford University Press, 1996), 177-85.
20 Sheila McIntyre, "Feminist Movement in Law: Beyond Privileged and Privileging Theory," in *Women's Legal Strategies in Canada*, ed. Radha Jhappan (Toronto: University of Toronto Press, 2002), 69.
21 Ibid., 72-73.
22 Although both Norberg and Wynrib were content to treat their dispute as a purely private law case without any public law implications, Justice Sopinka had granted LEAF leave to intervene precisely in order to raise Charter issues that the principal parties were uninterested in pursuing. See Ian Brodie, *Friends of the Court: The Privileging of Interest Group Litigants in Canada* (Albany: State University of New York Press, 2002), 68.

23 Factum of the Women's Legal Education and Action Fund, *Norberg* v. *Wynrib*, para. 14.
24 Ibid., para. 17.
25 Ibid., para. 30.
26 Ibid., para. 31.
27 Ibid., para. 32.
28 *Norberg* v. *Wynrib*, [1992] 2 S.C.R. 226, 246.
29 Ibid., 247.
30 LEAF Factum, *Norberg* v. *Wynrib*, para. 9.
31 [1992] 2 S.C.R. 226, 304.
32 Factum of the Women's Legal Education and Action Fund, *R.* v. *M. (M.L.)*, para. 19.
33 Ibid., para. 30.
34 Ibid., para. 60.
35 Ibid., para. 61.
36 *R.* v. *M. (M.L.)*, [1994] 2 S.C.R. 3. Justice Sopinka – ironically, given his position in *Norberg* – wrote the judgment.
37 Factum of the Women's Legal Education and Action Fund, *R.* v. *Whitley*, para. 10.
38 Ibid., paras. 13-15.
39 Ibid., para. 18.
40 Ibid., para. 30.
41 [1999] 1 S.C.R. 330.
42 Factum of the Women's Legal Education and Action Fund, *R.* v. *Ewanchuk*, para. 8.
43 Ibid., para. 11.
44 Ibid., paras. 14, 16.
45 Ibid., para. 18.
46 Ibid., paras. 21-22.
47 Ibid., para. 25.
48 Ibid., para. 27.
49 Ibid., paras. 33, 34.
50 Ibid., para. 36.
51 Ibid., para. 41.
52 Ibid., para. 51.
53 Ibid., para. 54.
54 [1999] 1 S.C.R. 330, at para. 18. Justice McClung went further, however, and addressed questions of intent and consent. This part of McClung's judgment would elicit a specific response from Justice L'Heureux-Dubé, discussed below.
55 Ibid., para. 21.
56 Ibid., para. 25.
57 Ibid., para. 26.
58 Ibid., paras. 27, 29.
59 Ibid., para. 39.
60 Ibid., para. 42.
61 Ibid., para. 47.
62 Ibid., para. 51.
63 Ibid., para. 65.
64 Ibid., para. 69.
65 Ibid., paras. 73-74.
66 Ibid., para. 82. Citing David Archard, *Sexual Consent* (Boulder, CO: Westview Press, 1998), 131. Two of the items referenced by L'Heureux-Dubé, Esterich's article and an article by Elizabeth Sheehy entitled "Canadian Judges and the Law of Rape: Should the Charter Insulate Bias?" *Ottawa Law Review* 21 (1989): 741-87, also appeared in LEAF's factum.
67 Ibid., para. 87.
68 Ibid., paras. 88-93.
69 Ibid., para. 95. L'Heureux-Dubé's judgment prompted an unprecedented public response by Justice McClung. In a letter to the *National Post* published on 26 February 1999, <http://fact.on.ca/newpaper/np990233.htm> (7 May 2002), McClung wrote that L'Heureux-Dubé's "graceless slide into personal invective ... allows some response." However, rather than rebut her characterization of his judgment in any substantive way, McClung chose to

respond bizarrely by linking the "personal convictions of the judge" to "the disparate (and growing) number of male suicides being reported in the Province of Quebec." Given that Justice L'Heureux-Dubé's husband had committed suicide in 1978, the comment was particularly cruel; nor did Justice McClung's insistence that he was unaware of this fact ring true, since he described L'Heureux-Dubé as a friend in both his original letter and an interview one day later.

70 Ibid., para. 103.

71 L'Heureux-Dubé refers to this in ibid., paras. 94-95.

72 The book also appears in other LEAF factums, and MacKinnon's association with LEAF was quite close during the 1990s.

73 *R. v. Seaboyer*, [1991] 2 S.C.R. 577.

74 Factum of the Women's Legal Education and Action Fund, *Seaboyer and Gayme v. The Queen*, [1991] 2 S.C.R. 577, para. 2.

75 Sheila McIntyre, "Feminist Movement in Law: Beyond Privileged and Privileging Theory," in *Women's Legal Strategies*, ed. Jhappan, 75.

76 Factum of the Women's Legal Education and Action Fund, *R. v. Seaboyer*, paras. 6-11. The treatise was J.H. Wigmore, *Evidence in Trials at Common Law*, vol. 3A, rev. J.H. Chadbourne (Boston: Little, Brown and Co., 1970), at 924a (736-37).

77 Ibid., paras. 21-23.

78 Ibid., paras. 24-31.

79 Ibid., para. 33.

80 Ibid., para. 39.

81 Ibid., paras. 42-43.

82 Ibid., para. 47. Citing Catherine MacKinnon, *Toward a Feminist Theory of the State* (Cambridge, MA: Harvard, 1989), 126-54.

83 See ibid., para. 44. Citing L. Vandervort, "Mistake of Law and Sexual Assault: Consent and Mens Rea," *Canadian Journal of Women and the Law* 2 (1987): 233-309 and T.B. Dawson, "Sexual Assault Law and Past Sexual Conduct of the Primary Witness: The Construction of Relevance," *Canadian Journal of Women and the Law* 2 (1988): 310-34.

84 See Harriett R. Galvin, "Shielding Rape Victims in the State and Federal Courts: A Proposal for the Second Decade," *Minnesota Law Review* 70 (1986): 763-916.

85 *R. v. Seaboyer*, [1991] 2 S.C.R. 577, 613.

86 Ibid., 634-36.

87 Ibid., 598.

88 Ibid.

89 Ibid., 647.

90 Ibid., 701.

91 Ibid., 684.

92 [1995] 4 S.C.R. 411.

93 [1991] 3 S.C.R. 326.

94 Justices Lamer, Sopinka, Cory, Iacobucci, and Major decided to discuss this issue. In their view, the fact of Crown possession attested to the relevance of therapeutic records while obviating any claims of privilege or privacy. Justices L'Heureux-Dubé, La Forest, Gonthier, and McLachlin simply declared that the case did not raise the issue and there was no need to consider it. They did not, however, dispute the strict application of *Stinchcombe* to therapeutic records held by the Crown.

95 Factum of the Women's Legal Education and Action Fund, *R. v. O'Connor*, para. 6.

96 Ibid., paras. 9, 8.

97 Ibid., para. 10. Citing *Dagenais v. Canadian Broadcasting Corp.*, [1994] 3 S.C.R. 835, 877.

98 Ibid., para. 14.

99 Ibid., para. 26.

100 Ibid., para. 35.

101 Ibid., paras. 41-49.

102 Ibid., paras. 17, 18, 24, 30, 32-33.

103 These sources were Committee on Sexual Offences Against Children and Youth, *Sexual Offences Against Children: Report of the Committee on Sexual Offences Against Children and Youth*, vol. 1 (Ottawa: Supply and Services Canada, 1984) and Temi Firsten, "An Exploration

of the Role of Physical and Sexual Abuse for Psychiatrically Institutionalized Women" (1990), unpublished research paper, Ontario Women's Directorate.
104 Factum of the Women's Legal Education and Action Fund, *R. v. O'Connor*, para. 65.
105 [1995] 4 S.C.R. 411, para. 17.
106 Ibid., para. 106.
107 Ibid., paras. 22, 29.
108 Ibid., para. 111.
109 Ibid., para. 24.
110 *R. v. Carosella*, [1997] 1 S.C.R. 80.
111 Ibid., para. 26.
112 Ibid., para. 38.
113 Ibid., paras. 40, 56.
114 Ibid., para. 56.
115 Ibid., para. 66.
116 Ibid., para. 68.
117 Ibid., paras. 71, 74.
118 Ibid., para. 76 (emphasis added).
119 Sheila McIntyre, "Redefining Reformism: The Consultations that Shaped Bill C-49," in *Confronting Sexual Assault: A Decade of Legal and Social Change,* ed. Julian V. Roberts and Renate Mohr (Toronto: University of Toronto Press, 1994), 295.
120 LEAF Factum, *R. v. Seaboyer*, para. 24.
121 McIntyre, "Redefining Reformism," 296-97.
122 Ibid., 297.
123 Ibid., 300.
124 Ibid., 302.
125 Evelyn Cronin, quoted in Sylvia Bashevkin, *Women on the Defensive: Living Through Conservative Times* (Toronto: University of Toronto Press, 1998), 154.
126 House of Commons, Minutes of Proceedings and Evidence of Legislative Committee on Bill C-49, An Act to amend the Criminal Code (Sexual Assault), 19 May 1992, 2:5. Testimony of Sheila McIntyre for LEAF.
127 Ibid., 2:16 (McIntyre for LEAF); ibid., 20 May 1992, 3:30. Testimony of Lee Lakeman for the Canadian Association of Sexual Assault Centres.
128 Janet Hiebert, "Debating Policy: The Effects of Rights Talk," in *Equity and Community: The Charter, Interest Advocacy and Representation,* ed. F. Leslie Seidle (Montreal: IRPP, 1993), 52.
129 Janet L. Hiebert, "Wrestling with Rights: Judges, Parliament and the Making of Social Policy," in *Judicial Power and Canadian Democracy,* ed. Paul Howe and Peter H. Russell (Montreal and Kingston: McGill-Queen's University Press, 2001), 187.
130 Ibid., 192-96.
131 Jodie van Dieen, "*O'Connor* and *Bill C-46*: Differences in Approach," *Queen's Law Journal* 23 (1997): 39.
132 Canada, Department of Justice, "Issues and Opinions: Confidential Records and Communications of Sexual Assault Complainants: Access and Disclosure," November 1995.
133 Van Dieen, "*O'Connor* and *Bill C-46*," 39.
134 Karen Busby, "Discriminatory Uses of Personal Records in Sexual Violence Cases," *Canadian Journal of Women and the Law* 9 (1997): 148-77.
135 National Association of Women and the Law, *Submissions to the Standing Committee on Bill C-46*, March 1997, 1; House of Commons, Evidence, Standing Committee on Justice and Legal Affairs, 6 March 1997, 106:6 (Testimony of Nicole Tellier, NAWL). NAWL attributed the same position to its "sister organization," LEAF.
136 NAWL, *Submission to the Standing Committee on Bill C-46*, 51.
137 House of Commons, Evidence, Standing Committee on Justice and Legal Affairs, 6 March 1997, 106:5-6 (Testimony of Sheila McIntyre, LEAF).
138 See *Globe and Mail*, 3 October 1997, A1, A12.
139 Rob Martin, "Bill C-49: A Victory for Interest Group Politics," *University of New Brunswick Law Journal* 42 (1993): 357-72; Douglas A. Alderson, "R. v. O'Connor and Bill C-46: Two Wrongs Do Not Make a Right," *Criminal Law Quarterly* 39 (1996): 181-226.
140 *Mills*, para. 17.

141   Ibid., para. 20.
142   Ibid., para. 57.
143   Ibid., para. 58.
144   *A.-G. Quebec* v. *Irwin Toy*, [1989] 1 S.C.R. 927, 993-94. See also Christopher M. Dassios and Clifton P. Prophet, "Charter Section 1: The Decline of Grand Unified Theory and the Trend Towards Deference in the Supreme Court of Canada," *Advocates' Quarterly* 15 (1993): 289-91.
145   Ibid., 994.
146   *R.* v. *Mills*, [1999] 3 S.C.R. 668, paras. 92, 113. See Karen Busby, "Discriminatory Uses of Personal Records"; Katherine D. Kelly, "'You Must Be Crazy If You Think You Were Raped': Reflections on the Use of Complainants' Personal and Therapy Records in Sexual Assault Trials," *Canadian Journal of Women and the Law* 9 (1997): 178-95; Busby, "Third Party Records Cases since *R.* v. *O'Connor*: A Preliminary Analysis," Research and Statistics Section, Department of Justice Canada, July 1998.
147   [1999] 3 S.C.R. 668, para. 90; LEAF Factum, *Mills*, para. 54.
148   [1999] 3 S.C.R. 668, para. 113; LEAF Factum, *Mills*, para. 24.
149   [1999] 3 S.C.R. 668, para. 92; LEAF Factum, *Mills*, para. 25.
150   [1999] 3 S.C.R. 668, paras. 119, 136; LEAF Factum, *Mills*, paras. 21-22, 26, 43-44.
151   [1999] 3 S.C.R. 668, para. 113.
152   Ibid., para. 125.
153   Ibid., para. 144.
154   *R.* v. *Darrach*, [2000] 2 S.C.R. 443, paras. 1, 20, 34.
155   Ibid., para. 32.
156   Ibid., para. 41.
157   Ibid., para. 44.
158   Ibid., paras. 54, 61.
159   Ibid., para. 59.
160   LEAF Factum, *Darrach*, paras. 7, 16.
161   [2000] 2 S.C.R. 443, para. 39; LEAF Factum, *Darrach*, para. 31.
162   [2000] 2 S.C.R. 443, para. 40; LEAF Factum, *Darrach*, paras. 36-38.
163   Hogg and Bushell, "The Charter Dialogue," 80.
164   *Vriend* v. *Alberta*, [1998] 1 S.C.R. 493, para. 138.
165   *Little Sisters Book and Art Emporium* v. *Canada*, [2000] 2 S.C.R. 1120, at para. 268. Even Iacobucci's enthusiasm for the dialogue metaphor may be fading. In *R.* v. *Hall*, 2002 SCC 64, he criticized the Chief Justice's reliance on the metaphor to uphold bail provisions on the grounds that the "mere fact that Parliament has responded to a constitutional decision of this Court is no reason to defer to that response where it does not demonstrate a proper recognition of the constitutional requirements imposed by that decision" (para. 127). In *Sauvé* v. *Canada*, 2002 SCC 68, he simply ignored the argument that Parliament had engaged in effective dialogue on the issue of inmate voting rights.
166   Roach, *The Supreme Court on Trial*, 273.
167   Ironically, this sequence is not a perfect example of the dialogue metaphor as conceptualized by Hogg and Bushell because *O'Connor* did not entail judicial nullification of a statute. Nevertheless, it has become so symbolic of dialogue for both judicial and scholarly supporters of the metaphor that one can ignore this detail.
168   Roach, *The Supreme Court on Trial*, 277-81.
169   Hogg and Bushell, "The Charter Dialogue Between Courts and Legislatures," 79, 80, 82, 88.
170   Roach, *The Supreme Court on Trial*, 242.

Chapter 6: Making a Difference

1   Women's Legal Education and Action Fund, *Equality and the Charter: Ten Years of Feminist Advocacy Before the Supreme Court of Canada* (Toronto: Emond Montgomery, 1996), xix.
2   Lori Joanne Hausegger, "The Impact of Interest Groups on Judicial Decision Making: A Comparison of Women's Groups in the U.S. and Canada" (PhD diss., Ohio State University, 2000), 72-77.
3   Ibid., 267.

4 *O'Malley* v. *Woodrough*, 307 U.S. 277, 281 (1938); Charles Evans Hughes, "Forward," *Yale Law Journal* 50 (1941): 727; *West Virginia State Board of Education* v. *Barnette*, 319 U.S. 624, 634-35 (1943).
5 Clement Vose, *Caucasians Only: The Supreme Court, the NAACP, and the Restrictive Covenant Cases* (Berkeley: University of California Press, 1959), 68-71; Richard Kluger, *Simple Justice* (New York: Vintage Books, 1975), 315-21.
6 *Reference re Anti-Inflation Act*, [1976] 2 S.C.R. 373, at 424-25. Laskin discusses the general question of extrinsic evidence at 422-27.
7 Colleen Sheppard, "Uncomfortable Victories and Unanswered Questions: Lessons from *Moge*," *Canadian Journal of Family Law* 12 (1995): 287.
8 *Pelech* v. *Pelech*, [1987] 1 S.C.R. 801; *Richardson* v. *Richardson*, [1987] 1 S.C.R. 857; *Caron* v. *Caron*, [1987] 1 S.C.R. 892.
9 Sheppard, "Uncomfortable Victories," 289.
10 *Boston* v. *Boston*, [2001] 2 S.C.R. 413; *R.* v. *Shearing*, 2002 SCC 58, File No. 27782.
11 The data were compiled by searching the Supreme Court judgment database maintained by the Centre de recherche en droit public at the Université de Montréal (for Supreme Court citations) and the Index to Canadian Legal Literature (for legal literature citations).

For comparative purposes, the table below indicates citations for some high-profile non-LEAF cases: *R.* v. *Oakes* (original, and still largely controlling, interpretation of section 1), *RWDSU* v. *Dolphin Delivery* (important statement on the scope of government action), *R.* v. *Big M Drug Mart* (first freedom of religion case), *Operation Dismantle* v. *The Queen* (important discussion of political questions doctrine), and *Law Society of Upper Canada* v. *Skapinker* (first case decided on Charter grounds).

Case	Supreme Court	Legal literature	Total
Oakes	35	14	49
Dolphin Delivery	17	23	40
Big M Drug Mart	21	1	22
Operation Dismantle	12	5	17
Skapinker	6	2	8

12 [1999] 1 S.C.R. 497.
13 Ibid., para. 39.
14 Ibid., para 53.
15 Thomas Flanagan, "The Staying Power of the Legislative Status Quo: Collective Choice in Canada's Parliament after *Morgentaler*," *Canadian Journal of Political Science* 30 (1997): 31.
16 See Eva Rubin, *Abortion, Politics and the Courts: Roe* v. *Wade and Its Aftermath* (Westport, CT: Greenwood Press, 1982).
17 Canada, *Report of the Committee on the Operation of the Abortion Law* (Ottawa: Supply and Services, 1977).
18 Ibid., 146-47.
19 Ibid., 310-11.
20 Ibid., 93, 109, 139.
21 Ibid., 141.
22 This is out of a total of nine provinces, since Ontario did not provide a complete report of abortions in 1999. Statistics Canada thus excluded Ontario from the analysis.
23 Ibid., 17.
24 Gerald Rosenberg, *The Hollow Hope: Can Courts Bring About Social Change?* (Chicago: University of Chicago Press, 1991), 33-35.
25 Sheila McIntyre, "Feminist Movement in Law: Beyond Privileged and Privileging Theory," in *Women's Legal Strategies in Canada*, ed. Radha Jhappan (Toronto: University of Toronto Press, 2002), 76.
26 Ibid., 79-80.
27 Ibid., 81.

28 Lise Gotell, "Towards a Democratic Practice of Feminist Litigation? LEAF's Changing Approach to *Charter* Equality," in *Women's Legal Strategies*, ed. Jhappan, 155. This "outrage" led to the establishment of the Ad Hoc Coalition of Anti-censorship Women. Ibid., 172 n. 114.
29 Ibid., 156.
30 See especially Janine Benedet, "*Little Sisters Book and Art Emporium* v. *Minister of Justice*: Sex Equality and the Attack on *R.* v. *Butler*," *Osgoode Hall Law Journal* 39 (2001): 187-204.
31 See <http://www.fin.gc.ca/budget96/chsup/chsupe.htm> (8 October 2002).
32 Statistics Canada, *Women in Canada, 2000: A Gender-Based Statistical Report* (Ottawa: Minister of Industry, 2000), 102.
33 Ibid.
34 See <http://socialunion.gc.ca/ecd/ch2_2_e.html> (8 October 2002).

Conclusion

1 Lise Gotell, "Towards a Democratic Practice of Feminist Litigation? LEAF's Changing Approach to Charter Equality," in *Women's Legal Strategies in Canada*, ed. Radha Jhappan (Toronto: University of Toronto Press, 2002), 140.
2 Miriam Smith, *Lesbian and Gay Rights in Canada: Social Movements and Equality-Seeking, 1971-1995* (Toronto: University of Toronto Press, 1999), 42.

Bibliography

Aggarwal, Arjun P. *Sexual Harassment in the Workplace*. Toronto: Butterworths, 1987.

Alderson, Douglas A. "R. v. O'Connor and Bill C-46: Two Wrongs Do Not Make a Right." *Criminal Law Quarterly* 39 (1996): 181-226.

Archard, David. *Sexual Consent*. Boulder, CO: Westview Press, 1998.

Atcheson, M. Elizabeth, Mary Eberts, and Beth Symes. *Women and Legal Action: Precedents, Resources and Strategies for the Future*. Ottawa: Canadian Advisory Council on the Status of Women, 1984.

Backhouse, Constance, and Leah Cohen. *The Secret Oppression: Sexual Harassment of Working Women*. Toronto: Macmillan of Canada, 1978.

Banks, Olive. *Faces of Feminism: A Study of Feminism as a Social Movement*. New York: St. Martin's Press, 1981.

Bashevkin, Sylvia. *Women on the Defensive: Living Through Conservative Times*. Toronto: University of Toronto Press, 1998.

Baum, Lawrence. *The Puzzle of Judicial Behavior*. Ann Arbor: University of Michigan Press, 1997.

Behiels, Michael D., ed. *The Meech Lake Primer: Conflicting Views of the 1987 Constitutional Accord*. Ottawa: University of Ottawa Press, 1989.

Benedet, Janine. "*Little Sisters Book and Art Emporium* v. *Minister of Justice*: Sex Equality and the Attack on *R. v. Butler*." *Osgoode Hall Law Journal* 39 (2001): 187-204.

Berry, Mary Frances. *Why ERA Failed: Politics, Women's Rights, and the Amending Process of the Constitution*. Bloomington, IN: Indiana University Press, 1986.

Bickel, Alexander. *The Least Dangerous Branch: The Supreme Court at the Bar of Politics*. 2nd ed. New Haven, CT: Yale University Press, 1986.

Bogart, W.A. *Courts and Country: The Limits of Litigation and the Social and Political Life of Canada*. Toronto: Oxford University Press, 1994.

Boles, Janet K. *The Politics of the Equal Rights Amendment: Conflict and the Decision Process*. New York: Longman, 1979.

Bork, Robert H. *Coercing Virtue: The Worldwide Rule of Judges*. Toronto: Vintage Canada, 2002.

Bozinoff, Lorne, and André Turcotte. "Support for Legalization of Abortion Is Increasing." *The Gallup Report*, 19 October 1992.

Brodie, Ian. "The Market for Political Status." *Comparative Politics* 28 (1996): 253-71.

–. "Interest Group Litigation and the Embedded State: Canada's Court Challenges Program." *Canadian Journal of Political Science* 34 (2001): 365-71.

–. *Friends of the Court: The Privileging of Interest Group Litigants in Canada*. Albany: State University of New York Press, 2002.

Brodsky, Gwen, and Shelagh Day. *Canadian Charter Equality Rights for Women: One Step Forward or Two Steps Back?* Ottawa: Canadian Advisory Council on the Status of Women, 1989.

Bryden, David. "Between Two Constitutions: Feminism and Pornography." *Constitutional Commentary* 2 (1985): 147-89.

Busby, Karen. "Discriminatory Uses of Personal Records in Sexual Violence Cases." *Canadian Journal of Women and the Law* 9 (1997): 148-77.

Canadian Center for Judicial Statistics. *The Juristat Reader: A Statistical Overview of the Canadian Justice System.* Toronto: Thompson Educational, 1999.

Cossman, Brenda, ed. *Bad Attitudes on Trial: Pornography, Feminism and the Butler Decision.* Toronto: University of Toronto Press, 1997.

Cover, Robert M. "The Origins of Judicial Activism in the Protection of Minorities." *Yale Law Journal* 91 (1982): 1287-1316.

Dassios, Christopher M., and Clifton P. Prophet. "Charter Section 1: The Decline of Grand Unified Theory and the Trend Towards Deference in the Supreme Court of Canada." *Advocates' Quarterly* 15 (1993): 289-91.

Dawson, T.B. "Sexual Assault Law and Past Sexual Conduct of the Primary Witness: The Construction of Relevance." *Canadian Journal of Women and the Law* 2 (1988): 310-34.

Day, Shelagh, and Gwen Brodsky. "The Duty to Accommodate: Who Will Benefit?" *Canadian Bar Review* 75 (1996): 433-73.

Dobrowolsky, Alexandra. *The Politics of Pragmatism: Women, Representation and Constitutionalism in Canada.* Toronto: Oxford University Press, 2000.

Ely, John Hart. "The Wages of Crying Wolf: A Comment on *Roe* v. *Wade.*" *Yale Law Journal* 82 (1973): 920-44.

–. *Democracy and Distrust.* Cambridge, MA: Harvard University Press, 1980.

Epp, Charles. *The Rights Revolution: Lawyers, Activists, and Supreme Courts in Comparative Perspective.* Chicago: University of Chicago Press, 1998.

Epstein, Lee, and Jack Knight. *The Choices Justices Make.* Washington, DC: CQ Press, 1998.

Epstein, Lee, and Joseph Kobylka. *The Supreme Court and Legal Change: Abortion and the Death Penalty.* Chapel Hill, NC: University of North Carolina Press, 1992.

Epstein, Lee, Thomas G. Walker, and William J. Dixon. "The Supreme Court and Criminal Justice Disputes: A Neo-Institutional Perspective." *American Journal of Political Science* 33 (1989): 825-41.

Flanagan, Thomas. "The Staying Power of the Legislative Status Quo: Collective Choice in Canada's Parliament after *Morgentaler.*" *Canadian Journal of Political Science* 30 (1997): 31-53.

Fletcher, Joseph F., and Paul Howe. "Public Opinion and the Courts." *Choices* 6:3 (Institute for Research on Public Policy, May 2000): 4-56.

Galanter, Marc. "Why the 'Haves' Come Out Ahead: Speculations on the Limits of Legal Change." *Law and Society Review* 9 (1974): 95-160.

Galvin, Harriett R. "Shielding Rape Victims in the State and Federal Courts: A Proposal for the Second Decade." *Minnesota Law Review* 70 (1986): 763-916.

Gates, John B., and Charles A. Johnson, eds. *The American Courts: A Critical Assessment.* Washington, DC: CQ Press, 1991.

Gibson, James. "Judges' Role Orientations, Attitudes, and Decisions: An Interactive Model." *American Political Science Review* 72 (1978): 911-24.

Gilligan, Carol. *In a Different Voice: Psychological Theory and Women's Development.* Cambridge, MA: Harvard University Press, 1982.

Gold, Alan D. "The Legal Rights Provisions: A New Vision or Déjà Vu." *Supreme Court Law Review* 4 (1982): 107-30.

Government of Canada. *Report of the Royal Commission on the Status of Women in Canada.* Ottawa: Queen's Printer, 1970.

–. Committee on the Operation of the Abortion Law. *Report of the Committee on the Operation of the Abortion Law.* Ottawa: Supply and Services, 1977.

Gunther, Gerald. "The Supreme Court, 1971 Term – Forward: In Search of Evolving Doctrine on a Changing Court: A Model for Newer Equal Protection." *Harvard Law Review* 86 (1972): 1-48.

Hausegger, Lori Joanne. "The Impact of Interest Groups on Judicial Decision Making: A Comparison of Women's Groups in the U.S. and Canada." PhD diss., Ohio State University, 2000.

Heard, Andrew. *Canadian Constitutional Conventions: The Marriage of Law and Politics*. Toronto: Oxford University Press, 1991.

Hennigar, Matthew A. "Value Hierarchy on the Supreme Court of Canada: Explaining *Seaboyer* and *O'Connor*." (Unpublished manuscript on file with the author, 1997).

Hickling, M.A. "Employer's Liability for Sexual Harassment." *Manitoba Law Journal* 17 (1988): 124-55.

Hiebert, Janet. *Limiting Rights: The Dilemma of Judicial Review*. Montreal and Kingston: McGill-Queen's University Press, 1996.

Hogg, Peter W. *Constitutional Law of Canada*. 3rd ed. Toronto: Carswell, 1992.

Hogg, Peter W., and Allison A. Bushell. "The Charter Dialogue Between Courts and Legislatures." *Osgoode Hall Law Journal* 35 (1997): 75-124.

Howe, Paul, and Peter H. Russell, eds. *Judicial Power and Canadian Democracy*. Montreal and Kingston: McGill-Queen's University Press, 2001.

Hughes, Charles Evans. "Forward." *Yale Law Journal* 50 (1941): 737-38.

Jhappan, Radha, ed. *Women's Legal Strategies in Canada*. Toronto: University of Toronto Press, 2002.

Johnsen, Dawn E. "The Creation of Fetal Rights: Conflicts with Women's Constitutional Rights to Liberty, Privacy and Equal Protection." *Yale Law Journal* 95 (1986): 599-625.

Kelly, Katherine D. "'You Must Be Crazy If You Think You Were Raped': Reflections on the Use of Complainants' Personal and Therapy Records in Sexual Assault Trials." *Canadian Journal of Women and the Law* 9 (1997): 178-95.

Kelly, James B. "The Charter of Rights and Freedoms and the Rebalancing of Liberal Constitutionalism in Canada, 1982-1997," *Osgoode Hall Law Journal* 37 (1999): 625-95.

Kluger, Richard. *Simple Justice*. New York: Vintage Books, 1975.

Knopff, Rainer. *Human Rights and Social Technology: The New War on Discrimination*. Ottawa: Carleton University Press, 1989.

Knopff, Rainer, and F.L. Morton. *Charter Politics*. Scarborough, ON: Nelson Canada, 1992.

Kome, Penney. *The Taking of Twenty-Eight: Women Challenge the Constitutional*. Toronto: Women's Press, 1983.

Lawrence, Susan E. *The Poor in Court: The Legal Services Program and Supreme Court Decision Making*. Princeton, NJ: Princeton University Press, 1990.

Lempert, Richard. "Mobilizing Private Law: An Introductory Essay," *Law and Society Review* 11 (1976): 173-89.

Levinson, Sanford, ed. *Responding to Imperfection: The Theory and Practice of Constitutional Amendment*. Princeton, NJ: Princeton University Press, 1995.

Lusztig, Michael. "Constitutional Paralysis: Why Canadian Constitutional Initiatives Are Doomed to Fail." *Canadian Journal of Political Science* 27 (1994): 747-71.

Lutz, Donald S. "Toward a Theory of Constitutional Amendment." *American Political Science Review* 88 (1994): 355-70.

MacKinnon, Catharine. *Sexual Harassment of Working Women*. New Haven, CT, and London: Yale University Press, 1979.

–. *Toward a Feminist Theory of the State*. Cambridge, MA: Harvard University Press, 1989.

Mahoney, Kathleen. "*R. v. Keegstra*: A Rationale for Regulating Pornography?" *McGill Law Journal* 37 (1992): 242-69.

Makin, Kirk. "Top Court Bows to Will of Parliament." *Globe and Mail*, 26 November 1999, A1.

Mallory, J.R. *Social Credit and the Federal Power in Canada*. Toronto: University of Toronto Press, 1954.

Mandel, Michael. *The Charter of Rights and the Legalization of Politics in Canada*. Rev. ed. Toronto: Thompson Educational Publishing, 1994.

Manfredi, Christopher P. "Institutional Design and the Politics of Constitutional Modification: Understanding Amendment Failure in the United States and Canada." *Law and Society Review* 31 (1997): 111-36.

–. *Judicial Power and the Charter: Canada and the Paradox of Liberal Constitutionalism*. 2nd ed. Toronto: Oxford University Press, 2001.

Manfredi, Christopher P., and Scott Lemieux. "Judicial Discretion and Fundamental Justice: Sexual Assault in the Supreme Court of Canada." *American Journal of Comparative Law* 47 (1999): 489-514.

Manfredi, Christopher P., and Michael Lusztig. "Why Do Formal Amendments Fail? An Institutional Design Analysis." *World Politics* 50 (1998): 377-400.

Mansbridge, Jane. *Why We Lost the ERA*. Chicago: University of Chicago Press, 1986.

Martin, Rob. "Bill C-49: A Victory for Interest Group Politics." *University of New Brunswick Law Journal* 42 (1993): 357-72.

McCann, Michael. "Reform Litigation on Trial." *Law and Social Inquiry* 17 (1992): 720-21.

–. *Rights at Work: Pay Equity Reform and the Politics of Legal Mobilization*. Chicago: University of Chicago Press, 1994.

McCormick, Peter. *Supreme at Last: The Evolution of the Supreme Court of Canada*. Toronto: Lorimer, 2000.

McRoberts, Kenneth, and Patrick Monahan, eds. *The Charlottetown Accord, the Referendum, and the Future of Canada*. Toronto: University of Toronto Press, 1993.

Monahan, Patrick. *Politics and the Constitution: The Charter, Federalism and the Supreme Court of Canada*. Toronto: Carswell/Methuen, 1987.

–. *Meech Lake: The Inside Story*. Toronto: University of Toronto Press, 1991.

Morton, F.L. "The Political Impact of the Canadian Charter of Rights and Freedoms." *Canadian Journal of Political Science* 20 (1987): 31-55.

–. *Morgentaler v. Borowski: Abortion, the Charter and the Courts*. Toronto: McClelland and Stewart, 1992.

–., ed. *Law, Politics and the Judicial Process in Canada*. 3rd ed. Calgary: University of Calgary Press, 2001.

Morton, F.L., and Avril Allen. "Feminists and the Courts: Measuring Success in Interest Group Litigation in Canada." *Canadian Journal of Political Science* 34 (2001): 55-84.

Morton, F.L., Peter H. Russell, and Troy Riddell. "The Canadian Charter of Rights and Freedoms: A Descriptive Analysis of the First Decade, 1982-1992." *National Journal of Constitutional Law* 1 (1994): 1-60.

Mossman, Mary Jane. "Gender Equality and Legal Services: A Research Agenda for Institutional Change." *Sydney Law Review* 15 (1993): 30-58.

–. "Gender Equality, Family Law and Access to Justice." *International Journal of Law and the Family* 8 (1994): 357-73.

Murphy, Walter F. *Elements of Judicial Strategy*. Chicago: University of Chicago Press, 1964.

Noble, Gayle. *Legal Literature and S. 15 Charter Litigation: An Interest Group Strategy*. MA research essay, Department of Political Science, McGill University, 1993.

O'Connor, Karen, and Lee Epstein. "Rebalancing the Scales of Justice: Assessment of Public Interest Law." *Harvard Journal of Law and Public Policy* 7 (1984): 483-505.

Olson, Susan. "Interest Group Litigation in Federal District Courts: Beyond the Political Disadvantage Theory." *Journal of Politics* 52 (1990): 854-82.

Ostberg, C.L., and Matthew Wetstein. "Dimensions of Attitudes Underlying Search and Seizure Decisions of the Supreme Court of Canada." *Canadian Journal of Political Science* 31 (1998): 767-87.

Pal, Leslie A. *Interests of State: The Politics of Language, Multiculturalism, and Feminism in Canada*. Montreal and Kingston: McGill-Queen's University Press, 1993.

Pal, Leslie, and F.L. Morton. "*Bliss v. Attorney General of Canada*: From Legal Defeat to Political Victory." *Osgoode Hall Law Journal* 24 (1986): 141-60.

Peacock, Anthony, ed. *Rethinking the Constitution: Perspectives on Canadian Constitutional Reform, Interpretation, and Theory*. Toronto: Oxford University Press, 1996.

Phillips, Susan D. "Meaning and Structure in Social Movements: Mapping the Network of National Canadian Women's Organizations." *Canadian Journal of Political Science* 24 (1991): 755-82.

Pollack, Nancy. "Business as Usual." *Ms.*, May/June 1995, 12.

Pritchett, C. Herman. *The Roosevelt Court: A Study in Judicial Politics and Values*. New York: Macmillan, 1948.

Rabin, Robert L. "Perspectives on Public Interest Law." *Stanford Law Review* 28 (1976): 207-61.

Raffel, M., ed. *Health Care and Reform in Industrialized Countries*. University Park, PA: Pennsylvania State University Press, 1997.

Razack, Sherene. *Canadian Feminism and the Law: The Women's Legal Education and Action Fund and the Pursuit of Equality.* Toronto: Second Story Press, 1991.

Roach, Kent. "The People versus the Supreme Court." *Literary Review of Canada* 9 (June 2001): 13-16.

–. *The Supreme Court on Trial: Judicial Activism or Democratic Dialogue.* Toronto: Irwin Law, 2001.

Roberts, Julian V., and Renate Mohr, eds. *Confronting Sexual Assault: A Decade of Legal and Social Change.* Toronto: University of Toronto Press, 1994.

Romanow, Roy, John Whyte, and Howard Leeson. *Canada Notwithstanding: The Making of the Constitution, 1976-1982.* Toronto: Carswell/Methuen, 1984.

Rosenberg, Gerald. *The Hollow Hope: Can Courts Bring About Social Change?* Chicago: University of Chicago Press, 1991.

–. "Hollow Hopes and Other Aspirations." *Law and Social Inquiry* 17 (1992): 761-78.

–. "Positivism, Interpretivism, and the Study of Law." *Law and Social Inquiry* 21 (1996): 435-55.

Rubin, Eva. *Abortion, Politics and the Courts: Roe v. Wade and Its Aftermath.* Westport, CT: Greenwood Press, 1982.

Russell, Peter H. *The Judiciary in Canada: The Third Branch of Government.* Toronto: McGraw-Hill Ryerson, 1987.

–. *Constitutional Odyssey: Can Canadians Be a Sovereign People?* Toronto: University of Toronto Press, 1992.

Scheingold, Stuart. *The Politics of Rights.* New Haven, CT: Yale University Press, 1974.

Schneiderman, David, and Kate Sutherland, eds. *Charting the Consequences: The Impact of Charter Rights on Canadian Law and Politics.* Toronto: University of Toronto Press, 1997.

Schubert, Glendon, and David Danelski, eds. *Comparative Judicial Behavior: Cross-Cultural Study of Decision-Making in the East and West.* New York: Oxford University Press, 1969.

Segal, Jeffrey A. "Supreme Court Justices as Human Decision Makers: An Individual-Level Analysis of the Search and Seizure Cases." *Journal of Politics* 48 (1986): 938-55.

–. "Separation-of-Powers Games in the Positive Theory of Congress and Courts." *American Political Science Review* 91 (1997): 28-44.

Segal, Jeffrey A., and Harold J. Spaeth. *The Supreme Court and the Attitudinal Model.* New York: Cambridge University Press, 1993.

Seidle, F. Leslie, ed. *Equity and Community: The Charter, Interest Advocacy and Representation.* Montreal: IRPP, 1993.

Sheehy, Elizabeth. "Canadian Judges and the Law of Rape: Should the Charter Insulate Bias?" *Ottawa Law Review* 21 (1989): 741-87.

Sheppard, Colleen. "Uncomfortable Victories and Unanswered Questions: Lessons from Moge." *Canadian Journal of Family Law* 12 (1995): 283-329.

Smith, Miriam. *Lesbian and Gay Rights in Canada: Social Movements and Equality-Seeking, 1971-1995.* Toronto: University of Toronto Press, 1999.

Statistics Canada. *Women in Canada, 2000: A Gender-Based Statistical Report.* Ottawa: Minister of Industry, 2000.

Steiner, Gilbert Y. *Constitutional Inequality: The Political Fortunes of the Equal Rights Amendment.* Washington, DC: Brookings Institution, 1985.

Sunstein, Cass. *One Case at a Time: Judicial Minimalism on the Supreme Court.* Cambridge, MA: Harvard University Press, 1999.

Tate, C. Neil, and Panu Sittiwong. "Decision-Making in the Canadian Supreme Court: Extending the Personal Attributes Model Across Nations." *Journal of Politics* 51 (1989): 900-16.

Tsebelis, George. *Nested Games: Rational Choice in Comparative Politics.* Berkeley: University of California Press, 1990.

Tushnet, Mark V. *The NAACP's Legal Strategy Against Segregated Education, 1925-1950.* Chapel Hill, NC: University of North Carolina Press, 1987.

van Dieen, Jodie. "*O'Connor* and *Bill C-46*: Differences in Approach." *Queen's Law Journal* 23 (1997): 1-65.

Vandervort, L. "Mistake of Law and Sexual Assault: Consent and Mens Rea." *Canadian Journal of Women and the Law* 2 (1987): 233-309.

Vickers, Jill, Pauline Rankin, and Christine Appelle. *Politics As If Women Mattered: A Political Analysis of the National Action Committee on the Status of Women*. Toronto: University of Toronto Press, 1993.

Vose, Clement E. *Caucasians Only: The Supreme Court, the NAACP, and the Restrictive Covenant Cases*. Berkeley: University of California Press, 1959.

Walker, Jack L., Jr. *Mobilizing Interest Groups in America: Patrons, Professions and Social Movements*. Ann Arbor, MI: University of Michigan Press, 1991.

Welch, Jillian. "No Room at the Top: Interest Group Interveners and Charter Litigation in the Supreme Court of Canada." *University of Toronto Faculty of Law Review* 43 (1985): 204-31.

Westmacott, M.W., and H. Mellon, eds. *Political Dispute and Judicial Review*. Toronto: Nelson, 1999.

Wilson, Bertha. "Will Women Judges Really Make a Difference?" *Osgoode Hall Law Journal* 28 (1990): 507-22.

Women's Legal Education and Action Fund. *Equality and the Charter: Ten Years of Feminist Advocacy Before the Supreme Court of Canada*. Toronto: Emond Montgomery, 1996.

Yogis, John A. *Canadian Law Dictionary*. Toronto: Barron's Educational Series, 1983.

Zemens, Frances Kahn. "Legal Mobilization: The Neglected Role of the Law in the Political System." *American Political Science Review* 77 (1983): 690-703.

Cases Cited

A. (L.L.) v. *B. (A.)*, [1995] 4 S.C.R. 536.
A.-G. Manitoba et al. v. *A.-G. Canada et al. (Patriation Reference)*, [1981] 1 S.C.R. 753.
A.-G. Quebec v. *A.-G. Canada (Quebec Veto Reference)*, [1982] 2 S.C.R. 793.
A.-G. Quebec v. *Irwin Toy*, [1989] 1 S.C.R. 927.
Action Travail des Femmes v. *Canadian National Railway* (1987), 40 D.L.R. (4th) 193.
Action Travail des Femmes v. *Canadian National Railway*, [1987] 1 S.C.R. 1114.
American Booksellers' Association v. *Hudnut*, 771 F.2d. 323 (7th Cir. 1975).
Andrews v. *Law Society of British Columbia*, [1989] 1 S.C.R. 143.
Benner v. *Canada (Secretary of State)*, [1997] 1 S.C.R. 358.
Blencoe v. *British Columbia (Human Rights Commission)*, [2000] 2 S.C.R. 307.
Bliss v. *A.-G. Canada*, [1979] 1 S.C.R. 183.
Borowski v. *Canada*, [1989] 1 S.C.R. 342.
Boston v. *Boston*, [2001] 2 S.C.R. 413.
British Columbia (Public Service Employee Relations Commission) v. *BCGSEU*, [1999] 3 S.C.R. 3.
Brooks v. *Canada Safeway*, [1989] 1 S.C.R. 1219.
Brown v. *Board of Education*, 347 U.S. 483 (1954).
Canada (Attorney General) v. *Mossop*, [1993] 1 S.C.R. 554.
Canada v. *Taylor*, [1990] 3 S.C.R. 892.
Canadian Council of Churches v. *Canada (Minister of Employment and Immigration)*, [1992] 1
    S.C.R. 236.
Caron v. *Caron*, [1987] 1 S.C.R. 892.
Cleveland Board of Education v. *LaFleur*, 414 U.S. 632 (1974).
Corbiere v. *Canada (Minister of Indian and Northern Affairs)*, [1999] 2 S.C.R. 203.
Dagenais v. *Canadian Broadcasting Corp.*, [1994] 3 S.C.R. 835, 877.
Edwards v. *A.-G. Canada*, [1930] A.C. 124.
Egan v. *Canada*, [1995] 2 S.C.R. 513.
Eisenstadt v. *Baird*, 405 U.S. 438 (1972).
Eldridge v. *British Columbia (Attorney General)*, [1997] 3 S.C.R. 624.
Ford v. *Québec*, [1988] 2 S.C.R. 712.
Forsythe v. *The Queen*, [1980] 2 S.C.R. 268.
Friends of Point Pleasant Park v. *A.-G. Canada*, Docket T-1235-00 (F.C.T.D., 21 August 2000).
Gordon v. *Goertz*, [1996] 2 S.C.R. 27.
Gould v. *Yukon Order of Pioneers*, [1996] 1 S.C.R. 571.
Griswold v. *Connecticut*, 381 U.S. 479 (1965).
Hunter v. *Southam* (1984), 11 D.L.R. (4th) 641.
Irwin Toy v. *A.-G. Quebec*, [1989] 1 S.C.R. 927.
Janzen v. *Platy Enterprises Ltd.*, [1989] 1 S.C.R. 1252.
Lavell v. *A.-G. Canada*, [1974] S.C.R. 1349.
Law Society of Upper Canada v. *Skapinker* (1984), 9 D.L.R. (4th) 161.

Law v. *Canada (Minister of Employment and Immigration)*, [1999] 1 S.C.R. 497.
Leatherdale v. *Leatherdale*, [1982] 2 S.C.R. 743.
Little Sisters Book and Art Emporium v. *Canada*, [2000] 2 S.C.R. 1120.
Lovelace v. *Ontario*, [2000] 1 S.C.R. 950.
M. v. *H.*, [1999] 2 S.C.R. 3.
M.(K.) v. *M.(H.)*, [1992] 3 S.C.R. 3.
Marbury v. *Madison*, 1 Cranch (5 U.S.) 137 (1803).
McCulloch v. *Maryland*, 17 U.S. 316 (1819).
Miller v. *California*, 413 U.S. 15 (1973).
Min. of Justice (Canada) v. *Borowski*, [1981] 2 S.C.R. 575.
Moge v. *Moge*, [1992] 3 S.C.R. 813.
Morgentaler v. *The Queen*, [1976] 1 S.C.R. 616.
Morgentaler, Smoling and Scott v. *The Queen*, [1988] 1 S.C.R. 30.
Murdoch v. *Murdoch*, [1975] 1 S.C.R. 423.
New Brunswick (Minister of Health and Community Services) v. *G.(J.)*, [1999] 3 S.C.R. 46.
Norberg v. *Wynrib*, [1992] 2 S.C.R. 226.
O'Malley v. *Woodrough*, 307 U.S. 277, 281 (1938).
Operation Dismantle v. *The Queen*, [1985] 1 S.C.R. 441.
Orr v. *Orr*, 440 U.S. 268 (1979).
Pappajohn v. *The Queen*, [1980] 2 S.C.R. 120.
Pelech v. *Pelech*, [1987] 1 S.C.R. 801.
Pittsburgh Press v. *Pittsburgh Commission on Human Relations*, 413 U.S. 376 (1973).
Planned Parenthood v. *Casey*, 505 U.S. 833 (1992).
Plessy v. *Ferguson*, 163 U.S. 537 (1896).
R. v. *Andrews and Smith*, [1990] 3 S.C.R. 870.
R. v. *Askov*, [1990] 2 S.C.R. 199.
R. v. *Big M Drug Mart Ltd.*, [1985] 1 S.C.R. 295.
R. v. *Butler*, [1992] 1 S.C.R. 452.
R. v. *Carosella*, [1997] 1 S.C.R. 80.
R. v. *Darrach*, [2000] 2 S.C.R. 443.
R. v. *Daviault*, [1994] 3 S.C.R. 63.
R. v. *Drybones*, [1970] S.C.R. 282.
R. v. *Edwards Books and Art Ltd.*, [1986] 2 S.C.R. 713.
R. v. *Ewanchuk*, [1999] 1 S.C.R. 330.
R. v. *Hall*, 2002 SCC 64.
R. v. *Keegstra*, [1990] 3 S.C.R. 697.
R. v. *M. (M.L.)*, [1994] 2 S.C.R. 3.
R. v. *Mills*, [1999] 3 S.C.R. 668.
R. v. *Morgentaler*, [1993] 3 S.C.R. 463.
R. v. *Oakes*, [1986] 1 S.C.R. 103.
R. v. *O'Connor*, [1995] 4 S.C.R. 411.
R. v. *S. (R.D.)*, [1997] 3 S.C.R. 484.
R. v. *Seaboyer and Gayme*, [1991] 2 S.C.R. 577.
R. v. *Shearing*, 2002 SCC 58, File No. 27782.
R. v. *Stinchcombe*, [1991] 3 S.C.R. 326.
R. v. *Sullivan and Lemay*, [1991] 1 S.C.R. 489.
R. v. *Whitley*, [1994] 3 S.C.R. 830.
Re Binder et al. and Canadian National Railways, [1985] 2 S.C.R. 561.
Re Ontario Human Rights Commission et al. and Simpsons-Sears Ltd., [1985] 2 S.C.R. 536.
Reed v. *Reed*, 404 U.S. 71 (1971).
Reference re Anti-Inflation Act, [1976] 2 S.C.R. 373.
Reference re Legislative Authority of Parliament to Alter or Replace the Senate, [1980] 1 S.C.R. 54.
Reference re s.94(2) of the Motor Vehicle Act (B.C.) (1985), 24 D.L.R. (4th) 536, at 554-55.
Reference re workers' compensation act, 1983 (Nfld.), [1989] 1 S.C.R. 922.
Reynolds v. *Sims*, 377 U.S. 533 (1964).
Richardson v. *Richardson*, [1987] 1 S.C.R. 857.

Robertson and Rosetanni v. *The Queen*, [1963] S.C.R. 651.

Roe v. *Wade*, 410 U.S. 113 (1973).

Roth v. *United States*, 354 U.S. 476 (1957).

RWDSU v. *Dolphin Delivery Ltd.*, [1986] 2 S.C.R. 573.

Sauvé v. *Canada (Chief Electoral Officer)*, 2002 SCC 68.

Schachter v. *Canada*, [1992] 2 S.C.R. 679.

Schachter v. *The Queen* (1988), 52 D.L.R. (4th) 525 (F.C.T.D.).

Schacter v. *The Queen* (1990), 66 D.L.R. (4th) 635 (F.C.A).

Shelley v. *Kraemer*, 334 U.S. 1 (1948).

Smith v. *Allwright*, 321 U.S. 659 (1944).

Stenberg v. *Carhart*, 530 U.S. 914 (2000).

Symes v. *Canada*, [1993] 4 S.C.R. 695.

Taylor v. *The Canadian Human Rights Commission*, [1990] 3 S.C.R. 892.

Thibaudeau v. *Canada*, [1995] 2 S.C.R. 627.

Tremblay v. *Daigle*, [1989] 2 S.C.R. 530.

United States v. *Carolene Products*, 304 U.S. 144 (1938).

Vriend v. *Alberta*, [1998] 1 S.C.R. 493.

Weatherall v. *Canada (Attorney General)*, [1993] 2 S.C.R. 872.

West Virginia State Board of Education v. *Barnette*, 319 U.S. 624 (1943).

Winnipeg Child and Family Services v. *G. (D.F.)*, [1997] 3 S.C.R. 925.

Index

Abella, Rosalie, 52
Aboriginal women: failure of Charlottetown Accord to ensure protection of,
under the Charter, 47. *See also Lavell
v. A.G. Canada* [1974]; *R. v. O'Connor*
[1995]; *Winnipeg Child and Family
Services v. G. (D.F.)* [1997]
Aboriginal Women's Council, 61, 130
abortion: "abortion injunction" cases,
69-71; as area of lesser LEAF influence
on courts, 150; in Canadian public
opinion, 66; and Criminal Code, s. 251,
67, 179-80; and Equal Rights Amendment (US), 38-9; feminist legal victories
as fuel for anti-abortion movement, xvi;
free parliamentary vote on, 67; hospital,
lack of availability, 180; LEAF intervention in cases, 31; LEAF opposition to
pro-choice advocates, 179; legal history
of, 178-83; litigation and change in
social policy, 195; as most successful
area for feminist legal mobilization,
192; nongovernment groups opposed to
LEAF's position, 30; rights, established
by Morgentaler cases, 178-9; therapeutic, statistics before and after decriminalization, 180-2. *See also Borowski v. Canada*
[1989]; fetal rights; *Morgentaler, Smoling
and Scott v. The Queen* [1988]; *Morgentaler
v. The Queen* [1976]; *R. v. Morgentaler*
[1993]; *Roe v. Wade* (US) [1973]; *Tremblay
v. Daigle* [1989]
ACLU. *See* American Civil Liberties Union
(ACLU)
*Action Travail des Femmes v. Canadian
National Railway* [1987], 6
addiction: and consent, in sexual assault
case, 117-18; and fetal rights, 72-4. *See
also Norberg v. Wynrib* [1992]; *Winnipeg*

Child and Family Services v. G. (D.F.)
[1997]
Allen, Avril, xv, xvii
American Civil Liberties Union (ACLU): as
model for LEAF, 45; use of legal
mobilization for social reform, 10
Anderson, Doris, on Meech Lake Accord,
47
Andrews, Mark, 51
Andrews (90). *See R. v. Andrews and Smith*
[1990]
Andrews v. Law Society of British Columbia
[1989]: equality, impact on definition of,
53-4; equality principles and legislation,
92; extrinsic evidence cited by LEAF,
51-2, 152; government participants in
case, 25; LEAF participation, position,
and success in Supreme Court; 16;
nongovernment intervenors in case,
27; origin and outcome of case, 19;
substantive equality and freedom of
expression, 193; Supreme Court citations
list, 167; Supreme Court and legal literature citation frequencies, 165, 166;
Supreme Court use of LEAF material and
arguments, 154; Supreme Court votes
on, 22
Anti-Inflation Reference [1976]. *See Reference
re Anti-Inflation Act* [1976]
Arbour, Louise (Justice): judgment in LEAF
cases, 5, 21, 25; on *Little Sisters*, 5, 81
Atcheson, Beth, 49
"attitudinal model," of judicial behaviour,
2-3, 6

Backhouse, Constance, 54, 55
Badgley Report. *See Report of the Committee
on the Operation of the Abortion Law
(Badgley Report)*

Baines, Beverley, 52
Barristers and Solicitors Act (BC), 49
Bastarache, Michel (Justice): support for LEAF positions, 21; support percentage for Charter claims, 4
Bayefsky, Anne, 52
Beetz, Jean (Justice): on *Morgentaler 2,* 66; support for LEAF positions, 21
Beharriel. See L.L.A. et al. v. Beharriel [1995]
Benedet, Janine, 81
Benner v. *Canada (Secretary of State)* [1997], 166
Bhinder. See Re Bhinder et al. and Canadian National Railways [1985]
Big M Drug Mart. See R. v. Big M Drug Mart [1985]
Bill C-23, and changes in benefits/ obligations of cohabiting couples, 191
Bill C-46: and *Mills,* 140-3, 145; as not challenging court's institutional authority, 194; rules of access to therapeutic records, 137-8
Bill C-49: changes to sexual assault law, 136, 137, 147; and *Darrach,* 143-5, 194; and definition of consent, 136-7, 184; and *Seaboyer,* 145; and sexual assault statistics, 185
Bill of Rights. *See* Canadian Bill of Rights (1960)
Bill 178 (Quebec), and use of Charter's "notwithstanding clause," 8
Binnie, Ian (Justice): dissent behaviour in LEAF cases, 25; on *NBMHCS,* 109; support for LEAF positions, 21; support percentage for Charter claims, 4
Blencoe v. *British Columbia (Human Rights Commission)* [2000]: and antidiscrimination policy, 193; extrinsic evidence cited by LEAF, 152; government participants in case, 26; LEAF participation, position, and success in Supreme Court, 18; origin and outcome of case, 20; Supreme Court citations list, 177; Supreme Court and legal literature citation frequencies, 165; Supreme Court use of LEAF material and arguments, 162; Supreme Court votes on, 24
Bliss, Stella, xiii
Bliss v. *A.-G. Canada* [1979]: and Brooks, 1-2; critique of decision to allow discrimination on basis of pregnancy, 54; and feminist legal mobilization in Canada, 91; and maternity leave under Unemployment Insurance Act, xiii
Bogart, William, xv, xvi
Borowski, Joe, 65

Borowski v. *Canada* [1989]: criteria for exercising judicial decision to decide otherwise moot cases, 109; extrinsic evidence cited by LEAF, 152; on fetal vs. mother's rights, 67-70; government participants in case, 25; LEAF opposition to pro-choice movement, 179; LEAF participation, position, and success in Supreme Court, 16; as LEAF victory, 193; nongovernment intervenors in case, 27; origin and outcome of case, 19; Supreme Court citations list, 167-8; Supreme Court and legal literature citation frequencies, 165; Supreme Court votes on, 22
Brandeis, Louis, 151
British Columbia Forest Service, occupational fitness test, 58
British Columbia Legal Services Society, and *NBMHCS,* 108
British Columbia Medical Services Commission, and sign interpreters for deaf patients, 103-4
British Columbia (Public Service Employee Relations Commission) v. *BCGSEU* [1999]: extrinsic evidence cited by LEAF, 152; government participants in case, 26; nongovernment intervenors in case, 29; occupational fitness and sex discrimination, 58-60; origin and outcome of case, 20; as successful case in antidiscrimination policy area, 18, 193; Supreme Court citations list, 176; Supreme Court and legal literature citation frequencies, 165; Supreme Court use of LEAF material and arguments, 161; Supreme Court votes on, 24
British North America Act (1867). *See* Constitution Act (1867)
Brodsky, Gwen: on accommodation and substantive equality, 59; and *Andrews,* 50; report on early sex equality litigation under Charter, s. 15, xv; and scholarly research on equality issues, 49; works cited as extrinsic evidence by LEAF, 153
Brooks v. *Canada Safeway* [1989]: cited in *Moge,* 92; extrinsic evidence cited by LEAF, 152; government participants in case, 25; LEAF participation, position, and success in Supreme Court, 16; origin and outcome of case, 19; and pregnancy benefits, 1; pregnancy discrimination as sexual discrimination, 54; references to *Andrews,* 166; as success in antidiscrimination policy area, 193; Supreme Court citations list, 168; Supreme Court and

legal literature citation frequencies, 165;
Supreme Court votes on, 22
Brown v. *Board of Education* (US) [1954], 10
Busby, Karen, 79-80, 83, 138, 142
Bushell, Allison, 112, 113, 146, 148
Butler. See R. v. *Butler* [1992]

CAC. *See* Canadian Advisory Council on
the Status of Women (CAC)
Campbell, Kim, 136
Can Courts Bring About Social Change?
(Rosenberg), 195
Canada (Attorney General) v. *Mossop* [1993],
81
Canada Customs, seizures of homoerotic
materials, 79, 80
Canada Health Act, and provision of sign
interpretation for deaf patients, 107
Canada Pension Plan, exclusion of able-
bodied claimants under 35, 166
Canada v. *Mossop* [1993], 81
Canadian Abortion Rights Action League
(CARAL): coalition with LEAF, 30; and
Daigle, 70; and *Morgentaler 3,* 31, 183
Canadian Advisory Council on the Status
of Women (CAC): and constitutional
interpretation of equality, xv, 44, 45;
establishment of, xii; and founding of
LEAF, 33, 49; opposition to Meech Lake
Accord, 47; report on use of Charter for
litigation-driven social change, 48-9;
and *Weatherall,* 193
Canadian Association of the Deaf, 107
Canadian Association of Sexual Assault
Centres: on Bill C-49, 137; and *O'Connor,*
130; and s. 15 of the Charter, 61
Canadian Association of Statutory Human
Rights, 63
Canadian Association of University
Teachers (CAUT), 50
Canadian Bar Association, and *NBMHCS,*
108
Canadian Bill of Rights (1960): and
Drybones, 4-5; enforcement, lack of
clarity in, 99; low litigation potential of,
41; and *Robertson and Rosetanni,* 4
Canadian Charter of Rights and Freedoms
(1982): as advance in constitutional
status of women's rights in Canada, xiii,
46; argument of sex discrimination cases
under, 7; and constitutional reform
process, 39-40, 42; criminal rights claims
under, 3; and evidence in sexual assault
cases, 129; feminist theory of, grounded
in social distribution of power, 194; and

implementation of UN Convention on
the Elimination of All Forms of Discrimination Against Women, 122; and
judicial-legislative dialogue, 112, 141,
146; post-Charter political activism by
women, xii; post-material claims, 3; s. 1,
right of legislatures to explore alternative means of achieving objectives, 112-
13; s. 1, and use of extrinsic evidence,
151; s. 7, and abortion law, 179; s. 7,
and access to legal aid, 108; s. 7, and
defendants' rights in sexual assault
cases, 116, 131; s. 7, and reproductive
choice and fetal rights, 67-8, 69; s. 15,
and access to legal aid, 108; s. 15, and
definition of equality, 51; s. 15, and
Divorce Act, 97; s. 15, input of women's
movement into wording, 46; s. 15, and
parental benefits, 102-3; s. 15, and provision of sign interpretation for deaf
patients, 107; s. 15, and sexual orientation, 81-2, 84; s. 15, and sources of inequality, 61; s. 24(1), and constitutional
violation resulting from acts taken under
a statute, 102-3; s. 24(1), and enforcement of rights, 99; s. 24(1), and UI
benefits for biological parents, 98-9; s.
24(2), compared with s. 24(1), 99-100;
s. 28, and access to legal aid, 108; s. 28,
input of women's movement into wording, 46; s. 33, "notwithstanding clause"
and equality rights, 46; s. 33, "notwithstanding clause" and judicial-legislative
relationship, 7-9, 112-13; s. 52, principle
of constitutional supremacy, 7; Supreme
Court as "trustee" of Charter, 88-9; types
of litigation claims, 3. *See also* constitutional reform
Canadian Civil Liberties Association
(CCLA): and *Daigle,* 70; frequent opposition to LEAF's position, 30; as intervenor
in Supreme Court cases, 15; opposition
to sexual assault law reform, 184; on
pornography, 78; and s. 15 of the
Charter, 61
Canadian Congress for Learning Opportunities for Women (CCLOW), 44
Canadian Council of Churches v. *Canada
(Minister of Employment and Immigration)*
[1992]: extrinsic evidence cited by LEAF,
151, 152; government participants in
case, 25; LEAF participation, position,
and success in Supreme Court, 16; nongovernment intervenors in case, 27;
origin and outcome of case, 19; Supreme

Court citations list, 171; Supreme Court and legal literature citation frequencies, 165; Supreme Court votes on, 23
Canadian Day Care Advocacy Association, 32
Canadian Disability Rights Council, 61
Canadian Hearing Society, 107
Canadian Human Rights Act, and sex discrimination cases, 6
Canadian Human Rights Commission, 63
Canadian Jewish Congress (CJC): coalition with LEAF, 30; and s. 15 of the Charter, 61
Canadian Journal of Women and the Law, 49, 126, 138
Canadian Labour Congress (CLC), 58
Canadian Newspapers Co. v. *Canada (Attorney General)* [1988]: extrinsic evidence cited by LEAF, 152; government participants in case, 25; LEAF participation, position, and success in Supreme Court, 16; origin and outcome of case, 19; Supreme Court citations list, 167; Supreme Court and legal literature citation frequencies, 165; Supreme Court votes on, 22
CARAL. *See* Canadian Abortion Rights Action League (CARAL)
cases (LEAF), by name: *Andrews* v. *Law Society of British Columbia* [1989]; *Blencoe* v. *British Columbia (Human Rights Commission)* [2000]; *Borowski* v. *Canada* [1979]; *British Columbia (Public Service Employee Relations Commission)* v. *BCGSEU* [1999]; *Brooks* v. *Canada Safeway* [1989]; *Canadian Council of Churches* v. *Canada* [1992]; *Canadian Newspapers Co.* v. *Canada (Attorney General)* [1988]; *Eldridge* v. *British Columbia (Attorney General)* [1997]; *Gordon* v. *Goertz* [1996]; *Janzen* v. *Platy Enterprises Ltd.* [1989]; *Little Sisters Book and Art Emporium* v. *Canada* [2000]; *L.L.A. et al.* v. *Beharriel* [1995]; *M.* v. *H.* [1999]; *M.(K.)* v. *M.(H.)* [1992]; *Moge* v. *Moge* [1992]; *New Brunswick (Minister of Health and Community Services)* v. *G.(J.)* [1999]; *Norberg* v. *Wynrib* [1992]; *R.* v. *Andrews and Smith* [1990]; *R.* v. *Butler* [1992]; *R.* v. *Darrach* [2000]; *R.* v. *Ewanchuk* [1999]; *R.* v. *Keegstra* [1990]; *R.* v. *Mills* [1999]; *R.* v. *M. (M.L.)* [1994]; *R.* v. *O'Connor* [1995]; *R.* v. *S. (R.D.)* [1997]; *R.* v. *Seaboyer and Gayme* [1991]; *R.* v. *Sullivan and Lemay* [1991]; *R.* v. *Whitley* [1994]; *Schachter*

v. *Canada* [1992]; *Taylor* v. *The Canadian Human Rights Commission* [1990]; *Thibaudeau* v. *Canada* [1995]; *Tremblay* v. *Daigle* [1989]; *Vriend* v. *Alberta* [1998]; *Weatherall* v. *Canada (Attorney General)* [1993]; *Winnipeg Child and Family Services* v. *G. (D.F.)* [1997]. For page references of cases, *see under* name of case
CAUT. *See* Canadian Association of University Teachers (CAUT)
CCLA. *See* Canadian Civil Liberties Association (CCLA)
CCLOW. *See* Canadian Congress for Learning Opportunities for Women (CCLOW)
Charlottetown Accord: and *Consensus Report of the Constitution,* 40; failure to pass, 40, 61-2; opposed by anglophone women's movement, 47-8; proposed constitutional amendments, 44
Charter Committee on Poverty Issues: and *Eldridge,* 107; and *NBMHCS,* 108; and s. 15 of the Charter, 61; and *Thibaudeau,* 96
Charter of Rights and Freedoms (1982). *See* Canadian Charter of Rights and Freedoms (1982)
child care expenses, as taxable, 31-2
child custody proceedings, and access to legal aid, 108-11
child support payments, as taxable, 23, 30-2, 95-8, 97, 189
citizenship, and s. 15 of the Charter, 61
Civil Rights Act (US), 38
CJC. *See* Canadian Jewish Congress (CJC)
CLC. *See* Canadian Labour Congress (CLC)
Coalition of Provincial Organizations of the Handicapped (COPOH): and *Andrews,* 50; partnership with LEAF, 30; and s. 15 of the Charter, 61
Cohen, Leah, 54, 55
Commission on Equality in Employment, 52
Consensus Report of the Constitution, 40
consent: *actus reus* and *mens rea* arguments, 120, 121-2; changes in sexual assault law, 137; definition, by Supreme Court, 117-24; "mistaken belief in consent," 119. *See also Norberg* v. *Wynrib* [1992]; *R.* v. *Ewanchuk* [1999]; *R.* v. *M. (M.L.)* [1994]; *R.* v. *Whitley* [1994]; sexual assault
Constitution Act (1867): and constitution reform process, 41, 42; and interpretation of "persons," xi

Constitution Act (1982): s. 52, and s. 24(1) of Charter, 102-3; s. 52(1), and constitutional supremacy, 99. *See also* constitutional reform

constitutional reform: amendment failure, causes, 62; formal amendment process, xviii, 35, 36-7, 43-4, 48; history, 1980-92, 39-3; and institutional design model, 36-9; judicial interpretation, xviii, 35, 37; low litigation potential of pre-1982 rules, 41; primary and secondary rules, 35; and provincial consent, 42. *See also* Canadian Bill of Rights (1960); Canadian Charter of Rights and Freedoms (1982); Charlottetown Accord; Meech Lake Accord

Convention on the Elimination of All Forms of Discrimination Against Women, 122

COPOH. *See* Coalition of Provincial Organizations of the Handicapped (COPOH)

Corbiere v. *Canada (Minister of Indian and Northern Affairs)* [1999], 166

Cory, Peter (Justice): on definition of spouse, as different from marriage, 89; on *Egan*, 81; on *M.* v. *H.*, 86-7; on *NBMHCS*, 109; on *Norberg*, 118; support for LEAF positions, 21; on *Vriend*, 84

Council of Canadians with Disabilities, 107

Court Challenges Program (CCP), 13, 14, 33

courts: judicial-legislative relationship, 7-9, 112-13, 136, 141, 142, 146-7, 184; and social policy, 196-7. *See also* justices, of Supreme Court; Supreme Court (Canada); Supreme Court (US)

Criminal Code: amendments in sexual assault cases, 146; levels of sexual assault, 114; privacy amendments, in cases of sexual assault, 112; s. 163, and pornography as violence, 76-7; s. 251, and abortion, 64-70; s. 251, as infringement of security of person, 179-80; s. 276 and s. 277, and complainants' right to privacy, 114, 125, 126, 127-9, 143-5; s. 278.5(2), on access to therapeutic records of complainant in sexual assault cases, 138, 139

Dagenais v. *Canadian Broadcasting Corp.* [1994], 131

Daigle. See Tremblay v. *Daigle* [1989]

Daigle, Chantal, 69-71

Darrach. See R. v. *Darrach* [2000]

DAWN. *See* DisAbled Women's Network (DAWN)

Day, Shelagh: on accommodation and substantive equality, 59; as one of LEAF's founders, 49; report on early sex equality litigation under s. 15 of the Charter, 1989, xv; works cited as extrinsic evidence by LEAF, 153

deaf persons, sign interpretation for patients, 103-7

Dickson, Brian (Justice): on *Big M Drug Mart*, 53; on *Brooks*, 1; on *Janzen*, 55; on judicial-legislative relationship, 141; on lack of abortion availability, 180; on *Morgentaler 2*, 65, 66-7, 72; support for LEAF positions, 21; support percentage for Charter claims, 3

Dignity Canada Dignité for Gay Catholics and Supporters, 83

disability: and limitations of accommodation, 104-5; physical and mental, and s. 15 of the Charter, 61

DisAbled Women's Network (DAWN): and *BCPSERC*, 58; and *Eldridge*, 104, 107; as frequent intervenor on LEAF's side, 30; and *NBMHCS*, 108; and *O'Connor*, 130; and s. 15 of the Charter, 61

discrimination: indirect, as unsuccessful in Supreme Court, 96. *See also* sex discrimination; sexual orientation

divorce: and *Moge*, 92-4; and relocation of custodial parent, 94-5; s. 15, and Charter of Rights and Freedoms (1982), 97; self-sufficiency model as superceding alimony, 151

Dobrowolsky, Alexandra, xvii-xviii

Dworkin, Andrea: on lesbian erotica, 79; on obscenity definition, 75

Eberts, Mary: and *Andrews*, 50, 52; and *Morgentaler 3*, 31; qualifications, 33; and *Schachter*, 98; scholarly research, 49, 52

Edwards, Henrietta, xi

Edwards Books and Art v. *The Queen* [1986], 51

EGALE. *See* Equality for Gays and Lesbians Everywhere (EGALE)

Egan v. *Canada* [1995], 3-4, 58, 81

Eisenstadt v. *Baird* (US) [1972], 64

Eldridge v. *British Columbia (Attorney General)* [1997]: extrinsic evidence cited by LEAF, 111, 152; and feminist legal mobilization, 107; government participants in case, 26; issues, 24, 193; LEAF participation, position, and success in Supreme Court, 17; nongovernment

intervenors in case, 28; origin and outcome of case, 19; and provision of health
benefits, 91, 103-7; references to *Andrews,*
166; and sign language interpretation
for deaf patients, 103-7; Supreme Court
citations list, 174-5; Supreme Court and
legal literature citation frequencies, 165;
Supreme Court use of LEAF material and
arguments, 159-60; Supreme Court votes
on, 24
Ely, John Hart: cited in *Schachter,* 100; on
Roe v. *Wade,* 73, 100-1; theory of judicial
review, 100-1
Employment Insurance Act. *See Brooks* v.
Canada Safeway [1989]; *Schachter* v.
Canada [1992]
Equal Rights Amendment (ERA) (US):
failure to pass, xiv, 37-8, 61-2, 62;
provisions, xiii-xiv
equality: and *Andrews,* 22, 53-4; and
Brooks, 1-2; cases under Charter, s. 15(1),
15, 61; development of theory of, by
women's movement, 49; expanded
interpretation of, xv, 1-2, 53-4; harms-
based equality approach, and pornography, 76; principles, as area of LEAF
influence on courts, 150; substantive,
59, 194
Equality for Gays and Lesbians Everywhere (EGALE), 30, 61
Equality Now, 81
*Equality Rights and the Canadian Charter of
Rights and Freedoms* (Eberts and Bayefsky),
52
equitable sharing, doctrine of, 93
Esterich, Susan, 123
Estey, William (Justice), on *Morgentaler 2,*
66
eugenics laws, compensation for Alberta
victims of, 9
Ewanchuk. See R. v. *Ewanchuk* [1999]
Ewanchuk, Steven, 120
extrinsic evidence: definition, 151; use by
LEAF, 150-3, 163

family law: as area of lesser LEAF influence on courts, 150; and *Murdoch,* 91-2;
as successful area of policy change for
women, xvii
Family Law Act (FLA) (Ontario): and *M.* v.
H., 163; and spousal support for same-
sex partner, 84-7
Family Law Committee, 189
family policy. *See* child support payments,
as taxable; family law; family relationships; parental benefits

family relationships. *See Gordon* v. *Goertz*
[1996]; *Moge* v. *Moge* [1992]; *New
Brunswick (Minister of Health and
Community Services)* v. *G.(J.)* [1999];
Thibaudeau v. *Canada* [1995]
Federated Anti-Poverty Groups of B.C.,
96
feminism: and legal scholarship, 153. *See
also* legal mobilization, and women's
rights; women's movement (Canada);
women's movement (US)
feminist organizations. *See* names of
individuals and organizations
fetal rights: LEAF case success rate, 63;
LEAF opposition to, 179; nongovernment groups opposed to LEAF's position,
30. *See also* abortion; *Borowski* v. *Canada*
[1989]; *R.* v. *Sullivan and Lemay* [1991];
Tremblay v. *Daigle* [1989]; *Winnipeg Child
and Family Services* v. *G. (D.F.)* [1997]
fitness test, and occupational qualifica-
tion, 24
Ford v. *Québec* [1988], 8
Foundation for Equal Families, 30
Frankfurter, Felix (Justice, US Supreme
Court), 150
freedom of expression: and issue of
pornography, 74-82; and liberal
democracy, 74-5; nongovernment
groups opposed to LEAF's position, 30.
See also Canadian Newspapers Co. v.
Canada (Attorney General) [1988]; *Little
Sisters Book and Art Emporium* v. *Canada*
[2000]; *R.* v. *Butler* [1992]; *R.* v. *Keegstra*
[1990]

gay equality rights. *See* sexual orientation
Gay and Lesbian Awareness Society of
Edmonton (GALA), 83
Gay and Lesbian Community Centre of
Edmonton Society, 83
Gayme. See R. v. *Seaboyer and Gayme* [1991]
Gayme, Nigel, 124-5
General Social Survey (GSS), and sexual
assault reports, 185-6
Gibson, James, 6
Gilligan, Carol, 5
*G.(J.) See New Brunswick (Minister of Health
and Community Services)* v. *G.(J.)* [1999]
Godin, Jeannine, 108
Goertz, Robin, 95
Gonthier, Charles (Justice): on *Butler,* 77;
on *Darrach,* 143-4, 147; dissent behaviour
in LEAF cases, 25; on *Egan,* 81; on
Ewanchuk, 122; on *Gordon,* 95; on *M.* v.
H., 87; on *NBMHCS,* 109; on *Norberg,*

118; on *O'Connor,* 139; support for LEAF positions, 21; on *Thibaudeau,* 96
Gordon v. *Goertz* [1996]: equality of female custodial parent and best interests of child, 94-5; extrinsic evidence cited by LEAF, 111, 151, 152; and family law, 91, 193; government participants in case, 26; LEAF participation, position, and success in Supreme Court, 17; legal literature citations list, 164; as lost case, but win on substantive issue, 20; origin and outcome of case, 19; principle of spousal support, 164; Supreme Court citations list, 174; Supreme Court and legal literature citation frequencies, 165; Supreme Court use of LEAF material and arguments, 159, 163; Supreme Court votes on, 23
Gotell, Lise: on contentiousness of pornography issue in feminist movement, 188; on critique of LEAF for "essentialism," 194; on LEAF strategies, xvi
Gould v. *Yukon Order of Pioneers,* 58
Govereau, Tracy, 54
government participants, in LEAF cases, 25-6
Griswold v. *Connecticut* (US) [1965], 64

Harris, Mike, 90
hate propaganda. *See R.* v. *Andrews and Smith* [1990]; *R.* v. *Keegstra* [1990]; *Taylor* v. *The Canadian Human Rights Commission* [1990]
Hausegger, Lori, 150
Hiebert, Janet, 137
Hogg, Peter, 51, 112, 113, 146, 148
Hollow Hope, The (Rosenberg), 11
homosexual equality rights. *See* sexual orientation
Hospital Insurance Act (BC), 104, 105
Hughes, Charles Evans (Justice, US Supreme Court), 150
human rights, unreasonable delay in proceedings. *See Blencoe* v. *British Columbia (Human Rights Commission)* [2000]

Iacobucci, Frank (Justice): on Bill C-46, 143; on definition of spouse, as different from marriage, 89; dissent behaviour in LEAF cases, 25; on *Egan,* 81; on *Law,* 166, 178; on *Little Sisters,* 81, 146-7; on *M.* v. *H.,* 86, 88; on *Mills,* 140, 142; support for LEAF positions, 21; on *Vriend,* 84, 146
In a Different Voice (Gilligan), 5

incest. *See M.(K.)* v. *M.(H.)* [1992]; sexual assault
Income Tax Act (ITA), 95-8
Indian Rights for Indian Women (IRIW), 44
Individual Rights Protection Act (IRPA) (Alberta), 83
IRIW. *See* Indian Rights for Indian Women (IRIW)
Irwin Toy v. *A.-G. Quebec* [1989], 76

Jackson, Robert (Justice, US Supreme Court), 150
Janzen, Dianna, 54
Janzen v. *Platy Enterprises Ltd.* [1989]: and antidiscrimination policy, 193; extrinsic evidence cited by LEAF, 152, 153; government participants in case, 25; LEAF participation, position, and success in Supreme Court, 16; origin and outcome of case, 19; sexual harassment and imbalance of power between sexes, 54-5; Supreme Court citations list, 168; Supreme Court and legal literature citation frequencies, 165; Supreme Court use of LEAF material and arguments, 154, 163; Supreme Court votes on, 22
JCPC. *See* Judicial Committee of the Privy Council (JCPC)
Jhappan, Radha, xvi, 33
judges. *See* justices, of Supreme Court; names of individual justices
judicial bias. *See R.* v. *S.* [1997]
Judicial Committee of the Privy Council (JCPC), xi
judicial-legislative relationship, 7-9, 112-13, 136, 141-2, 146-7, 184
justices, of Supreme Court: decisions, and "attitudinal model" of judicial behaviour, 2-3, 6; positions on LEAF cases, 20-5. *See also* names of individual justices; Supreme Court (Canada); Supreme Court (US)

Keegstra. *See R.* v. *Keegstra* [1990]
Kelly, James, 3
Klassen, Claire, 83

La Forest, Gérard (Justice): on *Andrews,* 52, 57; dissent behaviour in LEAF cases, 25; on *Egan,* 4, 58, 82; on *Gould* v. *Yukon Order of Pioneers,* 58; on *Morgentaler 2,* 57, 66; on *Norbert,* 118; on *O'Connor,* 139; on *Schachter,* 103; support for LEAF positions, 21; on *Thibaudeau,* 96; on *Weatherall,* 57-8

Lamer, Antonio (Justice): on *Andrews,* 52; dissent behaviour in LEAF cases, 25; on *Egan,* 81; on *Mills,* 142; on *Morgentaler 2,* 66; on *NBMHCS,* 109-10; on *O'Connor,* 132, 134; on *Schachter,* 102-3; on *Sullivan and Lemay,* 72; support for LEAF positions, 21, 22; as supportive of sexual orientation cases, 4

Laskin, Bora (Justice): on *Borowski,* 65; dismissal of extralegal evidence, 151; on *Murdoch,* 91-2

Lavell v. *A.G. Canada* [1974], xii

Law, Nancy, 166

Law v. *Canada* [1999], 87, 166

LEAF. *See* Legal Education and Action Fund (LEAF)

LeBel, Louis (Justice): dissent behaviour in LEAF cases, 25; on *Little Sisters,* 81; support for LEAF positions, 21

legal aid, access to, 108-11

Legal Defense and Education Fund (LDF) of NAACP, 10

Legal Education and Action Fund (LEAF): cases, by issue, 22-24; cases, list of (*see* cases [LEAF], by name); cases, losses, 97, 113; cases, origin and outcome, 18-20; cases, participation position, 16-18; cases, success rate, 16-18, 165; cases, winnability as criterion for selection, 196; cited reports on equal rights litigation, xv; criteria for measuring effectiveness, 149-50; criticized for "essentialism," 194; education activities, 15; effect on Charter litigation, 178; effect on legal rules, 191; effect on policy, 191, 196; equality, contribution to expanded interpretation of, xv, 1; equality, substantive principles, 22, 193; expenses, 13, 14, 15; extrinsic evidence, use of, 126, 131, 150-3, 163; focus on litigation, rather than community consultation and consensus, xvi; founding of, 33, 49; funding of, 33; geographic distribution of cases, 15; government departments, cooperation with, 33; government participants in cases, 22, 25-6; importance of cases, 164; as intervenor in Supreme Court cases, 15; legal defeats as political victories, 91, 193; legal expertise, 33; nongovernment groups frequently opposed to, 30; nongovernmental organization participation in cases, 22, 27-9; opposition to Meech Lake Accord, 47; organization of, 12-13; and politics of constitutional amendment, 193; principles underlying

litigation activity, 149; as repeat player (RP), 33; revenue, 13, 14; scholarship, impact on courts, 150; strategy in Supreme Court, 12; use of law as tool for egalitarian social change, 9, 34; women's rights in Canada, contribution to, xiv. *See also* cases (LEAF), by name; West Coast LEAF

legal mobilization, and women's rights: highest successes in private sector discrimination and family law, xvii; losses, between 1973-82, xii-xiii; repeat player (RP) litigants, and achievement of long-term objectives, 10-11; and social change, xvii, 9-12, 196; and social movements, 63; success, difficulty of measurement of, 12; success rate, under conservative government between 1984-93, xiii; use of litigation to interpret Canadian constitution, xiv

legislature, and courts, 7-9, 112-13, 136, 141-2, 146-7, 184

lesbians. *See Little Sisters Book and Art Emporium* v. *Canada* [2000]; *M.* v. *H.* [1999]; pornography; sexual orientation

L'Heureux-Dubé, Claire (Justice): on *Butler,* 77; on courts changing attitudes to same-sex marriage, 90; dissent behaviour in LEAF cases, 25; on *Egan,* 81; on *Ewanchuk,* 122-3; on *Gordon,* 95; influence on Bill C-46, 138; on *Keegstra,* 150; and *Law,* 87, 178; on *Little Sisters,* 81, 163-4; and *M.* v. *H.,* 87; on *Moge,* 93, 94; on *NBMHCS,* 109, 110; on *Norberg,* 118; on *O'Connor,* 132-3, 134, 135; on *Schacter,* 103; on *Seaboyer,* 6, 126, 129, 153, 163; on *Sullivan and Lemay,* 72; support for LEAF positions, 5, 21; support percentage for types of Charter claims, 3; and *Symes,* 31; on *Thibaudeau,* 95, 96-7; vote percentage on excluding evidence, 3

litigation, and women's rights. *See* legal mobilization, and women's rights

Little Sisters Book and Art Emporium v. *Canada* [2000]: as contentious case within feminist movement, 188, 193-4; contribution to judicial-legislative dialogue, 146-7; dissent vote by Justice Louise Arbour, 5; equality rights and lesbian erotica, 79-82; extrinsic evidence cited by LEAF, 152, 153; government participants in case, 26; LEAF participation, position, and success in Supreme Court, 18; as less "winnable" case, 196; nongovernment intervenors in case, 29; origin and outcome of case, 20; Supreme

Court citations list, 177; Supreme Court and legal literature citation frequencies, 165; Supreme Court use of LEAF material and arguments, 162, 163; Supreme Court votes on, 24

L.L.A. et al. v. Beharriel [1995]: as Charter case on sexual assault, 115; extrinsic evidence cited by LEAF, 152; government participants in case, 26; as LEAF case loss, 194; LEAF participation, position, and success in Supreme Court, 17; nongovernment intervenors in case, 27; origin and outcome of case, 19; Supreme Court citations list, 173; Supreme Court and legal literature citation frequencies, 165; Supreme Court use of LEAF material and arguments, 159; Supreme Court votes on, 23

Lovelace v. *Ontario* [2000], 166

M. v. *H.* [1999], 89, 193: as advancement for rights of gays and lesbians, 4, 164; and definition of spouse, 84-90, 164, 190-1; extrinsic evidence cited by LEAF, 152; government participants in case, 26; highly cited in legal literature, 164; LEAF participation, position, and success in Supreme Court, 18; nongovernment intervenors in case, 29; origin and outcome of case, 20; references to *Andrews,* 166; Supreme Court citations list, 177; Supreme Court and legal literature citation frequencies, 165; Supreme Court use of LEAF material and arguments, 160-1, 163; Supreme Court votes on, 24

McCann, Michael, 11-12, 196

McClung, John (Justice, Alberta Court of Appeal), 123

McClung, Nellie, xi

McCullough v. *Maryland* (US) [1819], 50-1

McIntyre, Sheila: on Bill C-46, 138; on importance of *Seaboyer* to sexual assault dialogue, 188; on LEAF and amendments to sexual assault law, 136; on LEAF strategies, xvi; testimony before legislature on Bill C-49, 137

McIntyre, William (Justice): on *Andrews,* 52-3; on *Morgentaler 2,* 66, 72; support for LEAF positions, 21; support percentage for Charter claims, 3

McKinney, Louise, xi

MacKinnon, Catherine: analysis of sexual harassment, 54, 55; as consultant on *Keegstra* and *Butler,* 79; critique of Court's definition of consent, 117; feminist legal scholarship on sexual

assault, 153; on lesbian erotica, 79; on obscenity definition, 75; on rape and power, 123, 124

McLachlin, Beverley (Justice): appointment as Chief Justice, 2000, 5; and *BCPSERC,* 59-60; on Bill C-46, 143; dissent behaviour in LEAF cases, 25; on *Egan,* 81; on *Ewanchuk,* 123; on *Gordon,* 95; on *Little Sisters,* 81, 163-4; on *Mills,* 140, 142; on *Moge,* 94; on *NBMHCS,* 109; on *Norberg,* 118; on *O'Connor,* 135, 139; on *Seaboyer,* 6, 123, 127-9; support for LEAF positions, 5-6, 21; and *Symes,* 31; on *Thibaudeau,* 95, 96, 97; on *Winnipeg Child and Family Services,* 73-4

McPhedran, Marilou, 49, 118

Mahoney, Kathleen, 76

Major, John (Justice): dissent behaviour in LEAF cases, 25; on *Egan,* 81; on *Ewanchuk,* 121-2, 123; on *NBMHCS,* 109; support for LEAF positions, 21; on *Vriend,* 84

Manitoba Human Rights Act, 1, 54

Marbury v. *Madison* (US), 50-1

marriage: definition, not affected by definition of spouse, 191; as disadvantageous to women, 92-4, 111; same-sex, 89, 90, 191

Marriage Act (Alberta), 89

Marriage Amendment Act (Alberta), 89

Marshall, John (US Chief Justice), 50-1

Mathen, Carissima, 149

Medical and Health Care Services Act (BC), 105

medical/therapeutic record disclosure: and Bill C-46, 147-8; changes to Criminal Code, s. 278.2(2), 138-9; and note-taking by sexual assault centres, 133-5; requirement to establish record's relevance, 140-3. See also *L.L.A. et al. v. Beharriel* [1995]; *R. v. Mills* [1999]; *R. v. O'Connor* [1995]; *R. v. Stinchcombe* [1991]

Meech Lake Accord: loss of support due to Charter's "notwithstanding clause," 8; opposed by anglophone women's movement, 46, 47-8; ratification failure, 40, 61-2, 62

Meiorin, Tawney, 58

midwives. See *R. v. Sullivan and Lemay* [1991]

Mill, John Stuart, 74

Miller v. *California* (US) [1973], 75

Mills. See R. v. Mills [1999]

M.(K.) v. *M.(H.)* [1992]: extrinsic evidence cited by LEAF, 152; government participants in case, 26; LEAF participation, position, and success in Supreme Court,

17; origin and outcome of case, 19; Supreme Court citations list, 171; Supreme Court and legal literature citation frequencies, 165; Supreme Court use of LEAF material and arguments, 158, 163; Supreme Court votes on, 23

Moge, Andrzej, 92

Moge, Zofia, 92

Moge v. *Moge* [1992]: extrinsic evidence cited by LEAF, 111, 151, 152; and family law, 91, 193; government participants in case, 26; LEAF participation, position, and success in Supreme Court, 16; origin and outcome of case, 19, 92-4; Supreme Court citations list, 171-2; Supreme Court and legal literature citation frequencies, 165; Supreme Court use of LEAF material and arguments, 157; Supreme Court votes on, 23

Mohr, Renate, 137

Monahan, Patrick, 8

Morgentaler, Dr. Henry, 65

Morgentaler, Smoling and Scott v. *The Queen* [1988]: and Bill C-43, 67; and *Borowski*, 69; and doctrine of judicial minimalism, 68; as key victory over abortion provisions in Criminal Code, 30-1; legitimization of private abortion clinics, 181, 183; nullification of Criminal Code's abortion provisions, 179; Supreme Court judgment, 65-7

Morgentaler 2. See Morgentaler, Smoling and Scott v. *The Queen* [1988]

Morgentaler 3. See R. v. *Morgentaler* [1993]

Morgentaler v. *The Queen* [1976], xii-xiii

Morton, F.L., xv, xvii

Mossman, Mary Jane, 52

Mulroney, Brian, 8

Murdoch v. *Murdoch* [1975], 91

Murphy, Emily, xi

NAACP. *See* National Association for the Advancement of Colored People (NAACP)

NAC. *See* National Action Committee on the Status of Women (NAC)

National Action Committee on the Status of Women (NAC): and amendments to sexual assault law, 136; and constitutional interpretation of equality, 43-4; established on recommendation of the Royal Commission on the Status of Women, xii; opposition to Charlottetown Accord, 47; opposition to Meech Lake Accord, 47; and s. 15 of the Charter, 61

National Association for the Advancement of Colored People (NAACP): and *Brown* v. *Board of Education* (US) [1954], 10; extralegal evidence, as tactic, 151; resources of, 11; use of legal mobilization for social reform, 10

National Association of Women and the Law (NAWL): and briefs on Bill C-46, 138; and constitutional interpretation of equality, 44, 45, 46; and *NBMHCS*, 108; opposition to Meech Lake Accord, 47; and scholarly research on equality issues, 49; sexual assault, Criminal Code amendments regarding, 136, 146; sexual assault cases, support for, 113; on strengths of Charter for enforcement of basic rights and freedoms, 48

National Consumer's League, 10

Native Women's Association of Canada (NWAC): and constitutional interpretation of equality, 44; and s. 15 of the Charter, 61

NAWL. *See* National Association of Women and the Law (NAWL)

NBMHCS. See New Brunswick (Minister of Health and Community Services) v. *G.(J)* [1999]

New Brunswick (Minister of Health and Community Services) v. *G.(J)* [1999]: and constitutional right to legal aid, 91, 108-11, 164; and family law, 193; government participants in case, 26; LEAF participation, position, and success in Supreme Court, 18; legal literature citations, 164; nongovernment intervenors in case, 29; origin and outcome of case, 20; policy changes as result of, 111; Supreme Court citations list, 176; Supreme Court and legal literature citation frequencies, 165; Supreme Court use of LEAF material and arguments, 161; Supreme Court votes on, 24

nongovernment intervenors, in LEAF cases, 27-8

Norberg, Laura, 117, 118

Norberg v. *Wynrib* [1992]: and definition of consent, 117-18, 120; extrinsic evidence cited by LEAF, 152; government participants in case, 25; LEAF participation, position, and success in Supreme Court, 16; origin and outcome of case, 19; as sexual assault case, 115; Supreme Court citations list, 172; Supreme Court and legal literature citation frequencies, 165; Supreme Court use of LEAF material and arguments, 157; Supreme Court votes on, 23

"notwithstanding clause" (s. 33 of Charter). *See* Canadian Charter of Rights and Freedoms (1982)
Nova Scotia Court of Appeal, 119
NWAC. *See* Native Women's Association of Canada (NWAC)

obscenity: and Criminal Code, 76; definition (US), 75. *See also* pornography
occupational standards, and sex discrimination, 58-60
O'Connor. *See R. v. O'Connor* [1995]
O'Connor, Hubert, 130
Old Age Security Act (OAS), 3-4, 81
O'Malley v. *Woodrough* (US) [1938], 6
On Liberty (Mill), 74
one-shot (OS) litigants, 11
Ontario College of Physicians and Surgeons, Task Force on Sexual Abuse of Patients, 118
Ontario Confederation of University Faculty Associations, 50
Ontario Litigation Fund, 13, 14

parens patriae principle, and fetal rights. *See Winnipeg Child and Family Services* v. *G. (D.F.)* [1997]
parental benefits. *See Schachter v. Canada* [1992]
parental relocation. *See Gordon v. Goertz* [1996]
parental right to security of person, in custody proceedings. *See New Brunswick (Minister of Health and Community Services)* v. *G.(J)* [1999]
Parlby, Irene, xi
Parliamentary Committee on Equality Rights, 52
"persons," in Constitution Act (1867), xi
Plessy v. *Ferguson* (US) [1896], 52
policy reform, and litigation by women's groups. *See* legal mobilization, and women's rights
Politics of Pragmatism, The (Dobrowolsky), xvii-xviii
pornography: as area of LEAF influence on courts, 150; charges, statistics on, 188-9; as divisive issue among feminists, xvi-xvii, 79-82, 188, 191, 193-4; as form of hate propaganda, 78; and freedom of expression, 74-82; harms-based equality approach, 76, 164; LEAF case success rate, 63; lesbian erotica and pornography debate, 79-82; role in gay and lesbian culture, 163; as violence against women, 76. *See also Little Sisters Book and*

Art Emporium v. *Canada* [2000]; obscenity; *R.* v. *Butler* [1992]
Pothier, Dianne, 153
pregnancy. *See* abortion; *Bliss* v. *A.-G. Canada* [1979]; *Brooks* v. *Canada Safeway* [1989]; fetal rights; *Tremblay* v. *Daigle* [1989]
prisoners, equal treatment of. *See Weatherall* v. *Canada (Attorney General)* [1993]
Pritchett, C. Herman, 2-3
pro-life movement. *See Borowksi* v. *Canada* [1989]
public interest groups, standing of. *See Canadian Council of Churches* v. *Canada (Minister of Employment and Immigration)* [1992]

Quebec: Bill 178, and use of Charter's "notwithstanding clause," 8; and constitutional reform process, 42; low profile of LEAF in, 32-3; multicultural rights and Meech Lake Accord, 47

R. v. *Andrews and Smith* [1990]: and anti-hate propaganda, 76; government participants in case, 25; LEAF participation, position, and success in Supreme Court, 16; nongovernment intervenors in case, 27; origin and outcome of case, 19; and substantive equality principles, 193; Supreme Court citations list, 168; Supreme Court and legal literature citation frequencies, 165; Supreme Court use of LEAF material and arguments, 155; Supreme Court votes on, 22
R. v. *Big M Drug Mart* [1985], 53
R. v. *Butler* [1992]: compared with *Little Sisters*, 163, 188, 196; effect of, 164; extrinsic evidence cited by LEAF, 152, 153; government participants in case, 26; highly cited in legal literature, 164; and issue of expressive freedom, 193; LEAF participation, position, and success in Supreme Court, 17; as lost case, but win on substantive issue, 20; nongovernment intervenors in case, 27; origin and outcome of case, 19; and s. 163 of Criminal Code, 76; Supreme Court citations list, 171; Supreme Court and legal literature citation frequencies, 165; Supreme Court votes on, 23
R. v. *Carosella* [1997], 133-4
R. v. *Darrach* [2000]: and Bill C-49, 147, 148, 194; extrinsic evidence cited by LEAF, 152; government participants in case, 26; LEAF participation, position,

and success in Supreme Court, 18; legal rights and equality rights, 184; nongovernment intervenors in case, 29; origin and outcome of case, 20; and "rape shield" provisions, 112, 143-5; and second-wave Criminal Code amendments, 146; Supreme Court citations list, 177; Supreme Court and legal literature citation frequencies, 165; as Supreme Court sexual assault case, 115; Supreme Court votes on, 24; as win for LEAF, 113, 194

R. v. Daviault [1994], 30, 115

R. v. Drybones [1970], 4-5

R. v. Ewanchuk [1999]: and definition of consent, 119-24, 147, 184; extrinsic evidence cited by LEAF, 152; government participants in case, 26; LEAF participation, position, and success in Supreme Court, 17; nongovernment intervenors in case, 29; origin and outcome of case, 19; and principle of substantive equality, 194; and second-wave Criminal Code amendments, 145-6; Supreme Court citations list, 176; Supreme Court and legal literature citation frequencies, 165; as Supreme Court sexual assault case, 115; Supreme Court use of LEAF material and arguments, 160; Supreme Court votes on, 24

R. v. Keegstra [1990]: extrinsic evidence cited by LEAF, 152; and freedom of expression, 193; government participants in case, 25; and hate propaganda provisions in Criminal Code, 76; LEAF participation, position, and success in Supreme Court, 16; nongovernment intervenors in case, 27; origin and outcome of case, 19; Supreme Court citations list, 168-9; Supreme Court and legal literature citation frequencies, 165; Supreme Court use of LEAF material and arguments, 154-5; Supreme Court votes on, 22

R. v. M. (M.L.) [1994]: and definition of consent, 119, 121; extrinsic evidence cited by LEAF, 152; government participants in case, 26; LEAF participation, position, and success in Supreme Court, 17; origin and outcome of case, 19; Supreme Court citations list, 173; Supreme Court and legal literature citation frequencies, 165; Supreme Court votes on, 23

R. v. Mills [1999]: and Bill C-46, 140-3, 147, 148, 194; compared with *Darrach*,

112-13; extrinsic evidence cited by LEAF, 151, 152; government participants in case, 26; LEAF participation, position, and success in Supreme Court, 18; legal rights and equality rights, 184; nongovernment intervenors in case, 29; origin and outcome of case, 20; and second-wave Criminal Code amendments, 145-6; as sexual assault case before Supreme Court, 115; Supreme Court citations list, 177; Supreme Court and legal literature citation frequencies, 165; Supreme Court votes on, 24; as win for LEAF, 113

R. v. Morgentaler [1993], 30, 31

R. v. Oakes [1986], 151

R. v. O'Connor [1995]: and Bill C-46, 143, 147; and change in rate of sexual assault, 195; extrinsic evidence cited by LEAF, 152; as frequently cited case, 164; government participants in case, 26; and judicial-legislative relationship, 112-13, 141, 142, 184; LEAF participation, position, and success in Supreme Court, 17; nongovernment intervenors in case, 27; origin and outcome of case, 19; and principle of substantive equality, 194; as sexual assault case before Supreme Court, 115; Supreme Court citations list, 173-4; Supreme Court and legal literature citation frequencies, 165; Supreme Court decisions, 129-35; Supreme Court use of LEAF material and arguments, 158; Supreme Court votes on, 23

R. v. S. [1997]: extrinsic evidence cited by LEAF, 152; government participants in case, 26; LEAF participation, position, and success in Supreme Court, 17; legal literature citations, 164; nongovernment intervenors in case, 28; Supreme Court citations list, 175; Supreme Court and legal literature citation frequencies, 165; Supreme Court use of LEAF material and arguments, 159; Supreme Court votes on, 24

R. v. Seaboyer and Gayme [1991]: and Bill C-49, 143, 145, 147, 184; extrinsic evidence cited by LEAF, 151, 152, 153; and feminist theory of Charter, 194; as frequently cited case, 164; government participants in case, 25; importance to sexual assault dialogue, 188; judgments by women Supreme Court justices, 6, 123; and judicial-legislative relationship, 113, 136; LEAF participation, position, and success in Supreme Court, 16; nongovernment intervenors in case, 27;

origin and outcome of case, 19; and production of third-party records, 132; and rights of defendants in sexual assault cases, 112; and role of courts as champion of vulnerable groups, 142; as sexual assault case before Supreme Court, 115; and sexual assault legislation reform, 184; and sexual assault statistics, 185, 195; Supreme Court citations list, 169-70; Supreme Court and legal literature citation frequencies, 165; Supreme Court use of LEAF material and arguments, 155-7; Supreme Court votes on, 23

R. v. *Stinchcombe* [1991]: and Bill C-46, 141; and medical/therapeutic record disclosure, 116, 130, 132, 134

R. v. *Sullivan and Lemay* [1991]: extrinsic evidence cited by LEAF, 152; and fetal rights issue, 71-2, 193; government participants in case, 25; LEAF opposition to extend personhood to fetuses, 179; LEAF participation, position, and success in Supreme Court, 16; nongovernment intervenors in case, 27; origin and outcome of case, 19; Supreme Court citations list, 170; Supreme Court and legal literature citation frequencies, 165; Supreme Court votes on, 22

R. v. *Whitley* [1994]: extrinsic evidence cited by LEAF, 152; government participants in case, 26; LEAF participation, position, and success in Supreme Court, 17; and "mistaken belief in consent," 119; origin and outcome of case, 19; as sexual assault case before Supreme Court, 115; Supreme Court citations list, 173; Supreme Court and legal literature citation frequencies, 165; Supreme Court votes on, 23

Radclyffe, Nancy, 15

rape. *See* consent; sexual assault

rape shield provisions. *See* R. v. *Darrach* [2000]; R. v. *O'Connor* [1995]; R. v. *Seaboyer and Gayme* [1991]

Razack, Sherene: on difficulty of making feminist gains in courts, xv; on internal contradictions in LEAF's strategies, xviii; on LEAF and the feminist community, xvi; on Symes case, 32

Re *Bhinder et al. and Canadian National Railways* [1985], 6

REAL Women, as frequent opposition to LEAF, 30

Reference re Anti-Inflation Act [1976], 151

repeat player (RP) litigants: and achieve-

ment of long-term objectives, 10-11; and interpretive flexibility of constitutional rules, 37; resources of, 11

Report of the Aboriginal Justice Inquiry of Manitoba, 131

Report of the Committee on the Operation of the Abortion Law (Badgley Report): as basis for decision in *Morgentaler 2*, 67; and decriminalization of abortion, 181, 183; on risk to health of mother, 179-80

reproduction choice. *See* abortion; fetal rights

Rights at Work (McCann), 12

Ritchie, Roland (Justice), 2; on *Bliss*, 5; career and major decisions, 4-5; on *Lavell*, 5

Roach, Kent, 146, 148

Robertson and Rosetanni v. *The Queen* [1963], 4

Roe v. *Wade* (US) [1973], xii, 38, 39, 64

Rosenberg, Gerald, 11, 195

Roth v. *United States* (US) [1957], 75

Royal Commission on the Status of Women, xi-xii

St. Lewis, Joanne, 137

Schachter, Shalom, 98

Schachter v. *Canada* [1992]: extrinsic evidence cited by LEAF, 152; government participants in case, 26; LEAF participation, position, and success in Supreme Court, 17; as legal defeat but political victory, 193; nongovernment intervenors in case, 27; origin and outcome of case, 19; and parental leave benefits, 91, 98; policy changes as result of, 111, 190; Supreme Court citations list, 172-3; Supreme Court and legal literature citation frequencies, 165; Supreme Court use of LEAF material and arguments, 157; Supreme Court votes on, 23

Scheingold, Stuart, 11, 196

Seaboyer. See R. v. *Seaboyer and Gayme* [1991]

Seaboyer, Steven, 124

sex discrimination: and Human Rights Act, 6; LEAF arguments under Charter, 6-7; as successful area of policy change for women, xvii. *See also Bliss* v. *A.-G. Canada* [1979]; *British Columbia (Public Service Employee Relations Commission)* v. *BCGSEU* [1999]; *Brooks* v. *Canada Safeway* [1989]

sexual assault: as area of lesser LEAF influence on courts, 150; Bill C-49, and

changes to sexual assault law, 136-7; change in attitude toward charges, 186-8; change in classification of behaviour defined as sexual assault, 184-5; changes in protection of complainants, 114; and complainants' previous sexual conduct, 124-9; conflict between legal rights and equality concerns, 184-9; as crime, history of, 113-14; and Criminal Code, 112, 114, 145-6; defendants, protection of rights by courts, 116-17; and feminist legal mobilization, 113, 195; LEAF education activities regarding, 15; non-government groups opposed to LEAF's position, 30; physicians, sexual abuse of patients, 117-18; reported and unreported cases, 113; and request for complainants' therapeutic records, 130-5; statistics 1983-2001, 184-6. *See also* consent; incest; medical/therapeutic record disclosure; *R.* v. *Darrach* [2000]; *R.* v. *Ewanchuk* [1999]; *R.* v. *M.* (*M.L.*) [1994]; *R.* v. *O'Connor* [1995]; *R.* v. *Seaboyer and Gayme* [1991]; *R.* v. *Whitley* [1994]
sexual harassment. *See Janzen* v. *Platy Enterprises Ltd.* [1989]
Sexual Harassment of Working Women: A Case of Sex Discrimination (MacKinnon), 153
sexual orientation: and definition of spouse, 24, 88, 89, 190-1; discrimination on basis of orientation, 83-4; "family status" and bereavement leave, 81; impact of changes in judicial changes in Supreme Court decisions, 3-4; LEAF case success rate, 63; LEAF coalition with nongovernment intervenors, 30; and Old Age pension rights, 81; and s. 15 of the Charter, 61; and same-sex marriage, 89; and spousal support, 84-90. *See also Egan* v. *Canada* [1995]; *Little Sisters Book and Art Emporium* v. *Canada* [2000]; *M.* v. *H.* [1999]; pornography; *Vriend* v. *Alberta* [1998]
Sheehy, Elizabeth, 153
Sheppard, Colleen, 52, 151
sign language, right to interpreter. *See Eldridge* v. *British Columbia (Attorney General)* [1997]
Smith, Lynn: legal scholarship contribution to Andrews, 52; qualifications, 33-4; and scholarly research on equality issues, 49
social movements: and legal mobilization, 63; policy-oriented litigation and social change debate, 195

Sopinka, John (Justice): on *Borowski,* 69; on *Butler,* 77-9; on *Carosella,* 134-5; dissent behaviour in LEAF cases, 25; on *Egan,* 4, 81; on *Norberg,* 118; support for LEAF positions, 21; on *Thibaudeau,* 96
spousal support. *See M.* v. *H.* [1999]; *Moge* v. *Moge* [1992]
spouse, definition of. *See M.* v. *H.* [1999]
Standing Committee on Justice and Legal Affairs, 138
Status of Women Canada, 33
Stevenson (Justice), 21
Strayer, Barry (Justice), on *Schachter,* 98-9, 100
substantive equality principles, 35, 59, 193, 194
Sunstein, Cass, 68
Supreme Court (Canada): appointment of women to, 4, 5; "attitudinal model" of judicial behaviour, 2-3, 6; composition, 2, 4-6; first Charter equal rights case, 1989, xv; and indirect discrimination claims, 96; judicial-legislative relationship, 7-9, 112-13, 136, 141, 142, 146-7, 184; "persons" interpretation, xi; and sexual assault cases, 114-17; traditional view on extralegal evidence, 151; as "trustee" of Charter, 88-9; use of LEAF material and arguments, 154-62. *See also* justices, Supreme Court; names of individual justices
Supreme Court (US): "case and controversy" doctrine, 68; feminist organizations as intervenors in cases, 30; judicial minimalism doctrine, 68; rulings on pornography, 75; standards of constitutional review, 45
Symes, Elizabeth, 31, 49
Symes v. *Canada* [1993], 30, 31-2

Tarnopolsky, Walter, 52
Task Group on the Taxation of Child Support, 189
Taylor v. *The Canadian Human Rights Commission* [1990]: extrinsic evidence cited by LEAF, 152; government participants in case, 25; as hate propaganda case, 76, 193; LEAF participation, position, and success in Supreme Court, 16; nongovernment intervenors in case, 27; origin and outcome of case, 19; Supreme Court citations list, 169; Supreme Court and legal literature citation frequencies, 165; Supreme Court use of LEAF material and arguments, 154; Supreme Court votes on, 22

Thibaudeau, Suzanne, 95
Thibaudeau v. *Canada* [1995]: child support taxation changes, as result of, 111, 189; extrinsic evidence cited by LEAF, 152; and family law, 91; government participants in case, 26; and Income Tax Act (ITA), 95-8; LEAF participation, position, and success in Supreme Court, 17; as legal defeat but political victory, 193; nongovernment intervenors in case, 28; origin and outcome of case, 19; Supreme Court citations list, 174; Supreme Court and legal literature citation frequencies, 165; Supreme Court votes on, 23
Toward a Feminist Theory of the State (MacKinnon), 117-18, 123, 124, 153
Tremblay, Jean-Guy, 69
Tremblay v. *Daigle* [1989]: extrinsic evidence cited by LEAF, 152; fetal rights and Charter, 69-71; government participants in case, 25; LEAF opposition to father input into abortion decision, 179; LEAF participation, position, and success in Supreme Court, 16; nongovernment intervenors in case, 27; origin and outcome of case, 19; as reproductive rights case, 193; as successful case for LEAF, 31; Supreme Court citations list, 168; Supreme Court and legal literature citation frequencies, 165; Supreme Court votes on, 22

Unemployment Insurance Act (UIA). *See Bliss* v. *A.-G. Canada* [1979]; *Brooks* v. *Canada Safeway* [1989]; *Schachter* v. *Canada* [1992]
United Nations Convention on the Elimination of All Forms of Discrimination Against Women, 122

Vriend v. *Alberta* [1998]: as advancement for rights of gays and lesbians, 4, 164; changes in rights regarding sexual orientation, 190; and court as "trustee" of Charter, 88; as discrimination case based on sexual orientation, 83-4, 193; extrinsic evidence cited by LEAF, 152; government participants in case, 26; highly cited in legal literature, 164; and judicial-legislative relationship, 146; LEAF participation, position, and success in Supreme Court, 17; nongovernment intervenors in case, 28; origin and outcome of case, 19; references to *Andrews*, 166; Supreme Court citations list, 175-6; Supreme Court and legal literature citation frequencies, 165; Supreme Court use of LEAF material and arguments, 160; Supreme Court votes on, 24, 89

Watch Tower Bible and Tract Society (Jehovah's Witnesses), 108
WCFS. See Winnipeg Child and Family Services v. *G. (D.F.)* [1997]
Weatherall v. *Canada (Attorney General)* [1993]: cross-gender searches of prisoners, and sex discrimination, 55, 58-60; and definition of equality as not necessarily identical treatment, 55-8; extrinsic evidence cited by LEAF, 152; LEAF intervention to prevent formal equality outcome, 193; LEAF participation, position, and success in Supreme Court, 17; nongovernment intervenors in case, 27; origin and outcome of case, 19; Supreme Court citations list, 173; Supreme Court and legal literature citation frequencies, 165; Supreme Court votes on, 23
West Coast LEAF: as direct sponsor of court cases, 15; and *NBMHCS*, 108
Wilson, Bertha (Justice): author of self-sufficiency model of post-marital support, 151; on importance of women judges, 5; on *Morgentaler*, 30; on *Morgentaler 2*, 66; support for LEAF positions, 21; vote percentage on excluding evidence, 3
Winnipeg Child and Family Services v. *G. (D.F.)* [1997]: extrinsic evidence cited by LEAF, 152, 153; government participants in case, 26; LEAF participation, position, and success in Supreme Court, 17; legal literature citations, 164; nongovernment intervenors in case, 28; origin and outcome of case, 19; and *parens patriae* principle, 72-4, 153, 164, 166, 179; as reproductive rights case, 193; Supreme Court citations list, 175; Supreme Court and legal literature citation frequencies, 165; Supreme Court use of LEAF material and arguments, 160; Supreme Court votes on, 24
Women's Access to Legal Services Coalition, 108
Women's Legal Education and Action Fund (LEAF). *See* Legal Education and Action Fund (LEAF); West Coast LEAF
women's movement (Canada): and constitutional interpretation of equality,

44; debate between "essentialism" and "particularism," 194-5; nineteenth-century reforms, xi; post-Charter feminist legal mobilization, xii-xiii, xiv-xviii; and Royal Commission on the Status of Women, xi-xii

women's movement (US): Equal Rights Amendment (ERA), xiii-xiv; political victories during 1970s, xiii
Women's Program, Secretary of State, 13, 14
workplace standards, 15
Wynrib, Morris (Dr.), 117, 118

Printed and bound in Canada by Friesens

Set in Stone by Artegraphica Design Co. Ltd.

Copy editor: Judy Phillips

Proofreader: Deborah Kerr

Indexer: Annette Lorek